SCOTLAND: A HISTORY

SCOTLAND

A HISTORY

EDITED BY

Jenny Wormald

OXFORD

UNIVERSITY PRESS

OXFORD
UNIVERSITY PRESS

Great Clarendon Street, Oxford OX2 6DP

Oxford University Press is a department of the University of Oxford.
It furthers the University's objective of excellence in research, scholarship,
and education by publishing worldwide in

Oxford New York

Auckland Cape Town Dar es Salaam Hong Kong Karachi
Kuala Lumpur Madrid Melbourne Mexico City Nairobi
New Delhi Shanghai Taipei Toronto

With offices in

Argentina Austria Brazil Chile Czech Republic France Greece
Guatemala Hungary Italy Japan Poland Portugal Singapore
South Korea Switzerland Thailand Turkey Ukraine Vietnam

Oxford is a registered trade mark of Oxford University Press
in the UK and in certain other countries

Published in the United States
by Oxford University Press Inc., New York

British Library Cataloguing in Publication Data
Data available

Library of Congress Cataloging in Publication Data
Data available

Typeset by SPI Publisher Services, Pondicherry, India
Printed in Great Britain
on acid-free paper by
Biddles Ltd., King's Lynn, Norfolk

ISBN 0–19–820615–1

1 3 5 7 9 10 8 6 4 2

Contents

       SALLY MAPSTONE

       Further Reading   335
       Chronology   351
       Illustration Sources   367
       Index   369

LIST OF COLOUR PLATES

List of Maps

LIST OF CONTRIBUTORS

DAVID ARMITAGE is Professor of History at Harvard University. He is the author of *The Ideological Origins of the British Empire* (2000) and *Greater Britain, 1516–1776: Essays in Atlantic History* (2004). He also edited *Theories of Empire, 1450–1800* (1998), and co-edited *The British Atlantic World, 1500–1800* (2002), among other books.

STEVE BOARDMAN is a Senior Lecturer in Scottish History in the University of Edinburgh, and Director of the Survey of Dedications to Saints in pre-Reformation Scotland. His major research interests lie in late medieval Scottish kingship, aristocratic lordships, particularly those of Gaelic Scotland, and the political and social aspects of saints' cults. He is author of *The Early Stewart Kings: Robert II and Robert III, 1371–1406* (1996) and *The Campbells* (forthcoming), and the co-editor of *The Exercise of Power in Medieval Scotland, c.1200–1500* (2004).

MICHAEL BROWN is Reader in Scottish History in the University of St Andrews. He works on kingship, politics, and the nobility in late medieval Scotland. His main publications are *James I* (1994), *The Black Douglases* (1998), and *The Wars of Scotland* (2004).

RICHARD FINLAY is Professor of Scottish History at Strathclyde University. He has co-edited with Ted Cowan *Scottish History: The Power of the Past* (2002), and is the author of *Modern Scotland, 1914–2000* (2004). He is currently working on Scottish national identity since the union of 1707.

KATHERINE FORSYTH is a Lecturer in the Department of Celtic, University of Glasgow. Her research interests lie in the history and culture of the Celtic-speaking peoples in the antique and early medieval periods, with a special focus on epigraphy. She has published on aspects of language, literacy, and epigraphy in early medieval Britain and Ireland.

I. G. C. HUTCHISON is a Reader in History in the University of Stirling. A former editor of the *Scottish Historical Review*, he has written three books: *A Political History of Scotland, 1832–1924: Parties, Elections, Issues* (1986); *The University and the State: The Case of Aberdeen, 1860–1963* (1993); and *Scottish Politics in the Twentieth Century* (2000).

SALLY MAPSTONE is a Fellow in English at St Hilda's College, University of Oxford. She is President of the Scottish Text Society. She has published widely on Older Scots literature, and has co-edited several books of essays on that literature.

ROGER MASON is Professor of Scottish History in the University of St Andrews. His wide-ranging publications on late medieval and early modern Scottish political culture include *Kingship and the Commonweal: Political Thought in Renaissance and Reformation Scotland* (1998) and an edition of the political writings of John Knox: *Knox: On Rebellion* (1994). His most recent publication is a critical edition and translation of George Buchanan's celebrated political tract, *A Dialogue on the Law of Kingship among the Scots* (2004).

RICHARD B. SHER is Distinguished Professor of History at New Jersey Institute of Technology and NJIT Chair of the Federated History Department of Rutgers University–Newark and NJIT. He has published extensively on the Scottish Enlightenment and other topics on eighteenth-century Scotland, and is the founding executive secretary of the Eighteenth-Century Scottish Studies Society.

KEITH STRINGER is Professor of Medieval History at Lancaster University. He works within the related fields of state-making, noble power structures, religious reform, cultural exchanges, and the construction of regional, national, and supra-national identities. His most recent publications include *The Reformed Church in Medieval Galloway and Cumbria: Contrasts, Connections and Continuities* (2003). He co-directs the Leverhulme-funded research programme 'Border Liberties and Loyalties in North-East England, 1200–1400', and is editor of the forthcoming *Regesta Regum Scottorum*, iii: *The Acts of Alexander II, King of Scots, 1214–1249*.

JENNY WORMALD is a Fellow in History at St Hilda's College, University of Oxford. She was President of the Scottish History Society, 2001–4. She has published widely on late medieval and early modern Scottish history, and early modern British history. She is currently working on a book on James VI and I.

1. Early Medieval Scotland

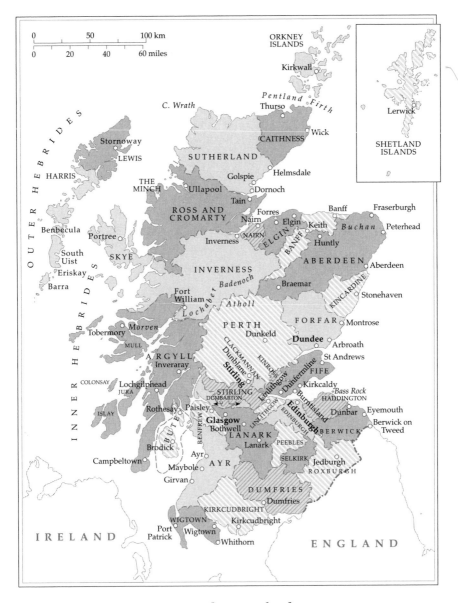

2. Modern Scotland

INTRODUCTION

'Stands Scotland where it did?' asked Macduff in Shakespeare's *Macbeth*. 'Alas, poor country!' answered Ross. 'Almost afraid to know itself!' This well-known quotation from that play which has given us so many quotations offers a quite remarkable number of interpretations when thinking about Scotland from the early medieval period to the modern age. *Macbeth* was, of course, written at one of the great pivotal times in Scottish history, shortly after the Union of the Crowns of 1603. Its author's attempt to dramatize 'real' Scottish history, its sympathetic portrayal of a kingdom rent by murder, self-ambition, total failure of loyalty, on the verge of being rescued by the great Malcolm Canmore—akin, in that sense, to the similar portrayal of that darkest of periods of English history, the reign of Richard III, before the advent of Henry Tudor—stands in very sharp contrast to the savage and utterly fictitious *James IV* by Robert Green of 1599; Green tapped into English hostility to the likely union with Scotland, Shakespeare to acceptance of it, however grudging. In other words, the English succession crisis made Scotland very centre-stage. That refers to a particular historical moment. But one might extrapolate from that the more general point that historiographically Scotland has had to fight hard against the normal instinct of marginalization; famously, Scots are very interested in their past, real or invented, but who else is? *Macbeth*, for example, picks up on Scottish witchcraft, and no wonder in view of the royal demonologist who inherited the English throne in 1603. But how many collections of essays on witchcraft trawl through Europe, include England, which was not a major witch-persecuting society, but ignore Scotland, which was? Scottish historians, especially in the last half-century, have been strenuously demonstrating that Scotland—Scottish history—does not stand where it did. 'To know itself' is not a matter of fear, but confidence. It is therefore very pleasurable to acknowledge Oxford University Press's agreement with that; already there is an *Oxford Illustrated History of Britain*, but that was based on the chronological history of England, although incorporating comment on Scotland, Ireland, and Wales. This volume, however, is one of a number of recent OUP publications on Scottish history, and the editors and contributors are very appreciative of the fact that when it devised its series of Illustrated Histories, it did not ignore Scotland.

This is not all that can be picked up from *Macbeth*. Shakespeare's *Richard III* had a message which would inform later historiography: that the fifteenth century—the end of the Middle Ages—was about to give way to the infinitely more civilized early modern world; he was writing about England, but the point can be made equally about historians of Europe, except perhaps of Italy with its precociously early renaissance. The second half of the twentieth century saw a sustained attack on that view, and no one now would subscribe to it. *Macbeth* takes us into a much more problematic world, the world of intractable sources which still present huge problems to those who engage with them. There has, therefore, lingered on the idea, thanks mainly to Bede, that pre-Conquest England was already in some sense a nation—I take refuge in 'in some sense' because I would not dare to try to define 'nation'. Scotland, by contrast, was a very ill-defined place, full of Gaels, Britons, Vikings, and, above all, those most problematic and most fascinating Picts, about to be pitchforked, as Shakespeare had heralded, into the more civilized world of English and European fashions, by Malcolm Canmore and his Anglicizing and Europeanizing successors. It is so much easier to deal with charters and chronicles than with sculptured stones. But this is now a matter of very considerable and exciting historical investigation; and Katherine Forsyth's chapter gives us a compelling insight into that investigation, and her own equally compelling answer to it. She demolishes the idea that Scotland before 1100 was, or ever had been, an isolated country.

Thus when Keith Stringer shows us the remarkable developments which did take place in the next two centuries, he does not lose sight of the past, and so brings out, to great effect, the distinctive nature of high medieval Scotland, drawing, as it did, on both its own traditions and the new attitudes which were sweeping Europe; and it should be emphasized, as Forsyth does, that it was not a question of Scotland belatedly coming into line, but taking part in the general changes, secular and ecclesiastical, detectable throughout Europe. These two articles replace the cloth so apparently rent *c*.1100 with a more seamless web, and Stringer's approach enables him to depict a kingdom whose keynote was a striking confidence. That confidence makes little sense if in fact, as has tended to be assumed, Scotland was no more than a marginal little kingdom, struggling to ape the really important players. Rather, changes were happening—which is to say no more than that change happens in every historical period—and Scotland was very much part of this. And that is why he can argue, at the end of his article, which deals with the period when Scotland had plunged down into very real threat from the imperialist designs of

Edward I, that 'the English colossus . . . had bitten off more than it could chew'. There were two flourishing and successful kingdoms, not one, within the British mainland.

This does not mean, of course, that we can simply paint a positive and rosy picture. Steve Boardman and Michael Brown, in their analysis of late medieval Scotland, bring out all too clearly the times when England seemed to 'chew' successfully, and the social and political dislocation caused by a century of war. And to that was added adverse climatic change and the scourge of plague. Moreover, by the end of the fourteenth century, when the external threat was largely over, an internal threat to political stability was created by the weakness of the first two Stewart kings, Robert II and the even more lamentable Robert III. Yet neither mighty English kings nor weak Scottish ones seriously threatened the Scottish kingdom. Confidence had by no means disappeared in the fourteenth century, and was remarkably in evidence in the fifteenth, with the recovery and, indeed, the strengthening of the power of the monarchy, freed from preoccupation with England and able to 'become a part of the monarchical club of Europe', and enhancing its prestige with its brilliant court and its shrewd instinct for making its presence felt in the localities, not least in identifying itself with regional saints.

Thus medieval Scotland offers a significant challenge to the normal historiographical rules of what made a successful kingdom; and it is a challenge all the more significant because it does not simply show that Scotland was different from kingdoms like England and France, with their greater governmental sophistication and increasing bureaucratic welter of red tape. Rather, the Scottish experience is extremely important because it provides an alternative model of how a medieval kingdom could flourish. That continues to be true in the sixteenth century, when, as Roger Mason points out, Scotland reached a high point of involvement with Europe, culturally as well as politically. Its scholars, its invocation of imperial iconography—probably the earliest north of the Alps—its dazzling architecture all fed in to the power of the monarchy and to its servants who created its up-to-date humanistic style. But sixteenth-century Scotland had every need of both the morale thus engendered and the long-standing pride in past achievements; for this century also saw a continuation of the minorities which had assailed the Stewart monarchy from 1406, on an even more extensive scale, the crisis created by Mary queen of Scots, and most dramatic of all, the trauma of Reformation. What is striking is that once again Scotland emerges as a kingdom able to survive its seismic shocks. In contrast to England, but more in keeping with European kingdoms, its nobility, brought into a new partnership with the crown in the fifteenth century—albeit with some tension—moved into the royal vacuum, and provided direction—even if not all nobles agreed with that direction. But there was nothing unusual about that. And when at last a strong monarchy, in the person of James VI, reasserted itself, once again political equilibrium was restored.

And then came, for the first time, the hiccough. The Union of the Crowns in 1603 was another high point, the culmination of the northern kingdom's success, which these articles have so clearly demonstrated, when the Scottish James inherited the dynastically bankrupt English throne. It was also a low point. For the monarchy moved to England. Scotland, that European nation, now had to redefine its identity, initially, under the first two Stuart kings, who maintained, in their different ways, an interest in Scotland and then under later 'British' kings, when Scotland began to experience for the first time monarchical neglect. Peace and supposed unity with England was more damaging to any sense of national unity than military threat from England had been, and was now sought, in the first half of the seventeenth century, in the purity of its reformed Kirk, and the oppressive regime of the covenanters. The myth of Scottish Calvinist godliness was born, and has never quite lost its power. Fortunately, it was never as monolithic as the myth would have it; and as the later articles show, godliness was in any case harnessed and turned to the use of Scottish assertiveness.

The depressing century which culminated in an attempt to redefine the constitutional relationship of Scotland and England, with the union of the parliaments in 1707, was succeeded by one which demonstrated all the former confidence of the Scots. As Richard Sher shows, it took time to adjust to the new form of union; and culturally, its scholars and writers could build on seventeenth-century advances. But the combination of adjusting and building produced an explosion of change and development, an opening up in all areas of life, economic as well as cultural, and even religious. Calvinist unity had disappeared by 1800. What had replaced it was a Scotland with an enhanced international role, merited not least by the dazzling brilliance of the Scottish Enlightenment which itself engendered a spirit which informed much of Scottish life, from agricultural, industrial, and urban development to the famed achievements of Scottish academics—such as Adam Smith. Nothing more encapsulates that renewed confidence than the easy acceptance, by the leading inhabitants of this most distinctive nation, that they were now 'North Britons'.

A rather more sombre note creeps into Ian Hutchison's analysis of the nineteenth century, the downside of success, with the combination of rapid population growth, and the move from countryside to town, both creating a new level of social hardship and economic pressure. Moreover, for those who benefited from burgeoning industrialization, capital rather than culture mattered most; and when Scottish identity became associated with the new romantic nonsense associated with the tartan, it 'teetered', as he says, 'on the comic'. Yet Scottish education was more advanced than that of England. There were notable scientific and medical advances. And above all, there was the staggering development of heavy industry. Small wonder, then, that the Scots remained at ease within the union, sure, as they were, of their prominent place in the Empire, and in the wider world.

Only in the twentieth century did doubts and uncertainties seriously dent Scottish confidence, in a way which had happened before only in the seventeenth century. Richard Finlay opens on the bleak note of political dislocation, as the Tories began to make inroads into Liberal dominance and, much more significantly, the spectre of class war, with the Red Clydesiders and the rapid rise of the Labour Party, terrified the upper- and middle-class elites. Heavy industry began to collapse, leaving little leavening against the horrors of appalling housing conditions, poverty, and bad health. Scotland, in the inter-war years, presented the chilling spectacle of a nation in decline, even terminal decline. Visibly it was an unfounded fear, thanks to the remarkable redefinition of social, economic, and new and vital cultural *mores*, beginning in the 1960s, and gathering political momentum as the gulf opened up between Conservative success in England, which meant that Labour dominance in Scotland was always undercut; and this was brought to a head by the brooding figure of Margaret Thatcher, with her infamous experiment of the poll tax in Scotland a year before its disastrous introduction in England. Union with England had already come into question, hesitantly with the botched referendum on devolution in 1979, but the need for change gathered pace in the 1980s and 1990s, partly fuelled by the increasing strength of the Scottish Nationalist Party. In 1997, the massively decisive vote for devolution—so very different from the cliffhanger in Wales—and the huge enthusiasm and emotion which surrounded the opening of the Scottish parliament in 1999, as Finlay concludes, 'completed the transformation of the nation at the end of a turbulent century'.

The final two chapters, David Armitage's on the Scottish Diaspora and Sally Mapstone's on Scottish literature before 1603, might at first sight look like that old-fashioned and pernicious practice of relegating to the end of a book such minor considerations, after giving pride of place to political narrative. This is wholly not the case. The *Oxford Illustrated* series inevitably takes a chronological approach—which is not the same as political narrative—and that has been followed here. But these authors were invited to contribute to this volume because the dimensions of the Scottish past which they discuss are every bit as much essential reading for anyone who wants to understand that past as the other chapters. How did the Scots express that confidence which is such a marked theme of this book? Not just by sitting at home, feeling pleased with themselves as they survived periods of adversity, and proud as they thought of themselves as an important European and imperial nation. They left Scotland, and made their presence felt abroad. 'Rats, lice and Scotsmen: you find them the whole world over', is the opening and arresting quotation of Armitage's article, from a French medieval proverb. He quickly corrects the indication of rapacity and poverty; and as he goes on to point out, not all Scots—the transported, for example—went willingly. But most did. As soldiers, doctors, scholars and students, industrialists, artists, preachers and missionaries, in West and East Europe, from the Americas to Australasia, there were the Scots, combining the ability to assimilate with the retention of Scottish identity.

If that offers considerable insight into Scottish identity, so also does Mapstone's chapter. This is not only a discussion of Scottish literature. It is a beautifully crafted analysis of the way in which Scottish writers used storytelling to invoke its past, to define its identity, and to comment on kingship and the community; and although Mapstone concentrates on the pre-1603 independent kingdom of Scotland, she rightly points out that this is a tradition which has continued into the eighteenth and nineteenth centuries, and indeed to the present day. One of her most interesting arguments—and one which tells us a lot about the Scottish political community and its attitudes to its kings—is that which deals with the impact of the Reformation, when Knox could detach the issue of national interest from the reigning monarch, Mary queen of Scots, and her mother, the regent Mary of Guise. This gives particular point and context to the discussions of the monarchy in the medieval and early modern chapters. Hence this chapter, like Armitage's, is not in any way an extra dimension to the book. Both are a crucially integral part.

With two brief—and even then partial—exceptions, this is a book about a remarkably positive, confident, and successful kingdom. It does not, of course, have all the answers. Research into the definition of the Scottish national identity—not, in any case, a static subject—is ongoing. But this book comes out at a time when Scotland has already experienced devolved government. Not all the hopes and aspirations of that heady day when the Scottish parliament opened in 1999 have been realized; there is the inevitable dissent, criticism, and grumbling on the part of the electorate, failures to deliver on the part of the Executive. What is not in doubt, however, is that aspiration, born of history and long tradition, to ensure Scotland's place on the international map. And it is perhaps a telling reflection on that history that despite the widely held belief in English superior constitutional sophistication, famed down the ages, the Westminster parliament is in a great deal more of a muddle over two current issues, foxhunting and smoking. In the first case, the Executive acted decisively, while Westminster dithered and debated. In the second, the Executive will realize James VI and I's dream of the Scottish part of a non-smoking Britain in 2006, while Westminster is giving itself two more years, until 2008, to find out what it is going to do. The Scots have always tended to worry less about constitutional niceties, concentrate more on political decisions; as these examples show, they still do. There is a lot to be said for that approach. 'Stands Scotland where she did?' It is of course a truism to say that she has never stood still. 'Almost afraid to know itself?' Manifestly not, either in the present or in the past which gave rise to that present, as the chapters in this book make so clear.

It is entirely normal for editors to offer their thanks to contributors, and genuinely so. And that I do, with great enthusiasm; it has been stimulating and rewarding to work with the contributors to this book. It is less normal for editors to mention strains and stresses in getting articles out of contributors. I invoke that consideration, but in reverse, and with considerable apologies; for personal and health reasons, this book has been held up by the editor. I want to thank the contributors, therefore, not just for the academic excitement of this book, but for their understanding and patience, which have considerably eased my embarrassment and which I have much appreciated. Equally, my appreciation is certainly due to Anne Gelling, Louisa Lapworth and Kay Rogers at OUP, and Anne Lyons, indefatigable picture researcher, who have shown the same kindness, and have been a pleasure to work with, and to Rosemary Dear, for her splendid index.

JENNY WORMALD

Oxford
January 2005

1 Origins: Scotland to 1100

Katherine Forsyth

The land and its people

'Scotland' has been a meaningless concept for eight of the nine millennia people have been living in the part of northern Britain now designated by the term. Only in the last thousand years has there been any discernible sense of 'Scottishness' above the more local, regional, and dynastic identities which shaped people's daily lives. Prior to this, not only was there no 'Scotland', but there was no 'England', no 'Wales', and no 'Ireland'. Nor is there much to suggest that the boundary lines between these entities as they are today were in any way inevitable. At various times, areas of modern Scotland have been ruled from Ireland, from England, or from Scandinavia, and conversely, parts of what are now England and Ireland have been ruled from Scotland.

Our perception of Scotland's early history is clouded, not only by the outlines of modern political geography, but perhaps more subtly, by the mental template of today's heavily urbanized population, concentrated as it is in the towns and cities of the central belt, accustomed to moving around by car, and able to convey a message to Berwick or Lerwick merely by picking up the phone. It is hard to re-imagine the forests uncleared, the bogs undrained, and the uplands without their metalled roads; hard to re-imagine the impediment these formed to ready communication. Conversely it is hard to appreciate how differently the landscape would be perceived when the movement of people and goods was most easily achieved on water: along rivers and firths, up and down the elongated lochs of the west, and around the sheltered waters of the coastal seas. In this land without towns, the population was dispersed through the landscape, housed in the farmsteads of a single extended family and their dependants. Almost everyone was directly involved in agriculture, and each locality effectively self-sufficient in producing what the people needed from the land. Of course, not all land was as good as the best, but before the uneven effects of the medieval economic boom, the relative impoverishment of regions like the Highlands was not so marked and the population was more evenly distributed across the country than today.

The first people to settle in Scotland were Mesolithic foragers who gradually ventured north around 7000 BC after the final retreat of the great ice sheet. Our increasing understanding of Scotland's rich archaeological record allows us to trace how the landscape was shaped by the descendants of these men and women and by the descendants of those who were to join them over the succeeding millennia in exploiting its natural resources. Any starting point for a 'history' of the people of Scotland can be only arbitrary, but the appearance of a first surviving fragment of language seems somehow to intensify our connection to the otherwise mute populations of our ancient past. The first documentary reference to Scotland, the first name we can apply, derives from an account of a voyage undertaken by the Greek mariner Pytheas about 320 BC. He mentions the name of the most northerly cape of the island of Britain: *Orcas*. That this Celtic word, apparently derived from the name of the local tribe, 'the young boars', survived to give modern 'Orkney' shows that it had real local currency and was not merely an external label. It probably implies that there were Celtic-speakers in the far north as early as the fourth century BC. This first reference, however, is precocious and we must wait almost four hundred years for further names to fill out the picture. When these come, in the first century AD, they show unequivocally that by the time of the first encounter with Rome a form of Celtic language was spoken all over Scotland, even in the extreme north and west. The handful of apparently pre-Celtic names, for instance *Ebudai* (the source of our 'Hebrides'), do not alter this picture. They reflect, not the survival of separate populations of pre-Celtic descent, but rather elements of an early prehistoric inheritance within the common (Celtic) culture of the Scottish Iron Age, in much the same way as modern place-names of Gaelic origin in, say, Fife or Aberdeenshire reflect the Celtic heritage of these now English-speaking regions.

There is much debate among archaeologists and historians concerning the correlations, if any, between the ethnic labels applied by external observers to the late prehistoric peoples of north-western Europe and their observed social and political structures, art, material culture, religion, and language. It is clearly significant, however, that places, persons, and tribes in Scotland mentioned in classical sources have Celtic names. Moreover,

THE MOST DISTINCTIVE ARTEFACTS of the 'Caledonian School' of metalworking are the 'massive' bronze armlets of the north-east. This example from Culbin Sands, Moray, was made in the first or second century AD. About two dozen survive, some with snakehead terminals, decorated in high relief with elaborate scroll and trumpet patterns.

familiar elements of pagan Celtic religion can be glimpsed in, for example, dedications to Celtic divinities such as *Lugos* and in places named *nemeton* 'sacred place/shrine'. A religious practice of far longer standing, the ritual deposition of material in pits, bogs, and rivers, has ensured the preservation of most of the fine objects to survive from this period. These technically impressive and aesthetically appealing pieces of 'Caledonian' metalwork are decorated in the international art style known as 'La Tène'. The spiral-ornamented war-gear (swords, horse-trappings, and battle-trumpets), jewellery, and mirrors comprise the portable wealth of a Celtic warrior aristocracy concerned with armed conflict and the ostentatious display of wealth about the person. In this increasingly competitive world it is perhaps no coincidence that the first named Scotsman, the leader of the Caledonians against the Roman army at Mons Graupius, had a name, Calgacus, meaning 'swordsman'.

In the early centuries of the first millennium, native society was undergoing profound political and social change. We see in the heightened development of social inequality and hierarchy the emergence of what anthropologists might term a 'chiefdom society'. The appearance of souterrains (large underground stores) in the eastern mainland is but one reflection of ongoing attempts to maximize the extraction of wealth from the land and concentrate it in the hands of the few. All over Scotland, small-scale power structures founded on face-to-face relations were being superseded by far-reaching systems of control, distant authority delegated to local leaders in return for a share of the tribute. The rise and fall of the famous brochs are an architectural manifestation of the beginning of this trend away from the intensive and towards the extensive exercise of power, as hierarchies of space *within* a settlement (internally differentiated sites of similar form throughout the landscape) were replaced by new hierarchies *between* settlements (major centres controlling dependent sites). Political units, however, remained comparatively small. Identity was vested at the level of the tribe whose members might have numbered only a few thousand. Writing in the early second century AD, the Greek geographer Ptolemy of Alexandria lists sixteen tribes in northern Britain, including the Uotadini (Lothian), Epidii (Argyll), and the Smertae (Sutherland), but there were surely more. The greater tribal confederacies glimpsed in the classical sources were loose and ephemeral, a response to the intervention of the Roman army and lasting only as long as the military threat.

The Roman interlude and its legacy

The knock-on effect in Scotland of the centuries of Roman occupation in southern Britain was considerable, but the actual Roman presence in the north was fleeting. The first incursion came in the summer of AD 79 when the Roman governor Agricola led his army deep into Caledonia. The campaign which followed was recorded by his son-in-law, the historian Tacitus, and culminated in Roman victory at the battle of Mons Graupius in AD 83. Roman priorities, however, lay elsewhere, and Agricolan ambitions to bring all of Britain within the Empire were abandoned. A frontier was established much further south with the building of Hadrian's Wall on the Tyne–Solway line in the 120s and 130s. In the middle of the second century southern Scotland was brought within the Roman province of *Britannia* when a second wall, of more modest construction, was built on the Forth–Clyde line, *c.*143. But this Antonine reoccupation lasted little more than a decade and the northern wall was abandoned in the mid-160s. A punitive campaign against the northern barbarians was waged by the Emperor Severus from 197, but his death at York in 211 brought the initiative to an end and Roman troops drew back to the Wall. In the extreme south-west of Scotland, around the western terminus of Hadrian's Wall, the Roman presence was strong because of the legionary fortress of Carlisle, and more or less continuous until the mid-fourth century. Further north, military intervention was limited to these few discrete episodes, all of them short.

In attempting to assess the impact of all this on native society it is easy to be misled by the impressive physical remains of the military majesty of the

THE SUBSTANTIAL DITCHED RAMPARTS surrounding the fort of Ardoch are among the most impressive of Roman military remains in north-west Europe. Yet the site was garrisoned for only a few years after its construction in the 80s AD. Re-occupied in the late 150s the fort was finally abandoned about 163 AD.

Empire: the enormousness of Hadrian's Wall itself, the monumental carved distance slabs from the Antonine Wall, the remains of the huge legionary fortress at Ardoch, Perthshire, the dazzling parade armour found at Newsteads in the Tweed Valley. Much harder to see is the kind of effect prolonged proximity to the Empire had on the society of northern Britain. It would be a mistake to assume constant local hostility to the 'imperial oppressor' for, in reality, the Empire held many attractions. The dichotomy was not so much between 'Roman' and 'Native', as between those inside and those outside the Empire. Recruits to the Roman army were drawn from all over the Empire including, after the initial period, Britain: a grave slab from Mumrills, on the Antonine Wall, commemorates a Briton, Nectouelius, serving in the Roman army in Scotland. From the very outset it is clear that some outsiders saw the Empire as something which they could exploit to their own advantage. One such was Lossio Ueda who proudly proclaimed himself 'a Caledonian' on an impressive Roman-style votive inscription at early third-century Colchester, Essex.

The impact of Rome on those who stayed behind in the north varied great-ly according to region. Archaeologists perceive a cultural boundary at the Tay, 100 miles north of Hadrian's Wall. There is no doubt that Roman influence on the 'near zone' of southern Scotland was profound. The presence there of low-value Roman items reflects the functioning in this frontier area of a lim-ited monetary economy, of markets and of merchants. In the unconquered 'far zone', north of the Tay, it is trinkets and a few luxury items which are found circulating amongst the elite, as far as Shetland and the Outer Isles. Prestige goods are found in the south too: the great early fifth-century hoard from Traprain Law, East Lothian, alone contains more than 50 lb of silver (it has been suggested, only half in jest, that Rome's biggest contribution to Scot-land consisted of silver plate!). Differential access to the great wealth and prestige of Rome had a disruptive effect on local politics. Those who failed to take advantage of these new resources to express and enforce their social position might find themselves squeezed out by more favoured rivals. A sim-ilar pattern of political and social destablization can be seen all round the rim of the Empire especially after imperial power began to collapse in the gener-ation before c.400. The complete lack of Roman pottery in the 'Inter-Wall' region from the second half of the fourth century suggests that trade had effectively ceased there by then. This decline in the ready supply of Roman goods may help explain the references in fourth-century Roman sources to devastating seaborne raids from beyond the Walls. The concerted attacks of the 360s were particularly intense and involved not only Picti and Scotti but also Saxons from across the North Sea.

The economic and political impact of Rome can be quantified to a greater or lesser extent, but what of the cultural impact? The Roman view of the Caledonians, as expressed by Tacitus, was as 'the last men on earth, the last of the free'. Participation in long-distance trade brought the inhabitants of northern Britain into contact with an international economic system which was centred on the Mediterranean. Did direct contact with Roman citizens give them, for the first time, a sense of their own peripherality? Without doubt the most important and enduring intellectual legacy of Rome dates from the end of the period: the introduction of Christianity. Since the early fourth century Christianity had been the prevailing religion of the Empire but we are sorely ignorant of the means by which it reached northern Britain. We have no contemporary accounts and are forced to rely almost exclusively on archaeology. The only documents we have were written centuries later and present a version of events tailored to fit greatly changed political circumstances. Mounting archaeological evidence reveals the osmotic spread of the new religion from Christian communities in the Roman frontier zone, focused on the bishopric at York, via Carlisle, to Galloway and along the river valleys of Liddesdale and the Tweed basin to Lothian. This first phase of Scottish Christianity can be traced in the new 'long-cist' cemeteries as far north as Angus. These were ordinary Christian cemeteries of slab-lined graves oriented east-west. The burials of the privileged few might also be marked by a cross-slab or inscribed stone. The earliest of these is the fifth-century memorial to Latinus and his young, unnamed daughter at Whithorn. In its lettering and layout this monument reflects the Roman roots of the new faith, but the family were not incomers. Although Latinus was given a name of Roman origin, the name of his grandfather is a Celtic one.

At about this time, British missionaries, most famously of course Bishop Patrick, were actively evangelizing beyond the Empire in Ireland, but we have no contemporary evidence for such campaigns among northern British pagans. Attempts have been made to find a north British equivalent of the missionary Patrick in the shape of Ninian of Whithorn, but on close inspection the evidence for such a figure is slight, some would even say non-existent. As we have it, the legend of Ninian is a creation of the eighth century, clearly shaped by the desire of both Picts and Angles to assert Christian origins independent of, and pre-dating, those of Gaelic Iona. The later prominence of the cult of Ninian has obscured the efforts of other early churchmen. The Briton Uinniau (Finnian), a major figure of the mid-sixth-century Church who was known as an early teacher of Columba, has strong associations with the southwest. Later in the sixth century Kentigern was head of an episcopal church associated with the British kingdom of Dumbarton, and further east, at least according to Brittonic sources, his younger contemporary Run, son of the British king Urien, worked among the Angles, baptizing the English king Eadwine (Edwin) and a great number of his followers.

The wine and oil required for the rituals of the new religion came to the lands bordering the Irish Sea from the eastern Mediterranean and, later, from the emporia of Atlantic Gaul. All that remains of this important, though short-lived, trade is the distinctive pottery which contained and accompanied it. Whatever perishables these commodities were exchanged for, long-distance trade was tightly focused on royal sites and, by allowing kings to control the flow of goods to their own ends, played a significant role in the political development of the Celtic West. Though direct contact with the Mediterranean can be traced only from the late fifth to mid-sixth centuries, links with Gaul were maintained till the end of the seventh and provided a conduit for artistic and intellectual innovations from the Merovingian Church, above all profoundly influential ideas about monasticism.

Britons and Picts

Though united by a common language, the Britons 'between the Walls' were politically divided. Straddling the modern Border, the Gododdin, descendants of Ptolemy's Uotadini, controlled a great swathe of the eastern coastal plain. The Rock of Dumbarton ('fortress of the Britons') was the focus of another kingdom encompassing the Clyde Valley. At times the reach of the Dumbarton kings may have included Ayrshire or even Galloway, but the extent and allegiance of the other British polities is far from clear. There are hints of unnamed kingdoms based in the upper Tweed basin, in western Dumfriesshire, perhaps, and round the mouth of the Solway and up the Eden Valley in Cumbria. With only dialectal variation, language and culture linked the people of these competing post-Roman Christian kingdoms to Britons in northern and western England, in Wales and the south-west, then on to the coast of Armorica and as far south as the Loire (in the early period at least, there were even Britons settled in north-west Spain). But what of their non-Christian, never-Romanized neighbours to the north?

The term Picti, 'painted people', was first used by Roman writers at the end of the third century. It was picked up in succeeding centuries by Christian authors to refer in an entirely derogatory fashion to the warlike tribes of the distant north. It seems unlikely to have been used with any precision by either group and may have been a rather elastic term signifying nothing more than 'free Britons' to the former, and 'pagan Britons' to the latter. To Tacitus, the people north of the Forth were 'Caledonian Britons' and it is clear that in

the Roman period they were also considered Brittonic by their neighbours. The early medieval Irish and Welsh terms for the Picts, respectively
Cruithne and Prydyn, both derive ultimately from the same word: Pretanni,
the root of our own 'Britain'. Yet if they had, at one time, been perceived to be
of common stock, by the eighth century at least, Britons and Picts were seen
by those around them as two distinctly separate peoples.

Archaeological support for such a distinction is hard to find. Many aspects
of material culture were common throughout northern and western Britain.
Others varied from region to region, distributions of different categories of
artefact cutting across one another. There seems no compelling reason to single out the Forth as a more fundamental cultural boundary than, say, the
Mounth, the Spey, or the Oykell. If anything the long-reaching firths of Forth
and Clyde united as much as divided and if a boundary is to be sought in prehistoric archaeology it would be at the Tay. On the basis of the surviving linguistic evidence, there seems little to distinguish the speech of those north
and south of the Forth. Place-name evidence presents many difficulties and
a great deal of work remains to be done, but the onomastic evidence we have
suggests any difference between the languages spoken either side of the
Forth–Clyde line represented no more than dialectal variation within the
greater Brittonic continuum. Elements such as *aber* 'confluence', *tre(v)*
'homestead', and *lanerc* 'glade' appear both north and south (Aberdeen,
Aberlady; Rattray, Ochiltree; Lendric, Lanark) and recorded Pictish personal names such as Drostan, Necton, Onuist, and Mailcon are drawn from a
common Brittonic pool.

This picture, however, is hard to reconcile with the explicit statement by
the early eighth-century Northumbrian scholar Bede that the Britons and the
Picts were two peoples speaking different languages. Perhaps political and
religious divisions caused Bede to see as separate languages what a linguist
might class merely as different dialects (cf. the distinction between Modern
Irish and Scottish Gaelic). Historians today can trace in Bede's writing a distinctly anti-British stance. He may have been at pains to recognize the distinctness of the Pictish *gens*, of whom he was more approving. Perhaps a key
reason may be that, as Bede wrote, Picts faced Angles across the Forth. A little over a generation earlier, the Brittonic continuum had been breached by
invading Germanic-speakers. With the old links severed, those on either side
had begun to develop along divergent lines. These redefinitions were part of
a much wider process, for it was in this period that the various peoples of
Britain, both incomer and native, were forging new ethnic identities for

themselves. The disparate Germanic tribes who had settled in eastern Britain were beginning for the first time to view themselves all as 'English', even though they remained politically divided. Perhaps in opposition to this, an anti-Anglo-Saxon ideology seems to have begun to bind together the different British-speaking polities of the west, and across the Irish Sea a new unifying 'Gaelic' identity was being fostered among the kingdoms of the Irish. It may be that a distinctive 'Pictish' identity, encompassing all the Brittonic territory north of the Forth, was being forged at the same time for similar reasons. In the scant documentary record, we can trace the metamorphosis of the old tribal affiliations into territorial identities. The contemporary sources refer to 'the men of Fife', 'the men of the Hebrides', 'the men of Orkney', 'the men of Moray'. These regional identities were strong and endured throughout the early medieval period, yet, transcending them, we see what might well have been an entirely new concept: a sense of common 'Pictishness', an identity which in some way united these people and distinguished them from their neighbours the Gaels, the Angles, and even the Britons, an identity which, following the Latin sources of the time, we label 'Pictish', but, ironically, for which the Pictish word has not survived.

Lacking surviving Pictish documents, it is hard to find indigenous expressions of this identity (we are entirely dependent on what the Picts' Gaelic-, British-, and English-speaking neighbours wrote of them). Except, perhaps, for what might be the most distinctive aspect of Pictish culture, their unique and compelling system of symbols: formalized, stereotyped designs carved on a variety of objects, but above all on upright stone monuments. The system's invention, perhaps as early as the sixth century, may have been part of a growing political and ethnic self-awareness. Its popularity is remarkable: it was used throughout Pictish territory as late as the ninth century and in a variety of contexts. Whatever the actual content of the messages conveyed by the symbols (and sadly this seems irrecoverable), the choice of this indigenous form of written communication, over, say the roman alphabet, may in itself have been an expression and assertion of the new 'Pictish' identity.

Facing: THIS PICTISH CARVED STONE, known as the 'Craw Stane', is one of eight from the Rhynie (Aberdeenshire) area. It stands beside the inner entrance of an earthwork enclosure. The vitrified remains of an Iron Age fort are visible in the distance on the summit of Tap O'Noth. Over 200 symbol-carved stones survive from Pictland, and though the meaning of the designs is unknown, the stones appear to function as individual memorials.

Anglian expansion in the east

The Anglo-Saxons have already been referred to as playing a decisive role in the shaping of northern Britain. In archaeological and written sources they are first detected in coastal Northumbria in the second quarter of the sixth century, establishing, at the expense of the Gododdin, the territory of Bernicia, centred on Bamburgh. To begin with, this site, the old British fortress of Dinguaroy, was little more than a pirates' lair and there can have been little hint of the control the Bernicians would come to exercise over vast tracts of formerly British territory. At a later stage, both sides were keen to present the struggles of the sixth and seventh centuries as a monolithic ethnic conflict, a 'cowboys and Indians' fight to the death, but the reality of the factionalized dynastic politics of the region was far more complex. The Anglian rulers of Bernicia had their own internal rivalries and vied with the Anglian kingdom to their south—Deira. As far as the different British dynastic interests were concerned, ethnicity was no bar to alliance with an Anglian warlord against a common rival. To some extent these processes can be reconstructed on the evidence of two remarkable cycles of early British poetry, one centred around the great king Urien, the other around his rivals, the Gododdin of Edinburgh. These heroic elegies, the earliest vernacular literature to survive from Britain, were composed by learned bards in the royal courts of the north. Their status as a wellspring of later British tradition ensured their copying as literary classics and consequent preservation in later Welsh manuscripts.

The death of Urien in or around the 580s, betrayed by a fellow Briton we are told, while besieging the Bernician Hussa at Lindisfarne, may have been the devastating turning point in British fortunes that is claimed in the poetry. Certainly the rapid expansion of Bernician control thereafter under the pagan king Aethelfrith (reigned 593–616) allowed the Anglians to consolidate their hold on the entire coastal region from Tyne to Tweed. By 603 the Anglian threat appeared sufficiently pressing that the Gaels of Dál Ríada, under their leader Áedán son of Gabrán, came from Kintyre to meet the Bernicians in battle at the unidentified Degsastan, only to be heavily defeated. Aethelfrith was ousted by the Deiran Eadwine but it was not until the reign of Aethelfrith's son Oswald that the Lothians were occupied and settled. Edinburgh was attacked in 638 and by the mid-seventh century the northern boundary of the Anglian kingdom was being maintained at the Forth. Identifiably early English place-names—containing elements such as *-ingaham* (Coldingham), *-ington* (Renton), *-ham* (Yetholm)—indicate that the main early settlements were on the best land, near the coast and along the main river valleys in East Lothian, Berwickshire, and Roxburghshire. Without any doubt, such inroads were achieved by violence and terror, but the local population was not exterminated. The survival of a great number of British names in these areas reflects not a cataclysmic break but a degree of acculturation and continuity. Gododdin antecedents can be seen, sometimes quite literally, to underlie structures of Bernician power, both secular and ecclesiastical. The invaders appear not to have built their own forts but rather to have taken over British strongholds. Archaeological excavation at Doon Hill near Dunbar (British *Din Baer*) showed a British timber hall superseded by an Anglian one.

Oswald was succeeded by his brother Oswiu (Oswy) (reigned 642–70) under whom expansion continued westward and north-westward along the Solway and into Galloway. Oswiu campaigned in Cumbria, taking in marriage a great-granddaughter of Urien, and advances in his reign, and in that of his son Ecgfrith, established Bernician control from coast to coast. By the 680s, after a series of military victories, Bernicia was claiming tribute rights over the southern Picts. In about 681 Ecgfrith established a bishopric at Abercorn on the southern shore of the Forth and installed the Anglo-Saxon Trumwine as 'Bishop of Picts'. The Anglian advance seemed inexorable. Until, that is, 20 May 685, when the Pictish king Bridei (Brude) son of Bili lured his cousin Ecgfrith and his army to their deaths at a great battle, known in British tradition as the mighty victory of *Linn Garan* ('the pool of the crane'), and to the English as the crushing defeat of *Nechtanesmere*. This battle was one of the major turning points of Scottish history. Thereafter the Bernicians were pushed definitively back across the Forth and the Abercorn bishopric was hastily abandoned. Intermittent hostilities persisted, interspersed with periods of more cordial relations between Angles and Picts, but thereafter the main thrust of Northumbrian ambitions was westward. Place-name and archaeological evidence reveals the progress of Anglian settlement in Galloway. In 731 an Anglian bishopric was established at the old British episcopal centre of Whithorn, where recent archaeological excavations have done so much to reveal the vibrant culture and economy of this region in the eighth and ninth centuries. In 750 Eadbert added Kyle to Northumbrian overlordship leaving only Clydesdale independent, the sole British kingdom to withstand the Anglian advance.

From the documentary sources the Northumbrian encounter may seem to consist entirely of violence and oppression but archaeology hints at the rich-

ness of the Anglian cultural legacy. From Aberlady and Morham, in Anglian East Lothian, there survive fragments of superb crosses which testify to the skill and artistry of eighth- and ninth-century stone-carvers. The status of Hoddom as a major centre of Anglian culture in Annandale is reflected in the quantity and quality of the Christian sculpture which survived there. Fragments of magnificent stone shrines survive at Abercorn, Mid-Lothian, and Jedburgh, Roxburghshire, but arguably the finest pieces of sculpture are the great early eighth-century crosses from Bewcastle in Cumbria and, most famously, from Ruthwell, Dumfriesshire. The latter is inscribed with a precious reminder of the lost literature of Anglian Scotland: a rendering in runic lettering of the Old English poem on the crucifixion', 'The Dream of the Rood'. The roots of modern Scots language and literature lie in this most northerly dialect of Old English spoken by descendants of Bernicians and Britons alike.

The Gaels of the west

The Anglo-Saxons were not the only newcomers in the post-Roman north. Latin sources of the period call the inhabitants of Ireland the Scotti and the people of Argyll, Scotti Brittaniae, 'Scots of Britain'. The presence of these Irish-speaking Scotti may, as tradition maintains, reflect an actual folk movement of settlers from Ireland to Argyll. Alternatively, the people of the region may always have been more closely linked to the inhabitants of north-east Ireland, with

THE EARLY EIGHTH-CENTURY RUTHWELL CROSS stands over 3.6m tall and is ornately carved with biblical scenes and inscriptions in both Latin and Old English. This detail shows runic lettering framing creatures who nibble at the fruits of a vine. This Mediterranean 'vine-scroll' ornament was also popular with Pictish sculptors.

whom they were united by the sea, than to the occupants of the Brittonic lands on the far side of the harsh mountains of Druim Alban. The distance separating the Mull of Kintyre from the Antrim coast is a mere 12 miles. It is not in the least surprising, therefore, that as early as the Neolithic there is archaeological evidence for contacts across the North Channel. The sixth and seventh centuries were a period of rapidly changing fortunes in Irish politics and it is against this background, specifically the rise of the Uí Néill dynasty, that we should view what appears to be the transfer of the ruling house of the kingdom of Dál Ríada to a new power-base in Scotland. This was not the abandonment of one territory and the taking of another, but rather a shift of emphasis, from the western to the eastern part of a wider territory encompassing both. Irish Dál Ríada continued, at least at first, to be ruled from the strongholds of Scottish Dál Ríada.

By the seventh century Dalriadic territory stretched in Scotland from the Mull of Kintyre to Ardnamurchan, including the adjacent islands. Its main political divisions are reflected in a remarkable tenth-century document which contains a probably seventh-century core. In addition to listing the manpower the households of Dál Ríada were obliged to provide for naval defence, this text, the *Senchus fer nAlban* ('The Tradition (or history) of the Men of Alba'), gives us a Dalriadic view of their own origins. As was common at the time, the metaphor of genealogy is used to express a fixed moment within the fluctuating relationships of contemporary power politics. The people of Dál Ríada are represented as being essentially unified by their common descent from one Erc son of Eochaid. That the different groups are actually named, however, after various alleged sons and grandsons of the legendary Erc, and not the man himself, suggests that the claimed unity existed, if at all, at the level of political ideology rather than political reality. The 'kindred of Oengus' (Cenél nOengusa) controlled Islay; the 'kindred of Loarn' (Cenél Loairn) held the mainland and islands to the north of Loch Awe, including the lands to which they gave their name; and the 'kindred of Gabrán' (Cenél nGabráin) occupied Kintyre, Knapdale, and Cowal. The sources we have make little mention of Cenél nOengusa and not much more is known about the Cenél Loairn. It is no coincidence that most of what survives concerns the kindred from which almost all the subsequent kings of Scots claimed descent: Cenél nGabráin.

Dál Ríada's place in the wider world of Gaelic language and culture means that through sources preserved in medieval Irish manuscripts we know a great deal more about the *Scotti* of Dál Ríada than we do about most of their neighbours. Much of our information goes back to a now lost chronicle of the mid-eighth century kept at the monastery of Iona. Such chronicles had their origins in 'annals', brief notes on major events kept year by year in manuscripts primarily used for fixing the dates of the movable feasts and rituals of the Christian year. These annals were later excerpted, collected, and copied, merged with other collections, recopied, and recopied. Modern historians have displayed considerable skill and ingenuity in untangling the complicated transmission of these texts, weeding out retrospective additions, and piecing together the oldest layers to form what they believe to be an accurate picture of events. Literary texts help flesh out the bare bones of annalistic history. Saints' Lives, heroic tales, and poems were written for specific patrons whose dynastic allegiances and ambitions they naturally reflect. The historian's task is to establish the context of these texts and why they were composed, preserved, and modified over time. Though our surviving evidence is entirely derived from ecclesiastical sources, it reveals a great deal about more 'secular' matters. Leading church personnel were drawn from the subsidiary branches of the local ruling families, ensuring a commonality of interest bolstered by the ideological and economic interdependence of the two spheres. A fitting example of this interdependence is the relationship between perhaps the most ambitious and successful of the Dalriadic kings, Áedán son of Gabrán, and certainly Dál Ríada's most famous churchman: Colum Cille, 'the dove of the church', in Latin, Columba. Áedán was, we are told, inaugurated by the saint in 574, and obtained victories through his prayers. Áedán's military successes were indeed impressive and his long reign (he ruled till about 608) reflects his enduring power. The sources record his campaigns against Orkney, the Isle of Man, in the Mearns, in the area around Stirling, and in Ireland. His only major setback seems to have been the terrible defeat at Degsastan in 603. Throughout the period direct control of Irish Dál Ríada was being contested by the increasingly powerful Uí Néill, the dynasty of which Colum Cille himself was a prominent member. King and saint met with the high-king of the Uí Néill at the Convention of Druim Cett, Co. Londonderry, in 575, at which a compromise was agreed whereby Irish Dál Ríada would be subject to an Uí Néill overlord while still rendering tribute to Áedán and his successors. Columba had prophesied the success of Áedán and his descendants for as long as they supported his foundation on Iona and his kin in Ireland. The disastrous defeats of Áedán's grandson Domnall Brecc were soon attributed to the betrayal of this pledge. Domnall's defeat at the hands of the Uí Néill in 637 at the battle of Mag Rath, Co. Down, meant the perma-

nent loss of Irish Dál Ríada; at least twice Domnall had been defeated in battle against Picts; and he was finally killed by the Strathclyde Britons at Strath-
carron, Stirlingshire, in 642.

The weakening of Cenél nGabráin seems bound up with the general
decline in the political fortunes of the Gaels since the attendant ascendancy
of the Cenél Loairn coincided with a period of sustained Pictish aggression
against Dál Ríada: the campaigns of Onuist son of Urguist (Oengus son of
Fergus) in the 730s and 740s. Quite what effect this Pictish expansion had on
Cenél Loairn is unclear. The ruling elite may have been squeezed north; certainly the later kings of Moray, at the opposite end of the Great Glen, traced
their ancestry to the dynasts of the Cenél Loairn. In the south, however, from
the 770s on, the story is once again that of the expanding power of the Cenél
nGabráin. Attempts to reconstruct exactly what happened in the following
decades are hampered by the extensive rewriting the sources have undergone in later centuries in attempts to present the ill-understood events of the
ninth century as the divinely ordained conquest and annihilation of the Picti
by the Scotti and the merger of two monolithic kingdoms into one inevitable
whole. For this reason any claims that in the period before the 840s certain
kings of Dál Ríada ruled in Pictland, or vice versa, must be viewed with
extreme suspicion.

Saints, scholars, and sculptors: the Church in the north

The ecclesiastical history of Dál Ríada is dominated by the figure of Columba and by his monastery on the island of Iona. In life, Columba was indeed a
great and influential figure and the legacy of his foundation was immense,
both as a centre of learning of European standing and as mother-house to a
far-flung family of monasteries in Dál Ríada, Ireland, Pictland, and Northumbria. The holy man is brought vividly to life in the pages of a three-part Latin
'Life' written about a century after his death in 597 by another Irish cleric,
scholar, and diplomat, Adomnán. So effective was the learned Adomnán,
ninth abbot of Iona, in ensuring the fame of his illustrious subject that his own
considerable achievements have been greatly overshadowed. He was known
to contemporaries as the author of an exegetical work on the holy places of
the Bible and, above all, as the author of a remarkable law, *Cáin Adomnáin*,
which, it was claimed, granted 'the lasting freedom of the women of the
Gaels'. Also known as 'the Law of Innocents', this text was a Geneva Convention of its day, intended to protect women and other non-combatants from

the horrors of war and guaranteed as such by kings and leading clerics from throughout the Gaelic world and Pictland.

As a result of the exile on Iona of the Bernician princes Oswald and Oswiu, the Columban Church played a defining role in the Christianization of Northumbria. Cuthbert's Melrose was a Columban foundation and the first monks of Lindisfarne were brought from Iona by the Irishman Aidán. Gaelic intellectual and administrative dominance of the Northumbrian Church lasted for thirty years till 664, when the Synod of Whitby brought a complete break with the old Celtic authority and a realignment towards the mainstream international Church.

Of course, not all Gaelic clerics active in northern Britain were part of the Columban confederation. The work of other monasteries is reflected in ancient church dedications to Mo-Luoc of Lismore (d. 592); to Máel-Ruba (d. 722), who came from Bangor, Co. Down, to found the monastery of Applecross in Wester Ross; and to his predecessor in the Pictish north-west, Donnán, martyred with his community on Eigg in 617. Such dedications, in the form of place-names, holy wells, and feast-day fairs, provide some of the most important evidence for the localized saints' cults of the Middle Ages. They must, however, be used with great caution, since these apparently long-lived traditions are very difficult to date and reflect, not the personal foundations of a saint during his or her own life, but the popularity and extent of their cult after death. Adherence to a particular saint was an important means of expressing identity and allegiance, and the later medieval prominence of saints such as Columba, Andrew, Kentigern, and Ninian has often all but obscured the more minor early saints and their intensely local cults.

Since other sources are few, place-names and saints' dedications are particularly important to any investigation of the Church in Pictland. An early stratum of British influence there is reflected in place-names incorporating the element eccles- (from Latin ecclesia 'church'), and links with Northumbria are reflected in Pictish Christian art. These important and continuing connections with the British and Northumbrian churches are sometimes overshadowed by the admittedly more pervasive and enduring influence of the Gaelic Church. The systematic conversion of Pictland was not, it seems, part of Columba's agenda, though an early source describes him as preaching to 'the

Facing: CLOSELY RELATED TO THE OUTSTANDING CROSSES of Iona, this well-preserved 'high cross' at Kildaltan (Islay) reflects artistic connections between the churches of Dál Ríada and those of Northumbria, Pictland, and, especially, Ireland. The devotional image of the Virgin and Child (at the top of the shaft) is typical of the 'Iona School'.

tribes of the Tay'. Other Gaelic influences came direct from Ireland. The royal monastery at Abernethy was traditionally founded about 620 by an abbess of St Brigid's, Kildare, Leinster. Irish churchmen and -women were active in Pictland, but the traffic was not all one way. A mid-ninth-century Pictish abbot of Orkney is recorded as having trained in Ireland in his youth and some Pictish clerics appear to have stayed on to work among the Gael. One such was Urguist (Fergus) 'the Pict', who attended a church council in Rome in 721 in his capacity as a bishop to the Scotti. Dedications in Pictland to Ethernan, Drostan, Nathalan, Devenec, and Serf are evidence of the early strength of the cults of 'home-grown' saints.

Perhaps the most important body of evidence for the history of the Church in Pictland comprises the hundreds of pieces of monumental sculpture which survive from ancient Pictish church sites. The most humble are simple slabs incised with the Christian cross; the most elaborate rank as some of the greatest works of art in early medieval Europe. Crosses and cross-slabs, such as those at Aberlemno, are justly famous. Less well known are the recumbent monuments and grave-covers which marked the burials of the powerful. The extant altar panels and composite shrines would have furnished churches made of timber, though a few surviving architectural elements indicate that some buildings at least were of stone. The sculptural art of the Picts reflects the interplay between metalworker, stone-carver, and manuscript illuminator and hints at the lost material culture of the Pictish Church. The recent archaeological discovery of a major monastery at Portmahomack goes some way to explaining the remarkable concentration of sculpture on the Tarbat peninsula in Easter Ross. Technically and stylistically these related monuments indicate close contacts with Iona and St Andrews. They exemplify the wealth of the Picts of the Moray Firth and their cultural interconnections with the rest of the Insular world. Other major collections of sculpture survive at Rosemarkie (Easter Ross), Kineddar (Moray), St Vigeans (Angus), and Meigle (Perthshire).

One feature which distinguishes the Pictish Church from its neighbours is the apparently exceptional degree of secular involvement in ecclesiastical affairs. In contrast to contemporary Ireland, major monasteries in Pictland were known as royal foundations (e.g. Abernethy, Dunkeld, and St Andrews). The juxtaposition of royal palace (*palacium*) and major church at ninth-century Forteviot, Perthshire, is indicative of the close relationship between the two powers, but the actions of the early eighth-century king Naiton (Nechton) in legislating on fundamental matters of ecclesiastical observance and discipline suggest that kings might hold the upper hand. Naiton's request for stonemasons to be brought from Northumbria is thought to have precipitated the efflorescence of Pictish cross-slabs carving. The art of these cross-slabs reflects to a remarkable extent the interests of secular patrons. Though scriptural scenes do, of course, appear, these are overshadowed by overtly secular themes and the repeated portrayal of members of the Pictish aristocracy in all their finery, hunting and waging war.

Life and society: the ruling and the ruled

Any attempt to write a narrative history of these Pictish lords is thwarted by the extreme paucity of documentary sources. The only kings about whom anything much more than a name is known are those who impinge upon the sources of their neighbours, for instance: Bridei (Brude) son of Mailcon, the pagan king who was visited by Columba at his court near Inverness; his southern namesake Bridei son of Bili who, a century later, expelled the Northumbrians back across the Forth; Naiton (Nechton) son of Derile, the learned Christian king who retired, after a long reign, to the royal monastery of Cennrigmonad (St Andrews); the mighty eighth-century Onuist (Oengus) son of Urguist (Fergus), known to his enemies as *carnifex*, 'butcher'.

By and large, pre-tenth-century texts from the British Isles have survived only in later transcriptions. If there was no reason to go to the effort of copying a manuscript then the texts it contained would be lost when, inevitably, the original got burnt, soaked, eaten by vermin, or simply fell apart from long use. Cultural obsolescence—in the eyes of the Gaelic-speaking clerics of the tenth and eleventh centuries, and *a fortiori* in those of the English-speaking clergy of later centuries—is the reason virtually nothing survives of a tradition of Pictish historical writing glimpsed in our sources. There is what purports to be a list of Pictish kings and their reign-lengths which does go back to a genuine Pictish source, but which in its present form (a highly corrupted fourteenth-century copy of a tenth-century text) has clearly been reshaped to give the impression that there had been a unified kingdom of the Picts with a single king. This was certainly not the case. Scraps of contemporary evidence, along with later territorial divisions and designations, indicate the existence of several regional kingdoms. Exceptional kings might establish over-kingship of neighbouring polities but such hegemonies were usually short-lived.

The Mounth remained a major division. According to a twelfth-century topographical survey, *De situ Albanie*, 'Concerning the situation of Alba', north of the Mounth there was *Ce* (Mar and Buchan), Moray (from the Spey to Druim Alban), and *Cat* (Caithness and Sutherland). Another text describes Orkney as Pictish, and there appears to have been a western Pictish province in Skye and Wester Ross. As for Shetland and the Outer Hebrides, the only evidence to go on is the presence there of 'Pictish' symbol stones. They may have been under the dominion of, or allied with, Orkney. South of the Mounth were *Circenn* (Angus and the Mearns), Atholl, Gowrie, Fife. The important kingdom of *Fortriu* (perhaps based on Strathearn, possibly further north) preserves the name of the tribe known to the Romans as Uerturiones. In the course of the 720s and 730s there appears to have been a power struggle among the royal kindreds of Fife, Circenn, and Fortriu for over-kingship in the south, a struggle eventually won by Onuist son of Urguist (d. 761). There is very little documentary evidence for the second half of the eighth century, but the battle between rival Pictish factions recorded in 789 implies that the matter was far from settled.

Though politically and ethnically divided, the societies of northern Britain had many traits in common. Above all, these were intensely hierarchical societies. Legal rights and duties, a person's very identity, were dependent on their social status, as determined by such factors as gender, age, wealth, family ties, dependence on the politically powerful, and the possession of a craft or specialized learning. In each society there were a few who were very wealthy, a goodly number who were fairly prosperous, and a great many who were very poor. The legal unit in these kindred-based communities was the family, with young men and all women subject to senior men. No one in society was fully independent and towards the bottom of the heap dependence could be near total. Real slaves, however, were those brought in from outside. Until at least the seventh century, slavery was a fact of life, and it became so again in the ninth century when unfortunates in northern Britain were seized for the slave markets of the Scandinavian world. Most slaves were captives in war; probably the majority were women.

All our documentary sources are male based and reflect cultural values linked to male roles. Because of this a whole realm of social relations controlled by women is not visible to us. By analogy with the contemporary legal traditions of Wales and Ireland it seems likely that women in Celtic-speaking north Britain had rather wider social roles than their Anglo-Saxon counterparts. The exceptional images of female aristocrats on Pictish sculpture hint at how these wealthy female patrons of the Church chose to present themselves: one is depicted sitting by her loom, another rides side-saddle in pursuit of deer.

Apart from the elite and the few who had specialized skills in craftworking, medicine, law, music, poetry, or religion, almost everyone was engaged in full-time agriculture. The particular mix of stock and arable farming depended on the local environment. Hunting provided food, sport, and training for war, and in coastal areas marine resources, including seals and whales, were exploited too. Already by the tenth century, everything points to a settled landscape of well-defined properties. In the absence of coinage, exchange was by barter, and renders to secular and ecclesiastical lords were paid in kind. True wealth was measured not so much in what one had but in what one was in a position to give away, and generosity was esteemed as one of the greatest of qualities. Extravagant hospitality was a demonstration of status. It attracted supporters and produced links of dependence. Wealth, however, was a means to an end: the source of status was lordship—dominion over other people. At many levels up and down the social scale people were bound together in dependent relationships. Our sources, especially heroic literature, emphasize the bond formed between lord and retainer by the gift of prestige goods—weapons, jewellery, clothing, horses—especially in the context of feasting. A lord could obtain luxury items such as these through war, by purchase from traders, or from his own specialist producers. Archaeological evidence of metalworking and other craft activity is an important feature of lordly sites throughout the period. Control of luxury goods was an essential prerequisite of political power, and the control of trade, especially foreign trade, was vital for political success, but what really mattered was power over land and those who worked it: in all periods wealth flowed from the land.

Conflict was a major component of society, not just conflict over land or property but rivalry over position, which had to be maintained in the context of constant competition. Military action, however, was not the only form of aggression. Fortified residences, military equipment, and highly schooled war horses performed a practical role in a society in which violence was endemic, but they also provided a medium for competitive public display, as did the patronage of poets and metalworkers, acts of charity, and liberality to the Church. A good reputation was vital for success. Not only could foes inflict practical damage, potentially even more serious was the loss of prestige which a defeat entailed. Lords retained poets who used the twin tools of praise and satire to ensure their patron's fame. The maintenance of honour

was a vital principle of the various legal systems. Appropriate restitution had to be made, not only to the victim of a wrong, but also to the lord or senior relative who had been slighted by this action against a dependant.

Kingship, like lesser forms of lordship, was personal and office could be sustained only as long as the current bearer was politically dominant. Any weakness would be exploited by the rival who was surely waiting to take his place. Though there were exceptional figures who held the kingship for decades and died in their beds, most met a violent end at the hands of their successor within a matter of years. In the Celtic-speaking areas, kingship was open to any man who had a grandfather who had held the kingship, and if one did not have a royal father through whom to claim, a royal mother would do. The closer the link to an earlier king the stronger one's claim, but ability (which might depend on age, military skill, or personal qualities) had also to be taken into account. The support of kin would be given with an eye to their own future chances or those of their descendants, and the support of political allies and dependants might not be forthcoming if a choice was likely to produce social strife. Dominance within the pool of potential successors was therefore achieved through a balance of hereditary legitimacy, personal ability, and access to resources. An outsider would be less likely to have an appropriate power base but if internal support was sufficient, his ethnicity need not disqualify him from the kingship. It was noble descent that mattered. Since the various royal dynasties of northern Britain were intricately interconnected by marriage, members may have felt unifying kinship and elite status more keenly than such ethnic identities as were meaningful to their subjects.

What kings were actually able to do developed over the centuries, as state structures began to emerge from the chiefdom societies of the Roman and sub-Roman north. Government was the king's will, but royal action was shaped by the need to retain support: there was always some rival ready to rally the disaffected. There was little bureaucracy, although, as the scale of territories expanded to a point where direct personal control became impossible, more reliance had to be placed on officials and local lords. It was the king's duty to maintain order and administer justice. In the Celtic-speaking areas, affairs were regulated according to a body of customary law, as interpreted by a learned caste of legal specialists, but it was the king's role to arbi-

Facing: THE WELL-GROOMED MALE NOBILITY of Pictland as they liked to see themselves: riding to hunt, long hair flowing. On this cross-slab from Kirriemuir (Angus) detail in the clothing and horse-gear has been carefully rendered.

trate in disputes. Kings had the authority to promulgate new laws but did so only rarely. Alliances between territories were the unstable personal achievements of the rulers concerned and had to be made anew on the death of either party. Kings had personal retinues of armed followers but there was no standing army. In time of military crisis each household could be called on to provide equipped fighters, but if the population felt sufficiently over-burdened by military demands it might withdraw support.

Kings were peripatetic, travelling round the realm to make their presence felt. They consumed the produce due to them and enjoyed the hospitality their dependants were obliged to provide. Kings spent time at the most important monasteries and at the residences of their leading dependants but royal power was centred on each dynasty's principal seat. Archaeological excavation at such sites as Dunadd (Argyll), Dundurn (Perthshire), Mote of Mark (Dumfriesshire), and the Brough of Birsay (Orkney) has done much to elucidate the functions of these major centres. Most simply, they were fortified residences for kings and their entourages, but they also provided a focus for control of the landscape's resources, a forum for trade, and facilities for specialist craft production. They constituted a political assembly point and a visual theatre for the display of royal power. The close proximity of important ecclesiastical sites to many royal centres underlines the growing interrelationship between the secular elite and the Church in this period. Kings celebrated the major rituals of the Christian year at favoured monasteries and leading clerics participated in the most important royal ceremonies. It was in the interests of both to promote social stability through strong rule and both were active in the development of an ideology of Christian kingship.

The impact of the Norse

Wealth passed through the secular power centres as it was collected and redistributed. In the major churches, however, it was amassed in large quantities in the form of precious metalwork decorating altars and saintly relics. The concentration of portable wealth at these unfortified sites made them the obvious target of the Scandinavian raiders who began to attack the British Isles, and much of northern Europe, at the very end of the eighth century. At first these attacks, though terrifying, were small-scale, the work of individual warbands under the control of a chieftain. Within two generations, however, great armies with permanent or semi-permanent bases in the British Isles were waging coherent and prolonged campaigns against the major kingdoms.

Their impact on native society was immense. Historians wrestle with the difficulty of reconciling the bloody image of the viking raider and warrior gleaned from the documentary sources with the more peaceful figures who emerge from the archaeological record, the accomplished mariners, resourceful farmers, skilled craftworkers, and enterprising traders. Though raiding, for goods and slaves, was and remained an important aspect of Norse social and economic life, the most important motive in coming to the British Isles was to acquire land for settlement.

From place-names and archaeological evidence, the history of Scandinavian settlement in northern Britain can be pieced together in its various phases from the ninth century to the thirteenth. The earliest and by far the most extensive settlements were in the north and west, but smaller and later settlement occurred around the mouth of the Tay. To begin with, the northern and western settlements appear to have been as opportunistic and uncoordinated as the early raids, but in time certain dynasties had gained sufficient power to

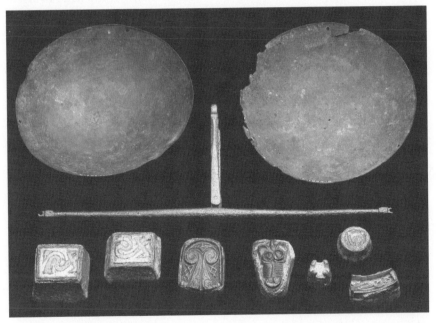

THIS SET OF WEIGHTS with balance-beam and pans, found in a Norse grave of the ninth–tenth century at Kiloran Bay (Colonsay), reflects the trading activities of Scandinavians settled in the Hebrides. Two of the weights are decorated with Insular enamelwork designs derived from Arabic script. Weighing equipment from this period has also been found in non-Norse contexts in Invernesshire and Kirkcudbrightshire.

take control and turn these scattered communities into permanent colonies. In Orkney the descendants of Rognvald of Møre grew rich and powerful by exploiting their pivotal position between Scandinavia and the rich Norse colonies of Ireland. The thirteenth-century Old Norse saga of these earls of Orkney, *Orkneyinga Saga*, records the traditional history of the family and their success in building on the framework of the older Pictish kingdom to establish dominance in the north, notably through the eleventh-century achievements of Earl Sigurd 'the Stout' and his illustrious son by the daughter of the king of Scots, Earl Thorfinn 'the Mighty'.

Undoubtedly initial land-grabbing was achieved by violence and maintained by the threat of military action, but there is no question of any attempt at genocide. Native leaders who posed a threat would have been removed, but where accommodation could be reached it may have been to the advantage of both sides to do so. Norse sources record a native lord, Dungadr/Donnchad, profiting from a marriage alliance with his new Norse neighbours in Caithness. Sculptural evidence shows wealthy native Christians living in Shetland a generation or more after the Norse settlement. Excavation of major sites such as Jarlshof, Shetland, or the seat of the Orkney earls at Birsay, has contributed to our understanding of life under Norse rule. Other, particularly informative bodies of evidence exist in the hoards of precious metalwork, buried and never recovered in unsettled times, and in the richly furnished graves of the Norse elite in the generations before they adopted the Christian religion of the locals. In the Northern Isles of Shetland and Orkney the indigenous language died out completely as the native population became completely assimilated to the language and culture of their new Scandinavian rulers. In the Western Isles, by contrast, Gaelic survived, not only as the speech of a Norse-ruled population of dependent Gaels, but also, in some areas, as the language of a Gaelic-speaking elite retaining power over their own people alongside politically independent Norse neighbours. By the eleventh and twelfth centuries, the intermingling of incomer and native had produced in the Isles a ruling class who were Gaelic-speakers of mixed Norse and Gaelic heritage, known to contemporaries as *Gall-Gaedhil* 'foreign (i.e. Scandinavian) Gaels'.

The birth of Alba and the death of Pictish

In the years when vikings were first raiding along the northern and western sea routes, the eastern mainland was enjoying a new stability under the dynasty of Urguist (Fergus). The culture of Pictland and its openness to out-side influences in this period is reflected in the magnificent cross erected by Custantin (Constantine), son of Urguist, at Dupplin, beside the Pictish royal centre at Forteviot, Perthshire. The Pictish artists have incorporated the lat-est styles from Northumbria and Ireland to create a unique and distinctive monument to faith and royal power. Traditionally, Custantin is credited with the foundation or refoundation of Dunkeld, which, by the middle of the ninth century, had replaced Abernethy as head church of the kingdom. In 820 Cus-tantin was succeeded by his brother Onuist (Oengus) whose patronage was directed more at St Andrews. Both brothers are also recorded as prominent benefactors of the Church in Northumbria. Their family monopolized the kingship until 839 when the dynasty was dealt a mortal blow with the slaying of the king, Uuen (Eógannán) son of Onuist, and his brother in battle against the Norse along with others 'beyond counting'.

At the beginning of the ninth century there were kings of Picti and of Scot-ti, but by the end of the ninth century both had disappeared, and instead the sources speak of a king of the people of Alba. There is still considerable dis-agreement among historians as to the reasons for this change in terminology. One thing is clear, however: the Norse were prime catalysts. The old regime was crushed by the events of 839 and the kingship lay open to whomever could take control of a desperate situation. The opportunity was seized by one Cinaed son of Alpín (Kenneth mac Alpin). Later sources claimed him for the Cenél nGabráin but his origins are obscure, and quite how he came to power remains unclear. Historians have traditionally seen his reign as a major break in Scottish history, crediting him with the 'Conquest' of the Picts and the 'Union' of their kingdom and the kingdom of the Scots. The later kings and queens of Scotland traced their ancestry back to Cinaed and it is from him that their reigns are traditionally numbered, but whatever hap-pened in the mid-ninth century, a close reading of the texts suggests that Cinaed's reign was not the vital watershed that his descendants' historians tried to present. It is clear that a Pictish identity endured till the time of his grandsons in the years around 900.

Cinaed died in 858 and was succeeded first by his brother Domnall (Don-ald) and then by his son Custantin (Constantine I). The kingdom was by now under viking threat from all sides. The Anglian kingdom of Northumbria had been destroyed by the Scandinavian capture of York in 866, and in the west, Olaf 'the White', king of Dublin, was vigorously extending his control over Scandinavians in both Scotland and Ireland. He defeated his father-in-law

Ketil 'Flatnose', ruler of the Hebridean vikings, in 857, and in the 860s campaigned in Pictland. Vital to Olaf's ambition was control of the Firth of Clyde and to that end he laid siege to Dumbarton. It took a gruelling four months before the stronghold of the Britons was finally sacked in 870. With the ancient power centre destroyed, a replacement was created further up the river at Govan. The Norse connections of the new Strathclyde regime are there exemplified in the remarkable collection of tenth- and eleventh-century sculpture which survives in the old parish church. By the late 870s rival groups of York-based vikings were once again devastatingly active in central Scotland. History appeared to be repeating itself, as political and social dislocation of the kind which had brought down the Pictish dynasty of Urguist threatened to destabilize the kingship of Cinaed's sons. Custantin died in 877, killed in a massacre of Picts by Hálfdan of York. He was succeeded by his brother Áed, but within months Áed was murdered by his own followers and for more than a decade the family lost control of the kingdom.

It is important to note that throughout this period contemporary sources continue to talk of 'Picts' and 'Pictland'. Not until the reign of Domnall son of Custantin (889–900) are the *Picti* and *Scotti* of the Latin sources superseded by the Gaelic term *Albanaig* 'people of *Alba*'. This emphasis on the *territorial* term 'Alba' may have been a useful distraction from ethnic ambiguities and sensitivities at a time when what was happening was not the replacement of an old Pictish identity by an existing Scottish one, but rather the forging of something new which transcended both. The language of the new kingdom was Gaelic, but in shape it was decidedly Pictish. The boundaries of tenth-century Alba were those of ninth-century Pictland: Argyll was not in Alba and the new Scottish kings turned their backs on the ancestral homeland. The territorial organization of the new Alba was rooted in the Pictish period, as reflected both in the retention of a Pictish term of land assessment—*pett* 'estate' (as in Pittodrie, Pitlochry, etc.)—and the continued importance of old centres of secular and ecclesiastical power. Even the form of Gaelic spoken in Alba may betray in its structure the heavy influence of Pictish.

Facing: THIS EXCEPTIONAL SURVIVAL from the church of Alba is a small Latin Gospel manuscript, written and illuminated in the tenth century, probably in north-east Scotland. It belonged to the monks of Old Deer, Buchan, who used it in the mid-twelfth century to record their rights in local properties as granted by the king, the mormaers of Buchan and Moray, and the leading families of the area. Some of these Gaelic notes can be seen here squeezed in the margin around the framed portrait of Abraham.

Yet despite the obvious strength of their Pictish inheritance, the inhabitants of tenth-century Scotland had forgotten, or suppressed, the fact that they were the descendants of Picts. Instead they had become the Gaels of *Alba* and the Picti were written out of history, their supposed disappearance a just fate ordained by God. In the ninth century no fewer than five languages were spoken in the territory of modern Scotland: the Celtic languages of Britons, Picts, and Gaels; and the Germanic tongues of Angles and Norse. It is more than a little paradoxical that the language which had the greatest number of speakers at that time was the only one subsequently to disappear. The causes of the demise of Pictish are still disputed among historians, but in any period linguistic change is merely a symptom of wider social change. Unfortunately we have as yet only a limited understanding of the turmoil in Pictish society in this period, but there is no reason why the elimination of the Pictish royal dynasty and their supporters should inevitably have resulted in the death of their language: after all the English language survived the Norman Conquest. For whatever reason, the dispossessed of mid-ninth-century Pictland clearly felt there was more to be gained from allying themselves with the culture of the new Gaelic ascendancy than from cleaving to the marginalized remnants of the discredited Pictish aristocracy. Once Gaelic was established as the language of prestige and advancement it was only a matter of time before Pictish was abandoned completely.

The MacAlpin dynasty and the consolidation of the kingdom of Alba

Cinaed's dynasty re-established their dominance in 889 when Domnall son of Custantin, grandson of Cinaed (Donald II), took the throne. On his death in 900, Domnall was styled *rí Alban*, 'king of Alba', the first to be accorded this title in our sources. It was in his reign that the foundations of the new kingdom of Alba were laid, but it was the remarkably long reign of his brother Custantin (Constantine II) which was crucial in ensuring that his legacy endured. Four years into his reign Custantin achieved a major victory against the Norse, the first in the heartland of Alba, and for almost half a century (he retired from the kingship in 943) he maintained the integrity of the kingdom by a combination of military might and diplomatic astuteness. By such means, the kings of Alba played a central role in the politics of the tenth-century British Isles, containing the expansion of the West Saxon dynasty to the south and the Norse to both north and west.

From the mid-ninth century to the millennium recognizable medieval kingdoms were taking shape throughout a Europe galvanized by Scandinavian incursion. As far as eastern Scotland was concerned, the need to participate in the defence of the realm may have been an important factor in the creation of a common culture: the aggression of their neighbours uniting the diverse peoples of Alba in obedience to a single king whose powers were enhanced in this time of crisis. Part of that process was the decline in status of the rulers of the former Pictish regional kingdoms. Authority over territories such as Atholl, Angus, and Mar was delegated by the king to officials known as *mormaer* (literally, 'sea, or great, steward'). This hereditary office had an important military function and we see in it the roots of the provincial earldoms of the later Middle Ages. The status of these regional magnates could, however, depend on one's perspective: as late as 1020 the kings of Alba considered Findláech (Finlay) of Moray no more than a mormaer but contemporary Irish chroniclers labelled him a king.

Blocked to the north, by the native rulers of Moray and the dynamic Norse earldom of Orkney, the kings of Alba sought to expand south. In the course of the tenth and early eleventh centuries, they gradually came to dominate and then absorb the kingdoms on their southern flank. Overlordship of the kingdom of Strathclyde, already long acknowledged, was extended southwards in 945 when Cumbria was granted to the king of Alba in return for supporting the Anglo-Saxons against the Norse of Dublin. With the death in 954 of Eirík 'Blood-Axe', viking ruler of York, the West Saxon kings now ruled to the Scottish border. Quite where that border should lie continued to be disputed as the kings of Alba and the kings of Wessex fought for control of old Bernicia. Lothian was annexed during the reign of Custantin's son Indulf (954–62) and control over it confirmed in 1018 when the victory of Máel-Coluim son of Cinaed (Malcolm II) at the battle of Carham, near Coldstream, established the Tweed, the 'line of Scottish exhaustion', as the new frontier.

Máel-Coluim, 'devotee of Columba', was succeeded after a long reign (1005–34) by his daughter's son Donnchad (Duncan). Like three of his predecessors, Donnchad was killed in the north fighting the men of Moray. What was different this time was that on his death the Moray dynasty was able to take control of the lands to the south. Mac-bethad (MacBeth), son of Findláech mormaer of Moray, ruled the whole of Alba 1040–57. The power of the northern dynasty did not outlast him, however, and the macAlpin line reasserted itself when, with English backing, Donnchad's son Máel-Coluim (Malcolm III) slew Mac-bethad's successor, Lulach. When he seized power in 1058, the most pressing problems for Máel-Coluim, known as ceann mór

(Canmore) 'Great Head/Chief', were to quash the resistance of the men of Moray in the north and to withstand the pressure of the Norse in the west. But the rest of his long reign, which lasted to 1093, was characterized by his increasingly hostile relations to the south with first Anglo-Saxon and then Norman England. Matters were not eased when in 1068 he married Margaret, sister to the refugee Edgar 'aetheling', princely symbol of Anglo-Saxon opposition to William the Conqueror. Only four years later Máel-Coluim was obliged to give homage to the new English king at Abernethy when William brought his army deep into Scottish territory. The political tensions of the period are reflected in the conflict which ensued when, in 1093, Máel-Coluim and his son were killed returning from raids in Northumbria. The succession was contested between his brother Domnall 'the Fair' (Donald Bán) (1094–7) and his English-supported sons: first Donnchad (Duncan II), son of Máel-Coluim's first wife Ingebjorg, Norse widow of the earl of Orkney; then Edgar (1097–1107), third son of Margaret.

Scotland in 1100

To what extent was the kingdom Máel-Coluim bequeathed to his successors something we could recognize as 'Scotland'? At the turn of the twelfth century the boundaries of 'Scotia' were still far from those of modern Scotland. Galloway did not come fully under the control of the Scots king for another sixty years. It would be for a further 160 years that the Western Isles remained under Scandinavian rule (till 1266), and a further 360 before the Northern Isles were once again ruled from Scotland (from the 1460s). The kingship was still based on the core Pictish areas between Spey and Forth: Moray was ostensibly under royal control but the provincial dynasty continued to flourish. Since the death of his grandfather and namesake in 1034, the kingdom of Alba had come to be known in Latin sources as *Scotia*. As king of the Scots, Máel-Coluim thus ruled over 'Scotia', 'Cumbria' (the old British territories of the west), and 'Lothian': only in the thirteenth century did Scotia, the lands of those who were subjects of the king of Scots, come to be applied also to the territory south of the Forth–Clyde line. Scotland was a kingdom first, and only then a land. Its diverse communities, speaking several languages, were brought together as one realm by their common allegiance to their king.

Wrapped up in the creation of Alba had been the promotion of Scone and St Andrews over the older Pictish centres, Forteviot and Dunkeld. Two centuries later the symbolic institutions of the kingdom were still centred on Scone (site of royal inauguration) and St Andrews (most senior bishopric). Other features had still deeper roots. By the late eleventh century there was very extensive organization and centralization of Scotland's agricultural produce: using an Anglo-Saxon terminology of 'thanes', 'thanages', and 'shires', but based on more ancient territorial units (as was the parish structure which we can first trace emerging in the decades after 1100). Wealth continued to flow from control of agricultural produce, those who owned land exploiting their resource by the labours of others, but we see at this time new attempts to expand the scale of lordship, often under direct royal authority. In the past the imposing nature of lordly residences had been achieved by siting them on craggy hills, as at Dunadd, Dundurn, and Dumbarton, but in the ninth century there had been a move down to more comfortable residences on the valley bottoms. It is a striking fact that no forts appear to have been built against the viking threat. In fact, in the two centuries 850–1050, there is no surviving trace of either church- or castle-building in stone. Structures, instead, were of timber. In the late eleventh century, however, the powerful and wealthy gradually turned, at key sites, to masonry architecture. Patronage of monumental sculpture declined over the eleventh century, and instead the elite began to sponsor the erection of church buildings, including impressively tall free-standing towers, both square, as at Dunblane and St Andrews, and round, as at Brechin and Abernethy. Though the growth of towns is more properly a phenomenon of the twelfth century and later, urban centres such as Perth had older origins. This seems particularly true of towns within the Scandinavian sphere, including Dingwall, Wick, and Kirkwall. Some of the economic and social functions of these later towns were performed in the tenth and eleventh centuries by the great monasteries, such as Whithorn and Brechin, with their important markets, dependent craftworkers and royal support. By 1100 the increase in trade had just begun to draw Scotland into a new 'European' economy.

From the reign of Mac-bethad, and to a greater extent that of Máel-Coluim, incomers from the south, loyal to the king, were being settled in areas where his authority was weak, especially in the south-west and north-east. The full impact of the immigrants' newly international culture was not felt until the twelfth century, though the ground was laid in the political developments of the second half of the eleventh. Yet this was still a profoundly Gaelic society. Everywhere except Lothian (and even there it was still expanding) Gaelic was the language, not only of everyday life but of the royal

court, of learning, and of law. The Church, too, was thoroughly Gaelic. Not only in culture but also in organization, the ecclesiastical foundations of Scotland, in all their diversity, still adhered to traditional Gaelic forms. Particularly prevalent were the houses of the *céli Dé* (Culdees), 'clients of God', whose origins lay in a monastic reform movement which had swept through the Gaelic Church from the ninth century. The twelfth-century spread of non-Gaelic-speaking clergy was to have a profound effect on Scottish culture, but in the eleventh century there was merely a foretaste when, in 1070, Margaret brought Benedictine monks from Canterbury to her new foundation at Dunfermline.

The twelfth century is often characterized as the period when Scotland opened up to outside influences, as if, previously, it had somehow been cut off from the wider world. Scotland had never been isolated, not since the Neolithic when the builders of stone circles and chambered tombs had participated in a religious and artistic tradition which stretched across Atlantic Europe from Portugal to Denmark. In the early medieval period, language linked Gaelic-speaking Scots to the Irish world, Norse-speakers to the far-flung colonies of Scandinavians to east and west, and Latin linked them all to the international culture of the Christian Church. It is true that the period around 1100 was a time of great change, but it was not just Scotland which was changing—it was the whole of Europe.

Facing: ALTHOUGH COMMON IN IRELAND, this eleventh century tower at Abernethy, Perthshire, is one of only two round towers to survive in Scotland. The function of these structures is debated, but in addition to housing bells they were probably 'treasuries' for the portable wealth of the monastery.

Legend:

- - - - Boundary of earldom. (Italic type=earldom held by native family)
✠ Bishopric (located by cathedral)
Stirling Main royal centre
● Seat of sheriffdom
□ Royal burgh
○ Major royal monastic foundation

ORKNEY

SHETLAND

LEWIS

CAITHNESS

SUTHERLAND

HARRIS

✠Caithness

ROSS

SKYE

✠Ross

✠Moray

BUCHAN

GARIOCH

GARMORAN

KNOYDART

M O R A Y

STRATH-
AVON

M A R

✠Aberdeen

BADENOCH

LOCHABER

Argyll

LORN

A T H O L L

Dunkeld✠

ANGUS

Brechin✠

Forfar

MENTEITH

STRATHEARN

Perth

St Andrews✠

FIFE

Dunblane✠

COWAL

Stirling

LENNOX

Edinburgh

KNAPDALE

BUTE

RENFREW

✠Glasgow

DUNBAR

Berwick

ISLAY

CUNNINGHAM

ARRAN

NORTH
KYLE

Selkirk

Roxburgh

CARRICK

ANNAN-
DALE

GALLOWAY

✠Whithorn

The Isles✠

MAN

0   25   50   75   100 km

0 10 20 30 40 50 60 miles

3.   Scotland in 1286

2 The Emergence of a Nation-State, 1100–1300

Keith Stringer

1100 and 1300

In effect, the twelfth and thirteenth centuries saw the birth of the modern West European state. The benchmarks included a well-defined national sovereignty, fully institutionalized administrative and legal systems, a commercialized economy, parliamentary representation, and a common sense of nationhood. Political entities unable to adapt to such norms were lucky to survive; but the Scottish kingdom rose, and the making of Scotland and the Scots in an ampler and (to us) more recognizable sense was one of the great state-building feats of these centuries.

By 1100 England under its new Norman rulers had extended its lead as the mightiest polity in the British Isles, and was claiming with unique forcefulness an imperial high-kingship over its 'Celtic' neighbours. In Wales, Ireland, and even northern Britain, the political landscape remained fragmented and multi-centred. Impressive as the reach of Scottish kingship had become, in 1100 there was no country like today's Scotland, and no nation such as today's Scots. Yet by 1286 all modern Scotland, save only Orkney and Shetland (Norwegian dependencies until 1468–9), had been transformed into a coherent, European-style nation-state. Scotland's rise is even more striking when set against the supremacy gained by the English crown in Wales and, from 1171, Ireland; and, famously, the kingdom had sufficient solidity to conduct an ultimately triumphant defence against concerted English attempts to extinguish its sovereign identity from 1296. In sum, after 1100 the old political order was gradually reshaped by *two* expansionist monarchies into a more manifestly bipolar world, with the result that the possibility of a single English kingdom of the medieval British Isles was never fully realized. The period 1100–1300 was therefore momentous not only in Scottish history but in British history as a whole, and the construction of a 'greater Scotland' is naturally our focal theme.

Crucial to this story are major shifts in Scotland's predominantly Gaelic culture and norms, processes accelerated by the arrival of ambitious colonists from as far afield as Normandy, Brittany, and Flanders. Thus, Scotland was increasingly affected by that broad expansionary and unifying phenomenon recently characterized as the 'Europeanization of Europe', and thereby shared more completely in the decisive political, religious, and socio-economic changes that moulded the dominant Western kingdoms from the 1060s onwards. Unsurprisingly, however, its chief source of new European ideas and technologies was Norman and Angevin England, the most 'advanced' European state. It was no accident that systematic change began in the pivotal reign of David I (1124–53), himself a leader of England's polit-ical elite as earl of Huntingdon and brother-in-law of King Henry I. Further-more, most of the knights, clergy, and townsfolk who flocked northwards were not Norman-French, but represented a second migratory incoming of English-speakers, albeit with more wide-ranging consequences than those of its sixth- and seventh-century forerunner.

Nevertheless, intensified Europeanization or, more aptly, Anglicization went only so far. Stress must be put on its gradual, uneven, and often non-revolution-ary nature; on the role played by existing forces, structures, and conventions in defining and shaping its impact; and on the essential distinctness of Scotland's experience. Most importantly, whereas Wales and Ireland witnessed Anglo-Norman conquests, in Scotland the Anglo-Normans settled by permission of the Scots kings, and recognized and advanced their superiority. So, unlike the more restricted and fragile native Welsh and Irish hegemonies, the Scottish kingdom had the capacity to absorb new influences and harness them to its own ends: a critical difference, and a forceful reminder that an earlier centralizing kingship had laid the groundwork for later success. More generally, in every sig-nificant sphere, developments after 1100 drew deeply on established modes and resources. Many initiatives involved regularizing entrenched practices, quickening existing trends, and augmenting proven strengths. The patterns of Scotland's past profoundly affected the nature of Scotland's future.

But it is one thing to highlight the continuities across the centuries; quite another to ignore the basic alterations society underwent. Nor was the emergence of an increasingly confident and far-reaching Scottish state by any means a foregone conclusion in 1100. The issue then was whether or not the gulf between the Scots realm and 'rising' European polities would expand apace. Specifically, a more assertive English monarchy had recently imposed humiliating treaties and agreements; it had seized Northumbrian territories—notably present-day Cumbria—claimed as rightfully Scottish. Customary norms and support systems no longer sufficed. After David I, the main innovators were Malcolm IV (1153–65) and William I 'the Lion' (1165–1214); Alexander II (1214–49) and Alexander III (1249–86) built on their policies and achieved more thorough and sustained advances in royal power. Accordingly, what was meant by Scotland and the Scots was radically redefined, and a kingdom largely divorced from the European mainstream in 1100 was transformed into one of Latin Christendom's strongest medium-sized states. Yet the fact remains that the creation of this new realm, country, and people rested throughout on the fusion of 'modern' ideas and a vigorous 'Celtic' legacy.

Scottish kingship: ideal and practice

An idealized account of David I's kingship was written by his English friend Ailred, the Cistercian abbot of Rievaulx in Yorkshire. He saw David as the only rightful king in northern Britain, whose firm but humane rule created a unified, well-ordered, and prosperous polity. Aided by Anglo-Norman knights and churchmen, he subdued 'many barbarous tribes', including the men of Moray and the Isles, and lorded it over Galloway and Argyll. But David was a true king to all his peoples, regardless of language, culture, and ethnic origins; he governed them justly, and 'always wished to be loved rather than feared'. His greatest virtue was his exemplary piety. He revitalized a moribund Church in accordance with new European paradigms, and ultimately tamed the 'barbarity' of the Gaelic–Norse kindreds 'by means of the Christian religion'. In such ways, Ailred believed, David ruled for the common good, groomed native society in genteel virtues, and instilled a strong sense of collective unity and identity:

He brought about [peace] with such authority among barbarous peoples with diversities of language and customs that . . . we have scarcely ever seen even among closely related peoples . . . of the same race and language such harmony being observed for such a long time.

Finally, for Ailred economic progress was a natural concomitant of 'civilized manners':

You who were formerly a beggar among all other countries . . . have relieved the poverty of neighbouring regions from your abundance. King David adorned you with castles and towns . . . enriched your ports with foreign merchandise, and added the riches of other lands for your delight.

Ailred, a leading publicist for the reforming European clergy and the benefits of a specifically English civility, shamelessly exaggerated to advance his own agenda. Yet, for all its hyperbole, his account undoubtedly represented David as the sort of ruler he aspired to be. Indeed, it powerfully evokes all the major elements at the heart of post-1100 Scottish kingship, and underlines how firmly David secured the basis for a fully fledged Scottish state. Four interlocking policies, all of which promoted a form of kingship superior to traditional Celtic-style kingship, can be highlighted straightaway.

The most obvious novelties concern the practical reinforcement of regnal power in the religious, economic, and other spheres, and ample evidence underscores the importance of the Davidian contribution on which later kings would build. Briefly, David strengthened the diocesan structure of the Scottish Church and planted in the eastern Lowlands major abbeys for the reformed European religious orders, notably the Augustinians and the Cistercians (the great Melrose was Rievaulx's daughter-house); he promoted an English-type market economy by minting the first Scottish coinage and founding royal burghs (including Berwick, Edinburgh, Perth, and Aberdeen); he settled in Lothian, Strathclyde, and lowland Moray trusted Anglo-Norman nobles who established strong local lordships based on castles, and supplied knights to his army; and he methodically experimented with the instruments and procedures of English administrative kingship. As an admirer in Normandy succinctly declared, David 'increased his power and was exalted above his predecessors'.

Second, David and his successors claimed a more exacting, monopolistic, and formalized royal lordship throughout a 'greater Scotland'. Their centralizing ambitions left no room for surviving local 'kings', and in general older notions of domination and subjection were redefined in stricter terms. They likewise institutionalized their hold on kingship by bringing an unprecedented orderliness to the royal succession, a vital requirement for national monarchy. No reminder was needed that the uncertainty and competitiveness of earlier practice had disrupted the systematic development of royal authority as recently as the 1090s, when William Rufus had exploited segmentary rivalries to England's advantage. Imitating Capetian custom, David pre-emptively made his only son Henry co-ruler in about 1135; on Henry's untimely death

ONE OF THE FINEST PIECES of Insular metalwork, this large gilded-silver brooch was made *c*.700. It is decorated with panels of intricate gold filigree work and amber mounts. In the tenth century the brooch belonged to the Gaelic-named *Máel-Brigte*, a fact recorded on the reverse in a Norse runic inscription.

THIS TINY PORTABLE SHRINE, the 'Monymusk reliquary', housed one of the chief relics of Scotland. Its hereditary keeper was charged with taking it into battle with the Scottish army, as was done at Bannockburn (1314). The reliquary was made *c*.750 and consists of a wooden casket, now empty, covered with silver and copper-alloy. Its decoration represents a fusion of Pictish and Gaelic artistic traditions.

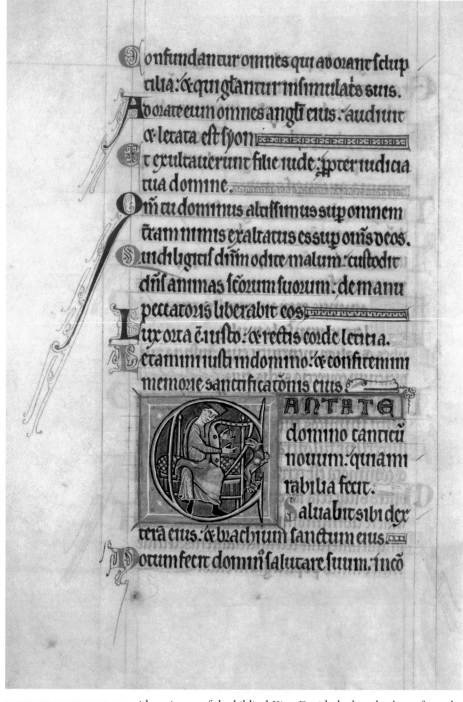

ILLUMINATED INITIAL, with an image of the biblical King David plucking his harp, from the 'Iona Psalter'. This devotional text is assumed to have been produced in Oxford for Beathag, first prioress of the Augustinian nunnery on Iona, founded by 1208. She was the daughter of Somerled, king of the Isles, and her cosmopolitan religious culture—albeit combined with devotion to St Columba—attests to the successes of European-style church reform in penetrating the Gaelic West.

Above: EDWARD III of England and David II of Scotland from a late fourteenth-century Book of Statutes. Anglo-Scottish relations in the fourteenth century were generally far less cordial than this depiction of the two kings might suggest.

Left: THE ARMS of the Douglas earls of Moray, Douglas, Ormond and the lord of Balvenie feature prominently in this mid-fifteenth-century armorial. By 1455 all these men had forfeited their lands and titles to the crown.

JAMES IV gifted a beautiful Book of Hours to his bride Margaret Tudor in 1503. Among its many stunning miniatures is this study of the king, flanked by St James, wearing an arched imperial crown and kneeling before an elaborate version of the royal arms displaying the same imperial motif.

in 1152, he had his oldest grandson recognized as heir presumptive, and Malcolm IV, though only 12, duly became king in 1153. Dynastic continuity was upheld even in the case of a child, unthinkable elsewhere in the 'Celtic' world, and a watershed for Scottish monarchical authority. Thereafter, the throne was held in the direct line until Alexander III's death in 1286. Alexander himself had succeeded unopposed as a 7-year-old in 1249. More remarkably, he successfully settled the succession on his baby granddaughter Margaret, the 'Maid of Norway', in 1284. Rebellions by rejected segments of the royal kin did not peter out until 1230; but the kingdom suffered far less than did other 'Celtic' polities from debilitating dynastic upheaval.

Third, it was a basic maxim that Scottish kingship was the equal of English kingship—be it to affirm its superiority vis-à-vis other power-holders in Scotland, to reply to the post-Conquest English monarchy's imperialist pretensions, or generally to bolster awareness of the independent status and identity of the kingdom. David's sovereign authority was fully accepted by Ailred, who in fact commended the Davidian concept of kingship to *English* monarchs. The Scots kings' insistence on parity was vividly expressed in their efforts to

THE SECOND GREAT SEAL OF ALEXANDER III. Scottish royal seals conformed to the double-sided English model by 1124, with the monarch depicted enthroned in majesty (front) and as a mounted knight (back). This seal, struck in *c.*1260, is a notably emphatic statement of sovereign authority. Alexander is crowned, with foliated sceptre, on a throne surmounted by four fleurs-de-lis; on back: his shield and the horse's trappings bear the royal arms within a tressure.

secure the pope's permission for the crowning and unction that proclaimed the semi-sacred aura of most other European monarchs as the Lord's anointed. Although English lobbying delayed papal approval until 1329, the conviction that their kingship was divinely ordained could not be gainsaid. Thus, in their charters they asserted their supremacy as direct intermediaries between God and their subjects by parading their majesty and glory as kings 'by God's grace'. On their seals and coins they likewise displayed the badges of regal authority familiar in Western Europe. More practically, they upheld their sovereign dignity by shielding the Scottish Church from the grasp of Canterbury or York; by prosecuting their historic rights to the 'English' Border shires; and, above all, by resisting the English crown's claims to the overlordship of Scotland—in marked contrast to the Welsh and Irish kings, who were much less reluctant to accept subordinate status. When in 1278 Alexander III was pressed to subject himself to Edward I, he bluntly retorted: 'No one has the right to homage for my kingdom save God alone.'

Lastly, the Scots kings promoted their kingliness by embracing new European courtly fashions and playing an international role with an assurance other rulers in the outer zone of the British Isles could only envy. David was the first Scottish king to win genuine respect on the wider European stage, and saw himself (according to Ailred) as a potential leader of the Second Crusade. French, and more especially English, became the stock languages of political society; the *Roman de Fergus*, a parody of knightly conventions, was written for the court's amusement in about 1200. David, knighted by Henry I of England, conferred knighthood on Henry's grandson, the future Henry II. Malcolm IV and William I, the sons of an Anglo-Norman mother, Ada de Warenne, adopted chivalric values with exceptional gusto. One English commentator even thought that they 'regarded themselves as . . . Frenchmen in race, manners, language, and culture'. There was already a demand for Scottish royal brides from continental princes; William I inaugurated the Auld Alliance by joining forces with Louis VII against Henry II in 1173. The two Alexanders married English princesses as their first wives and (to avoid over-dependence on England) high-born Frenchwomen as their second; Alexander III wed his daughter to Eric II of Norway.

Thus did the Scots kings seek and attain full membership of the community of West European rulers. Yet, on a broader view, it would be rash to overstate the novelty of royal ambitions, or—more importantly—the modernity of Scottish kingship in practice and style. David, as Ailred himself conceded, was as much a traditional Celtic-type ruler as a 'progressive' European monarch. No ruthless innovator, he worked with the grain of existing modes wherever practicable, and his successors followed suit. They normally ruled from ancient royal seats; a native elite remained influential alongside the Anglo-Normans; and an older layer of officialdom coexisted with the sheriffs, justiciars, and other new crown officers. Such continuity enhanced their legitimacy and support; but, in addition, they appreciated and capitalized on established strengths, including the old systems for securing tribute and military service.

They also invoked time-honoured rituals, images, symbols, and values, partly to validate their kingship by broadcasting its antiquity, partly to assert or reaffirm a potent sense of Scottish self-identity and cohesion. A classic instance concerns the act of royal inauguration. Ailred records that, albeit reluctantly, David accepted his bishops' advice to be enthroned in the customary manner; and the ceremonial of later king-makings conformed in essence to ancient rite. But, above all, the traditional face of Scottish kingship is seen in the fact that it never sought to match the increasingly authoritarian, interventionist, and confrontational ethos of English kingship. If this was partly a matter of resources, it was also a matter of choice. Royal prestige and authority still rested in good measure on the charismatic and relatively non-bureaucratic qualities of 'Celtic' rulership; and whereas English monarchs were often much feared, Scots kings were more truly, to adopt Ailred's biblical imagery, 'all things to all men'. They did not simply bask in the warm glow of David's holy kingship. Malcolm IV's reputation for chastity won admiration from native and English clergy alike; while Adam of Dryburgh (d. 1212) concluded that Scotland was second only to France for the saintliness of its kings. They reinforced regnal solidarity and loyalty by routinely stressing the immemorial 'tribal' bond between king and people. Ailred applauded David not only for treating his knights as equals, but for dispensing justice in person to ordinary folk at the door of his hall—often, surely, in fluent Gaelic. Significantly, the royal title 'king of Scots' was retained whereas from 1199 the English style was the more aloof 'king of England'; and perhaps nowhere does the affinity between ruler and ruled resonate more powerfully than in the praise given to Alexander III for governing Scotland 'in love and law'.

Admittedly, the expansion of the kingdom was a far less peaceful process than is often supposed, and individual Scots kings were no doubt perceived by their Gaelic–Norse enemies as iron-handed modernizers. Even the youthful Malcolm IV, so it was reported, 'terrorized the wicked and insolent by his royal authority and sternness'. But the fact remains that Scottish kingship fol-

THE INAUGURATION OF ALEXANDER III (1249), a representation of c.1440 illustrating Walter Bower's description of the ceremony, drawn from a contemporary account. Alexander is crowned, with sceptre, like a 'modern' monarch; but he sits in the cemetery of Scone Abbey, and the scene captures a focal stage in the ancient king-making ritual: the Highlander's recitation in Gaelic of Alexander's genealogy back to Iber Scot, the first Scot. Though the Stone is not shown, Alexander was undoubtedly enthroned on it.

lowed a different trajectory from that of its markedly more abrasive English counterpart. The Scottish heartlands never saw epic struggles like the Barons' Wars against royal overmightiness in thirteenth-century England. The factional squabbles of Alexander III's minority (1249–60) were kept within bounds; and overt conflict was confined largely to peripheral regions. Even then, political unification was based not simply on military conquest, but on respect for provincial interests; while, as a normal course, the crown still relied for much of its influence on power-sharing with local potentates, albeit in more structured ways. For all its coercive features, state-making in twelfth- and thirteenth-century Scotland thus displayed a lightness of touch more reminiscent of pre-1100 Scots statecraft than of contemporary English strategies.

Such aspects of Scottish kingship, however outmoded in Westminster terms, were in reality a major source of empowerment. And, most vitally, whereas the English regimes in Wales and Ireland ultimately created deeply fractured societies through a form of 'anti-Celtic' apartheid, that never happened in Scotland. Ailred trumpeted the superiority of Englishness; but, crucially, he believed that Gaeldom was inferior for socio-cultural, not racial, reasons, and that Scottish kingship could—and must—surmount ethnic divisions. Such views were basic to David and his successors who, notwithstanding their Anglicizing ambitions, dealt with all the peoples within their ambit more or less even-handedly. That had cardinal importance for the shaping of a new Scottish kingdom and people; it also epitomizes the greatest strength of this emerging nation-state: the judicious balance maintained between old and new.

Anglo-Scottish warfare and diplomacy

The main shifts in Anglo-Scottish relations from 1100 to 1300 provide a broader context for Scotland's political development—and a sharp reminder that it depended on a complex mix of design and chance. In 1296 Edward I attacked Scotland, followed up victory at Dunbar with King John Balliol's enforced abdication, and resolved to rule the country as its sovereign lord. But previous English monarchs, after William Rufus's drive to the Solway (1092), preferred peace to aggression. Given their continental priorities, it was imperative to stabilize relations with the developing Scottish state by treating it more gently than they treated native Wales and Ireland. One way of keeping the Scots kings in line was to make periodic demands for recognition of English overlordship; another diplomatic weapon was the earldom of Huntingdon. Acquired in 1113, it secured their dependence as the English crown's vassals; conversely, however, it enabled them to rebut the claims of English high-kingship by insisting that homage was due for English lands alone. English armies did invade Lothian (1138, 1173, 1216), but actually to check Scottish expansion into England—a very different story from that of Wales and Ireland. Ultimately, of course, northern England remained under the English crown. But if in retrospect that outcome seems inevitable, it was not so obvious to contemporaries, especially during David I's reign.

While all the Scottish offensives exploited English political turmoil, they nevertheless registered the increasingly bipolar nature of contemporary 'British' politics. Unlike Malcolm Canmore's attacks on Northumberland, David's campaigns against King Stephen resulted in extensive conquests. Despite the battle of the Standard near Northallerton (1138)—the only large-scale Scottish defeat in this period prior to Dunbar—David annexed the 'English' north to the Ribble and the Tees. From 1141 he kept court at Newcastle and Carlisle, replaced Stephen's kingship by his own, and, combining firmness with conciliation, won the northerners' respect and loyalty. This major shift in political geography threatened to curb the English crown's predominance for good; in 1149, indeed, David came close to seizing Yorkshire. But unforeseen calamities then occurred—notably the premature death of David's able son Henry in 1152 and the peaceful accession to the English throne of Stephen's former enemy, the formidable Henry of Anjou, in 1154—and, on Henry II's insistence, the boy-king Malcolm IV withdrew to the Tweed–Solway line in 1157.

In 1173–4 William I invaded Northumberland and Cumberland in an ill-starred bid to reassert Scottish control. Captured unawares at Alnwick (the bulk of his army was elsewhere), he regained his liberty only after acknowledging by the Treaty of Falaise (1174) that he was Henry II's liege vassal for Scotland—an unprecedented formal surrender of Scottish independence, reinforced by the handover to English garrisons of Berwick, Roxburgh, and Edinburgh castles. Yet Henry did not press his luck, and prudently refrained from exercising his overlordship to the full. Moreover, in 1189—for a hefty cash payment—Richard I restored Scottish independence, which was not to be relinquished again until 1291. The ageing William suffered from King John's bullying tactics; but in 1215 Alexander II regained the initiative by invading in alliance with the rebel barons of Magna Carta, who recognized Scottish claims to Northumberland, Cumberland, and Westmorland. In

1216 even the Yorkshire rebels entered his allegiance and, in a signal feat of Scottish arms, he marched the length of England to Dover to meet the pretender to the English crown, Prince Louis of France, who confirmed his right to the three Border counties. Yet the hated John's sudden death was a major blow for the Scots: Alexander's allies rapidly fell away; and in 1217 he made peace—the more readily because the pope had subjected him and his subjects to excommunication and interdict (suspension of public worship).

What were the long-term consequences of these wars for Scotland? David I's control in the 1140s of the rich Pennine silver mines near Carlisle stimulated rapid development of the Scottish economy, accentuating the crown's wealth and authority, and attracting Anglo-Norman adventurers into its service in increasing numbers. But the inglorious campaigns of 1173–4 and 1215–17 quashed the old dreams of southern expansion, and royal resources were concentrated more exclusively on power-building in Scotland's north and west. England, however, had been repeatedly reminded that the strengthened Scottish state was more valuable as an ally than an enemy.

The final outcome was unbroken peace between the crowns from 1217 to 1296—the longest period of Anglo-Scottish harmony in the entire Middle Ages. Accord was cemented by Alexander II's marriage to Henry III's sister Joan (1221), and by Alexander III's marriage to Henry's daughter Margaret (1251). And, strikingly, whereas the English crown's attitude towards the residual Welsh and Irish 'kingships' became increasingly uncompromising, it normally respected Scotland's status as a distinct self-governing realm. When it revived claims to overlordship (1235, 1251, 1278), these were quickly dropped after Scottish protests. The Treaty of York (1237), whereby Alexander II accepted for good that the Border counties were English shires in return for a Cumberland lordship based on Penrith, was an honourable settlement between sovereign polities. During Alexander III's minority, Henry III restrained his meddling, and often expressed his respect for Scottish laws and liberties. However reluctantly, the English crown was accepting the existence of a viable polity able to sustain an alternative supremacy to its own. Another stabilizing influence was an increasingly prominent body of landowners with Anglo-Scottish estates; yet the Border itself was an international frontier, and cross-Border lords, unlike English barons in Wales and Ireland, owed a dual loyalty to two sovereign rulers.

An extraordinary series of dynastic accidents destroyed this equilibrium. Aged 44, Alexander III was killed by a fall from his horse in 1286; his three

children had already died, and his only descendant was the 3-year-old Maid
of Norway. Margaret's betrothal to Edward I's son and heir Edward of
Caernarfon (later Edward II), agreed by the Treaty of Birgham (1290), was
expected—with appropriate safeguards of Scottish autonomy—to perpetu-
ate peace; and a lasting Anglo-Scottish union, similar to the Union of the
Crowns of 1603, might have resulted. But Margaret died while travelling
from Bergen to Scotland in September 1290. On this further catastrophe, the
Scottish state was left without an obvious monarch, and John Balliol, lord of
Galloway, and twelve others claimed the crown. Scotland's predicament was
England's opportunity. Edward I insisted on adjudicating in the succession
debate (the 'Great Cause') as Scotland's superior lord; and Balliol had to give
homage as a client-king immediately after his enthronement in 1292. Edward
interpreted his right to control Scottish affairs far more rigorously than Henry
II had done in 1174–89, but gravely misjudged the Scots' determination and
ability to defend their independent identity and nationhood. In 1295 their
leaders repudiated English overlordship in the name of the 'community of
the realm', and concluded an alliance with France. From 1296 it was England's turn to overreach itself in costly Anglo-Scottish warfare.

The territorial definition of the kingdom

Basic to the regnal solidarity that upheld Scottish independence after 1296
was the emergence of 'greater Scotland' as a single kingdom and country. Yet
in the twelfth century a fully united state remained an uncertain prospect.
Anglicization then underpinned Scottish rule primarily in the eastern Lowlands and Strathclyde. That gave it the boon of a larger and more powerful
core, but left a vast, largely unassimilated Gaelic–Norse sector. Disaffected
segments of the royal house, operating from Moray and especially Ross, periodically took the offensive. The MacHeths were still troubling the crown in
1215; the MacWilliam pretenders were not finally trounced until 1230. Even
more daunting were the obstacles to unity represented by the maritime polities of the far north and west. However much the Scottish government
believed otherwise, their ambitious rulers saw themselves as exercising legitimate authority independently of the Scots king within a western-sea zone
sweeping across the extremities of the British Isles from Man to Shetland.
Most flaunted royal titles as a matter of right; all commanded substantial
fleets, had their own courts and administrations, controlled the Church in
their territories, and negotiated freely with external powers.

These twelfth-century potentates included Harald Maddadson (d. 1206), the Norse earl of Orkney and Caithness; Fergus (d. 1161), king of the Gallovidians; and Somerled (d. 1164), king of the Isles, whose sea-kingdom included a vast tract of the mainland from Kintyre to Knoydart. Although Somerled's domains fragmented in 1164, his powerful descendants, the Mac-Donalds of Islay, the MacDougalls of Lorn, and the MacRuaries of Garmoran, for long strove to uphold regal authority and governmental autonomy, as did the Manx kings, whose dominions normally incorporated Skye, Harris, and Lewis. The capacity of such rulers to compete successfully with a stronger Scottish crown was questionable; but David I and his successors were not the only ones busy modernizing. Fergus of Galloway, who married an illegitimate daughter of Henry I of England, sponsored a concerted programme of ecclesiastical reform. No less impressively, by the 1250s the Mac-Dougalls and other western chieftains had reinforced their power-bases with mighty stone-built castles such as curtain-walled Castle Sween, Mingary, and Dunstaffnage. On this perspective, Scotland might be seen as containing one major kingdom and several 'proto-states', with each seeking by broadly similar means to assert and magnify its hegemony. And, finally, from about 1230 the Scots crown had to contend with a resurgent Norwegian monarchy anxious to restore its much-eroded authority over the Hebrides and Man.

Yet if Scottish unification involved a more radical reworking of the established order than is sometimes assumed, there is no doubting who presided over the shape of the political map. In the twelfth century, military challenges to the Scots kings' dominance usually ended in swift and expensive defeats. It was another index of their supremacy that the hostility encountered was often a defensive reaction to centralizing pressures. Save only in 1130—when Angus of Moray (a 'king' in Irish sources) was killed near Brechin—enemies lacked the means to strike in strength and depth into the royal heartlands. David I's takeover of the Moray lowlands, secured with castle-burghs and Anglo-Norman colonists, clipped the wings of the MacHeths and MacWilliams. Such was the crown's superior ability to project force that in a series of campaigns between 1179 and 1215 they were harried by armies operating forward of Inverness. Fergus of Galloway renounced his royalty following Malcolm IV's south-western offensives (1160); Somerled's counter-strike against encroaching Scottish power ended when he was slain near Renfrew (1164). Galloway threw off Scottish rule in 1174 and subjected itself to the English crown; but William I weathered this grave crisis, and had effectively re-established his control by 1186. In 1196–7 Harald Maddadson was severely disciplined for invading Moray. By 1179 royal castles guarded the Beauly and Cromarty Firths; in 1196 a royal army even sacked Thurso.

The decisive period nevertheless came later. Profiting from stable relations with England and a greater command of resources, Alexander II secured an uncontested dominance over the entire Scottish mainland—finally pacifying Ross and Caithness by the 1220s, quashing the vestiges of Galloway's autonomy in 1235, and bringing Argyll definitively within the orbit of crown authority by 1249. Hebridean sea-kings still contended for pre-eminence, and an increasingly confident Hakon IV of Norway was playing a more interventionist role. But such was Alexander's military reach that when he took ill (and died) on Kerrera in Oban Bay (1249), he was leading a great fleet and army poised to assault the Isles. The momentum was resumed when, after his lengthy minority, Alexander III applied pressure on Skye in 1262; Hakon's large-scale counter-attack faltered at Largs in 1263, precipitating the withdrawal of his armada to Orkney where he died; Scots war captains briskly took control of the southern Hebrides, and the king of Man came to terms. Then, by the Treaty of Perth (1266), Magnus IV of Norway ceded to the Scottish crown the Hebrides and Man in full sovereignty.

This landmark event defined the kingdom's western frontier as firmly as the Treaty of York had defined the Anglo-Scottish Border. Alexander III had finally eliminated all rival and lesser kingships in northern Britain; he had truncated the sovereign jurisdiction of the Norwegian monarchy, whose British sphere of influence was now reduced to Orkney and Shetland; and he had effectively secured Scotland's identity as a unitary state by bringing nearly all its inhabitants and territories under his sole and undisputed authority. The impressiveness of the intensification of Scottish dominion from David I's reign to its triumphant conclusion in 1266 is often obscured by the Anglocentric assumptions of British historiography. England's vastly superior strength was acknowledged by Alexander II in 1237 when he renounced all claims to northern England; it had to be recognized again in 1290 when Edward I seized Man. To this extent, Scotland was 'made' by English might. But the English polity was not the only dominant power able to usurp other royalties with a thoroughness previously unseen. Whereas in 1100 multiple kingships had been the norm in the British Isles, royal authority was now largely concentrated in the hands of two centralizing monarchies; by 1266 an essentially bipolar world had truly arrived.

There was, however, much more to the securing of Scottish unity than military conquest. The crown employed age-old devices of political coercion:

hostage-taking, forfeiture, punitive tributes, and calculated brutality—shockingly, in 1230 a MacWilliam baby girl had her skull smashed against Forfar's market cross. It benefited from Norway's strategic overextension; it also capitalized on the volatile alliances and chronic segementary feuding of Gaelic–Norse politics. But this merely highlights the fact that, despite concern to innovate, political units in Scotland's 'Celtic fringe' fell far short of overcoming their historic limitations, and amounted in practice to little more than increasingly unviable chiefdoms. Thus, on the one hand, concepts of royalty and power remained loose and insubstantial. On the other, the centralizing capacity of Scottish kingship was unrivalled—not least in terms of the cultivation of political support, the mobilization of economic resources, and the expansion of royal governance.

The Anglo-Norman nobility

Vital to Scottish state-making was the creation of a new Anglo-Norman nobility alongside the old native nobility. By 1200 the imprint of these assertive and acquisitive colonists had in many respects transformed Scotland as radically as that of their counterparts had transformed Wales and Ireland. That they did not come as conquerors needs no further emphasis; but Scottish society was nevertheless deeply affected by the aristocratic ethos and conventions of England and France. Many knightly incomers were themselves of Norman-French descent: for example, the Bruces, Colvilles, and Mowbrays hailed originally from Normandy; the Stewarts from Brittany; the Balliols from Picardy; the Douglases and Murrays from Flanders. Yet most belonged to English—or at least England-based and Anglicized—families and contributed, as did numerous other newcomers, to the diffusion of English speech over much of Lowland Scotland. The Giffards, Lindsays, Morvilles, Olifards (Oliphants), Ridels, and some others arrived from the earldom of Huntingdon; but many English counties, especially Yorkshire and Somerset, were represented. Crown favour was by far the surest route to landed wealth, and though immigration had slackened by about 1200, established settler families continued to earn substantial rewards thereafter.

Foremost was a small group of magnates like the Comyns and Stewarts, who held their vast estates directly of the king and served him as trusted advisers and officials. Their cosmopolitan outlook is amply reflected in the career of Robert Bruce of Annandale (d. 1295), grandfather of King Robert I, whose lands reached from Aberdeenshire to Middlesex. He married the earl

KNIGHTS PURSUING a defeated enemy at the points of their lances, from an English manuscript of *c.*1135. By this date David I had added a new cutting-edge to his war machine in the form of some 200 Anglo-Norman knights. At the battle of the Standard (1138), the bravery of his son Henry in leading a cavalry charge against the English army's flank was widely admired.

of Gloucester's daughter, was sheriff of Cumberland, fought for Henry III at the battle of Lewes (1264), went on crusade to the Holy Land (1271–2), granted lands in Annandale to Clairvaux Abbey in Burgundy, and was buried at Guisborough Priory, Yorkshire. In general, however, noble interests and attachments were primarily Scottish, due partly to the Scots kings' shrewd policy of recruiting lesser English landowners, often younger sons, whose loyalties centred on the Scottish court as their essential source of patronage and power. Such were Abbot Ailred's kinsman Robert son of Philip, raised to the nobility thanks to his 'great wealth' as a Lothianer; and, more notably, David I's constable Hugh de Morville, and his steward Walter son of Alan, first of the Stewarts.

Anglo-Norman colonization brought to Scotland an intensified form of power-building historians once confidently called 'feudalism'. Nowadays the word (a modern construct) is often avoided; but such terminology remains useful, provided it is accepted that 'feudal' power was varied, flexible, and adaptable. Land was granted by the lord (king or magnate) to his man or vassal as a fief or feu (Latin, *feudum*) on clear-cut conditions, the most basic being loyalty and counsel, subjection to the lord's jurisdiction, and specified service, normally (though by no means invariably) knight-service. What did the Scots king gain from this? He affirmed his political supremacy over noble society by recasting old-established notions of hegemony and clientship in stricter rule-bound (and written) terms. His 'feudal' rights allowed him to collect inheritance levies known as reliefs; to take minors and their lands into wardship; to demand special payments or aids when need arose; and to influence the descent of properties, most notably by upholding the claims of female heirs and controlling their marriages. In addition, he asserted his overriding judicial superiority by insisting on settling disputes about estates and a general licence to regulate his vassals' affairs. He also secured, in the form of mail-clad knights trained in the European arts of cavalry and castle warfare, a potent new weapon for crushing rebellions; and, above all, he gained new allies who extended the reach of his power by imposing in the localities a firmer territorial lordship of the sort familiar to them in England.

This updated system of delegated governance came into its own on the frontiers of crown authority. Very different from the tangled landholding pattern typical of Anglo-Norman colonization from Lothian to the Mearns were the concentrations in remoter areas, where the king installed hand-picked vassals in strategically commanding 'provincial lordships', complete with extensive jurisdictional rights. By 1165 Anglo-Norman lieutenants controlled a network of such fiefs stretching from the western Borders to the Firth of Clyde: Liddesdale (Soules), Upper Eskdale (Avenel), Annandale (Bruce), North Kyle (Stewart), Cunningham (Morville), and Renfrew (Stewart). By the 1230s the great Highland lordships of Badenoch and Lochaber had been created for, or taken over by, the Comyns; earlier, probably in the 1190s, the Murrays had begun to ensconce themselves in Sutherland. In the south-west Highlands, the expansion of the kingdom was spearheaded by the Stewarts, who had gained Bute by about 1200 and mastered Arran, Knapdale, and Cowal by the 1260s.

AERIAL VIEW OF THE MOTE OF URR in Galloway, the finest of all surviving Scottish motte-and-bailey castles. Such structures, built to master space and people, represented a major intensification of lordship and control. Urr was fortified by Walter de Berkeley (Barclay), who had come to Scotland from Somerset in c.1165. He was William I's chamberlain, and carried crown influence into Galloway by marrying a granddaughter of 'king' Fergus.

INVERLOCHY CASTLE in Lochaber, controlling the Great Glen's southern entrance, was one of several first-class stone strongholds erected by the Comyns, the greatest noble castle-builders in thirteenth-century Scotland. Begun in *c*.1275, it has a quadrangular plan, with a round tower at each corner of the curtain wall. Horatio McCulloch's painting conveys an apt image of power and wealth, despite the structural damage, and shows the castle before further alterations to its fabric in the late nineteenth century.

Incoming nobles bolted their rule on the countryside and its inhabitants by building castles, the pre-eminent symbols and tools of 'feudal' domination. The typical early castle (about 300 sites exist) was the motte—a large mound, man-made or natural, topped by a timber tower—and some were erected with baileys, enclosures housing barns and other service facilities. Parts of the south-west and north-east bristled with them; in securer areas, ringwork castles with simple banks and ditches often sufficed. From about 1200, leading Anglo-Norman lords (and the crown itself) reinforced their prestige and power in stone, as at Lochmaben (Bruce), Rothesay (Stewart), Inverlochy, and Lochindorb (Comyn). The big advantage of castles was their multi-functional role in maximizing lordly authority as military/policing strong-points, seats of justice, and hubs of sterner economic regimes. 'Provincial lordships' might be furnished with other new instruments of control and exploitation: burghs, reform monasteries, English-style estate bureaucracies, and large Anglo-Norman tenantries of knightly followers.

So Anglo-Norman might complemented royal might and played a key role in unifying the kingdom. In the thirteenth century, indeed, the exceptionally powerful Comyns and a few others also exercised lordship as earls (see below). But some crucial riders must promptly be added. There remained vast areas outside the southern Lowlands and the east midlands where Anglo-Norman settlement was limited or non-existent; and there was much adjust-ment to local conditions. That applies especially to lordships like Badenoch and Sutherland, whose holders fitted comfortably into the role of Highland chiefs, wielding a more or less traditional hegemony over largely Gaelic-speaking clients. In less far-flung regions, Anglo-Norman control and innova-tion went deeper; but everywhere novel forms were superimposed on an essentially unchanged base of customary arrangements and support systems. Most 'provincial lordships' corresponded to pre-existing regional power structures; many smaller fiefs were developed from 'shires' or thanages. Native and Anglo-Norman forms of lordship were harnessed, just as the crown itself found in the ancient obligations of clientship a ready-made framework from which a more demanding royal superiority could be fash-ioned. Scottish 'feudalism' was a distinctive synthesis of old and new.

Native lords and encounters with change

Farquhar MacTaggart, a native leader in Ross, suppressed a MacWilliam uprising in 1215, was rewarded by Alexander II with a knighthood and an earl-dom, and went on to rout rebels in Galloway in 1235. For all the crown's reliance on Anglo-Norman nobles, regnal unity and loyalty also rested on co-opting the old political elites, and drawing them into a closer relationship of 'feudal' dependence and service. Chief among the native nobility were the earls. Most twelfth-century earldoms were based on pre-1100 mormaerships, and 'earl' is merely the English term for 'mormaer'. But the crown flexed its muscles by suppressing Gowrie, Moray, and Ross; in about 1136 David I re-granted Fife to Earl Duncan as a fief subject to definite services. In the thir-teenth century, it was assumed that earldoms were normally held of the crown 'in feu', albeit not for knight-service. Intensified royal lordship was vividly reflected in the imposition of 'feudal' inheritance practices to rework local power balances, as when, by royally arranged marriages, Buchan passed to the Comyns (1212), Angus to the Umfravilles (1243), and Menteith to the Comyns (c.1234), then to the Stewarts (1261). A new earldom, Sutherland (c.1235), was created for the Murrays at the expense of the earls of Orkney/Caithness.

Yet crown policy expressed itself in ways many native lords found accept-able. 'Feudal' submission was probably seen as no more dishonourable than clientship, especially since it reinforced the right to royal protection. That above all was what most local leaders wanted, and that in essence was what they got. The Scots kings had the strength and foresight to moderate Anglo-Norman ambitions, minimize antagonisms, and ensure that even formerly independent rulers identified their interests with the crown's. Countless native landowners survived unmolested in the Lowland core itself; while, until 1212, only native magnates (often the descendants of pre-1100 mor-maers) enjoyed the special status of earls. Furthermore, of the thirteen earl-doms in 1286 eight (including Ross, revived for Farquhar MacTaggart) remained in native hands. There was thus no parallel to the imperialist Eng-lish political and cultural supremacy in Wales and Ireland, which polarized groups into 'insiders' and 'outsiders' by ostracizing old dynasties from public life and dispossessing many of their wealth and power. Mutual accommoda-tion between native and settler lords was the predominant theme and, despite the gravity of occasional rebellions in its borderlands, Scotland never saw general 'Celtic reactions' comparable to the anti-English risings else-where in the British Isles. To put it in Abbot Ailred's terms, 'the harmony of the nobles is the firm foundation of a kingdom'.

More specifically, the crown reconciled old and new elements by spread-ing its patronage widely, encouraging mixed marriages, and fostering a sense of common loyalty, fellowship, and identity. The key unifying role of the royal court was strengthened by the lack of major competition from other courts, and by the appeal of its cosmopolitan modes, including a chivalrous etiquette underwriting respect for the crown and aristocratic solidarity. As importantly, native lords could acclimatize to Anglo-Norman ways without having to renounce too much of their Gaelic distinctiveness, and could rap-idly adapt them to enhance their own standing. In twelfth-century eastern Scotland, most took change in their stride. The earls of Fife and Strathearn adopted the status and ethos of knights, married prominent Anglo-Norman ladies, built castles, recruited Anglo-Norman dependants, and eventually acquired English lands, in Yorkshire and Northumberland respectively. The Fifes profited steadily from royal favour, and by 1214 had gained two 'provincial lordships'—Strathavon and Strathbogie—in advance of that of Garioch (Aberdeenshire) created by William I for his brother, Earl David of Huntingdon, in about 1180. For men like these, the court lost none of its allure. They served as royal confidants alongside the king's Anglo-Norman intimates, and generally played an equivalent 'feudal' role in anchoring royal authority more effectively.

Court society also found a niche for Gaelic–Norse princelings from beyond the Scottish heartlands, where the processes of 'conquest' involved peaceful assimilation as much as military expansion. In Galloway, Carrick, the Highlands, and the Isles, the survival of an intensely Gaelic-dominated socio-economic and political culture can hardly be gainsaid. Yet Roland (d. 1200) and Alan (d. 1234) of Galloway, successors of 'king' Fergus, found the magnetism of the court and its fashions irresistible—the more so because they were allowed to retain much of their regional authority. At once Gaelic chiefs and Anglicized nobles, they bestrode the two cultural traditions and reaped the rewards of both. Their seals depicted them as mounted knights; their marriages tied them to the Morvilles and the royal house itself; their retinues included Anglo-Normans closely connected with eastern Scotland; and their support for European monasticism further blurred distinctions between Galloway and the kingdom's core. Acquisition of the Morville fiefs of Cunningham and Lauderdale brought them major new sources of affluence and influence; they also held the unique dignity of 'constable of Scotland', a great office reserved for the Scots king's chief war captain. Alan campaigned for Alexander II in the Hebrides, Man, and northern England; Roland had presented Donald MacWilliam's head to William I in 1187. Although Fergus's family was shorn of its royal rank, submission brought benefits as well as costs, and the Galloways collaborated with the crown to their mutual advantage.

The gentle side of royal policy had its limits. The Gallovidian revolt of 1234–5 was not separatist in origin but provoked by Alexander II when, ignoring native custom, he disinherited Alan of Galloway's bastard son and partitioned the province among Alan's daughters and their English husbands—a classic example of the tightening of the 'feudal' screw. Soon after, however, the king wisely granted to the Galloway kindreds the right to retain their own laws. A major reason for King Hakon's defeat in 1263 was that some western sea-lords had already been lured into the Scottish court and its service; and in the Treaty of Perth (1266) Alexander III ensured the Islemen's loyalty by offering terms even erstwhile enemies could readily accept. The MacDougalls are an instructive case. Ewen MacDougall, sometime 'king of the Isles', entered the Scottish allegiance as lord of Argyll in 1255; he named his first son in Alexander III's honour, and rebuffed Norwegian overtures in 1263. Alexander MacDougall—who was knighted like his father—married a Comyn, attended parliament as a 'baron of the realm of Scotland', and served as the crown's chief governor in the western seaboard. A broader, more homogeneous aristocratic community had emerged, linked by shared experiences and priorities, by an intricate web of kinship bonds, and by growing recognition of a common Scottish identity. Nor was acculturation a one-way process. The Anglo-Normans had adjusted successfully to their neighbours, even (in some instances) by learning Gaelic. Effectively, Scotland by 1286 had been shaped into a new political world in which the king stood at the head of a single nobility: a court-oriented, Anglo-Norman-Gaelic elite.

Church and crown

Religious change was no less pivotal to the making of Scotland and the Scots. However overdrawn, the deficiencies of 'Celtic' Christianity scathingly decried by charismatic reformers like Abbot Ailred prompted and justified the lead taken by the crown in bringing the Scottish Church into closer conformity with English and broader European norms. In practice, tradition and innovation were intermixed, partly because frameworks were found which could easily be rationalized and extended—even Ailred admitted that a few tolerably well-organized bishoprics existed in 1124 (St Andrews is an obvious example). Nevertheless, Scotland's ecclesiastical face was reshaped to an extent that had no parallel until the Reformation itself.

By 1200 the diocesan structure of mainland Scotland comprised eleven continental-type territorial bishoprics, nearly all directly under the Scots king; parish formation, boosted by David I's legislation enforcing payment of teinds (tithes), was far advanced; and there had been a dramatic proliferation of reform monasteries, two-thirds of them crown foundations. The Cistercians of Coupar Angus and Melrose benefited greatly from sustained royal favour, as did the Augustinians of Holyrood, St Andrews, and Scone, and the Tironensians of Arbroath and Kelso. Alexander II (1214–49) took firm control of the bishoprics of Argyll, Dunblane, and Whithorn/Galloway; co-founded Balmerino Abbey, the last of Melrose's four Scottish daughter-houses; set up Pluscarden Priory for the Valliscaulians, a new Burgundian monastic order; and introduced the mendicant friars, the first Dominicans perhaps coming from Paris.

Most twelfth-century bishops and abbots, and many rank-and-file clergy, were English incomers. The thirteenth-century Church, staffed largely from the Anglicized Lowlands, was hardly less noted for its reforming zeal. So marked was the spread of pastoral provision that by 1300 there was a

AERIAL VIEW OF JEDBURGH ABBEY, including the claustral area (domestic quarters) excavated in 1984. It was founded by David I in *c*. 1138 for Augustinian canons from Beauvais in Picardy. A century of intensive building work, incorporating the most fashionable English and continental motifs, brought the abbey to its glorious prime; and to stand today in its imposing kirk—a rich surviving example of medieval monastic architecture—is to appreciate how far the Scottish Church had set itself on a new course.

nationwide parish system, essentially the same as today's. Glasgow and Dunkeld cathedrals adopted the constitutions of Salisbury; Moray those of Lincoln. English architectural styles left an indelible mark in the magnificent abbeys and kirks that from about 1130 began to transform the Scottish landscape. Cistercian abbots were required to join their fellows from elsewhere in Europe for regular meetings at Cîteaux in Burgundy, to whose running costs Alexander II himself contributed. Clergy educated at newly founded universities like Oxford, Paris, and Bologna applied their expertise to governing the Scottish Church and kingdom. The pope asserted an unparalleled authority over the Scottish priesthood. In these ways and others, Scotland was drawn firmly within the West European religious scene.

But whereas in Wales and Ireland church reform underwrote Anglo-Norman conquests, in Scotland the crown's directing influence never faltered, and royal piety and bounty were repaid with respect and support. William I angered Rome by insisting too blatantly on control of church appointments; and the thirteenth-century papacy sometimes seemed too pro-English for comfort. Yet the crown's senior clergy, for all their supranational affiliations, took a markedly royalist stance, identifying themselves with the kingdom and a distinct 'national' Scottish Church.

Accordingly, a major impetus was given to the close church–king alliance characteristic of Scotland's Gaelic religious tradition. With their stronger institutional structures and greater resources, reform churchmen advanced monarchical authority and generally promoted the concept of a unitary state and people. Deeply committed to peace and good governance, they held important offices in the king's central administration, while their advanced literate mentality and record-keeping skills added a new incisiveness to his power. The consolidation of monastic estates and dioceses gave abbots and bishops a primary role alongside the greater nobles in sustaining royal authority locally. By about 1200, the 'frontier' bishoprics of Moray, Ross, and Caithness were sufficiently well established to carry crown influence far into the periphery. Bishop Adam of Caithness's murder by the earl of Orkney's henchmen in 1222 was a brutal tribute to the reformed Church's potency as a state-building tool; his successor Gilbert Murray (d. 1245), so it was said, 'supervised the government of the north, and built several royal castles for the kingdom's security'.

Also vital were the reformers' successes in crossing ethnic, even political, boundaries by winning the support of Gaelic lords and chiefs. Besides founding eight new monasteries, Fergus of Galloway and his family were protectors of the bishopric of Whithorn, revived in about 1128 under York's metropolitan jurisdiction. Ranald, Somerled's son, brought the Benedictines and Augustinians to Iona, planted a Cistercian abbey at Saddell in Kintyre (albeit colonized from Mellifont in Ireland), and perhaps founded the bishopric of Argyll (c.1193). However much such potentates sponsored reform to serve their own ambitions, the crown increasingly reaped the benefit, as in Galloway in 1235–6 when Alexander II appointed the bishop of Whithorn and the Cistercian abbots of Dundrennan and Glenluce. When Alexander III gained the Norwegian diocese of the Isles (1266), ecclesiastical Scotland—except the see of Orkney—was politically united, and the unity of the Church under the king powerfully upheld the idea of one country and polity.

No less importantly, reform churchmen were the crown's chief allies in articulating and cultivating stronger notions of Scottish independence and identity. Unusually, Scotland had no archbishopric. But attempts to subordinate the entire Scottish Church to York were defeated through the acquisition of a unique national exemption, confirmed by the famous bull *Cum universi* (1192), which guaranteed the constitutional freedom of the *Scoticana Ecclesia* (excluding Whithorn and the Isles) as a 'special daughter' of Rome. The securing of St Margaret's papal canonization (1249) was a triumphant affirmation of the sacred grandeur of Scottish kingship, and of regnal pride and loyalty. The reform elite also fostered national solidarity by adopting more accommodating ecclesiastical policies than is sometimes thought. While they deplored certain 'barbarous' Gaelic customs, notably concubinage and divorce, such views merely fortified their evangelizing commitment to cross-cultural Christian unity, and never grew into the stark racial hostility characteristic of the English clergy in Wales and Ireland. Indeed, for all the disparagement of the older Scottish Church, there were marked continuities in ecclesiastical organization, ethos, and personnel. The native religious past was thus enlisted in ways that respected local sensibilities, and reinforced with increasing effectiveness a new sense of collective Scottishness.

Cathedrals and monasteries were often constructed on or near long-established holy sites; while in Moray, Perthshire, Argyll, and elsewhere the parish system was developed from an existing nexus of Gaelic local churches and chapels. Ancient saints' cults central to popular piety were solicitously nurtured. Ailred himself produced a revised *Life of St Ninian*; the bishops of Glasgow venerated St Kentigern by building a sumptuous cathedral as his shrine-church; Arbroath Abbey associated itself with the Columban tradition as custodian of the *Brecbannoch Coluim Chille*—now usually assumed to be the 'Monymusk Reliquary'—which was still carried by the Scots army into battle (most famously at Bannockburn). Nor were Gaelic church communities necessarily proscribed, for some—as at Abernethy and Monymusk—survived until they opted for a reformed rule in the mid-thirteenth century.

Facing: ST ANDREWS CATHEDRAL, begun in the 1160s, completed in 1318, was built on an exceptionally grand scale, as befitted the long-established prestige and sanctity of the site. The design, based on French styles brought to northern England by the Cistercians, served in turn to inspire work at Jedburgh and Arbroath. St Rule's (centre), with its tall tower beckoning pilgrims to the blessed Andrew, was the cathedral of Bishop Robert (1127–59), and probably incorporated a church dating from before 1100.

Numerous parish clergy were recruited from Gaelic society; and many reform monasteries were or became mixed Anglo-Norman-Gaelic houses. Even at Melrose Abbey, in the heart of 'English' Lothian, it was gladly accepted, at any rate by the 1280s, that all Scotland's inhabitants—regardless of ethnic-cultural differences—belonged to the same nation of Scots. Holyrood Abbey registered its devotion to Scottish unity as early as the 1160s by assuming pastoral responsibility for much of Galloway. Yet nowhere was the cultivation of religious, cultural, and national cohesion more graphically displayed than at the old head-bishopric of St Andrews. The great new cathedral of the Augustinian canons, alongside whom a *Céli Dé* community resided until about 1200, majestically enhanced the centrality of St Andrews in Scottish religious life, and represented Andrew to all as the spiritual father of the enlarged state and nation. By 1286 the superiority of his cult was unchallenged: Scotland and the Scots had found their special intercessor and protector—a patron saint who, as it were, embodied reconciliation between the old order and the new.

Economic take-off

Englishmen like Abbot Ailred associated a modern kingdom with economic opulence and, by their standards, only in David I's reign did Scotland become 'pleasant and fruitful'. Of course, the earlier prosperity of much of eastern Scotland—for long the economic powerhouse of Scottish royal authority—is now well recognized. Nevertheless, between 1100 and 1300 the Lowlands saw a decisive acceleration of earlier expansive trends, resulting in the development of an English-type economy and full involvement in the 'commercial revolution' of contemporary Western Europe. This remarkable transformation—the most important shift in the tempo of the Scottish economy prior to the eighteenth century—was not merely a natural consequence of a European-wide surge in population, markets, and trade. It was actively promoted by a reinvigorated monarchy and governing elite with the enterprise and authority to develop their economic roles; and the increased wealth thereby generated was central to the shaping of a unified kingdom and people.

Institutionalized marketing arrangements and a national coinage, quintessential ingredients of mature medieval polities, were both introduced by David I. He founded royal burghs—fully franchised markets—in most Lowland areas, and with their appearance the history of the Scottish town effectively begins. Some of his fifteen or so foundations were old trade centres with 'proto-urban' functions; but burghal privileges, including defined trading precincts and monopolies, supplied greater potential for genuine urbanization. Royal burghs continued to be created in significant numbers, and the typical conjunction of burgh–castle–sheriffdom formed a potent new source of royal substance and power. By 1296 fifty-two burghs existed, eighteen of which had been founded on royal licence by lay lords and churchmen. The king's burghs, often occupying prime locations near the North Sea for trade with England, the Low Countries, and the Baltic, were as English in business practices and ethnic make-up as were, say, Newcastle and Carlisle. Berwick, Perth, and Aberdeen commanded major economic hinterlands, and virtually cornered overseas commerce. Berwick, the biggest town, also developed an industrial base in cloth-making, as did Perth. Middle-ranking burghs included Stirling, Dundee, and Elgin, all with merchant guilds by 1286. Even minor burghs like Jedburgh, Selkirk, and Lanark, though semi-rural, were geared to market-oriented activities, at once servicing and stimulating the local economies.

Another index of accelerating commercialization is the remarkable growth of Lowland Scotland's monetary sector. As in England, the standard coin was the sterling or silver penny; and only rising cash revenues made possible the large-scale building of stone castles, abbeys, and churches by the crown and other landlords. Coin flowed into their coffers from the burghs, where money could easily be extracted through rents, market tolls, and produce sales. But, from about 1170, a money-based economy became entrenched throughout the Lowlands as coin-use spread to the peasantry. Money-rents replaced food-rents; mills, fisheries, saltworks, and the profits of justice also provided substantial cash returns. In the 1250s, mints were active in burghs as far afield as Dumfries and Inverness. By the 1280s, some forty million sterlings (c.£180,000) may have circulated; and if allowance is made for Scotland's smaller population—perhaps doubling between 1100 and 1300 to a peak of one million—the volume of coin per head was possibly the same as it was in England. At least for the king and other lords, boom conditions had indeed arrived.

So much for any notion that thirteenth-century Scotland was England's poverty-stricken neighbour, a label much more applicable to native Wales. Whence came the silver? David I's annexation of the north Pennine silver mines supplied copious treasure for the first Scottish coinage. After 1157 bullion was increasingly earned abroad through a favourable balance of trade

THE CISTERCIANS stressed the virtues of manual labour, and aimed to transform the countryside into a Garden of Eden. This scene from an English source of *c*.1250 shows monks and lay brothers clearing woodland for cultivation; but it was the Cistercians' all-round commitment to businesslike farming that gave a major boost to the Scottish economy.

dependent chiefly on exploiting the land and its peasantry more systematically. The basic economic organization and technologies of rural society remained largely unchanged. But commercially conscious landlords gained fuller control over peasant surpluses and labour, and maximized output through more intensive forest clearance, drainage of carselands, and upland cultivation. In 1150 Melrose Abbey had sheep, cattle, and pigs in abundance; its barns at Eildon and Gattonside overflowed with wheat and rye. By 1290 Kelso Abbey had a large farm, including arable and a mill, at 1,000 feet in the Cheviots. In particular, wool production became heavily commercialized, the lead being taken by the Cistercians who, on the Sidlaws and the Southern Uplands, organized sheep-farming into very efficient large-scale concerns. As a result, only England outclassed Scotland as a wool producer for European markets, and the dramatic expansion of the wool trade, primarily to supply the Flemish textile towns (especially Bruges and Saint-Omer), was basic to the kingdom's growing wealth.

While the Anglicized Lowlands set the pace of economic expansion, were Gaelic-speaking areas poor? Too stark a contrast must not be drawn. The Atlantic mountain-maritime economy produced large surpluses in cattle and fish; informal markets, fairgrounds, and long-distance trade were scarcely unknown; and individual chieftains undoubtedly amassed great riches. Alan of Galloway had his own chamber (financial office); the spending power of the Hebridean sea-lords was vividly displayed in their castle-building programmes. Yet efficient wealth creation was curtailed by geography, weaker governmental systems, persistent political instability, and the survival of a piratical warrior-pillage economy abandoned as outmoded in most of Western Europe. Gaelic–Norse grandees did not mint their own coins, and the only western burghs were those licensed by the crown—notably Ayr (c.1205) and Dumbarton (1222)—in order to extend its economic-cum-administrative stranglehold. Thirteenth-century tax assessments fully confirm the economic ascendancy of the Lowland core: in 1292, for example, St Andrews was pre-eminently the richest Scottish diocese—and proportionally wealthier than many an English one.

The real differences in economic development and performance between 'royal' Scotland and its fringes had profound political effects. They intensified traditional disparities of power by forging a stronger monarchy and simultaneously arresting any tendency of the Gaelic-Norse chiefdoms (with the marginal exception of the Northern Isles) to become durable polities. Above all, the rising prosperity of the urbanized, monetized, and semi-manorialized Lowlands explains the crown's ability to keep on building up military and political support by dispensing extensive patronage. Such a command of wealth left room for only one obvious focus of royalty and allegiance in northern Britain. The growth of a robust market economy bred a sturdy nation-state.

Governing the kingdom

By 1296 the governmental underpinnings of Scottish unity were securely in place. Although the elements of continuity are striking, stress must first be put on the Scots kings' ability to regularize and extend existing systems of governance by selective adoption of English modes and models. They were especially well placed to do so because, judged by the norms of the northern and western British Isles, the functions and responsibilities of Scottish kingship were already exceptionally developed by 1100. But equipped with more streamlined and rational routines and structures, they reinforced their authority and expanded its range, centralized royal rights in their own hands, and bound outlying provinces more firmly to the kingdom.

From David I's time onwards, the king's itinerant court became increasingly institutionalized and dominant as the effective hub of Scottish government and political authority. The royal household was headed by officers of an English type who ran the king's central bureaucracy and shared with other courtiers in his counsels and judgements. Enlarged courts (great councils) transacted important public business in consultation with a broader cross-section of notables. These forums ultimately became formalized as parliamentary sessions, as in England; and so well established was the Scottish parliament by the late thirteenth century that it was attended by most leading men of the realm, and met frequently during the crisis years 1286–1306 to govern the kingdom and uphold its sovereign identity.

David I's reign also saw the transition from a largely pre-literate governmental culture to regular use of written records, a turning point whose importance for effective command and control cannot be overstated. The highly trained clerks of the king's 'chapel' or chancery, directed by the chancellor, went on to produce a much bulkier mass of documentation: in 1292 almost 800 rolls of charters and other records were stored in Edinburgh Castle. As the kingdom expanded, so did the crown's fiscal organization and grasp. Its chief financial officer, the chamberlain, held regular exchequer audits or accounting sessions (introduced by the 1180s), and also had overall responsibility for managing the king's own lands and burghs. The growth of monarchical authority, as well as the influence of English ideas and methods, was displayed even more emphatically in the systematic extension of the crown's judicial supremacy through regular lawmaking and the bringing of all parts of the kingdom within its jurisdictional reach. The mid-thirteenth-century realm had a unitary royal law, a single 'common law' superior to regional laws, which persisted only at royal pleasure; thus, the 'laws and customs of the kingdom of Scotland' were automatically imposed on the Islemen in 1266. Royal courts proliferated and expanded their competence, especially through the new English-inspired actions of novel dissasine and mortancestry, swift and popular remedies introduced by Alexander II to protect all freeholders against unlawful dispossession. The king's justiciars, dispatched on regional ayres or circuits twice yearly, played a major part in enforcing justice, and also monitored the conduct of lesser royal officials.

All this amply testifies to greater central direction and control; and the scope and intensity of Scottish royal governance did indeed see more spectacular development than at any time before or since. Locally, moreover, the sheriff (another borrowing from England) had a focal role in dispensing justice, revenue-raising, and mustering military levies. The sheriffdoms, normally based on royal castles, numbered twelve by 1165 and no fewer than thirty by 1296—a particularly graphic illustration of the spread of government power. While most were situated in the Lowland core, Dingwall and Cromarty were sheriffdoms by 1264; the west-coast network comprised Ayr (*c.*1200), Dumbarton (1237), Wigtown (1263), and Skye, Lorn, and Kintyre (1293). Royal burghs and their courts were other essential instruments of local control.

But Scottish government fell far short of duplicating the rapid expansion of post-Conquest English government. Monarchical rule advanced across Scotland slowly and circumspectly, and remained deeply dependent on old obligations and dues, old structures such as earldoms and many surviving thanages, and a considerable complement of old officials, including the *brithem* (Latinized to *judex*) and *maer*. Scots law itself was a synthesis of Gaelic and English usages; even the remodelled royal household retained a nucleus of traditional offices. Nor, by much-governed England's standards, did the crown's administrative role become highly developed; and there was an obvious contrast between the Lowlands, with their greater density of royal residences, sheriffdoms, and burghs, and outer regions, where the stamp of royal authority was less marked. In consequence, the most powerful earls and lords, though subject to increasing royal oversight and control, maintained levels of 'self-government' that had very few parallels in England after 1154. Indeed, one result of the enlargement of the kingdom was that the crown's age-old dependence on power-sharing with leading landowners actually became more pronounced.

How effectively overall was the kingdom governed? It is a fallacy that the only satisfactory type of medieval state was a highly centralized one. Intrusive and demanding royal rule could easily reveal its inadequacy, as was shown explosively in the English polity by recurrent major rebellions. Moreover, onerous continental commitments largely explain the elaboration of English state power and organization. Scotland did not need to follow suit and, all in all, the mix of English-style innovation and 'Celtic' practice served it well. Low-key governance eased the absorption of provinces characterized by diverse political traditions. Above all, since the crown did not intervene relentlessly in their affairs, the regional elites had more respect for it, and could usually be relied on to uphold its authority locally; that magnates—not professional bureaucrats—monopolized the plums of royal patronage, and often served as chamberlains, justiciars, and sheriffs, reinforced a sense of government in the king's name. Paradoxically, the 'limitations' of central power strengthened rather than weakened the unity and integrity of the kingdom.

More precise indicators exist in the crucial spheres of justice, finance, and force. While the Scottish legal system was relatively simple, there is no mistaking the gradual emergence for the whole realm of an interlocking hierarchy of royal and subordinate courts, linked ultimately by processes of appeal and judicial review to the king's council or parliament; the growing success of new legal norms in protecting property rights and correcting miscarriages of justice; the productive collaboration between royal and lords' courts in maintaining public peace; and the relative absence of major problems like those generated in the English state by protracted legal delays, conflict between royal and local jurisdictions, and perceptions of the law as a tool of royal oppression. Additionally, Scots law promoted a greater sense of national cohesion because, unlike English law in Ireland, it did not discriminate against the king's Gaelic subjects by withholding its protection from them.

The Scottish fiscal system never approached its much more formidable English counterpart in income or rapacity. Despite the early appearance of new cash renders, crown revenue for long came mainly from traditional sources, including the ancient cain-conveth tributes. Yet royal monetary initiatives greatly facilitated revenue collection, especially after 1200 when produce-rents were often converted to cash. Customary public dues were transformed into regular national exactions; general taxation was introduced for special purposes; and new mechanisms were developed for tapping the profits of economic expansion. In about 1280, immediately after their launch in England, Alexander III imposed customs duties on wool and leather exports. Even by the 1180s, it was becoming clear that money incomes usually met royal needs. William I found £6,667—roughly £25 million today—to restore Scotland's independence (1189), and then offered £10,000 for the English Border shires (1194). Furthermore, unlike England, Scotland escaped the escalating costs of major wars in France; there was less call for stringent fiscal policies—and less cause for political discontent. What mattered most was ensuring that in wealth the crown dwarfed all other power-holders in northern Britain, and this was achieved.

Scottish military organization was based on the 'feudal' machine of knights and castles and on the old-established common army. The English state increasingly replaced unpaid forces by more professional troops, and clearly had far greater war-making potential. Yet the reliance of the semi-modernized

Scottish system on unwaged manpower allowed for less heavy-handed governance. More importantly, successive kings from David I to Alexander III—in contrast to their predecessors—had the fighting power to dispatch political enemies in Scotland, and thus gradually secured that monopoly of force basic to a unified nation-state. Nor should the 'feudal' contribution be allowed to obscure unduly the importance of the common army, whose peasant spearmen and bowmen greatly outnumbered the knights. Virtually national mobilization was possible even in 1138, when David I led warriors into Northumbria from all the main Scottish provinces. The English chronicler Matthew Paris, writing in about 1250, did not doubt Scotland's military effectiveness when he described the Scots army as 'huge and powerful', and pointedly stressed the resolve of its peasant levies to die for 'their homeland'. The two Alexanders developed a formidable fleet, a decisive factor in the winning of the Hebrides; while the extensive emergency measures taken by Alexander III to protect the kingdom against Norwegian attack in 1263 suggest a well-organized scheme of national defence. Last but hardly least, Edward I's attempts at conquest embroiled the English in a strength-sapping and ultimately fruitless struggle, a foretaste of which was given at Stirling Bridge (1297), where the common army under William Wallace upheld the cause of Scottish independence by brilliantly defeating an English cavalry army. On this view, even under the gravest pressure the organizational capacity of the Scottish state was not ill adapted to its needs.

The kingdom of Scotland and the Scots

Under Alexander III (1249–86) the unified Scottish polity envisaged by David I finally emerged. It was a relatively loose-jointed realm. But royal power was unprecedentedly penetrating and all-encompassing; while even its suppleness gave the state a legitimacy that enhanced its integrative force. Separatist yearnings were extinguished or muted. Regnal cohesion was fortified by clearly defined frontiers, unitary legal and administrative frameworks, a 'national' Church, and the unmistakable imprint of a single sovereign authority. The name Scotland, *Scotia*, no longer excluded regions such as Galloway, Moray, and Caithness, but routinely approximated to its modern sense; and even the west Highlands and islands were more firmly incorporated than the 'Gaelic problem' of later centuries might suggest. Nor, by contemporary European standards, did the kingdom lack the requisite economic and military resources for a medium-sized power; and in the Treaty of

Birgham (1290) Edward I would himself acknowledge Scotland's identity as a fully developed state 'distinct and free from the realm of England', with its own 'rightful boundaries' and 'laws, liberties, and customs'.

Scotland's political coherence and maturity are seen again in a national parliament where the kingdom's elites claimed to speak for the 'community of the realm'. This novel idea of a unified political society, however narrow or broad that happened to be, mirrored developments in thirteenth-century England, though significantly the Scottish 'community' lacked the oppositional overtones of its English equivalent. And so vibrant was the concept that during the climactic events from 1286 it assumed a more vital constitutional significance, Guardians (regents) being appointed, in the absence of an effective monarch, to sustain the crown and kingdom in the community's name. Especially after John Balliol's departure (1296)—and despite serious rifts and other severe setbacks—personal devotion to a ruler was superseded by a greater allegiance: loyalty to the state and the political community that personified it.

Yet already by the 1280s nothing reflected and reinforced Scottish solidarity more amply than the fact that 'greater Scotland' was now the land of one people, the Scots. The forging of a single Scottish identity out of multiple peoples, categorized in twelfth-century charters as English, French, Flemings, Scots, Welsh (Britons), and Gallovidians, was a rich tribute to the potency of state-making processes that combined the unifying force of a stronger crown and its structures with sensitivity to plural traditions, aspirations, and attachments. Above all else, the Scots kings have to be credited with controlling the impact of change and successfully resolving the tensions between old and new. Unlike in Wales and Ireland, there was no question of the intrusion of colonialist Anglo-Norman enclaves and the development of an institutionalized schism between the English and the 'uncivilized Other'. All parties were equally under the crown's rule and protection. There emerged a hybrid kingship, a hybrid Church, and hybrid systems of law and government, which different groups could easily relate to, and which intensified or instilled a perception of collective Scottishness. Nation-building scarcely eliminated linguistic and cultural diversity; but ethnic-cultural boundaries were relatively easy-going and porous. Even in the Lowlands north of the Forth, English cultural domination over Gaelic speech and customs was less suffocating than is often realized; while, by the later thirteenth century, 'Celtic' traditions were increasingly exploited by the intelligentsia to supply the symbols, images, and mythologies deemed necessary for national identification. Thus did two

THE SEAL OF GUARDIANSHIP (1286–92). Guardians first took responsibility for upholding crown rights and regnal unity on Alexander III's death; and this celebrated icon of Scottish statehood and identity encapsulated their role and obligations. *Front*: shield of the royal arms, with legend meaning 'Seal of Scotland appointed for the rule of the kingdom'. *Back*: St Andrew as the focus for national cohesion, with legend (see text) representing him as both protector of the Scots and a Scot himself.

vibrant cultures coexist and intermingle, and Anglicization was matched by degrees of Gaelicization—a phenomenon deplored by English officials in Ireland as 'degeneracy', but not so regarded in Scotland, where Anglo-Normans became Scots in a way they did not become Irish or Welsh.

The kingdom of Scotland and the Scots as it existed in the 1280s was undeniably a recent creation; national consciousness had yet to be tempered in the furnace of sustained English aggression; and loyalties remained more complex and ambiguous than historians sometimes imagine. Yet there seems little doubt that, no less than in other European polities where people and kingdom appeared to correspond, the Scots already saw themselves as an established nation, entitled to their separate identity in a defined territory which they collectively embodied as a sovereign nation-state. Nowhere were such notions more emotively expressed than in the inscription on the reverse of the seal struck for the Guardians in 1286: '[St] Andrew be leader of the Scots, your fellow countrymen.' And, after all, the Wars of Independence were fought not just by lords (who had often to submit to the English) but by lesser folk, too. When it was said that in 1297–8 'the community of the land followed Wallace as their leader', lairds and better-off peasantry were primarily meant. Thus, a deep-rooted patriotic spirit was more a cause than a product of the wars—to Matthew Paris, indeed, the readiness of ordinary Scots to die for their country had been self-evident half a century before.

Predictably, the English did not view the Wars of Independence as a conflict between two autonomous states and peoples—the Scots, denied rights of belligerent status, were treated as rebels against their lawful ruler, the king of England. Yet, in reality, by 1296 the British Isles contained not one but a pair of those well-grounded kingdoms from which the modern West European state was born. The English monarchy saw itself as the strongest fiscal-military polity in Latin Christendom; but when it sought to master Scotland, conquest was attempted on a quite different scale from what it had achieved in politically fragmented Wales and Ireland. Even then, this superpower had scarcely subdued the whole of Ireland, while in north Wales in 1277–83 it had taken a vast mobilization of state resources to stifle the remnants of native independence. All told, it is perhaps little wonder that when the English colossus went on to try to devour the nation-state that was Scotland, it ultimately found that it had bitten off more than it could chew.

3 Survival and Revival: Late Medieval Scotland

MICHAEL BROWN AND
STEVE BOARDMAN

War and the fourteenth-century kingdom

During the century from 1296, Scotland was a kingdom at war. The conflict was rooted in the efforts of Edward I of England to establish his personal dominance in Scotland, and the claims of the rulers of England to authority over the northern kingdom were never fully abandoned in the later Middle Ages. From Edward I in the 1290s and 1300s to Henry IV in 1400 all the kings of England led armies northwards to press their rights to Scotland in war. All these attempts failed in the face of Scottish resistance. However, warfare in fourteenth-century Scotland was not simply a case of the opposition of a unified community to foreign conquest. In the opening decades of the century, Scottish political society was split by civil war, and local warfare persisted as a fact of life in many places. If the outcome of these wars was the survival of Scotland as a separate realm and community, it was one which was significantly altered in structure and outlook from the thirteenth-century kingdom.

The key moment in the wars was the seizure of the Scottish throne by Robert Bruce in early 1306. In late 1305 Scotland appeared to be a conquered land. Through war and diplomacy, many Scots had opposed Edward I's attempts to gain control of their country during the previous decade. The lightning campaign of 1296 in which Edward defeated and deposed King John of Scotland proved a short-lived triumph. The uprisings across the kingdom in 1297 erupted in opposition to the absorption of Scotland into the Plan-

THE BUTE MAZER, an early fourteenth-century drinking cup, provides one of the earliest examples of Scottish heraldic decoration. Around the lion couchant in the centre are the arms of noble families from south-western Scotland. The shield of the Stewart family, a chequered band of blue and white on a golden background, is accompanied by those of neighbours and kins like the Lindsays, Douglases, and Hamiltons. The rise of all these families during the fourteenth century would be a major consequence of Robert Bruce's success and his dependence on the Stewart family connection.

tagenet state. These risings were fuelled by the active participation of many lesser men in renewing the war, as symbolized by the emergence of the Lanarkshire squire William Wallace as war leader in the victory at Stirling Bridge (1297) and then guardian of the realm. He and his aristocratic successors as guardians put up dogged resistance to Edward on behalf of the exiled Balliol king. Their ability to withstand repeated major offensives suggests the depth and durability of the support they received from many Scots. However, after eight years of war, abandoned by European allies, divided amongst themselves, and ultimately defeated by Edward I's devastating campaign of 1303–4, the last Scottish leaders had reached the end. Though Edward made some concessions to secure peace, 1305 marked the defeat of his Scottish enemies.

The war that was renewed in 1306 was Bruce's war. He launched it to secure the throne for himself. His usurpation of the crown united Edward I and those Scots who still adhered to Balliol against him and Bruce was initially defeated by the coalition. However, as Robert I, Bruce could call on traditions of kingship established during the previous two centuries. From 1307 Robert skilfully exploited these traditions to achieve his aims; the expulsion of English lordship and English garrisons from the kingdom, and the secure establishment of his dynasty as rulers of Scotland. In achieving these goals, Robert altered the shape of his realm. In fighting the English, he learned from past lessons, using ambushes, night attacks, and raids, and defending prepared ground. By 1314 these tactics had reduced English control to Berwick (itself captured in 1318) and Bruce had inflicted a crushing defeat on Edward II at Bannockburn near Stirling. Bannockburn did not end the war but it confirmed that military initiative had passed to Robert. He took the war onto Edward II's ground. Northern England was systematically devastated by raiding, and Robert's brother Edward sought, ultimately unsuccessfully, to replace the English king as the lord of Ireland. Robert's main goal was English recognition of his rank and rights as ruler of Scotland. It took fourteen years of war after Bannockburn to secure this. The peace of 1328 was the final and greatest achievement of Robert I, who died the next year.

Peace outlived Robert by only three years. In 1332 Edward Balliol, son of the king accepted by most Scots before 1306, invaded Scotland, defeated a far larger Bruce force at Dupplin Moor near Perth, and was crowned king at Scone. His invasion triggered the intervention of Edward III of England who regarded the peace of 1328 as 'shameful'. In return for English support, Balliol ordered the cession of southern Scotland and recognized Edward III's overlordship. In 1333 these allies crushed a second Bruce army at Halidon outside Berwick and overran much of Scotland. The young king, David II, was sent to France for safety. Yet, as in 1296 and 1305, final victory eluded the English. Though Edward III led an army to the Moray Firth in 1336, he found his grip on Scotland slipping. Under a series of competent guardians and skilled local captains, the Bruce regime defeated Balliol partisans and English garrisons. When David II returned in 1341 he found his realm had been largely recovered. Keen to emulate his father and his lieutenants, David led a series of invasions of England. The last, and most ambitious, of these in 1346 ended at Neville's Cross outside Durham, where the Scottish army was defeated and David captured. Earlier in the century, the capture of the Bruce king would have spelled disaster for his cause. However, though Balliol renewed his claims and Edward III led a final invasion in 1356, there was no fresh effort to subjugate Scotland after Neville's Cross. From the 1340s Anglo-Scottish war was largely confined to the marches of the two realms. Campaigns like those of 1356, the Scottish offensives of the 1380s or Richard II's invasion of 1385 were increasingly rare. The war was mostly fought between small, local forces over the allegiance of Scottish border communities and control of the last English strongholds. By 1409 only Roxburgh and Berwick remained of English lordship in Scotland.

Despite the disparity in resources, the subjugation of Scotland had proved a task beyond the Plantagenet kings of England. From Dunbar in 1296 to Neville's Cross fifty years later the English found it impossible to turn battlefield success into decisive victory. Armies were kept in the field and strongholds taken and garrisoned but these repeatedly proved to be insufficient to deliver complete control of the country, especially the north and west. The reach of such forces was limited. Their cost placed massive strains on the Plantagenet state. Moreover, only in the early 1300s and mid-1330s was the Scottish war the prime concern of the English kings. Continental wars and domestic conflicts detracted from the war effort in Scotland. Significantly, when he freed himself to concentrate on the Scots in 1303, Edward I unleashed a campaign which forced his enemies to seek peace.

Yet even this effort failed before renewed rebellion. English victory ultimately depended on Scottish submission and, though there were always Scots supporting the Plantagenets, even at the point of apparent defeat some Scots still resisted, continuing to place strains on their enemies' resources. What linked these Scots together was a desire to uphold the Scottish realm and its rights. This was no abstract ideal but a fight for established laws and customs, structures of government and local community, even for personal and family loyalties, which depended on the existence of a kingdom of Scotland and were threatened by the English king's lordship. It was not always easy to agree on this Scottish cause or its leaders. The roots of war lay in a dispute for the kingship that divided Scots from the 1280s to the 1350s, and when Bruce seized the throne in 1306 he was rejecting the rights of John Balliol and the efforts made on his behalf. To many who had fought hard in the previous decade, this made Bruce a criminal, and they now sided with Edward I against the usurper. Bruce's struggle to secure recognition from Scots was as hard as the war with England.

Throughout his reign Robert I sought to turn his personal search for power, the Bruce cause, into the Scottish cause. At first, authority rested predominantly on success in war. Between 1307 and 1309 Robert took on and defeated his Scottish enemies. Some of these, like the earls of Ross and Sutherland, accepted his kingship, others, like his main rivals the Comyns, were driven from the land. Moreover, Robert's victories over the English, culminating in Bannockburn, must have convinced many doubters that his leadership was the best way of preserving the Scottish realm. Yet military success was an uncertain basis for claiming royal rights. Robert also tried to justify his rule in other terms. In documents like the Declaration of the Clergy (*c*.1309) and the Declaration of Arbroath (1320), statements were made on behalf of the community which identified Robert as their rightful king by inheritance and by delivering his people from oppression. A king, like Balliol, who submitted to England was said to have forfeited his rights, and Bruce was presented as chosen defender of the realm whose chief duty was the maintenance of freedom from English lordship.

Despite the claims of Bruce propaganda, the survival of the dynasty remained uncertain for many years after 1306. Robert I never freed himself from doubts about his usurpation. His disinherited enemies, led by Edward Balliol, waited in exile, and many who had submitted to his rule were disenchanted with the unremitting warfare he offered. The conspiracy of 1320, mere months after the Declaration of Arbroath, aimed to replace the king with Balliol and secure a peace with England. Its suppression did not end Robert's anxieties and the king's lack of an adult heir added to his difficulties. Three years after he died Scotland received its second Balliol king. Edward Balliol's return renewed internal dynastic conflict. However, Edward depended increasingly on English backing, and by the late 1340s it was clear that a Balliol restoration was impossible. Balliol's failure was testament to Robert's achievement. If he never won the total support of his subjects which his propaganda claimed, Bruce promoted those subjects whose support he had secured. Civil war had cut a swathe through the great families of thirteenth-century Scotland and Robert used their lands and his own to build a new Bruce nobility. His brother Edward and nephew Thomas Randolph received vast principalities in the south-west and north respectively. Robert's lieutenant James Douglas was given lordships along the exposed English Border, while a host of the king's lesser allies were promoted from lands forfeited by his enemies. The marriage of Robert's daughter to Walter Stewart linked the Bruces' west-coast allies to the new royal line. All these lords had a stake in the survival of Bruce rule. The defeats of 1332, 1333, and 1346 shook but never broke their allegiance to Robert's son. Success for Edward Balliol and his supporters would mean loss of lands and status for this Bruce establishment.

This land settlement also concentrated power in the hands of a close-knit group of families. Robert was ruling a kingdom at war and wanted trusted deputies who could defend his interests in vulnerable parts of his realm. The absence of active royal leadership for most of the three decades after Robert's death demonstrated the importance of this approach. Bruce's grandson Robert Stewart, his brother-in-law Andrew Murray, and the Randolphs led the Bruce party in the warfare of these years. However, Bruce's patronage followed by his son's absences from Scotland altered the balance between the crown and its greatest subjects. For example, while the successors of James Douglas inherited his adherence to the Bruce party, they developed their role as leaders of this party in the Borders. Between 1332 and 1357 as they waged war against the English in the region, Douglas magnates annexed lands and extended their lordship throughout the south. They were winning the war, they were ensuring Border communities remained in Scottish allegiance, and, as the murder of the sheriff of Roxburgh by William Douglas of Liddesdale in 1342 demonstrated, external interference, even from the king, was unwelcome. In the Borders war had altered local society and placed limits on royal authority.

The lords of the Isles and Gaelic Scotland

The years of war also left their mark on Gaelic Scotland. The thirteenth-century kings had drawn the rulers of the Western Isles and western Highlands into their orbit, reinforcing their lordship by sponsoring bonds between these dynasties and the lords of neighbouring Gaelic-speaking lands, the Comyns and Stewarts. However, after 1286, these bonds cut both ways. Old emnities between the Hebridean lords, never fully settled, re-ignited in the 1290s and became bound up with the rivalry between Bruce and Balliol. The MacDougall lords of Argyll were allies of the Comyns and amongst Robert I's fiercest opponents. Their rivals the MacDonalds of Islay and MacRuaries of Garmoran consistently supported Robert. The actions of these Hebridean magnates were not peripheral to the wars. They were the leaders of a militarized society with fleets of longships and armies of mailed axemen at their disposal. By 1300 these axemen already had a reputation as professional soldiers, galloglasses, in Ireland and they provided Robert I with the hard core of many of his armies, the king himself leading a force of Islesmen at Bannockburn. Robert's victory was a victory for Clan Donald and the MacRuaries and ended the power of the MacDougalls in Gaelic Scotland. At stake for the lords of the Western Isles was not the Bruce cause or the survival of the Scottish community, but primacy in their own region. The fall of the MacDougalls left Clan Donald as the greatest family in the Hebrides, and when war resumed in Scotland in the 1330s, the head of Clan Donald, John of the Isles, used his primacy to wring concessions in land and title from both Bruce and Balliol regimes. By 1346, when John secured the MacRuarie lands, his authority stretched throughout the Hebrides.

While the wars brought greater political unity to the Isles, they had a reverse effect in the neighbouring regions of Gaelic Scotland. For the Highlands between the Great Glen and the upper valleys of Tay and Forth war brought social and political dislocation. Families that had dominated the region for a century or more disappeared in the conflicts of the early fourteenth century. The Comyns of Badenoch and the earls of Atholl and Strathearn all paid for their opposition to the Bruces, while Robert's great northern creation, the earldom of Moray, survived only two generations before the death in battle of the last Randolph earl led to its dismemberment. The fall of these great houses had a deep effect on the region. Such magnates were the link between the largely Gaelic populations of their lordships and the king's government. Their absence left Badenoch, Atholl, and Strathearn, the geographical heart of Scotland, without established structures of authority, disrupted Anglicized patterns of law, settlement, and power, and encouraged the rise of new lords. In many districts, Gaelic tenants of the old lords, lesser kinsmen or officials, like *Clann Donnachaidh* (the Robertsons of Atholl) or the MacKintoshes of Badenoch, became heads of local society. The emergence of these kindreds represented both the fragmentation of Highland lordship and the loosening of ties between crown and regional communities. Instead of lords ruling defined provinces, the new Gaelic magnates were the heads of personal followings whose success was measured in terms of local warfare. The changing conditions of the Highlands also drew in lords from outside the region. Through Lochaber Clan Donald and men from the Isles entered the Highlands as allies, mercenaries, and overlords of local kindreds, while during the 1340s and 1350s Robert Stewart acquired rights and influence in Atholl, Strathearn, and Moray. Though Bruce's grandson and head of the king's government, Stewart did not seek to re-establish earlier styles of lordship. Instead he sought to draw local kindreds into his orbit after the fashion of the lord of the Isles.

This new order in the north and west had a major impact on Scotland's history. Complaints in parliament and elsewhere characterized the Highlands as a source of lawlessness which spilled over in raids on the surrounding Lowland districts. Before 1286 there is little evidence of tension between Gaelic- and English-speaking communities, but the rise of Highland lords, whose power rested on their ability to maintain bands of fighting men, altered the situation. The raids of caterans, lightly armed Highland warriors, became a long-running grievance in the north-east Lowlands. For these districts, the principal task of the royal government became their protection from the 'wyld wikked hielandmen'.

Kingdom and communities

The experience of many Scots in the fourteenth century was shaped against a background of war. The effects of Bruce's ravaging of the province of Buchan in 1308 were still felt locally half a century later, while in the late 1330s Scottish heartlands like Angus, Fife, the Mearns, and Lothian were reduced to desolation by English and Scottish armies. Lothian suffered again in 1356 at 'Burnt Candlemas', Edward III's winter devastation of the province, which forced many inhabitants to flee across the Forth for safety, and, as late as the 1400s, Lothian was the target of sustained raiding by English forces based in Berwickshire. The effect of conflict was aggravated, perhaps even outweighed, by those other scourges of late medieval Europe, famine and plague. The fourteenth century brought a change across northern Europe to a colder and wetter climate. In Scotland, wet summers and poor harvests were exacerbated by the damage and demands of warfare. Many Scots faced starvation, and during the siege of Perth in 1339 reports of cannibalism surfaced amongst local populations stripped of their supplies. In addition, lands high in the southern uplands or in the valleys of the Highlands which before 1300 had been under the plough were now only suited as pasture for herds. The changes in climate and the needs of war in both these upland regions increased the significance of local societies based on extended and militarized kindreds, equipped for herding and the raiding of animals and goods. Overall, by the middle of the century, Scotland was confirmed as an importer of grain from England, an exporter of wool and other animal products.

In the autumn of 1349 the Black Death reached Scotland. The plague had

already killed millions in its spread from China across Asia to the Mediterranean and the Scots were clearly aware of its impact in neighbouring realms.
According to an English account, the disease was carried home by a Scottish
army which had gathered to exploit the effect of the plague on their southern
enemies. Contemporary accounts spoke of a disease that killed in two days
and struck hardest at the poor in town and country, slaying as many as a third
of the total population. Yet commentators in other European lands spoke of
far higher levels of mortality and Scotland, with its dispersed population and
cooler climate, may have suffered less from the plague than its neighbours.
Any limit to the death toll was purely relative. If the plague of 1349 killed only
a fifth of Scotland's population, a conservative estimate, this still made it
the greatest cataclysm to strike the land at any point in the kingdom's history.
With renewed outbreaks of pestilence in every generation, the plague continued as a feature of late medieval life, forcing the great to flee and still causing
greatest suffering among lesser Scots.

War, plague, and climatic change all left their mark on Scottish kingdom
and people but the impression given to a modern observer is of the resilience
of the structures of society and community. By the 1360s indeed the realm
was enjoying a period of relative peace and prosperity. The 1357 truce with
England ended major warfare for a quarter-century, while exports of wool
began to rise to a peak in the 1370s, bringing in greater profits and providing
the smaller population of post-plague Scotland with a plentiful supply of
meat.

This recovering prosperity had a political importance. In 1357, Scotland's
king, David II, was released from England after a decade in captivity. He
found the authority of his crown much reduced. The succession crises of 1286
and 1290, the fall of Balliol, Bruce's usurpation, and even Robert I's generosity with the lands and rights of the monarchy, diminished the resources and
standing of the crown. David's own long absences from his realm had compounded this situation and from 1357 onwards he sought to rebuild royal
power by tapping the wealth of his subjects. Though saddled with a ransom
owed to England, through almost annual taxes on lands and rents, the levying
of increased duties on exported wool, and by reclaiming former royal lands,
David massively increased his income. Amongst other things, he used these
funds to assemble a large personal following of knights and clerics that
enforced royal demands and judgements and upheld David's authority. The
king's men had previously served those who dominated Scotland in David's
absence. The old lieutenant of the realm, David's nephew and heir Robert

THE GREAT CASTLE OF DOUNE in the earldom of Menteith was probably built by
Robert Stewart, son of Robert II, earl of Menteith and, from 1398, duke of Albany. The
scale and sophistication of the fortress reflects the power, wealth, and importance of the
Albany Stewarts in fourteenth- and early fifteenth-century Scotland.

Stewart, and William earl of Douglas, the greatest magnate in the south, had defended and led the realm while the king was a prisoner. They felt ill paid for their service and in 1363 expressed their hostility to David's policies in rebellion. The king and his knights defeated the rebels and forced Stewart into a humiliating surrender. However, despite his victory, David had the appearance of a ruler seeking to turn back the clock. His failure to produce a child to succeed him remained a nagging worry, but the effort to block the succession of his enemy, Stewart, by arranging for Edward III of England or one of his sons to inherit Scotland was unrealistic. An English succession was acceptable to Scots in 1290, but the intervening years had made it abhorrent. David, who had spent little time in his realm and identified with international bonds of kingship and chivalry, may have underestimated the impact of decades of conflict on the attitudes of his subjects. Even the restoration of royal authority may have been shakier than it appeared and David never felt strong enough to launch a direct, irreversible assault on the magnates whose influence still dominated much of Scotland. Though his death in early 1371 found David still at the height of his power, neither his style of kingship nor the Bruce dynasty survived him.

The new king and the new dynasty came in the person of Robert Bruce's grandson, Robert II of the house of Stewart. If David II's rule appeared as an attempt to reverse the impact of preceding decades, Robert's was the culmination of recent change. For most of his fifty-four years, Robert had been heir to the throne, for fifteen of them he had acted as guardian for the absent king. These years were spent building his private power as a lord of many followers and estates, and producing a massive family of thirteen legitimate and nine illegitimate children. This experience as lord and dynast shaped his approach to kingship. He was determined that the throne should remain with the Stewarts by insisting on succession in the male line and sought to increase the status and extent of his family even further. Daughters were married to the lord of the Isles, the heir of the earl of Douglas, and other magnates, and his sons, who between them held eight earldoms, were appointed as his principal lieutenants in the realm. The eldest, John earl of Carrick, was made lieutenant in the marches with England, his brother Robert earl of Fife was head of royal finances, while the king's third and favourite son, Alexander earl of Buchan and lord of Badenoch, was named lieutenant of the king in the north. While David II had kept his hands tightly on royal government and relied on lesser men as royal officers, Robert dispersed power over whole regions of Scotland to his kinsmen. The funds that had supported David's government were gifted as patronage amongst Robert's extended family. Rather than an assertive monarchy able to enforce its will, Robert based his rule on the mutual interests of his wide network of kin.

In the 1370s this approach produced an atmosphere of political stability. The threat to it came when the solidarity of the royal family broke down. In 1384 complaints against Robert's slack rule prompted his heir, the earl of Carrick, to remove his father from active rule and to take power as lieutenant. Only four years later, in 1388, Carrick himself fell victim to family rivalries. He was ousted from the lieutenancy, ostensibly because of ill health, really because of the machinations of his younger brother Robert of Fife. The coups of 1384 and 1388 were not just about family rivalries. They were also about the failure of kings and lieutenants to meet the demands of regional communities, demands which resulted from the long crisis of war and society earlier in the century. In the north, burgesses, churchmen, and Lowland lords made increasingly strident calls for the crown to control the activities of magnates and kindreds from the Highlands. South of Forth, magnates like the earls of Douglas and March sought support and licence for war in the marches against England. Robert II's delegation of power to regional lieutenants was designed to meet these needs. Instead it created problems. His son Alexander, lieutenant of the north, built an impressive following amongst the Gaelic lords of Moray but used it to wage war against his local enemies, earning the nickname of the 'Wolf of Badenoch' for his support of cateran raids. In the south, the lieutenant, Carrick, used his alliance with the earl of Douglas to oust his father from power. The price for southern backing was major war against England which led to Douglas's death and Carrick's own loss of office in 1388.

Between 1388 and 1420 Scottish politics were dominated by Robert earl of Fife, later the duke of Albany. Though never king, Fife was never far from power. His career reflected the changed face of Scotland since the 1280s. The needs of war and frequent absence of active kingship meant that politics had become more regionalized. Thus, instead of the lords of the Hebrides and of provinces like Moray, Lochaber, and Ross being drawn into the orbit of royal government, by 1390s, these regions were dominated by the Clan Donald lords of the Isles, expansionistic, assertive, even separatist, with their own claims to kingly authority. To the English-speaking communities north of Tay, the failure of the crown to protect them from this threatening Gaelic society encouraged the search for local protectors against caterans and Islesmen. The need for leadership in war also shaped southern Scottish politics. Lothi-

LATE MEDIEVAL SCOTLAND   89

an and the Borders, heartlands of the thirteenth-century kingdom, were now on a military frontier and looked to magnates like the Douglases for protection and lordship in war and peace. The rest of Scotland, from Argyll and the Clyde across to Fife, looked predominantly to Robert earl of Fife. His power came less as a royal prince than as a great lord, whose retainers and allies included the leading men of these communities.

At the same time, though, Robert of Fife did represent the crown. Between 1388 and 1420 he acted as lieutenant or governor for his father, his brother (Carrick, crowned as Robert III in 1390), and nephew (James I). In this Fife reflected another change from earlier centuries. After over a century and a half of unbroken kingly rule before 1286, during the next 138 years Scotland experienced active kingship for less than six decades. For most of these years royal authority was vested in deputies. The crises of Alexander III's death and John's capture prompted the appointment of the first guardians but, especially after 1329, guardians, lieutenants, and governors gained a significance of their own. By the 1380s it was clearly acceptable to remove adult kings from power in favour of lieutenants appointed by the estates of the realm. Poor Robert III, twice declared unfit to rule in humiliating terms, never seems to have grasped the reins of royal government fully. It had become normal for the duties of kingship, justice and war, to be removed from the king's hands in circumstances that emphasized the reduced status of the monarchy and the blurring of distinctions between the king and his chief subjects.

The reduction in the effectiveness and reach of royal government represented a loosening of the bonds holding the kingdom together. It did not mean anything like a collapse of the idea of Scotland as a single, unified realm. With the possible exception of the lords of the Isles, the magnates who dominated Scotland's regional societies in 1400 were acutely aware of their ties to king and kingdom. If they demanded recognition of their own rights and role in Scotland, they never challenged the standing of the crown in whose service they had built their own lands and influence and, despite the appointment of lieutenants, neither Robert II nor Robert III was ever totally excluded from power. Moreover, the image of Scotland's kings as the focus of Scottish people and realm was maintained in works of historical writing produced in the second half of the fourteenth century. *The Chronicle of the Scottish Nation*, compiled by John of Fordun in the 1380s from a number of sources, formed a history of the Scots from their mythical origins to the fourteenth century. It is the earliest survivor of a series of national histories and, like its successors, proudly related the achievements of the Scots, identifying the unity and security of the nation with its unbroken line of kings. John Barbour's epic poem *The Bruce* dealt with parallel themes by relating the deeds of Robert I. The exploits of the hero-king of late medieval Scotland, and of his noble companions, were told and glorified for the enjoyment of their heirs, the Stewart king and his aristocracy. The relation of both recent events and centuries of national history served a common function. In their different ways they stressed the separate identity and existence of Scotland and the efforts made to preserve crown, realm, and nation.

Church and churchmen

Fordun and Barbour were churchmen. Their attitudes reflected the identification of the Scottish Church with the survival of the realm. In the early conflicts with England, clerics, from Bishops William Lamberton of St Andrews and Robert Wishart of Glasgow down to the friars and hedge priests who preached in favour of Robert I, gave vital support for the Scottish cause in defiance of church law and papal authority. For most of his reign, Robert I was under sentence of excommunication for his murder of John Comyn in church and his usurpation. Between 1319 and 1328 an interdict was imposed by the pope on Scotland, suspending church activities. However, during this period, almost all the Scottish bishops remained steadfast supporters of the king. Adherence to the man who was protecting the separate existence and rights of the Scottish Church was placed above obedience to papal judgements. In common with other Western European realms, the crown was increasingly able to exert greater influence over the Church, a process accelerated by the disruption of papal government caused by rival popes elected during the Great Schism of 1378–1418.

The fourteenth century was a difficult era for the Scottish Church. War and the associated social and economic change brought disruption and impoverishment. The great religious houses of the Borders suffered from internal conflicts between English and Scots and the damage done to their lands and buildings by rival armies and raiders. As late as 1385 Melrose Abbey was destroyed by the troops of Richard II, perhaps the third time it had suffered major damage in the century. In the north too church institutions were affected by changes in local society. Deterioration in climate and political disruption meant that churchmen were often unable to collect revenues from their upland estates. Attempts to collect such income and preserve their rights led to conflict with local magnates. The most infamous of these, between the bishop of Moray and the 'Wolf of Badenoch', ended in the destruction of Elgin Cathedral in 1390.

Despite these difficulties, the Scottish church was hardly an institution in crisis during the fourteenth century. Patrons still existed to found new institutions, for example Archibald third earl of Douglas who founded collegiate churches at Lincluden and Bothwell. Bishops of ability continued to be chosen, like Walter Trail, bishop of St Andrews, a 'pillar . . . and defender of the Church', and Walter Wardlaw, cardinal bishop of Glasgow. There is no evidence to suggest either challenges to church authority like those launched by the Lollards in England, or a decline in standards of clerical learning. Indeed, the later fourteenth century saw Scottish students studying in considerable numbers, moving from cathedral schools at home to universities on the continent, in particular Paris, Cologne, and Orléans. When the disruption of the papal schism caused difficulties for Scots in these centres in the early fifteenth century, sufficient Scottish masters existed to lobby for the foundation of a university at St Andrews.

The desire for Scottish universities, like the writings of Barbour and Fordun, symbolized the renewed confidence of Scots in their survival as an independent community. The key development in fourteenth-century Scotland was the detachment of the realm from the orbit of the Plantagenets. By the 1370s England was firmly fixed as the enemy and, in the politics of Western Europe, Scotland's principal foreign connection was with England's other foe, the kingdom of France. A formal military alliance with France was first negotiated in 1295 and was renewed by Robert I in 1326. Its value was demonstrated in the 1330s when the French gave refuge to David II and refused to abandon the Scots to Edward III, adding to the tensions which precipitated the Hundred Years War. In the 1330s, 1350s, and 1380s, France sent military forces to Scotland, and David II repaid French help in 1346 by invading England to aid his ally. The success of such endeavours was, at best, limited. However as a diplomatic and cultural link with the continent and as a guarantee against military isolation in the face of England the French alliance was of vital significance for Scotland's physical security and status in Europe.

Scotland, 1400–1500: a European monarchy

If the fourteenth century could be characterized as an era in which the realm came to be dominated by a number of great magnate houses, then the fifteenth century can be seen as a period in which the monarchy reasserted itself as the focus of active government. The most obvious manifestation of this change was the steady eclipse of the aristocratic supremacies that had grown out of the Wars of Independence era. The transformation, however, was about much more than the redrawing of the relative balance of power between the crown and its greatest subjects and the achievement of personal political dominance by a sequence of monarchs. The aims and ambitions of kingship were also remodelled and expanded, and the institutions associated with the crown began to reflect and promote important long-term changes in the economic, social, and political life of the kingdom. By the end of the fifteenth century Edinburgh had emerged as a royal capital, a focus for the judicial business of the kingdom and an increasingly dominant economic centre. A glittering royal court by turns beguiled, wooed, and intimidated the kingdom's aristocrats, who came more and more to see honour and reward in crown service. However, the growing power of the Stewart kings and their relentless search for the resources required to sustain an increasingly expensive royal lifestyle also created new political tensions.

The new level of influence achieved by the crown in secular affairs was mirrored in the increasing ability of the king to control appointments to the major benefices of the Scottish Kirk. When, in 1487, the papacy conceded that the Scottish king should have an uncontested eight-month breathing space in which to present candidates to newly vacant Scottish bishoprics and abbacies, the gift largely served to confirm existing practice. Long before 1487 Stewart kings had acquired the ability to reward loyal clerical servants in the royal bureaucracy with bishoprics and abbacies, and by the end of the century James IV was even able to provide senior ecclesiastical appointments for members of his own family. The status of the Scottish Kirk as a distinct and autonomous ecclesiastical province was reinforced, albeit against the wishes of James III, with the creation of the archbishopric of St Andrews for Patrick Graham in 1472. Before the end of the century, resentment at St Andrews' primacy would result in the emergence of a second archbishop in Glasgow.

The assertion of some measure of royal control over the staffing of great ecclesiastical institutions may have been accompanied by a more complex attempt to ride the changing currents of piety and to harness popular devotion to regional saintly cults. The cult of St Duthac of Ross, for example, was used to secure the influence of royal lordship in a troublesome region. One aspect of the endeavour to place the royal line at the centre of the religious life of the kingdom was the consistent emphasis in fifteenth-century Scottish sources on the fact that the Stewart kings were the living descendants of the saintly line established by St Margaret (d. 1093).

In 1400 the Stewart monarchy was less influential and active in continental diplomacy than the earls of Douglas. By 1500 the royal dynasty had forced its way onto the European stage, became a part of the monarchical club of western Europe, secured marriage partners from the same elite rather than its own aristocracy, and promoted a cult of monarchy designed for both domestic and external consumption. Scotland's diplomatic relations, which in the fourteenth century had revolved entirely around Anglo-Scottish hostility and Franco-Scottish military and political cooperation, became more fluid and complex. By the opening of the fifteenth century the prospect of English overlordship being enforced by military conquest was effectively dead. Henry IV's ineffective expedition into Scotland in August 1400 in support of his supposed rights as an overlord was not the opening of a new phase of intense Anglo-Scottish conflict, but a faint and final echo of the early fourteenth century when the very survival of the Scottish kingdom and dynasty had been at stake. August 1400 was the last occasion on which an English king personally led a military invasion of Scotland. Conversely, Scottish confidence in promoting large-scale warfare to recover Scottish burghs and castles still in English hands and to force a formal recognition of the kingdom's independent status from the English crown was severely dented by the battle of Humbleton (Homildon Hill) in 1402. Battles between large Scottish and English armies did not occur again until the equally impressive disaster at Flodden in 1513. In the meantime Anglo-Scottish relations were characterized by a kind of 'cold war', interrupted by occasional outbreaks of more intense hostility.

The territorial issues souring Anglo-Scottish relations were relatively minor but hugely symbolic and emotive. The English hold on the castles of Jedburgh, Roxburgh, and Berwick (with its burgh) and the Isle of Man was an important irritant. Although Jedburgh was captured and destroyed in 1409 the other locations continued to be a source of dispute. Continued English occupation was an affront to the territorial integrity of the Scottish kingdom as it had stood in 1286. Perhaps more importantly, the political culture of the Scots polity embraced, by 1400, a profound and institutional Anglophobia. Despite a shared language and regular contacts in trade and pilgrimage, the English were identified as the Scots' natural enemies. Works such as Andrew of Wyntoun's vernacular verse chronicle from the 1410s and Walter Bower's *Scotichronicon* (*c*.1445) celebrated the alleged ancient history of the Scottish kingdom and the long unbroken line of monarchs who had defended the kingdom against a series of aggressors, Picts, Danes, Norwegians, and, latterly, the English. The *Scotichronicon* included a long digression on the treacherous and duplicitous nature of the English. Such attitudes made the conduct of profitable diplomacy unlikely even when there were few issues of substance to prolong conflict. The continued strength of this Anglophobia was most obvious in the reign of James III. That king's open promotion of a more conciliatory policy towards the English crown and a more hostile approach to the French provoked widespread internal opposition and was implicitly criticized in Blind Hary's *Wallace* (*c*.1477), a bloodthirsty literary evocation of the age of Anglo-Scottish warfare.

Scotland's Auld Alliance with the French also underwent a transformation. Although the relationship generally remained cordial, by the second half of the century the Scottish crown had established direct and independent links through dynastic marriages and trade with a number of other European states, most notably Burgundy and Denmark. By the end of the century James IV was a confident and largely autonomous player in the diplomatic chess games of Renaissance Europe. The kingdom was dwarfed in economic and military terms by its southern neighbour and the French realm, but through its independent monarchy and Kirk and its sense of a unified national history it could justifiably claim a full place as one of the sovereign kingdom-states of Western Europe.

Kings and nobles

At the opening of the fifteenth century the Scottish kingdom was dominated by a series of major magnate families. The dukes of Albany and earls of Mar (both cadets of the royal house), the Douglas earls, and the MacDonald lords of the Isles exercised extensive regional power and their lordship provided a focus for the social and cultural life of lesser men within their respective spheres of influence. The governance of Scotland had always depended, and would continue to depend, on a high level of cooperation between the king and territorial magnates and lords who dominated their own localities. What was perhaps unusual in the early fifteenth century was the extent to which the Albany Stewarts and the Douglases, in particular, were able to control wider royal resources and influence the conduct of government in key areas such as diplomacy and the defence of the realm.

The ascendancy of the Albany Stewarts and Douglas earls had been secured during the reign of Robert III (1390–1406). Hampered by ill health and political misfortune Robert was unable to exert his personal authority over royal government. For most of the reign effective power lay in the hands of the king's brother Robert duke of Albany. The impotence of Robert III in the face of the entrenched power of the cadet branches of the Stewart family and other regional magnates was evident in the fate of his sons. Robert's eldest son and heir David duke of Rothesay died in suspicious circumstances in March 1402 in the custody of his uncle Albany. In 1406, the ailing King Robert secretly attempted to transfer his remaining son James to the custody of the French king in an effort to keep the young heir to the throne out of the hands of his likely guardian, Albany.

However, the heir to the throne was captured at sea by English pirates and delivered into the custody of Henry IV of England. On 4 April 1406, shortly after hearing news of his son's capture, Robert III died in Rothesay Castle on Bute. For the next eighteen years James would languish as a prisoner in England. In Scotland, Albany became governor of the realm and, when he died in 1420, his son Murdoch succeeded him in the office.

Despite the problems caused by Robert III's incapacity and the prolonged absence of James I as an English prisoner between 1406 and 1424 it would be wrong to suggest that Scottish kingship experienced an irreversible institutional crisis or that the political unity of the kingdom was threatened. In theory at least, guardians and governors were appointed to preserve the unity, administration, and institutions of the realm only in the absence of a king capable of discharging his duties. The glowing report on Robert duke of Albany's conduct as governor provided by the chronicler Andrew of Wyntoun made great play of the prestige attached to the governor because of his membership of the royal dynasty and, most particularly, his direct descent from St Margaret. For Wyntoun, the duke's behaviour as governor meant that he resembled 'a mychty King'. Support and sympathy for the 'ideal' of a legitimate, capable adult king ruling in cooperation with his estates remained intact.

What was at stake then, when James I was eventually ransomed and returned to his kingdom in 1424, was not the integrity of the Scottish realm or, indeed, the adherence of the vast majority of Scottish noblemen to the idea of loyalty to the Scottish crown and king. Instead the years after 1424 saw a sustained royal campaign to reclaim full control of crown resources and the functions of royal government from major magnate houses which had an established and, as far as they were concerned, historically justified and ben-

THE RETURN OF THE KING. The building of Linlithgow Palace attests to the renewed confidence and ambition of the Scottish crown in the reign of James 1. The creation of an elegant residence with few defensive features has been seen as a symbolic demonstration and assertion of a belief in the invulnerability of the monarch. If so, the confidence was misplaced, for the king would be assassinated in 1437.

eficial role in the governance of the realm. James I's kingship was energetic, aggressive, and ruthless. In the year after his return James forced through the execution of the principal members of the Albany Stewart family, including his own cousin, Duke Murdoch. The earldoms of Fife, Menteith, and Lennox were forfeited by the Albanys and their supporters and annexed to the royal patrimony while control of the castles of Stirling and Dumbarton was reclaimed for the king. For the remainder of the reign James intimidated and terrorized real and potential opposition until, in February 1437, he was assassinated by men acting with the connivance of the king's uncle, Walter earl of Atholl.

Atholl's attempt to claim the guardianship of the king's young heir James II was defeated by an aristocratic coalition ostensibly representing James's mother Queen Joan. Earl Walter was executed for his role in the death of James I; his earldoms of Atholl and Strathearn were added to the swelling royal patrimony. Thereafter, the minority of James II saw the rise of the Douglas family to a new level of political and territorial prominence. When James assumed the reins of government, however, he immediately became embroiled in a dispute with William eighth earl of Douglas, which climaxed with the king personally leading a fatal assault on Douglas while he and the earl discussed affairs of state in Stirling Castle in February 1452. A protracted military and political struggle with the Douglas family over three years culminated in the forfeiture and permanent exile of Earl William's brother and successor, James, and the deaths of Earl James's brothers, the Douglas earls of Moray and Ormond. Once again, the forfeited estates of the Douglas earls were added to the crown lands. The reigns of James III (1460–88) and James IV (1488–1513) saw the crown involved in repeated clashes with the lordship of the Isles. In 1475–6 the MacDonald lords lost their hold on Ross and Kintyre, while in 1493 the lordship of the Isles itself was forfeited to the crown.

It would be dangerous to generalize about the cause of these disputes and the motivation of the protagonists, since each confrontation had its own dynamic and political context. It would also be misleading to see all these developments as part of a general struggle between the monarchy and the aristocracy as a class, or as a linear process that saw the triumph of royal lordship over aristocratic independence and pretension. Nevertheless, the cumulative effect of these episodes is clear enough. By the end of the century the economic and political resources of the crown massively outstripped those available to any individual aristocratic family. The creation and naming of royal heralds and pursuivants also suggests a deliberate attempt to emphasize the primacy of royal jurisdiction in peripheral, contested, or recently annexed areas at the limit of royal authority. Thus, alongside heralds and pursuivants named after royal castles or lordships such as Snowdoun (Stirling), Rothesay, and Bute, we find Marchmont herald (constituted before 1438), a creation which reflected the Scottish king's claims to the English-garrisoned castle at Roxburgh (i.e. Marchmont) and the aspiration to remove the last vestiges

THE TOMB OF ARCHIBALD, fifth earl of Douglas and second duke of Touraine in France, lies in his family's mausoleum at St Bride's Kirk in Douglas. At the time of his death in 1439 Douglas was the lieutenant-general of Scotland, ruling for the young James II. Douglas's sudden removal from the scene opened the way for political violence both to secure power on the royal council and within the Black Douglas family.

of English occupation in the south of the kingdom. Similarly, the extension of crown claims to direct authority over areas which had been subject to the lordship of the Isles stimulated the creation of a number of heraldic officers who were, quite literally, symbolic of the advance of royal sovereignty. Ross and Islay heralds (created around 1476 and 1493 respectively) were joined by Dingwall, Kintyre, and Ormonde pursuivants (from circa 1460, 1494, and 1501) to press home the message of ultimate royal supremacy (if not always effective control) in the north and west of the kingdom.

The Court

The royal ascendancy of the fifteenth century, however, was not built simply through conflict, coercion, and intimidation. The four king Jameses, in differing ways and with varying degrees of success, sought to enhance, promote, and justify royal power and the king's place as the natural and accepted leader of the kingdom's elite. The military and social values of chivalry were heavily exploited as a means of instilling devotion and deference. Scottish kings, like other great lords across western Europe, had long used knighthood to draw men into a personal relationship of lordship and service. James I continued the tradition, conducting large-scale knighting ceremonies to focus loyalty on king and dynasty. In 1430, at the baptism of his infant sons, James I knighted the sons and heirs of a number of noblemen. The chronicler Walter Bower was aware of the personal ties and obligations which this ceremony was intended to promote when he noted that 'All of these [new knights] were of tender years and are now fellow soldiers with our reigning king' (i.e. James II). A similar mass knighting ceremony accompanied James II's coronation in 1437. Fifteenth-century kings had as yet no formal monopoly on the creation of knights, but there are hints that the more exclusive and honourable form of knighthood bestowed by the monarch was increasingly desired as a mark of social distinction. The fidelity of those in royal service was marked, rewarded, and symbolized by the distribution of livery collars and other insignia.

Beyond the creation of individual and collective ties with a wide circle of noblemen through knighting, chivalric display could also be used to enhance the standing of the king in a more general sense. The royal court became an unrivalled centre for the entertainment of the kingdom's martial aristocracy. James IV in particular dazzling his subjects and promoting his image as king through a series of chivalric spectacles and mock tournaments. The settings for these displays also reflected the growing affluence and confidence of the crown. The construction of the royal palaces of Linlithgow, Falkland, and Holyrood House, and new halls and accommodation blocks in Stirling and Edinburgh castles, not only allowed the royal household greater privacy and comfort, but also provided impressive formal arenas where the king met his own subjects and received foreign ambassadors.

In the second half of the fifteenth century magnatial displays could scarcely compete with the architectural and ceremonial sophistication of the crown. Until the events of 1452–5, the Douglases provided a possible alternative focus for chivalric and martial sentiment in Lowland Scotland. The earls were the established leaders of the chivalry of southern Scotland with a European-wide reputation and an impressive array of diplomatic links to the continent. The Douglas earls justified their lordship and made service to their house attractive and glamorous by cultivating a reputation as a warrior dynasty that

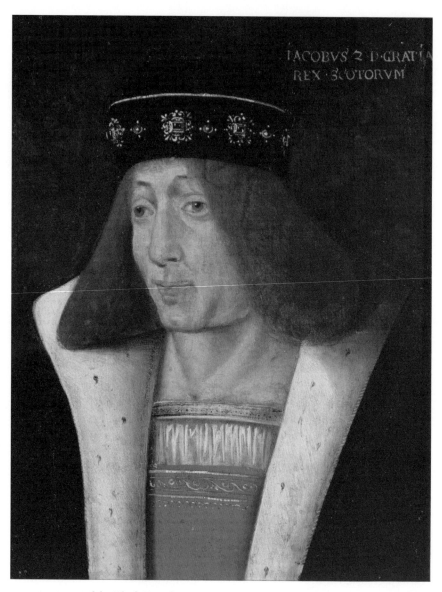

THE NEMESIS of the Black Douglases. James II's struggle with the Douglas family dominated the politics of the mid-fifteenth-century kingdom. The destruction of Douglas power was largely complete by 1455. The king had little time to savour his triumph, as he was killed in 1460 by the explosion of one of his own artillery pieces during a siege of the English-held castle at Roxburgh.

played a crucial role in the defence of Scotland's liberty and territory against English aggression. The huge retinue that accompanied William eighth earl of Douglas on pilgrimage to Rome in the jubilee year of 1450 points to his status and social influence. But after the destruction of the Douglas lordship there was no aristocratic court that could remotely rival the prestige and honour attached to the royal house.

Centre and locality

There were other means by which the royal dynasty sought to augment its standing within and out with the realm. The manipulation or promotion of saints' cults was one. In the fifteenth century there were at least two cults focused on the royal dynasty itself. The most significant and enduring was that of St Margaret who had been canonized in the mid-thirteenth century. In fourteenth- and fifteenth-century literary works it was common shorthand to describe the royal dynasty as 'Margaret's heirs'. Descent from saintly Margaret allowed Scottish kings to promote the notion that they held a claim to the English throne as a result of Margaret's membership of the Anglo-Saxon royal house, and also to emphasize that the same saintly blood continued to run in their veins. Thus Andrew of Wyntoun's tribute to the character of Robert duke of Albany described the duke as a lineal descendant of St Margaret in the tenth generation who replicated many of her qualities.

In contrast to St Margaret, the godliness of David duke of Rothesay, the ill-fated son of Robert III who gained a posthumous popular reputation as a 'saint' and a royal martyr, was much disputed. David received little or no official ecclesiastical recognition as a suitable subject for veneration, but there was undoubtedly a cult centred on his miracle-working tomb at Lindores in Fife in the second half of the fifteenth century.

The Scottish crown could also identify itself profitably with regional saints. The association of royal authority with saints such as St Ninian and St Duthac, figures who commanded great devotion in Galloway and Ross respectively, undoubtedly made other aspects of royal government in these regions seem less intrusive and alien. A series of earlier secular lordships had bolstered their hold in Ross by linking their power with St Duthac's cult, his relics, and his shrine at Tain. In the fourteenth century the earls of Ross had ridden out to war wearing what was reputed to be St Duthac's shirt. Early in the fifteenth century the Douglas family, which had acquired extensive estates in the Black Isle and the area around Inverness, also displayed an attachment to the Duthac cult. For most of the fifteenth century, however, control of the earldom of Ross was a matter of political dispute between the royal dynasty and the MacDonald lordship of the Isles. One element in the struggle for the support of the local communities was the Stewart monarchy's veneration of St Duthac. In the reign of James IV the absorption of Ross and Galloway into a more direct relationship to the crown was symbolized and reinforced by the king's almost annual pilgrimages to the cult centres of Duthac and Ninian at Tain and Whithorn. In fact, during the fifteenth century, these shrines came to define the northernmost and southernmost limits of a unified and national system of pilgrimage, the so-called 'four chief heidis', which attracted the devout and could be imposed on the penitent.

James IV's regular visits to Tain reinforced the message that Ross was now firmly within the sphere of royal lordship. For much of the period after 1400 the northern earldom had seemed destined to become part of the regional empire of the lord of the Isles. By 1500 the earldom, although still vulnerable to incursions from the west, was effectively under royal control. The crown's authority in the region was symbolized and proclaimed by the local heraldic officers, Ross herald and Dingwall and Ormonde pursuivants, by royal patronage of the collegiate kirk at Tain, and by the elevation of the cult of St Duthac to the point where it was integrated into the royal itinerary and, indeed, the religious life of the kingdom as a whole.

The creation of a more unified society centred on institutions associated with the crown was, in fact, under way at many different levels. By the early fifteenth century the circle of provincial earls and lords that had formed the highest level of the thirteenth-century aristocracy had been destroyed through failure of male lines, forfeiture, and political exile. The forfeiture of earldoms and lordships to the crown during the fifteenth century (by 1455 the monarchy held nine earldoms and numerous territorial lordships) exacerbated and made permanent the depletion of the traditional landowning elite. In the fifteenth century this vacuum was filled by the emergence of a parliamentary peerage, the so-called lords of parliament, and by the creation of a number of honorific rather than territorial earldoms. The lords of parliament created in the 1440s and 1450s were not really a 'new' nobility in the sense that most of the men ennobled were already highly influential and well established in local society. In some cases a family's rise to dominance could be charted through the bonds of manrent given to them by other men in the locality, offering service and loyalty in return for protection and 'good lordship'. Nevertheless, honorific earldoms and lordships of parliament did establish the principle that aristocratic title and status could be directly created by royal gift. As the century progressed it became obvious that entry to the parliamentary peerage could be won through dedicated service to the crown or as a whim of royal patronage as much as through the establishment of a local social supremacy that demanded royal recognition. The elevation, shortly before 1464, of the Fife laird William Monypenny to the rank of William Lord Monypenny after a career as a royal diplomat is a case in point.

The relationship of the crown with different areas of the kingdom was also slowly transformed in the judicial and financial spheres. As the crown's reach lengthened so did the usefulness of judgements underwritten by royal authority. The volume of civil law cases brought before royal courts increased dramatically in the second half of the fifteenth century, requiring the creation of a more or less permanent, increasingly professional, and Edinburgh-based judicial committee, the Lords of Council (effectively the forerunner of the court of session). The recorded verdicts of the Lords of Council represent the tip of an iceberg, for it is clear that many disputes were being settled by informal arbitration in and around Edinburgh as litigating parties sought to postpone or avoid expensive proceedings and judgements before royal courts. The increasing influence and accessibility of royal judgement was reflected in the way in which private contracts and arbitrations began to include penalty clauses designed to give the crown a financial inducement to enforce the terms of the agreement, or to guard against the possibility of agreed settlements being challenged and overturned in the king's courts. As the level and importance of litigation increased, major aristocrats established links with legal specialists who could act on their behalf in the Edinburgh courts. In the first decade of the sixteenth century, for example, the north-eastern earls of Erroll and Huntly received bonds of service from, respectively, Mr Richard Lawson and Sir William Scott of Balwearie, both regularly employed as legal representatives before the Lords of Council.

The increased number of tenurial disputes coming under the review of royal judges allowed the crown to enforce its own extensive rights as a feudal overlord in a more systematic way. In the reigns of James III and James IV many men involved in cases brought before the royal court soon found themselves being pursued for technical breaches of feudal law by the king's advocates. The heavy and sometimes crippling financial penalties exacted for these abuses helped to sustain the crown's increasing levels of expenditure, but the cost may well have been a growing resentment of the workings of the royal administration. The story of George Lord Seton, harried to distraction by James IV's advocate over a debt to the crown, rounding on his tormentor in court and enquiring exactly what service the lawyer's ancestors had rendered to Robert I at Bannockburn may be apocryphal, but it was presumably preserved to make a point about the attitudes of the representatives of long and noble lineages with a proud history, brought to bay by upstart lawyers because of technical infringements of feudal law.

The development of policies designed to exploit royal resources more vigorously had an impact on local society in a number of other ways. By the second half of the fifteenth century the crown had accumulated vast tracts of territory, but many of the new royal estates were in areas where the notion of efficient exploitation had traditionally taken second place to the need to maintain local social structures. Lords able to control or regulate troublesome areas and populations had been given privileged tenurial terms and wide-ranging judicial rights through which they entrenched their local power. In the years after 1450, a general economic upturn and a growing population produced a buoyant land market that placed pressure on privileges and exemptions established in periods of economic stagnation or local disorder. In the reigns of James III and James IV a growing number of charters were said to be issued 'for the profit of the crown' and the 'augmentation of the rentals'. The concern with maximizing profit saw a more widespread use of feu-ferme tenure in which the crown's tenants could transform their fixed-term leases into heritable possession of their land in return for a large initial cash payment and an increased annual 'rent'. In some areas the conversion of royal lands to feu-ferme tenure proceeded smoothly, but in others, such as the Appin of Dull in Highland Perthshire, the existing tenants lost out to men in favour with James IV who were capable of offering better financial returns to the crown. The result was widespread dispossession of sitting tenants and, in 1502, a violent rebellion in Perthshire that saw royal lands ravaged and the castle of the king's chief local agent, Sir Robert Menzies of Weem, burnt to the ground.

The potentially destabilizing effects of the crown's patronage and search for profit extended beyond the lands held directly by the king. Early in the

Facing: THE FUNERAL OF THE SCOTTISH KING. The illustration of a dirge for a king of Scots has been taken to represent the funeral at Cambuskenneth abbey of James's father, James III, who was killed at the battle of Sauchieburn in 1488. In fact the scene seems to employ a stock image customized for James and Margaret's Book of Hours by the inclusion of Scottish armorial banners.

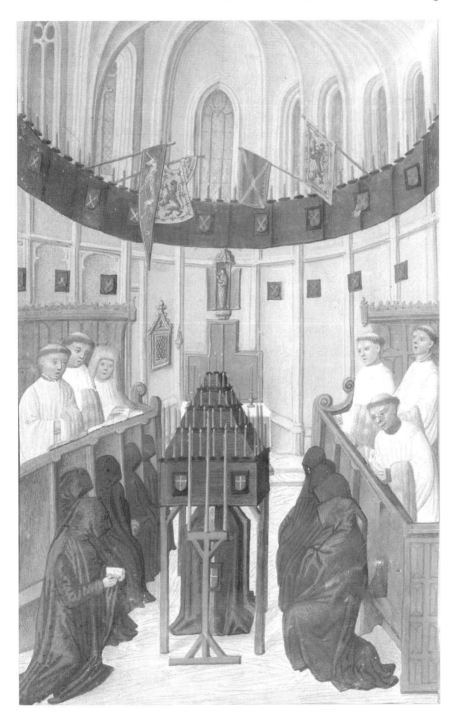

century the distribution of grants of land, local offices, and the lucrative marriages and wardships of heirs and heiresses which fell to the crown as a feudal overlord had been heavily influenced by the great regional magnates, and the process had therefore tended to consolidate their local power. By the end of the century, however, the crown was exploiting these resources either to provide patronage for its own retainers or to maximize revenue, often with little regard for established patterns of political influence in the localities. Many of the most serious baronial feuds of the second half of the fifteenth century were sparked by the deliberate or inadvertent intrusion of men with good connections to the royal court into estates or offices coveted by a powerful local rival. The necessity of obtaining the goodwill of the king in order to preserve or enhance local power became more obvious, and it hardly seems coincidental that the reign of James III saw the first indication of disquiet over the issue of royal favourites who monopolized access to the monarch. As the royal court became the centre of an intense bidding war for offices, lands, feudal rights, or even claims to enforce judgements delivered by royal courts, it also became the focus for political competition and tension. The great rebellion of 1488 that ended with the death of James III at the battle of Sauchieburn was largely fuelled by a series of local disputes in which the king was closely identified with one or other of the principal protagonists. The increasing influence of the crown on the distribution of resources within the kingdom brought with it dangers as well as opportunities.

Left: THE GERMAN INSCRIP-
TION of this portrait of 'Jacob der
Sechts Konning von Schottland'
suggests that it might be connected with James VI's Danish
marriage in 1589. The king's
youthful appearance, however,
conveying a watchful innocence,
indicates a date in the early 1580s,
when James would have been
fourteen or fifteen.

Below: DESIGNS for the British
flag, *c.*1604, with the earl of Not-
tingham's note of his choice. The
obvious attempts to give either the
St Andrew's or St George's cross
prominence in the heraldically
most important part of the flag,
the top part nearest to the flagpole,
give immediate visual expression
to determined Anglo-Scottish
rivalry. The final flag, the Union
Jack, is therefore a model of
heraldic compromise. The Irish
cross was not added until 1801.

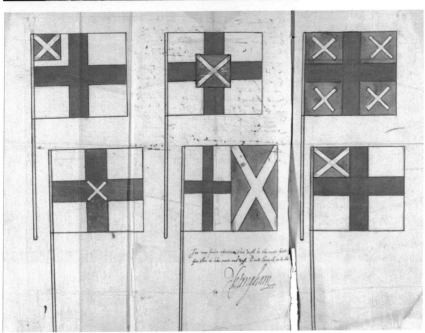

PARCHMENT COPY of the National Covenant, 1638, made for the Burgh of Peebles and signed by the provost, baillies, and town councillors.

HIGHLAND CULTURE. David Allan, the greatest product of the Foulis brothers' arts academy in Glasgow, captured several features of Highland popular culture in a series of pictures showing weddings and dances in Perthshire around 1780. In *The Highland Wedding*, the bride is attended to by family and friends while a piper and the famous fiddler Niel Gow play music, and guests in various forms of Highland dress celebrate with ale, whisky, and gunfire.

A BURGEONING CONSUMER CULTURE. Although both the artist and the sitter are unknown, this painting of a Glasgow shopkeeper in the 1790s says a great deal about the effects of commerce and overseas trade on urban social life. Lemons, tea, and cone-shaped loaves of sugar are among the items for sale, and the grocer's stylish clothing and gold jewellery are indications of considerable prosperity.

GLENCOE (detail), 1864, by Horatio McCulloch depicts the Highlands in romantic perception, with no vestige of humankind in the brooding, majestic landscape.

4 Renaissance and Reformation: The Sixteenth Century

ROGER MASON

In the course of the sixteenth century, Europe impacted on Scotland, and Scotland on Europe, in ways quite unprecedented in the kingdom's history. Just as the lottery of dynastic inheritance catapulted Mary queen of Scots onto the European stage, so her kingdom assumed a strategic importance far in excess of its intrinsic wealth and resources. In the 1540s and 1550s, more-over, the contest between France and England for control of Scotland assumed a religious dimension that propelled the kingdom to the forefront of a confessional conflict that was ripping contemporary Europe apart. Matters came to a head in the 1560s, during Mary's personal rule, which witnessed a series of interrelated crises that culminated in the deposition of a reigning monarch, and saw the country transformed from a Catholic kingdom allied with France to a Protestant kingdom tied to England. The eventual outcome was the union of the Scottish and English crowns under James VI and I in 1603, the belated fulfilment of the dynastic promise of the marriage, exactly a century earlier, of James IV and Margaret Tudor. It is, however, only with hindsight that Scotland's Protestant Reformation and the subsequent Anglo-Scottish union appear at all inevitable. Seen from the perspective of the early sixteenth century, a very different picture emerges. For the reigns of James IV and James V saw the consolidation of a Scottish Renaissance monarchy under a Stewart dynasty that was both formidably well established and deter-mined to play an independent role on the European stage.

Renaissance monarchy, 1488–1513

To mark his marriage to Margaret Tudor in 1503, James IV gave his bride an exquisitely illuminated Book of Hours commissioned from a Flemish *atelier* closely connected with Hugo van der Goes who, a generation earlier, had painted a magnificent altarpiece for Trinity Collegiate Church in Edinburgh. Both works are evidence of Scotland's close cultural links with the Low Countries. But they are significant for another reason. For when van der Goes painted James III kneeling at prayer with his young son in the Trinity altarpiece, he depicted the king wearing a crown in the form of an open circlet. By contrast, the Book of Hours contains a fine portrait of James IV, not only wearing an arched 'imperial' crown, but praying before an elaborate version of the royal arms displaying the same imperial motif.

The significance of this is that the arched crown, traditionally worn only by the Holy Roman Emperor, was fast becoming a symbol of the complete 'national' sovereignty being claimed by Europe's Renaissance monarchs. Such claims, recalling the authority of the Roman emperors of antiquity, were founded more immediately on the civil law doctrine that 'the king is emperor in his own kingdom'. Well known in Italy and France, it was from French law schools that the idea came to Scotland where, in 1469, parliament first declared that James III possessed 'full jurisdiction and free empire within his realm'. Fittingly, in the last coinage of his reign (*c.*1485), the same king was portrayed wearing an arched imperial crown in what was possibly the earliest Renaissance coin portrait minted outside Italy. By 1500, the image of the closed crown was becoming ubiquitous, a potent symbol of the Scottish kingdom's territorial integrity and the Stewart monarchy's jurisdictional supremacy within it. Definitively incorporated within the royal arms by James IV, it was also, and quite literally, set in stone. To embellish the belltower of his new university chapel at Aberdeen, Bishop William Elphinstone capped it with an impressive steeple in the form of an imperial crown.

In fact, King's College Chapel was only one of a number of churches for which such crown steeples were built in the late fifteenth and early sixteenth centuries. St Giles's, Edinburgh, and St Michael's, Linlithgow, were likewise embellished with the same highly visible symbol of royal authority. The proliferation of imperial iconography on ecclesiastical buildings is testimony to the success of the aggressive policies pursued by successive Stewart monarchs towards the weakening authority of the papacy. In Scotland, as in Europe generally, the balance of power between crown and papacy was shifting decisively in favour of the former. St Andrews' elevation to archiepiscopal status in 1472 was followed by an Indult of 1487 by which the papacy effectively surrendered to James III the right of appointment to his kingdom's richer ecclesiastical benefices. The result was the creation under James IV of what amounted to a royally appointed episcopate, which was, understandably, fiercely loyal to the imperial monarchy to which it now owed its primary allegiance.

The crown's new-found ability to exploit the Church's enormous riches had crippling long-term consequences for the clerical estate. More immediately, however, it helped crystallize a renewed sense of Scottishness among the clerical elite. The clergy had always played a crucial role in developing the myths and symbols of Scotland's independent identity. Not only were they society's educated elite, but the predatory ambitions of York and Canterbury had led them to invest heavily in a mythologized version of the Scottish past aimed at countering English claims to lordship over Scotland. It is no surprise that William Schevez, the cultured clerical careerist who became the second archbishop of St Andrews in 1478, was an avid collector of Scottish chronicles. Very much a man of the Renaissance, Schevez not only commissioned a striking portrait medal of himself from the distinguished Flemish artist Quintin Matsys, but also sought to rebuild in deliberately antique form the shrine of St Palladius, the legendary first bishop of Scotland. His interest in celebrating the Scottish past was shared by Bishop Elphinstone whose extensive historical research was prompted by a keen interest in developing native devotional practices. The result was the publication in 1509–10 of the Aberdeen Breviary, a deliberate attempt, backed by James IV, to create a national liturgy for Scotland.

While the closed imperial crown provided an ideal symbol for a Church that was both more self-consciously Scottish and more subservient to the royal will than ever before, the usefulness of the idea of empire was not confined to asserting royal authority in ecclesiastical affairs. It might also serve to underwrite territorial consolidation such as James III's acquisition of Orkney and Shetland in 1468 or James IV's suppression of the lordship of the Isles in 1493. As emperors in their own realm, Stewart monarchs were understandably concerned to extend and define the bounds of their kingdom. Equally, however, they were concerned to ensure the supremacy of royal authority within it. Thus the same 1469 parliament which asserted James III's imperial status also set up a commission to codify a uniform body of Scots law. While no such digest was immediately forthcoming, repeated efforts were made to eliminate the local laws and customs which persisted in outlying regions of the kingdom. The Scottish kingdom, as James IV's parliament of 1504 asserted, was to be 'ruled by our sovereign lord's own laws and [the] common laws of the realm and by no other laws'.

Such a statement tells us more about royal aspirations than about the realities of governing the Stewart *imperium*. After all, impressive though the iconography of empire might be, it did not equip the monarchy with the power or resources to impose royal authority on the localities. Admittedly, in the fifteenth century, royal aggression had gradually eliminated the great regional magnates, but the new parliamentary peers who emerged triumphant from the wreckage, though individually less threatening to the crown, retained formidable power in their own backyards. The localities were now the preserve of the new noble families—Campbells, Gordons, Hamiltons, Humes, and Kennedys—who would dominate early modern Scotland, and whose interests the crown could not ignore. Possessed of their own franchise courts, and often exercising regalian rights over their estates, their local authority was further extended by bonds of kinship and manrent. Within (and between) their respective spheres of influence, it was not the public justice of the king's law which necessarily prevailed, but the often violent though effective private justice of the feud.

In a society of local lordships, where kin-groups were frequently at daggers drawn, and where violence was second nature to a highly militarized elite, the crown interfered at its peril. Yet interfere it frequently did. Stewart kings proved highly assertive and predatory, determined to rule as well as reign, and quite prepared to play an intrusive role in local politics whether to pacify feuds or to extend royal income and authority. Friction between crown and nobility was no aberration in Scottish politics, but the norm. Moreover, it was triggered less by the irresponsible antics of over-mighty subjects than by the crown's aggressive pursuit of royal interests. That said, however, no contemporary monarch could rule without the cooperation of barons who were both the leaders of local society and the king's natural-born counsellors. The Stewarts could and did employ *force majeure* to destroy individual magnates, but violent confrontation was exceptional. The real key to effective royal government lay in the crown's ability to maximize its resources (often at the nobility's expense), while managing its leading subjects through force of personality and the judicious distribution of wealth and patronage.

James IV was an acknowledged master of these arts of government. During his reign (1488–1513), he exploited every device available to him to raise royal revenues to unprecedented levels—from around £13,000 in the 1490s to as much as £40,000 by 1513—while successfully retaining the loyalty of his leading subjects. The contrast with his father is stark and revealing. In many respects, James IV built on the fiscal practices pioneered by James III, supplementing traditional sources of income such as feudal casualties and the profits of justice with higher clerical taxation and innovatory schemes such as the feuing of royal estates. But while James III's exactions often seemed arbitrary and unjust, and his static and reclusive style of kingship created mistrust, James IV was tirelessly peripatetic and his administration of justice was backed by a council more representative of the territorial interests of his kingdom than that of any of his predecessors. As adept at the distribution of reward as he was at the accumulation of revenue, James IV never fell victim to the kind of coalition of disaffected magnates that destroyed his father.

Effective kingship, however, entailed more than the equitable distribution of patronage. Just as important was the creation of a royal court at once inclusive of competing factions and projecting royal authority over them. James IV invested heavily in the architectural settings, such as the magnificent Great Hall at Stirling Castle, where the splendour of Stewart kingship could best be displayed. At the same time, he encouraged a flamboyant courtly lifestyle, animated by his own considerable intellectual energy, and typified as much by the failed alchemical experiments of John Damian as by the stunning virtuosity of the court poet, William Dunbar. The Spanish ambassador, Pedro de Ayala, commented favourably on the king's intellectual accomplishments, and it may be that he was genuinely interested in such cultural innovations as the establishment of a printing press in Edinburgh and the foundation of King's College, Aberdeen. Ultimately, however, James IV saw himself as a warrior prince, not only presiding over but participating in the spectacular tournaments that he held in 1507 and 1508. The cult of chivalry provided a welcome outlet for the martial aggression of the nobility; but it also reinforced the king's position as the leader of the aristocratic community and the fount of honour within it.

Yet the king's interest in martial affairs extended well beyond chivalric pageantry. Throughout his reign, he spent heavily on military technology, stockpiling formidable arsenals of state-of-the-art weaponry, while also creating a navy of unprecedented size, with a flagship, the 'Great' *Michael*, launched in 1511 at a cost of some £30,000. James was undoubtedly a charismatic monarch, capable of imposing his personality on his subjects; but he was also formidably well resourced, able to dominate at home, while project-

THE GREAT HALL at Stirling Castle, recently restored to something approaching its original glory, was the largest hall of its kind ever built in Scotland. An appropriate setting for the display of royal magnificence, it was completed for James IV around 1503.

ing abroad the image of an imperial Renaissance prince. That he could do so owed much to the French king, Louis XII, who supplied the wherewithal to build his military strength. Despite marriage into the English royal house, Scotland remained closely tied to France, and it was on Louis XII's behalf that in 1513 James broke off relations with his young brother-in-law Henry VIII and invaded England. It is a measure of the king's popularity that he took with him on his Flodden campaign almost the entire leadership of the Scottish political community. Equally, it is a measure of the disaster that occurred on 9 September 1513 that that leadership was almost entirely eliminated. Thousands of common soldiers died at Flodden, and so too did the king, his bastard son (the archbishop of St Andrews), a bishop, two abbots, nine earls, and fourteen lords of parliament.

The effect of such carnage was devastating. Both at local and national level Scottish politics were destabilized overnight, the kingship nominally in the hands of a year-old infant, James V, who immediately fell prey to competing magnate interests headed by inexperienced politicians. The lengthy minority that ensued was dominated by conflict between the Hamiltons and Douglases in particular, and it was from the clutches of Archibald Douglas, sixth earl of Angus, that the sixteen-year-old James V engineered his own escape in 1528. But, while the minority did much to weaken royal authority, it is important not to exaggerate Flodden's long-term impact. Not only did the Stewart dynasty survive, but in the 1530s James V was able to reimpose the crown's authority with remarkable speed and to embark on policies of royal aggrandizement that are strikingly continuous with those of his father. Moreover, just as Scotland's Renaissance monarchy survived Flodden, so the country remained open to a range of cultural influences that were slowly transforming the society over which the Stewart kings presided.

Humanism and reform, 1513–1542

These continuities are evident in the magnificent heraldic ceiling constructed around 1520 for St Machar's Cathedral, Aberdeen. Designed by Alexander Galloway, a protégé of Bishop Elphinstone, the ceiling's three parallel rows of heraldic shields depict the pope and the hierarchy of the Scottish Church, the secular leaders of Christendom headed by the Emperor Charles V, and the leaders of the Scottish political community headed by James V. Of the princes of Christendom, aside from the Holy Roman Emperor, only the king of Scots is represented with a coat of arms surmounted by an arched imperial crown. Despite Flodden, Scots continued to see their kingdom as a secular *imperium* on a par with the Renaissance monarchies of Europe generally. The ceiling's design was probably directly indebted to Elphinstone, whose interest in imperial ideas is evident from the crown steeple of King's College. Certainly, Elphinstone's career neatly illustrates the sophisticated self-confidence that exposure to European learning had instilled in Scotland's elite. Although more influential than most, Elphinstone was not untypical among Scottish clerics in using a continental education as a stepping stone to advancement in the royal bureaucracy as well as the Church. Trained in law at Glasgow, Paris, and Orléans, he became both bishop of Aberdeen and, as keeper of the Privy Seal from 1492, a leading figure in James IV's government. A lawyer and royal servant, Elphinstone was primarily concerned with exacting obedience to the king's authority. More broadly, however, he was keenly interested in the promotion of a more 'civilized' society through the education of the lay elite. Thus the foundation of King's College in 1495 was

THE MAGNIFICENT HERALDIC CEILING at St Machar's Cathedral, Aberdeen, constructed around 1520, provides evidence of the high status that the Scots accorded their monarchy; while the shield of the English king, Henry VIII, is capped by a traditional open circlet, that of James V bears an arched imperial crown.

followed in 1496 by the passing of the celebrated Education Act, encouraging barons and freeholders to send their eldest sons to university to study 'arts and jure'.

The civilizing influence of an education based on classical literature was fundamental to the humanist programme that lay at the heart of Renaissance culture, and experience abroad ensured that educated Scots were well aware of the 'new learning'. Just as Elphinstone possessed a copy of one of the most influential texts of humanist Latinity, Lorenzo Valla's *Elegances of the Latin Language* (*c*.1440), so the Cologne-educated Archibald Whitelaw, royal secretary from 1462 to 1493, amassed a classical library which included a manuscript copy of Cicero's works as well as printed editions of Horace, Lucan, and Sallust. The influence of the printing press was only just beginning to make itself felt in Europe, but the ability to mass-produce printed texts rather than rely on laboriously copied manuscripts was a technological innovation with massive cultural repercussions. The availability of printed books ensured the rapid circulation of ideas and, for the Scots, opened up a relatively cheap and easy means of keeping abreast of continental cultural developments. Chepman and Myllar's Edinburgh printing press proved short-lived and, aside from the Aberdeen Breviary, confined itself to publishing vernacular poetry and romance literature. Yet, as Whitelaw's library suggests, Scots now had ready access to the printed texts which, whether produced in Paris, Antwerp, or Venice, lay at the heart of the 'new learning'.

While often rarefied and arcane, such learning did have direct practical application. Whitelaw's long tenure of the royal secretaryship, for example, ensured that humanist rhetorical skills became institutionalized in the Scottish chancery just as they were in the chanceries of Europe generally. Thus among Whitelaw's successors as royal secretary was the highly accomplished Latinist Patrick Paniter, a trusted confidant of James IV who held the post from 1505 until 1519. Paniter was among a remarkable group of Scots who in the 1490s were fellow students in Paris of the great Dutch humanist Erasmus of Rotterdam, and it was probably Paniter who persuaded James IV to send his illegitimate son Alexander, the eleven-year-old archbishop of St Andrews, to study with Erasmus in Italy. Alexander's death at Flodden—lamented in a celebrated panegyric by Erasmus—cut short a promising career that had already in 1512 witnessed the foundation of St Leonard's College, St Andrews. Yet humanism had already gained a foothold in the universities just as it had in government. For in 1497 Bishop Elphinstone recruited Hector Boece, another of Erasmus' Paris circle, to teach at King's College, Aberdeen, promoting him to principal in 1505. Boece served as principal until his death in 1536, composing the first humanist history of Scotland, the *Scotorum historia* (Paris, 1527), and establishing Aberdeen as the main Scottish centre for the dissemination of humanist ideas.

Not all the Scottish universities proved so receptive to the classically based humanist curriculum. The dominant figure at St Andrews was John Mair, who had again studied with Erasmus in Paris, but who remained deeply sceptical of the humanist movement's championing of rhetoric over logic. Mair taught at Paris for twenty-five years, establishing a towering reputation as a logician and theologian, before returning to Scotland in 1518 to teach initially at Glasgow and then St Andrews. For all his commitment to scholastic method, however, Mair's best-known work, his Latin *History of Greater Britain* (Paris, 1521), betrays considerable sympathy for the humanists' social agenda.

While his view of contemporary Scotland was decidedly bleak, leading him to promote at length the cause of Anglo-Scottish union, his belief that a more civil Scottish society could be created through the education of the lay elite was one that was becoming widespread. Gradually, St Andrews and Glasgow Universities were to follow Aberdeen in fashioning arts curricula that, heavily influenced by humanism, were aimed at the laity as much as the clergy.

The emergence of a literate, often highly educated, lay elite was the most significant cultural development of the era. The spread of literacy from the upper nobility and merchants to a wider population of lesser landowners and burgesses is evident in the adoption of vernacular Scots as the language of government as well as in the explosion of vernacular writing, for and by the laity, that occurred in the century after 1450 and that found its most memorable expression in the verse of the great 'makars', Henryson, Dunbar, and Douglas. Of the 'makars', only the aristocratic Douglas (the uncle of the sixth earl of Angus) was deeply touched by humanism, translating Virgil's *Aeneid* into Scots for his lay patron, Lord Sinclair. Crucially, however, many laymen were becoming sufficiently accomplished in the language of learning to read such classical texts for themselves. By the 1530s, it was common for laymen not only to have graduated in arts, but also to have studied law, often in France or Italy. Thus Sir James Foulis, the son of an Edinburgh burgess and an accomplished Latin poet, studied law in Paris and Orléans before serving as clerk-register from 1532 until 1549, while from 1526 to 1543, the post of royal secretary was held for the first time by a layman, Sir Thomas Erskine, a minor Angus landowner who had studied law at Pavia.

These developments began to bear significant fruit during the personal rule of James V (1528–42). Not only did the spread of literacy have a profound impact on the religious climate of the 1530s, but lay lawyers such as Erskine and Foulis were to play a prominent role in the young king's government following his escape from the Douglases in 1528. The vindictive pursuit of his former Douglas captors is often seen as the leitmotif of James's personal rule. However, the king's justifiable suspicion of the Douglases' treasonable dealings with England amounted to less than an obsessive vendetta, while the charge that a paranoid fear of the nobility led to the arbitrary appropriation of their lands needs to be treated with caution. The king has generally been portrayed as vindictive, cruel, and sadistic, but it is more accurate to see him as a highly effective Renaissance prince.

After a long and fractious minority, James was, understandably, a young king in a hurry, intent on reasserting royal authority with all the vigour and resources at his disposal. The tone was set in 1530 by a punitive expedition to the Borders which vividly demonstrated the king's determination that the royal writ should run throughout his kingdom. At the same time, he ensured that royal revenues, grossly mismanaged during his minority, were restored to the levels enjoyed by his father. Of course, in recovering crown lands and revenues, he ruthlessly exploited the full repertoire of legal and fiscal devices employed by his predecessors. As a result, some noblemen undoubtedly did suffer. But the aggressive pursuit of royal interests was nothing new and, if it proved particularly effective in James V's reign, the reason probably lies less in the king's alleged paranoia than in the skill of the lay lawyers on whose expertise he was able to draw. Like his equally ruthless and acquisitive father, James V saw the need to work with rather than against his leading subjects.

In fact, it was the clergy rather than the nobility who had reason to fear both the king and the lesser laymen who were colonizing his bureaucracy. Although James's former tutor Gavin Dunbar, archbishop of Glasgow, remained chancellor throughout the reign, the clergy's monopoly of administrative expertise was being steadily eroded. At the same time, the spread of reforming opinion, both outright Protestantism and the evangelical humanism that proved so appealing to anticlerical laymen, threw them further on the defensive. In 1525 parliament had legislated against the import of Lutheran literature, while three years later Patrick Hamilton was burned at the stake for espousing Luther's doctrines. But the undercurrents of reforming opinion, fuelled by the spread of print, could not easily be controlled, and James exploited the weakness of his own ecclesiastical hierarchy and the papacy's growing fear that he might follow the example of his uncle Henry VIII and repudiate papal authority altogether. As a result, with papal blessing, James was able further to consolidate royal control over appointments to major benefices, milk the revenues of the wealthiest religious houses to provide for his growing brood of bastards, and levy the heaviest tax on clerical income—£72,000 over four years—that the *Ecclesia Scoticana* had ever experienced.

Even with greatly augmented revenues, James was hardly able to compete with contemporary monarchs like Henry VIII, Charles V, or Francis I. Nevertheless, the intense rivalry between France, England, and the Empire, compounded by heightened religious tensions and the nervousness of Rome, lent the Scottish king unwonted diplomatic weight. His shrewd exploitation of the marriage market led to his securing in 1536 the hand of Francis I's eldest surviving daughter Madeleine, as well as a massive dowry from the French

FALKLAND PALACE, a former hunting lodge, was a favoured retreat for Stewart monarchs. James V employed French masons to reconstruct it in the 1530s, adding this fine classical façade to the courtyard side of the south range.

king. The glitter of this stunning dynastic coup was dimmed by Madeleine's death within months of her arrival in Scotland, but undeterred, in 1538, James married Mary of Guise-Lorraine, renewing Scotland's ties with France in return for a further substantial dowry. Despite Henry VIII's attempts to sever them, Scotland's links with France and Rome remained intact, the bargain sweetened by two generous dowries and lucrative papal concessions. Fittingly, the huge financial rewards of James's diplomacy were spent on restocking the royal arsenal, maintaining a lavish royal household, and creating the architectural settings in which the full majesty of his kingship could best be displayed.

The results of the king's building programme were some of the finest examples of Renaissance architecture in Britain: the extravagantly decorated Palace Block at Stirling and the more refined classical façades of the courtyard at Falkland. Both projects were heavily influenced by the king's sojourn at the court of Francis I during the winter of 1536–7. His nine-month absence, unprecedented for a reigning Scottish monarch, while giving the lie to those who doubt the stability of his regime or the loyalty of his leading subjects, also exposed James to the full panoply of Renaissance monarchy as practised at the Valois court. That he sought to recreate such a monarchy within his own kingdom, and that he sought to define it in the imperial terms employed by his father and grandfather, is hardly surprising. Not only does the closed imperial crown appear with increasing frequency on his coinage, but it also features in royal portraiture such as that of James and his second bride Mary of Guise. Indeed, to mark the latter's coronation in 1540, the king had the Scottish crown itself refashioned as an arched imperial one. Significantly, the same year saw the king personally leading a heavily armed seaborne expedition to Orkney and the Western Isles. James was intent on ensuring the submission of the outlying regions of his realm to royal authority, but his circumnavigation of the kingdom suggests a monarch beating the bounds of his *imperium* and asserting his jurisdictional supremacy within it.

Behind such confident displays of royal power, however, the glittering court of James V remained fraught with tension. Despite the renewal of Scotland's ties with France and Rome, the Church was still a target for anticlerical courtiers keen to persuade the king to follow the example of Henry VIII by asserting the crown's supremacy over the Church at the papacy's expense. After all, despite the renewal of anti-heresy legislation in 1535, and despite show trials of alleged heretics in 1534 and 1541, James continued to be an astute if fickle patron of anticlerical sentiment. It was the king who commissioned from George Buchanan the series of blistering attacks on the Franciscans that both established the young humanist's reputation as a Latin poet of prodigious talent and forced him into continental exile. More fortunate was the courtier-poet Sir David Lindsay, a lifelong confidant of the king, whose vernacular verse was increasingly characterized by a scathing Erasmian anticlericalism that would eventually, in the final version of his brilliant *Satyre of the Thrie Estaitis* (1552), spill beyond the confines of the royal court and address lay society at large.

So long as James was alive, his authoritarian style of kingship kept humanist and Protestant calls for reform in check. His sudden death, however, aged only 30, on 14 December 1542, left as his sole legitimate heir the week-old Mary Stewart, and the ensuing minority saw the religious tensions that had been simmering throughout his reign finally boil over. It was probably plague or cholera that killed the king rather than, as legend has it, nervous exhaustion arising from the loss of his two male heirs and a military reversal at the hands of the English at Solway Moss. Nevertheless, his reputed quip when told of the birth of his daughter—that the crown had 'come wi' a lass and would pass wi' a lass'—was not far off the mark as regards the future of Scotland's imperial monarchy. For the succession of a female infant precipitated a prolonged crisis that threatened the survival of both the Stewart monarchy and an independent Scottish kingdom.

Dynasticism, diplomacy, and war, 1542–1558

Mary queen of Scots is probably the most mythologized monarch in history. Mythology, however, has served simply to obscure the fact that to contemporaries Mary was much more important as a dynastic entity than a human personality. Within Scotland, from the moment her father died, her chances of survival were a matter of vital concern to princes of the blood such as James Hamilton, second earl of Arran, great-grandson of James II and heir presumptive to the throne, and Matthew Stewart, fourth earl of Lennox, likewise descended from James II, and married to Margaret Douglas, daughter of Margaret Tudor and her second husband, the exiled sixth earl of Angus. Whether through Mary's death in infancy or through her betrothal to one of their kin, Arran and Lennox had much to gain from the succession of a baby girl to the Scottish throne.

It was not just Scottish nobles, however, who saw Mary's dynastic inheritance as a prize worth coveting. In the 1530s, James V's success in punching well above his diplomatic weight had highlighted Scotland's strategic significance on the European stage. To Henry VIII, frustrated by James's refusal to break his alliances with France and the papacy, and ever more isolated by his own defiance of Rome, Mary's accession offered the chance of finally sealing his troublesome northern frontier through the betrothal of the Scottish queen to his own son and heir, Prince Edward. With the 'postern gate' to England closed, and Scotland reduced to a satellite of the English crown, Henry could pursue unhampered his warlike ambitions in France. Understandably this was an outcome that Henry's European rivals wished to avoid. To them, moreover, Mary's dynastic value was immeasurably enhanced by her descent from Margaret Tudor and consequent place in the English succession. In Catholic eyes, Henry VIII's divorce of Catherine of Aragon was illegal, and any children of subsequent marriages illegitimate and barred from the succession. Thus only the unmarried Mary Tudor, Henry's sole child by his first wife, stood between Mary Stewart and the English throne.

The prospect of absorbing England as well as Scotland into a French imperial system proved a powerful incentive for the Valois dynasty to maintain a

IACOBVS · 5 · DEI GRATIA
REX SCOTORVM

MR

JAMES V MARRIED MARY OF GUISE-LORRAINE in 1538. Following his death in 1542, his widow continued to play a key role in Scottish politics, representing French interests in Scotland and Scottish interests in France.

keen interest in Scottish affairs. Likewise, the powerful Guise family, for whom militant Catholicism went hand in hand with dynastic ambition, was acutely aware of Mary of Guise's position as queen dowager of Scotland. Following James V's death, however, it was neither the queen mother nor the leading proponent of a Catholic, pro-French policy in Scotland, the cardinal archbishop of St Andrews, David Beaton, who took control. Rather, it was the heir presumptive, Arran, a man both sympathetic to religious reform and open to overtures from England, who was appointed governor in January 1543. Within months an Act had been passed allowing the free circulation of vernacular bibles—a key reformist plank implacably opposed by the Catholic hierarchy—and commissioners were on their way to negotiate a marriage alliance with England. On 1 July 1543, the Treaties of Greenwich were drawn up and the infant queen of Scots was promised in marriage to the heir to the English throne.

Arran was riding the crest of the wave of reforming opinion unleashed by James V's death. That opinion was as much anticlerical and anti-papal as it was

ACCESS TO THE VERNACULAR was a key demand of religious reformers. While no Scots version of the bible was printed in the pre-Reformation era, Henry VIII and Protector Somerset were keen to see English versions, presumably Henry's Great Bible of 1539, circulating in Scotland.

Protestant, but the circulation of vernacular English bibles and of other 'bills, writings, ballads and books' caused sufficient concern to prompt Arran's council to forbid the possession of heretical literature. A Scottish regent, however, particularly one as irresolute as Arran, was ill placed to stamp his authority on a fluid religious climate. Arran, moreover, found himself caught between the intimidatory demands of Henry VIII and an upsurge of popular Anglophobia fuelled by fears that the English king was intent on making good England's age-old claim to suzerainty over Scotland. While Arran was forced to reject Henry's demand to hand Mary over to his safekeeping, and though the laws and liberties of the ancient Scottish kingdom were safeguarded by the treaty, it proved to no avail. By December 1543, Beaton and the queen dowager had so successfully exploited the growing opposition to Arran's policies that the Scottish parliament threw out the English treaties, reaffirmed the French alliance, and re-enacted James V's anti-heresy legislation.

Arran's 'godly fit' had proved short-lived, and Scotland was once again officially both pro-French and Roman Catholic. The wave of reforming zeal that had driven Arran in the direction of England had rapidly given way to one that aligned powerful patriotic sentiment with the religious and diplomatic status quo. There were, of course, dissenting voices. Between 1544 and his martyrdom in 1546, the preaching mission of George Wishart clearly tapped a reservoir of hard-line Protestant conviction. Lacking effective national leadership, however, it remained localized among the east-coast burghs and a scattering of Lowland lairds. It was not Protestantism that posed the most serious threat to Arran's regime, but rather the towering wrath of the ageing Henry VIII. In 1544–5, his diplomacy scuppered by Arran's timidity, and rightly distrustful of his other Scottish clients, Henry launched a series of savage military strikes designed to bring the Scots forcibly to heel.

The 'Rough Wooing', however, proved as counter-productive as it was destructive. Immense material damage was inflicted, particularly on the Borders, but Arran's shaky regime survived, propped up by the popular perception of Henry VIII as a brutal tyrant intent on subjecting Scottish right to English might. His death in January 1547, while welcomed by most Scots, in fact offered scant relief, for the accession of the nine-year-old Edward VI brought to power Henry's former commander in Scotland, the new king's uncle, Edward Seymour, earl of Hertford and now duke of Somerset. Somerset's protectorate, markedly more Protestant than anything Henry VIII would have tolerated, also saw a change in policy towards Scotland. On the one hand, Somerset orchestrated a concerted propaganda campaign in which the marriage of Mary and Edward was cast as a God-given opportunity to create a united Britain ruled by a Protestant and imperial monarch; but on the other, leaving no doubt as to England's predominant place in this visionary new Britain, Somerset inflicted a bloody defeat on the Scots at Pinkie in September 1547 and proceeded to establish permanent garrisons throughout the Lowlands. Some Scots tolerated military occupation for the greater good of the Protestant cause; others collaborated because they had no choice. Yet the dynastic prize at the heart of Somerset's British project was snatched from his grasp. In July 1548, by the Treaty of Haddington, Mary was betrothed to the Dauphin Francis, heir to the French throne, and dispatched immediately to France.

It is a measure of Mary's dynastic significance that Somerset's huge investment in his Scottish policy was more than matched by the French king, Henry II. In the event, the latter's greater resources proved decisive: financially overstretched and faced with internal rebellion, Somerset's regime collapsed and in 1550 English troops withdrew from Scotland. The French monarchy celebrated its victory by proclaiming Mary's right to the English throne, a declaration of intent that would animate Valois thinking throughout the 1550s. At the same time, Henry assumed the full protectoral role in Scotland that the Treaty of Haddington had conceded, taking control of its civil as well as military and diplomatic affairs. While Scots were not excluded from the government, the pliant Arran was bought off with the duchy of Châtelherault, and the way prepared for the establishment of what amounted to French colonial rule in Scotland. The Scots had little choice but to accept French terms, their dependent status within the Valois empire made more palatable by the generous distribution of French pensions and the appointment of Mary of Guise as regent in 1554. Dedicated above all to advancing her daughter's dynastic interests, the queen mother's opposition to an English match had seen her stock rise steadily in the eyes of both the French government and the Scottish nobility. Respected on all sides, and with her brothers, the duke of Guise and the cardinal of Lorraine, powerfully ensconced at the French court, there was no one better placed to represent France's interests in Scotland or Scotland's interests in France.

Maintaining this delicate balance, however, would not prove easy, and was made more difficult by the changing diplomatic scene. Guise's assumption of the regency not only followed hard on Edward VI's death in 1553 and Mary Tudor's accession to the English throne, but coincided with the latter's marriage to Philip of Spain. One result of the marriage was the forced re-

Catholicization of England that earned the Tudor queen her reputation as 'Bloody Mary'. Another was England's incorporation into a Spanish imperial system that turned the Anglo-Scottish Border into a frontier of Habsburg–Valois ambition. Whatever domestic agenda Mary of Guise had planned for Scotland—and she was evidently concerned to repair the damage of a decade of war—such matters took second place to policing the highly militarized frontier across which the European superpowers now eyed each other. The cost of border fortifications fell largely on the French. Yet the Scots too were asked to pay. A 'perpetual tax' was mooted in 1556 which would have hit the nobility particularly hard, and which they resolutely resisted. However, alternative taxes were successfully levied, stoking up resentment against Guise, and leading the nobility to oppose any military intervention in England on France's behalf.

It was to this highly charged atmosphere that John Knox returned, surreptitiously, from exile in the winter of 1555. A renegade Catholic priest, who had been associated with Wishart's ministry in 1544–5, Knox had subsequently taken refuge in St Andrews Castle, joining the Protestant lairds who had avenged Wishart by assassinating Cardinal Beaton in May 1546. On the fall of the castle to the French, Knox was forced to serve as a galley slave before being released in 1549 and settling in Edward VI's Protestant England. Hardly had he established his reputation as an outstanding preacher, however, than the accession of Mary Tudor forced him into exile. It was from Calvin's Geneva that he returned to Scotland, retracing Wishart's steps among the cells of committed Protestants that had maintained an underground existence in the Lothians, Fife, Angus, and Ayrshire. His whirlwind tour helped endow the scattered congregations with a renewed sense of purpose, but just as importantly, it enabled Knox to make contact with sympathetic noblemen—the future Lords of the Congregation—who alone were capable of turning an inchoate movement for reform into a significant political force. In securing the support of earls such as Glencairn and Argyll, and the queen's bastard half-brother Lord James Stewart, Knox laid the foundations of the Protestant party that in 1559–60 would embark on revolution.

In 1555–6, however, this small but powerful lobby of reform-minded nobles was not yet prepared to exploit the growing discontent with Guise's regime to lead a Protestant insurrection. Significantly, when the Scottish bishops summoned Knox to answer a charge of heresy, Guise had the proceedings quashed, allowing Knox to return to Geneva, from where he berated the Scottish lords for not advancing their 'godly' cause by force, while

JOHN KNOX was to lament that his *First Blast* had 'blown from me all my friends in England'. He was probably right. He and his fellow Genevan exile, Christopher Goodman, were depicted blowing their trumpets in a contemporary woodcut. The caption reads: 'No queene in her kingdom can or ought to syt fast, If Knokes or Goodmans bookes blowe any true blast'.

penning his infamous denunciation of female rulers, *The First Blast of the Trumpet against the Monstrous Regiment of Women* (1558). Knox's Scottish allies, however, remained unmoved by his prophetic denunciations. After all, Guise was unlikely to antagonize the powerful Protestant lobby, and thus jeopardize her dynastic ambitions, by emulating Mary Tudor's bloody persecution. In fact, Guise was invariably inclusive in her distribution of patronage, Protestants as well as Catholics benefiting from French largesse. Her *politique* attitude effectively forestalled rebellion by holding out to Protestants the hope of gradualist reform. It did little, however, to rehabilitate the Catholic Church in the eyes of the many disaffected Scots whose religious allegiances remained in the balance.

Recent historiography, reacting strongly against centuries of Protestant prejudice, has done much to cast the pre-Reformation Church in a more favourable light. Yet no amount of apologetics can disguise the grave problems confronting the Catholic Church. The crown's crushing fiscal demands, for example, had led to the widespread feuing of church lands in order to raise ready cash. While the wealthier 'middling sort' prospered as a result of a more active land market, some 40 per cent of tenants of the Church's feued estates found themselves evicted. The ranks of the dispossessed, already swollen by demographic growth and the social dislocation of war, were increased still further by the policies pursued by the only institution remotely equipped to help them. If anything, growing disparities of wealth in society generally were even more pronounced in the Church, where the system of appropriation had systematically drained the parishes of revenue in order to endow the new universities and collegiate churches and to fund the luxurious lifestyles of the higher clergy. Appropriation was an ancient practice, but the demands being made on it by the cash-strapped Church were increasing just at a time when, faced with an educated laity, the clerical elite could ill afford to allow impoverished parish priests to supplement their meagre incomes through pluralism or the exaction of unpopular charges on disaffected parishioners.

Of course, neither abuses such as these nor the greater availability of printed English bibles necessarily led the laity to embrace Protestantism. In such a volatile religious climate, however, it was imperative that the Church respond to lay demands that it reform its house. Its ability to do so was undoubtedly hampered by the crown's success in wresting from the papacy control of appointments to higher ecclesiastical benefices. The leadership of the monastic orders was vitiated by such appointments as Lord James Stewart as prior of St Andrews, while the elevation of Arran's bastard half-brother John Hamilton to the archbishopric of St Andrews in 1547 was further evidence that ecclesiastical offices were prizes in a domestic political game. To his credit, Hamilton did recognize the urgent need for reform, summoning provincial church councils in 1549 and 1552 to address the problem. One tangible result was Hamilton's *Catechism* of 1552, a vernacular primer setting out the basics of the Catholic faith for the benefit of clergy and laity alike. Yet, while the councils issued and reissued ordinances regulating the clergy's behaviour, they did little to grasp the financial problems that had left the parishes desperately under-resourced. The Church remained as vulnerable as ever to the attacks of its increasingly vociferous lay critics.

No doubt, had Guise seen the reinvigoration of the Church as a priority, more could have been done to address its problems. However, dynastic imperatives dictated a more cautious approach. The result was not so much deadlock as drift: while the Catholic hierarchy had its hands tied, the Protestant lobby preferred to bide its time, pushing for concessions but not forcing a confrontation. The drawing up of the famous First Band in December 1557 may suggest that some feared that the impending realization of Guise's dynastic ambitions, the marriage of Mary to the Dauphin Francis, would result in a backlash against them. The marriage duly took place in April 1558, yet still Guise showed no signs of turning on religious dissidents. On the contrary, in response to renewed Protestant agitation, she summoned another church council to reassure them of her continuing goodwill. By the time the council met in March 1559, however, yet another throw of the dynastic dice had significantly altered the situation. For in November 1558, Mary Tudor died childless and her half-sister Elizabeth, the last of Henry VIII's children, and an avowed Protestant, was crowned in her place.

In retrospect, 1558 marks the highpoint of Mary of Guise's regency and of the imperial ambitions of the Valois monarchy. To contemporaries, however, it looked more like the beginning than the end of French dynastic expansionism. Some weeks before the marriage of Mary and Francis in April 1558, the Scottish queen had signed a 'secret' document bequeathing her kingdom to the French crown should there be no children of the marriage. Together with the Scottish parliament's bestowal of the crown matrimonial on Francis in November 1558, this bound Scotland in perpetuity to the French monarchy, a provincial outpost of the expanding Valois empire. To the prospect of uniting the French and Scottish crowns, moreover, was added the possibility of ousting Elizabeth from the English throne in favour of Mary Stewart's Catholic claim. The French monarchy's ostentatious quartering of Mary's arms with those of England was more than a display of heraldic bravura. Following the duke of Guise's triumph in retaking Calais, England's last foothold on French soil, it was a serious declaration of dynastic intent. The prospects for the Valois monarchy had never looked brighter than they did in 1558— and at their heart lay the dynastic inheritance of the fifteen-year-old queen of Scots.

Reformation and revolution, 1558–1578

The euphoria that gripped Valois France in 1558 did not last long. The next year brought a welcome respite from conflict with Spain and England, but the celebrations were cut short when Henry II was fatally wounded in a tournament held to mark the peace. On his death, on 10 July 1559, Mary queen of Scots became also queen of France. Although her striking good looks belied a history of indifferent health, her physical frailty was as nothing compared to that of her husband, the new French king, Francis II. Only fifteen, and mentally as well as physically immature, Francis was patently unfit to govern. Instead, power was seized by his close relatives, Mary's uncles, the duke of

Guise and the cardinal of Lorraine. While the triumph of 'Les Guises' seemed complete, however, their power and ambition, as well as their militant Catholicism, were deeply resented by rival factions at the French court, whose sympathies were increasingly Protestant. Long before the outbreak of France's convulsive Wars of Religion in March 1560, the Guise regime was being undermined from within. Ironically, however, it was rebellion in Scotland that offered the first sustained challenge to its authority. It was, for the Scots, the beginning of a fifteen-year struggle that saw, not only a revolution against France and Rome, but the deposition of a queen regnant and a bloody civil war.

Initially, the rebellion that began in Perth in May 1559 hardly seemed to threaten Guise's Scottish regency, far less the French monarchy. Cautious as ever, the Protestant nobility preferred to wait on events rather than try and shape them. Unplanned and unwanted, the rebellion was triggered by the iconoclastic preaching of John Knox, who had returned to Scotland only because his incendiary *First Blast* had left him friendless in Elizabeth's England, and whose expectations of widespread noble support were quickly dashed. While the fifth earl of Glencairn rallied to the cause, he was the only nobleman of stature to do so. By contrast, Archibald Campbell, fifth earl of Argyll, and Lord James Stewart, two of the most influential Protestant lords, initially went to Perth to negotiate a settlement on the regent's behalf. Their later defection to the Congregation, followed by the recruitment of Châtelherault and the Hamiltons, lent the revolt much-needed credibility. But the rebels were still outgunned by a regent who, following her daughter's accession to the French throne, prevailed on her brothers to send military aid from France.

The arrival of French troops in the summer of 1559 prompted a significant change of tack from the Congregation. Having tried unsuccessfully to win their countrymen's support by stressing the limited, religious nature of their revolt, they now chose to appeal to them on the more emotive grounds that they were defending the commonweal and liberty of the realm, and it was as an enemy of the commonweal rather than of God that, in October 1559, they formally 'suspended' Guise from the regency. In one sense, this was a purely paper transaction that did nothing to hinder the regent's increasingly effective military efforts against them. Yet, in another sense, it marked a crucial turning point. For the Congregation were now claiming to act as a provisional government under a prince of the blood, Châtelherault, and to be doing so in the name of their sovereigns, Mary and Francis. Fiction though this was, it

was only under the guise of such constitutional legitimacy that the Congregation's true leader, Lord James Stewart, could realistically expect to persuade
the English government to intervene on their behalf.

While English aid was a practical necessity for the Congregation, Anglo-
Scottish cooperation also had significant ideological purchase. As much an
Englishman as a Scot, Knox saw a union of the two kingdoms as essential to
safeguarding Protestantism in both. Not all members of the Congregation
shared his vision of a Protestant British monarchy, but both Lord James
Stewart and his able lieutenant, Maitland of Lethington, were committed to
promoting union with England. Moreover, the Hamilton interest was easily
won over by the prospect of setting aside Mary's claim to the Scottish throne
and cementing dynastic union through the marriage of Châtelherault's young
son Arran to the English queen. The plan had sufficient merit to attract the
attention of Elizabeth's influential secretary William Cecil. A veteran of Somerset's Scottish campaigns of the late 1540s, Cecil was likewise committed to
Anglo-Scottish union, his British policy based on a clear grasp of Scotland's
strategic significance to England but also informed by a deep commitment to
Protestantism. Elizabeth, however, was not persuaded. Cash-strapped and
insecure, she had no wish to repeat the mistake of the 1540s, embroiling England in an expensive war with France, or to set a precedent that might re-
dound on herself by meddling in the internal affairs of a sovereign kingdom.

That Elizabeth did eventually intervene owed much to Cecil's tenacity. For
him, the need to counter Mary's Catholic claim to Elizabeth's throne was
itself a persuasive enough reason for intervention in Scotland; but for the
queen's benefit he could also argue that the domestic problems besetting 'Les
Guises' would severely hamper France's ability to respond. It was a calculated risk that paid off handsomely. By the Treaty of Berwick of February 1560,
Elizabeth undertook to provide military aid to Châtelherault's provisional
government: while offering no challenge to Mary's sovereignty in Scotland,
England would help rid the country of French troops. The following month
an English army crossed the Border, and though the military action that
ensued proved indecisive, France's response was hamstrung, not just by the
predicted domestic turmoil, but by the untimely death of Mary of Guise on
11 June 1560. Her demise left French policy in tatters. The following month,
by the Treaty of Edinburgh, France capitulated: French and English troops
were to withdraw from Scotland, but Elizabeth's right to the English throne
was formally recognized. It was an outcome with which Elizabeth was well
pleased. She had achieved her own security at minimal expense, while leav-

ing Scotland in the hands of a government that, if still nominally in allegiance to the French crown, owed its existence to the English queen.

Although essentially an Anglo-French settlement, the Treaty of Edinburgh did provide for the summoning of a Scottish parliament, which duly met in August 1560. Forbidden to meddle with religion, the Reformation Parliament nonetheless proceeded to repudiate the pope, outlaw the mass, and adopt a Protestant Confession of Faith. It was a remarkably well-attended assembly, the high turnout bolstered by the unusual presence of 101 lairds, most of them from Lowland areas that had long harboured Protestant sympathies. Even such a packed assembly, however, was unlikely to countenance the total reform of Kirk and kingdom envisaged by Knox. His blueprint for reform, now known as *The First Book of Discipline*, was not even considered by the Reformation Parliament. For his reformed commonwealth, in which a well-paid ministry would work hand in hand with an educated laity to create a new 'godly' society, was based on the assumption that all the revenues of the old Church would be made over to build the new. Such visionary economics held little appeal to landowners who had been engrossing ecclesiastical lands and revenues for years. To the preacher's disgust, vested interest prevailed, jeopardizing the godly alliance of ministers and magistrates on which the Reformation was founded.

Disputes over finance strained the Protestant alliance, but it was the events following the sudden death of Francis II in December 1560 that broke it beyond repair. The French court was plunged into confusion by the young king's death, while the widowed queen was left personally distraught and politically powerless. Her decision to return to Scotland, where she arrived in August 1561, was based on complex negotiations between Mary and the provisional government in Scotland represented by the queen's half-brother Lord James Stewart. For her part, Mary was permitted to hear mass in private, but undertook to leave undisturbed the Protestant settlement of 1560 and to rule through an essentially Protestant council. For his part, Lord James undertook to use his influence with Elizabeth to have Mary's place in the English succession formally recognized. It was an astute enough deal, avoiding the perils of further civil war while alienating only those, like Knox, who could brook no compromise with divine law. Lord James himself faced down the riot that Knox incited against the queen's first mass, an intervention that marked the end of any cordiality between them. Knox aside, however, for most Scots the return of an adult monarch, albeit a Catholic and a woman, promised a welcome respite from two decades of crippling civil disorder.

Mary's return also marked her emergence as a political player in her own right. Estimates of her capabilities have varied hugely, but in the early years of her personal rule she handled a potentially explosive situation with some aplomb. Although she refused to ratify the Acts of the Reformation Parliament, she gave tacit support to the reformed Kirk through a financial settlement that left existing benefice-holders in possession of two-thirds of their revenues, while dividing the remainder between the Protestant ministry and the crown itself. Together with her substantial French jointure of some £30,000, this enabled Mary to re-establish a lavish royal court without having recourse to unpopular taxes. Protestant opinion was further reassured by the destruction of the Catholic Gordon family in 1562: Huntly's forfeiture and Lord James Stewart's elevation to the earldom of Moray effectively nullified the north-east as a power-base for a Catholic counter-revolution. Mary, moreover, travelled incessantly around the kingdom, her progresses making clearly visible the re-establishment of royal authority and reinforcing her personal popularity. There remained, however, the anomaly of a Catholic queen ruling with a Protestant council, a constant reminder of the fragile base on which the Marian regime rested. Inevitably, it was the issue of her marriage and the succession—English as well as Scottish—that brought to the surface the tensions that underlay, and would finally undermine, her queenship.

Whatever one makes of Mary's personal piety, her continued adherence to Catholicism had distinct diplomatic advantages: it gave her leverage over Elizabeth. Just as Mary refused to ratify the acts of the Reformation Parliament, so she refused to ratify the Treaty of Edinburgh and thus recognize her cousin as the rightful English queen. Moray's hopes that Elizabeth could be persuaded to recognize Mary's place in the English succession in return for Mary dropping her immediate claim to Elizabeth's crown proved illusory, falling foul of the marital politics into which the two queens were inevitably drawn as pressure mounted on them to ensure the succession to their respective thrones. Both were well aware of the personal costs as well as the dynastic advantages of marriage. As it became clearer, however, that Elizabeth was not prepared to name her Stewart rival as her heir presumptive, it was Mary who eventually broke the diplomatic stalemate. In July 1565, she married by Catholic rite Henry Stewart, Lord Darnley, heir to the earl of Lennox and, as grandson of Margaret Tudor, second only to Mary in the English succession. Darnley's dazzling good looks clearly captivated Mary, initially blinding her to the meretricious personality that lay behind them; but the marriage did have political benefits. Not only did it avoid the pitfalls of a foreign match, but the rehabilitation of the Lennox Stewarts, in English exile since the 1540s, gave Mary a much-needed magnate power base within her kingdom. Moreover, while aligning Mary's claim to the English throne with that of her nearest rival, the marriage simultaneously appeared to fulfil the promise of 1561 by allowing Mary to pose as a 'patriot queen' ruling an independent Scottish kingdom.

Not just a patriot queen, however, but a Catholic one. Predictably, radical Protestants such as Knox feared the worst of a Catholic marriage; but so too, and more dangerously for Mary, did Knox's former noble allies. The restoration of the Lennox Stewarts posed a serious threat to their deadly Hamilton rivals, while the Darnley marriage dealt a mortal blow to Moray's policy of amity with England. Mary, however, easily rode out the ensuing storm. The efforts of Moray and Châtelherault to raise rebellion proved abortive, resulting only in the farce of the 'Chaseabout Raid' and their own exile. Elizabeth refused to intervene, while Mary was able to reassure moderate Protestants that the marriage did not signal the Catholic counter-revolution prophesied by Knox. Nevertheless, Protestant concerns were far from groundless. Increasingly overt displays of Catholicism at court culminated, in February 1566, in Darnley's investiture in the French Order of St Michael, the ceremony preceded by a solemn mass, and followed by the queen's consort boasting that he had returned the kingdom to the 'true faith'.

This was one of many indiscretions that soured relations between Mary and Darnley. Although styled *Rex Scottorum* on a commemorative medal struck for the marriage, Mary denied 'King Henry' the crown matrimonial—and the royal authority—that he believed his due. Within weeks of proclaiming himself a Catholic champion, Darnley had joined the Protestant conspirators who, in March 1566, vented their fears by brutally murdering Mary's Italian secretary, David Riccio, in the presence of the now heavily pregnant queen. Fearful that events might spiral into bloody religious war, Mary immediately sought reconciliation with Darnley and the Protestant nobles involved in both the Riccio conspiracy and the Chaseabout Raid. The search for consensus continued either side of the birth of her son on 19 June 1566 and culminated in the spectacular baptismal celebration held at Stirling in December. The Catholic baptism of the future James VI and I was the undoubted high point of Mary's personal rule. Not only did the Scottish succession seem assured, but the triumphal celebrations pointedly signalled to Elizabeth that James would also inherit her English throne. Moreover, in a bravura display of royal self-confidence, the banquet following the baptism was choreographed as a feast of reconciliation in which the Scottish nobility, Protestant and Catholic alike, celebrated the continuance of the Stewart line. The occasion was marred only by the absence of the prince's father: once more estranged from the queen, ill and politically isolated, Darnley refused to attend his son's baptism.

It is impossible now to tell when exactly the plot to murder Darnley was conceived. Likewise, neither the extent of Mary's complicity nor the precise identity of the murderer(s) can be established with certainty. What is clear, however, is that Darnley's death on 10 February 1567 was mourned by few, and that Mary was not among them. Only the Lennox family had reason to lament his passing, and their vested interest in his son, the heir to the throne, suggested that family honour might be satisfied by a show trial of the man believed to have been responsible for the deed. James Hepburn, fourth earl of Bothwell, however, proved an elusive scapegoat. Acquitted of the murder by a blatantly rigged court in April 1567, he subsequently 'abducted' the queen and married her by Protestant rite on 15 May 1567. Mary's role in this extraordinary sequence of events is hard to fathom. Pregnant again, and in very poor health, her political judgement following Darnley's murder proved as weak as her grip on power.

Mary might well have survived the fallout from the murder of an unwanted husband, but her marriage to the suspected murderer alienated her supporters abroad just as it united against her a range of conflicting Scottish interests. Even then, however, all was not entirely lost. The Confederate Lords, the coalition of nobles that confronted Mary and Bothwell at Carberry near Edinburgh on 15 June 1567, were more concerned to 'liberate' the queen from an unsuitable husband than to depose her. Her decision to surrender, having negotiated a safe-conduct for Bothwell that would take him into exile and death in a Danish prison, was met with widespread relief. But the events that followed—her 'voluntary' abdication on 24 July, the hurried coronation of her son on 29 July, and Moray's acceptance of the regency on 22 August—were not universally welcomed. In fact, the political community was deeply divided by what was a constitutional revolution as well as a Protestant coup. Indeed, in ideological terms, it was not so much confessional differences as the legitimacy of Mary's enforced abdication that proved critical, giving rise to an unprecedented debate over the nature of monarchical authority that was to have a profound impact on European as well as Scottish political consciousness. But it was not only, or even primarily, high principle that divided Scottish opinion. Equally important were the personal and familial ties that bound individuals to the deposed queen or the infant king.

In the early months of Moray's regency, many Scots, still shaken by the enormity of what had occurred, remained uncommitted. But Mary's sensational escape from Lochleven Castle in May 1568 demonstrated that, to a conservative political community, the queen's cause was much more attractive than the king's. Moray could rally Knox and the Protestant clergy to the side of the new godly prince, but only a handful of magnates, notably Lennox and Morton, were prepared to join them. It was Mary who commanded the loyalty of the majority of the kingdom's leading men, from the vast Hamilton network to nobles as diverse in their religious persuasions as the Catholic Huntly and the Protestant Argyll. Indeed, the groundswell of support for Mary was such that, within days of her escape, she had mustered an army more than capable of meeting Moray in the field. Her defeat at Langside on 13 May was the result of military incompetence and need not have proved conclusive; had she remained in Scotland, there is every likelihood that Mary could have overthrown Moray's shaky regime. As it was, she abandoned her Scottish supporters and threw herself instead on the mercy of Elizabeth.

For Elizabeth, Mary's flight to England was as unwelcome as it was unexpected. What was to be done with a Catholic queen who was, in her eyes, the rightful monarch of Scotland, but who had also, and more dangerously, a powerful claim to her throne? It was a dilemma that was only resolved in February 1587 when, after much intrigue on Mary's part and much agonizing on Elizabeth's, the Scottish queen was executed. The short-term solution, however, was to place her under house arrest and to extend initially tacit but increasingly tangible support to her enemies in Scotland. As a result, the queen's friends were left to fight a bitter civil war on behalf of an absentee queen whose chances of being restored to her kingdom diminished year by year. Despite claiming the lives of two regents—Moray was assassinated in 1570 and Lennox in 1571—Mary's was an increasingly desperate cause. Support for the exiled queen gradually ebbed away until, in 1573, with the help of English artillery, Edinburgh Castle, the last stronghold of the Marian party, was pounded into submission. The previous year, James Douglas, fourth earl of Morton, a convinced Protestant and friend of England, had been appointed regent. His six-year regency did much to impose peace on a disordered kingdom and to cement its dependence on England. As James VI was groomed to rule as a godly Protestant prince, his mother's cause, and with it hopes of a Catholic revival, slowly withered on the vine.

Empire, order, and authority, 1578–1603

In March 1578, as James VI neared his twelfth birthday, a coalition of Mor-ton's enemies declared the king of age and stripped the regent of his authori-ty. Their putsch proved premature, however, and within months Morton was back in power. This failed attempt to oust Morton was symptomatic of the factional politics that characterized the king's transition from adolescence to adulthood. Between 1578 and 1585, there occurred half a dozen palace revolutions as the nobility vied for advantage through seizing control of the king's person. James was not an entirely passive pawn in these factional manoeuvres. It was at his instigation that his Catholic French kinsman Esmé Stewart, sieur d'Aubigné, his father's cousin, was made earl of Lennox in 1580 and elevated to a dukedom in 1581. Lennox's meteoric rise, while prompted by the king's adolescent crush on his exotic relative, had serious repercus-sions. In June 1581 Morton was executed for his alleged involvement in Darnley's murder, and fears of a pro-Marian, Catholic reaction were rife. To counter them, both James and Lennox subscribed the so-called King's Con-fession (an abjuration of Catholicism also known as the Negative Confes-sion), but this failed to reassure those nobles who felt their power as much as their Protestantism threatened by Lennox's influence. In August 1582, James was seized by the 'Ruthven Raiders', led by William Ruthven, earl of Gowrie, and held captive for ten months.

His escape in June 1583 saw the king achieve a degree of independence that had hitherto eluded him. Lennox had fled back to France and was fol-lowed into exile by the leaders of the Ruthven Raid. Although James contin-ued to rely on James Stewart, a favoured courtier made earl of Arran in 1581, the regime that Arran headed implemented policies that bear the stamp of the king's own mind. One must beware of reading back to the early 1580s the view of kingship that James set forth in the late 1590s, notably the assertion of his divine right to rule in *The True Law of Free Monarchies* (1598) and his more down-to-earth advice on governing the kingdom in *Basilikon Doron* (1599). Yet this most cerebral of monarchs had long been obliged to reflect on the nature of kingly power. From 1570 to 1582, he was tutored by the formi-dable George Buchanan, a humanist of European stature, who had returned to Scotland in 1561 to grace Mary's court only to emerge as the leading pro-pagandist of the revolution against her. His Latin dialogue *De jure regni apud Scotos* (1579) was among the most radical statements of popular sovereignty to be penned in the sixteenth century, while his *Rerum Scoticarum historia*

(1582) was a history of Scotland deliberately designed to justify the constitutional revolution of 1567. James knew both works intimately and was well aware of the threat they posed to Stewart kingship. From the outset, his agenda was shaped by the need to reassert royal authority in the face of challenges that were ideological as well as practical.

The most dangerous of these challenges was not the factionalism of truculent noblemen, but the more sustained assault on royal authority represented by a Church over which the crown had lost control. James would later bemoan the fact that Scotland's Reformation had been initiated from below and made secure by a rebellion against his mother. The result had been the creation of a Protestant Kirk that was not just wary of royal control but firmly committed to maintaining its independence of it. Morton had attempted to introduce a system modelled on England in which the crown's supremacy over the Church was secured through royally appointed bishops. But this met with considerable clerical resistance, which hardened with the return to Scotland in 1574 of the brilliant young academic Andrew Melville, a former student in Beza's Geneva who added heavy intellectual weight to the Kirk's opposition to both bishops and the royal supremacy. Although not the only begetter of *The Second Book of Discipline* (1578), Melville was the driving force behind a militant tendency within the Kirk that believed in ministerial parity (and abhorred episcopal hierarchy) just as it was committed to the theory of the two kingdoms. A close friend of Buchanan, whose political theory he enthusiastically espoused, Melville's passionate advocacy of Presbyterianism posed a threat to James's kingship that could not be ignored.

Nor was it. In May 1584, parliament not only banned Buchanan's subversive writings, but also reaffirmed the authority of bishops and passed an Act of royal supremacy. If Arran, and the archbishop of St Andrews, Patrick Adamson, were behind this blatantly anti-Presbyterian programme, it surely met with the king's approval. As Melville and his hard-line colleagues fled the kingdom rather than accept the implications of what they dubbed the 'Black Acts', Adamson invoked the example of the first Christian emperor, Constantine the Great, as a model for the king's authority over both Church and state. Such comparisons, recalling the imperial claims of James IV and James V, would continue to inform the thinking of James VI. Like his Stewart predecessors, though in an ideologically more highly charged atmosphere, James VI pressed his claim to be emperor in his own kingdom, meeting the twin challenge of Buchanan's republicanism and Melville's Presbyterianism with assertions of his imperial sovereignty. To be sure, again like the most effective

THE
TRVE LAWE OF
free Monarchies:

OR,

THE RECIPROCK AND
MVTVALL DVTIE BE-
twixt a free King, and his
naturall Subiectes.

EDINBVRGH

Printed by Robert VValde-
grane Printer to the Kings Majestie.
Anno Dom. 1598.
Cum Privilegio Regio.

A PROLIFIC AUTHOR, whose education at the hands of George Buchanan he never forgot, James VI published this terse statement of his divine right to rule in 1598 as an answer to both his former tutor and his presbyterian critics. Although printed anonymously, its authorship was no secret.

of his predecessors, James sought to be inclusive rather than exclusive in his exercise of power, but the limits of royal tolerance were defined by acknowledgement of the king's sovereignty and obedience to his law.

It was on this basis that both the Melvillian clergy and the aristocratic Ruthven Raiders were allowed to return to Scotland in 1585. Arran fell from power and the king himself, supported by his able secretary, John Maitland of Thirlestane, took personal control of the government. In keeping with the king's desire to be 'a universal king', ruling above faction, privy council membership was extended to encompass a variety of magnate interests, Catholic and Protestant, while a compromise church settlement allowed for the continuing establishment of presbyteries answerable to the king's bishops rather than the Kirk's general assembly. This consensual approach was reflected in James's own accessibility: just as he relished intellectual debate, happily trading theological points with Andrew Melville, so he was a passionate huntsman, ready to ride out with favoured courtiers like the Catholic George Gordon, sixth earl of Huntly. The same philosophy underlay the lavish court that the king maintained. A considerable patron of literature, James was as happy to favour Catholic poets like Alexander Montgomerie as to relish the Protestant epics of the French Huguenot Salluste Du Bartas. While James's own 'poetical exercises' were undistinguished, those of Montgomerie and his fellow court poets were not. Significantly, however, it was James who dictated the framework of literary discourse, publishing his *Reulis and Cautelis of Poesie* in 1585 as a handbook of correct poetic practice. In literature as in politics, authority flowed from the sovereign, and it was the king's laws that defined the parameters of acceptability and inclusion.

The settlement of domestic affairs was facilitated by an easing of relations with England. Fears of Marian involvement in Spanish conspiracies to dethrone Elizabeth had made the English government understandably anxious over James's intentions. For his part, James was just as aware as his mother of his place in the English succession and, in order to pressurize Elizabeth, was equally prepared to maintain links with Catholic powers abroad as well as influential Catholics at home. Elizabeth still refused to name a successor, but an Anglo-Scottish league of 1586 offered James acknowledgement in the form of an annual pension, while providing England with reassurances as to his reliability. It was almost immediately put to the test when, in February 1587, Elizabeth was finally persuaded to have Mary executed. James's protests were muted; fundamentally, both then, and in the crisis sparked by the Spanish Armada the following year, he remained loyal to the league with

England. His marriage in 1589 to Anne, daughter of the Protestant Frederick II of Denmark, was a gesture of diplomatic independence that, significantly, posed no threat to Elizabeth.

It was a mark of the stability that had returned to the Scottish kingdom that James, like his grandfather before him, felt able to leave the country for six months to fetch his bride in person from the Danish court. The apparent success of James's rule in the later 1580s, however, masked internal tensions that in the 1590s were to destroy the consensus that he and Maitland had so carefully constructed. The king's tolerance of Catholic earls such as Huntly, long resented by the Kirk, exploded in his face when local feuding between Huntly and the Protestant 'bonnie earl' of Moray led to the latter's murder in 1592. A local crisis became a national one when Moray's cause found a champion in Francis Stewart, fifth earl of Bothwell, the extraordinarily quixotic figure who was outlawed in 1590 for allegedly attempting to sink by witchcraft the vessel on which James and his bride returned from Denmark. Bothwell's defiance of the king found support from the Kirk which used it as leverage to extract what it saw (mistakenly) as major concessions to an independent Presbyterian polity in the so-called 'Golden Act' of 1592. The crisis was only resolved when in 1594, to the Kirk's dismay, Bothwell joined forces with Huntly in open rebellion against the king. Both were forced to flee abroad in 1595 and, while Huntly subsequently made his peace with James, Bothwell died in exile. As for the Kirk, despite the Golden Act, James never conceded the principle of the royal supremacy and would make increasingly successful efforts to tighten royal control over the general assembly and re-establish diocesan episcopacy.

It was following these crisis years that James published his works on kingship, reflecting in the *True Law* on the necessity of obedience to his divinely ordained authority and in *Basilikon Doron* on the challenges of managing an unruly Kirk and powerful nobility. If the former suggests a monarch deeply frustrated by his subjects' lack of respect for the crown's authority, the latter shows his determination to 'civilize' his kingdom by bringing Scotland's remote and semi-autonomous localities under more direct royal control. As his predecessors had discovered, this was a tall order for a monarchy with limited resources that had traditionally relied on the nobility to exercise justice in their own backyards. Yet, in his efforts to eliminate feuding and curb the nobility's independence, James VI found himself better placed than either James IV or James V. Ironically, he found a key ally in the Kirk, equally determined to 'discipline' local society, whose developing system of session and presbytery courts, gradually extending over Lowland society, provided an unprecedented means of intruding central control into the localities. Just as importantly, however, local society was itself in the throes of a major transformation. Population growth and price inflation, together with the increasingly active land market created by feuing and the secularization of church lands, were slowly commercializing Lowland society and eroding the kin-ties that had traditionally bound local communities together and made the private justice of the feud both meaningful and workable. In the more commercial environment that was emerging in Lowland Scotland, great magnates continued to dominate their localities, but they were increasingly forced to exercise their lordship differently: clientage rather than kinship, money rather than blood, were becoming the new measures of noble power.

James exploited the financial worries of his nobility, while also ensuring their dependence on the crown, by making available on an unprecedented scale the patronage needed to secure clients' loyalty and fund the nobility's own acutely fashion-conscious lifestyles. It also, of course, created major financial crises as the costs of the king's largesse far outstripped the revenues available to pay for it. Although taxation was by the 1590s an all but annual occurrence, the spiralling costs of James's kingship ensured that royal finances remained firmly in deficit. Nevertheless, whether calculated or otherwise, James's willingness to try and satisfy the landed elite's insatiable demand for pensions and sinecures had the effect of knitting centre and localities together. Just as the nobility became more amenable to royal control, so the talents of lesser lairds were needed to service a burgeoning bureaucracy that penetrated ever more deeply into rural society. Highly educated, and with sophisticated cultural tastes, the lairdly lawyers who had first come to prominence in James V's reign were now the mainstays of a government from which the clergy had been obliged to withdraw. While some might be described as 'new men', most were from old landed families, their rise to national prominence a measure of the major social and cultural shifts that were transforming local society as well as the politics of the court.

Scotland's sixteenth century is usually characterized as the era of the Reformation, but it was equally—perhaps above all—the era of the Renaissance. For it was the educational revolution inspired by Renaissance humanism that transformed the manners and mores of the landed elite just as it had fuelled calls for religious reform. By the end of the century, James VI's overriding concern with extending law, order, and civility into the localities had begun to resonate with landowners for whom a humanist education was now the

CHANGING SOCIAL AND CULTURAL TRENDS are reflected in architectural fashion. Fyvie Castle, Aberdeenshire, was remodelled in the late 1590s for Alexander Seton, Lord Fyvie, a cultivated lawyer who, despite his Catholicism, served on the privy council from 1585 and headed the Octavians (eight men appointed as the king's financial advisers) in 1596. One of James VI's most trusted counsellors, he was made earl of Dunfermline in 1606.

norm. As the king's justice began to supplant the feud, and as Lowland society slowly demilitarized, so the elite began to remodel their stark but defensible tower-houses or to abandon them altogether in favour of more luxurious country dwellings. Such developments pre-dated 1603, though the king's removal to England accelerated the process and encouraged him to extend it forcibly into the Highlands and Islands. In his attitude to his Gaelic subjects, however, as in so much else, James VI was acting out the imperial role scripted by his Stewart predecessors.

5 Confidence and Perplexity: The Seventeenth Century

JENNY WORMALD

As the chapters so far demonstrate, Scotland was a flourishing and vibrant society, one which had sustained a notable level of cultural activity, maintained its independence from its ambitious and mightier southern neighbour England, and made its mark in Europe. In the eighteenth century, it would once again become vibrant. Despite the heady moment in 1603 when a Scottish king succeeded to the English throne, the seventeenth century, by contrast, seems to be overhung with an air of bleakness, even joylessness, as a stern and godly Calvinist Kirk imposed a new level of discipline, launching an unprecedented attack on immorality and on hitherto unquestioned pleasurable pursuits such as music, dancing, drama, and drinking. In the late sixteenth century, the poet and government official Sir Richard Maitland of Lethington had lamented the dreariness which had overtaken reformed Scotland: 'Quhair is the blyithnes that hes beine' now that 'all merines is worne away' in a land where he no longer saw the celebration of Christmas and Easter, but only kirkmen 'cled lyik men of weir'. In the mid-seventeenth, the elect and covenanted followers of a Calvinist God, aided by the follies of the second Stuart king of Britain, Charles I, turned vitality into stagnation and intolerance. Charles II's horrible experience, after his father's execution in 1649, as a convenanted king in Scotland in 1650–1 meant that Scotland never saw its king again, paving the way for the new sense of political marginalization in late seventeenth-century Scotland. That in turn led to the ultimate decision in the early eighteenth century that the personal Union of the Crowns, with all its political and religious confusion, must be shored up by the constitutional confusion of the union of the parliaments in 1707.

That is too stark a picture. Yet a hitherto confident nation did become a

JAMES VI AND I, by Daniel Mytons, 1621: the king who created the union.

very worried one. For the first time, the Scots, in seeking to define their identity, began to show that introspection which had been such a feature of English self-propaganda in the sixteenth century. No longer a major European power after the loss of the Hundred Years War, the English started to emphasize their superiority over all others, claiming even God himself as English and linking national pride to their place as God's elect nation. In the seventeenth century, the new experience of being part of a composite monarchy created among the Scots the same need to assert their own superiority. Like other nations, they did it primarily through their Church. If they did not quite give God honorary nationality, they strenuously insisted on the purity of their Kirk, as asserted in the Confession of 1616, and were even more passionate about themselves as God's elect and covenanted nation, a nation far more thoroughly reformed than England. This reached its height in 1643, when, with the Solemn League and Covenant, they came down on the side of the English parliament against the king, and dedicated themselves to 'the preservation of the Reformed Religion in the Church of Scotland' and to 'the Reformation of Religion in the Kingdoms of England and Ireland'. One can see, in this remnant of the outward-looking tradition of the Scots, the echo of the mighty claim of the Spanish Habsburgs to a special divine mission. Yet such rhetoric was very different from the high morale which had been so obvious a feature of earlier political reality and the epic poetry and chronicles extolling Scotland's greatness. Although at one level the Reformation looked like a triumph, given the speed and vigour with which the Calvinist Kirk established itself, there were struggles over its polity from the beginning, and after 1596 the king was winning the battle with the radical Presbyterians. The impassioned and vitriolic Presbyterian historian David Calderwood exemplifies what had changed. Unlike earlier writers who lauded the victory of the Scots over external foes, Calderwood's account of the vicissitudes of the godly brethren in his epic history of the Kirk showed that it was the enemy within— the crown—which appeared to triumph. The myth of the godly and embattled Kirk was born. It was the ideology needed to cloak the reality of divisions within the Kirk, and the loss of independent political status. It would prove remarkably enduring.

Trying to make union work

As James himself said, it was the English who rejoiced at his coming in 1603, the Scots who wept at his departure. Neither was the whole truth; both had considerable reason for ambivalence. There was no question of annexation. Two independent kingdoms now came together under one king, as James VI and I repeatedly emphasized. It left neither in an easy position, although initially it was the English who were distinctly more concerned about how to cope with a Scottish, and therefore, from their point of view, inexperienced king. The Scots could feel considerable pride in seeing their king peacefully seated on the English throne. And as he was their king, who had manifestly regarded himself primarily as king of Scots rather than heir to the English throne, there was no immediate reason to fear that his move to London would mean that he would neglect, let alone forget, his northern realm.

Moreover, Scotland was peculiarly suited to coping with the problem of absentee kingship. Its unique record of royal minorities in the fourteenth, fifteenth, and sixteenth centuries had a profound impact on the nature of Scottish government and the balance of power between crown and aristocracy, which was still very much in evidence in 1603; *faute de mieux* the government of the country devolved on the nobility in the absence of an adult king. James VI, when he emerged from his minority, found himself presiding over an aristocracy with a tradition going back over forty years of coping with the seismic shocks of religious reform, war with England, and then the redrawing of the diplomatic map as the old alliance with Catholic France gave way to the new amity with England, as well as the disturbed years of Mary's personal rule. It did not worry him. Before 1603 his government was markedly more aristocratic than that of Elizabeth, more in line with that of France. From his point of view, it was a good foundation for rule from England.

Those who served him before 1603 also included members of the lesser aristocracy, the lairds who from the reign of James V were steadily replacing the clergy in government. Those humanistically educated men were the real beneficiaries of the Union of the Crowns under a king whose way of enhancing their authority was to raise them to the highest ranks of the peerage, creating, in effect, a *noblesse de robe* alongside the older landed aristocracy. After 1603 there were eighteen peerage creations, half of them in 1604–5, going to men like George Hume, earl of Dunbar, and Alexander Seton, Lord Fyvie, earl of Dunfermline. They were not a different breed from the rest of the nobility; they all formed part of the same status-group. But they were the ones who were prepared to do the donkey work of government, and now became the backbone of the government of an absentee king. Dunbar undoubtedly fitted best with James's original intentions about composite rule. Until his death in 1611, he was an Anglo-Scottish politician, moving between Edinburgh and London, negotiating, discussing policy directly with both Scots and English. But he was a unique figure, and that in itself points to the problems of composite monarchy. The king's attempts at the beginning of his reign in England to bring Scots onto the English privy council, to give them English government offices, met with intense English hostility; relatively few Scots were able to hold office in England. His hopes of creating an Anglo-Scottish court were rather more successful but not entirely so. Ludovic, duke of Lennox, steward of the household until his death in 1624, was one of the big Scottish figures at court, close to the king and therefore influential in policy-making and patronage, and he had his successor, James marquess of Hamilton, in Charles I's court. But below that level there was considerable Anglo-Scottish rivalry and mutual antagonism. James's way round this, which was to staff his bedchamber with Scots, was no solution at all for his English subjects, for it denied them access to that inner sanctum of politics, where men could talk freely to the king; and giving his Scots money instead of office was equally offensive. What the Union of the Crowns produced, therefore, was not the joy and peace of new Anglo-Scottish friendship. It meant loss of face on both sides. The English saw their court and government threatened by the influx of the Scots. The Scots were all too aware that they were unwelcome in London.

Those who remained in Scotland had a better time of it. Apart from Dunbar, those who had served James before 1603 lived on, like him, until the 1620s. Despite his physical absence, therefore, they still had the great advantage, only possible under the first British king, of working with someone whom they knew well; and physical absence was compensated for by the continuous correspondence between London and Edinburgh, facilitated by the improved postal service which the king set up in 1603. In sharp distinction from his son Charles I, these letters make it clear that James was still willing to listen to and discuss policy with his councillors. The problem was that he was no longer only king of Scots. Of the two major policies which affected Scotland, the first, his desire for a closer union, was undoubtedly designed to do what he could to protect Scottish interests and prevent his ancient kingdom simply becoming, as he himself said, 'as the northern shires, seldom seen and saluted by their king'; the second, his ecclesiastical reforms, looked much more motivated by greater enthusiasm for the English Church than the Scottish kirk. Not even the first reassured the Scots.

The problem was that the dominant players in the king's union game were the English. 'One king, one people, one law' was his slogan; king of Great

Britain was his desired title, taken by proclamation when the English House of Commons refused it to him in 1604; again by proclamation, the king's British flag, the Union Jack, was to fly from English and Scottish shipping. These were the high-profile demands made in the first years of the reign. The English liked none of them, being particularly fearful of the use of proclamation to checkmate the Commons. The Scots' initial reaction was to approach the idea of union very seriously, in this being closer to their king than were his new subjects, but to insist on the independent sovereignty of their kingdom and to argue against any immediate unity of the laws of the two realms. The great academic lawyer Sir Thomas Craig of Riccarton in *On the Union of the Kingdoms of Britain* and *Jus feudale*, and the advocate John Russell, with *The Happie and Blissed Unioun*, both defended the viability of union under one king, Craig being more explicit about the idea of an incorporating union, Russell echoing James's vision of a union of hearts and minds. But both were certain about the impossibility of the king's 'one law', for how could English common law be brought into conjunction with Scots law, grounded in Roman law and the Acts of the Scottish parliament? Craig himself was one of the Scottish commissioners who came to London in 1604 to join English commissioners in treating of union. A particularly telling irony is that they were assigned to the building in which the Gunpowder Plotters were originally planning their act of fanatical terrorism, and the latter were forced to move out to the notorious cellar in the House of Lords, to continue to plot that act which in part they justified on the grounds of getting rid of the Scots. Neither enterprise succeeded.

English hostility pushed the Scots into fear and resentment. By 1607, when James was making the most moving of his speeches to the English parliament arguing for the viability of union, the Scottish parliament was arguing passionately against being relegated to the status of a province. It was now important to remind the king that Scotland was his 'ancient and native kingdom' which should not be 'disordered and made confused'. The passion was irrelevant. The union project was dead, killed by, among others, the English MP Sir Edwin Sandys who took up the idea of an incorporating or 'perfect' union with the fatal twist that this would involve Scotland giving up its sovereignty. The king lost out twice over, to English subjects antagonistic from the beginning and Scottish subjects made antagonistic. Yet it is unlikely that James ever seriously envisaged an incorporating union. This shrewd operator knew how to negotiate, beginning with huge demands which could be scaled down. This benefited the Scots, because what was achieved was dual nationality and, until 1610, free trade, both of which certainly meant more to them than to the English. These were relatively small victories, however. But the Scots could blame the English, not the king who attempted to be even-handed, and who had manifestly not forgotten that he was king of Scots. Thus he forcibly demonstrated the continuing importance of his Scottish subjects in the field of foreign relations; Scottish needs certainly informed his foreign policy and Scotsmen replaced Englishmen as envoys and ambassadors, notably but not exclusively in Scandinavia.

It was a very different matter in his dealings with the Kirk. Andrew Melville and his principal supporters were finally trounced when summoned to the 'second' Hampton Court Conference in 1606, and imprisoned or exiled. From 1610, full diocesan episcopacy was restored. In 1612, the king asserted his position as supreme head of the Kirk, although in a fairly *sotto voce* manner. Then came the huge row over the Five Articles of Perth, introduced in 1617.

For good Presbyterians—and good Presbyterian historians—these articles, forced on a hostile Kirk by a determined king, were anathema. The purity of the Kirk, the source of its strength at home and of admiration by like-minded puritans abroad, was now to be destroyed by Articles which included restoration of holy days, and, most inflammatory, kneeling at communion. Even James's loyal ally John Spottiswoode, archbishop of St Andrews, expressed profound unease about the Articles. There were three fundamental objections. They were redolent of popery. They showed that the king preferred the English Church to 'one of the purest kirks under heaven'. And although James had successfully asserted his authority over a Church with an influential wing which denied that authority, he had never before demanded so openly that support for his ecclesiastical policy was a matter of obedience to the king. Moreover, this was accompanied by dangerous enthusiasm about English practice, with the statues and organ he planned to install in the chapel at Holyrood, and even in the relatively moderate proposals for a new liturgy in 1616 and 1617. James gave way on these, though he reacted furiously to the suggestion that there was any taint of popery in his hope of introducing into Scotland what he had become accustomed to in England. The Articles were rejected by the general assembly of the Kirk in 1617, forced through its successor in 1618, and passed by a reluctant and highly managed parliament in 1621. Formally, therefore, the king emerged victorious in this notorious *cause célèbre*. But the Articles and the unpalatable use of the royal diktat symbolized what the king had become: the king distracted and seduced by English ways. It has been generally agreed, from then until now, that this was a battle he should never have fought.

So why did he do it? James's insistence on the Five Articles sits very oddly with his flexibility over other matters. Moreover, there was at the same time a remarkably efficient effort, initiated by James in 1616 and completed in 1618, to raise clerical stipends. It was something on which the Scottish king, his Scottish councillors, and the Scottish Kirk were at one; and their record was distinctly better than in England. Their success led to the sour comment in 1628 by the English MP Benjamin Rudyerd that James's efforts meant that ministers 'through all Scotland' had annual stipends of £30 sterling, while many English vicars still struggled on £5. The instinct which saw the need to enhance the Kirk's prestige and authority by providing a well-paid and, indeed, well-educated ministry, shared by James and even his clerical opponents, was well on the way to being realized. Had the union never happened, the king might have had more credit. But the union had happened; and a consequence was the Five Articles.

Ironically, they were the Scottish parallel to James's union problem in England a decade earlier. In 1607, he complained that he had been misled by his advisers into thinking that there was less objection to his union policy than was the case, and that his honour was involved. Something of the same happened with the Articles, because of his Scottish advisers. Spottiswoode, Patrick Galloway, king's chaplain, and Dunfermline all concealed the level of hostility until too late. Once again his honour was involved, the honour this time of the Lord's anointed, with his responsibility for the religious as well as the secular well-being of his realm. His determination to push them through was therefore heightened. Yet even so, he promised to make no further changes, a promise which he kept; and the whole business virtually fizzled out, because attempts to enforce the Articles were at best sporadic and, after 1622, hardly made at all.

Indeed, what has tended to be played down is the extent to which the affair brings into welcome focus resistance to the hardliners in the Kirk. Their attempts to abolish Christmas and Easter go back to the *First Book of Discipline* of 1560. Agonizing by successive assemblies about continuing 'superstition and idolatry' shows what they were up against. Many Scots were not impressed with the much-vaunted advantage of being members of the elect nation. It is telling that in the 1618 assembly which passed the Articles there was a sizeable presence of laymen. 'Stern daughter of the voice of God', as Wordsworth wrote, was what the Kirk wanted to be, and sometimes briefly managed to be. But it never wholly succeeded. Indeed, lay insistence in, for example, Aberdeen and Perth, on continuing to celebrate Christmas, went beyond the king's Article, which demanded only preaching on holy days, while enjoining the ministers to 'rebuke all superstitious observation and licentious profanation'. Any observance was abolished by parliament in 1637, and again—after it had been restored in 1661—in 1690, while the covenanters in 1643 insisted that England too abolish Christmas. The Calvinist insistence on abolition was to allow enough time to elapse for the faithful to forget the papist associations of the feast. The time-lag in Calvinist Scotland was almost four centuries: Christmas did not become an official holiday until 1958. But the impression of Scotland as wholly dour and joyless, pervasive though that image is, is misleading. Nothing reveals better the limitations on the efforts to create a godly society than the continuing celebration of that wholly pagan feast, Hogmanay.

There is more to it, however. The godly aspirations of the extremists among the Presbyterians who captured the power of the printed word tell us one side of the story. The other side presents a much less stark picture. The Jacobean era dispels another long-lasting Presbyterian myth, that bishops were always anathema to the Kirk. In 1617, an English observer noted in Edinburgh that bishops were 'misliked'—but for their persons rather than their calling. But Edinburgh was not Scotland. James's bishops were low-key and moderate men, dressed in the plain black gown of the minister—Spottiswoode refused to walk in the funeral procession of the king he admired, rather than wear English episcopal dress—and working, often effectively, with the local courts of the Church. Concerted resistance to episcopacy would come, in Scotland as in England, in the reaction to Charles I and Archbishop Laud. Moreover, the ecclesiastical courts might impose tough discipline, but they also showed an impressive concern with social welfare which, because of their very existence, was much more effective than in the pre-Reformation past. Marital counselling, help for unmarried mothers, and care for orphans was very much the business of kirk sessions, and continued to be so. And while the Kirk set its face resolutely against the secular justice of the feud, paradoxically it ran with enthusiasm the imposed arbitration to resolve dispute which had been such a feature of that traditional secular justice. An active Kirk, involving itself in the lives and problems of its members, is much more attractive and convincing than the embattled Kirk of the Presbyterian writers, and explains its considerable appeal.

In secular society, another apparently Anglicizing move was the introduction of justices of the peace. First mooted in the 1580s, a much more comprehensive scheme was introduced in 1609 and repeated in 1617. Neither succeeded. By 1625, JPs were established in less than a quarter of the shires, and were notably ineffective. As Archbishop Gledstanes had said, in a furious row with Thomas Hamilton in the council of 1611, 'the realm had many hundred years been well governed without Justices of the Peace'. Nevertheless, the move reflects the new attitudes to government, beginning before the union but gaining pace after it, of the men who were ennobled after 1603, some themselves trained in the law; and they were backed by that new success story, the legal profession, recruited from cadet branches of the nobility, but carving out their distinctive identity, especially in Edinburgh, and rising to greater and ever wealthier heights. The combination was to mount a formidable challenge to local autonomy and traditional local means of self-help. Not only was the justice of the feud visibly in decline by the early seventeenth century, in the Lowlands at least; bonds of manrent and maintenance—local agreements between nobles and lairds offering protection and service—died out at the same time. Ironically, what did not was the equally long-standing practice of making contracts of friendship, designed to bring men together to act in a common purpose, originally for local concerns but from the mid-sixteenth century for national ones, and in particular in order to advance the Reformation. That practice fitted well into developing covenanting theology. Its apogée was the National Covenant of 1638. It still had a *raison d'être*, therefore. For those who sought to change the relationship between centre and locality, other bonds did not.

None of this was an attempt to make Scotland a pale reflection of England; the rapid shifts came from the new aspirations of influential members of the political elite and the changing mores of Scottish society. But it did produce a veneer of similarity, one which the king's hard-worked politicians and administrators saw value in encouraging. Just as James had argued to unconvinced English MPs in 1607 that Scotland was both civilized and governable, so men like Dunbar and Dunfermline had an obvious interest in demonstrating to the English politicians and administrators who were now the men in regular direct contact with their king the similarity of their approach. Hence when in 1605 the king unusually snubbed George earl of Huntly, his former favourite, Dunfermline seized the chance to tell Robert Cecil, earl of Salisbury, that 'it will make the courses of all our great hidalgos the more temperate'. As it turned out, Charles I would make his 'great hidalgos' anything but 'temperate'. But that was not the prevailing mood in James's reign.

Indeed, on James's death in 1625, Scotland, having been ruled by a king whose actions and policies could be traced back to the days when he was exclusively a Scottish monarch, could still view the union with some confidence. That would change dramatically under his successor.

The king and the theocrats

Charles I was a disaster, and not only in Scotland. Infinitely more Anglicized than his father, he was hardly a successful king of England. Indeed, by 1629 mutual suspicions produced the complete breakdown of 'king-in-parliament', and his religious changes were beginning to turn his opponents into anti-episcopal and anti-ornate hardliners on the Scottish model. The first four years of his Scottish rule were less dramatic, although his actions visibly worried the Scots; and the transference of power from the king they had known to the king they did not was not helped by the foolish entry into the Thirty Years War, pressed by Charles, Buckingham, and the bellicose parliament of Protestant Englishmen in 1624, a war which was inglorious and short-lived, but meant high taxation and the interruption of Scottish trading links with France. The paradox of his reign is that although he was more visibly in difficulties in England in these years, it was in Scotland, which took longer to react, that he was embroiled in his first civil war and constitutional revolution.

He was the king of the immensely tidy mind. All had to be ordered, dignified, and ritualistic. So the sloppy ways of his father had to be remedied. In England, that meant, initially, a dramatic change in court style. In Scotland, it involved unnecessary meddling with government; noblemen and councillors could no longer be members of the court of session. Breaking the close link between the two deprived the council of its trained lawyers, while the court of session was threatened by the king's statement that its judges would no longer be appointed for life but at his pleasure. Weakening both would provide him with a council and court more amenable to a remote king's fiats from London—or so he hoped. What it in fact showed was his ignorance of the way in which Scottish government worked. The emerging legal profession was closely bound by ties of kin, that fundamental source of social cohesion which now operated in this new area. It was also firmly enmeshed in government: James's last two leading ministers, Dunfermline and Melrose, were presidents of the court of session. Worries under James about rule from London now seemed very small, when the political nation was suddenly dis-

The high & mighty Monarch. CHARLES by ye grace of GOD king of Great Brittaine France & Ireland Defendor of the Fayth. etc.

EDYNBURGH

Ce. v. Dalen sculp:

CHARLES I, in front of Edinburgh, by Cornelius van Dalen, probably 1633 or 1641 when he came to Edinburgh: the king who almost smashed the union.

rupted by the arbitrary act of a king who neither knew nor cared about his northern kingdom—'your nation', he called it in 1625.

He did it in order to ease the passage of an even more monstrous and disruptive action. Charles was 24 when he succeeded, the first king since 1406 who was not a minor. Nevertheless, he chose to assert the legal fiction of minority, so that he, like his predecessors, could issue an Act of revocation, that Act by which kings could revoke minority grants over which they had had no control. Although not strictly adhered to, there was the idea that it should be done on the king's twenty-fifth birthday and apply only to the specific minority. No one, in the few months of Charles's twenty-fifth year, had granted anything in his name. But Charles spectacularly changed the rules: he dated his revocation back to 1540 in the case of feudal tenures, and 1455 for ecclesiastical property and heritable rights. Thus what had been a fair deal struck between the landowners and the crown now became a shattering destruction of the security of the landed classes, plunged into the nightmare of uncertainty about their titles to their property. His justification was the restoration of ecclesiastical revenues to the Kirk. His method ensured the failure of a scheme which would have been intolerably complex and difficult to implement had he got cooperation. He did not; the whole dreadful business simply dragged on until 1637, after twelve years of doubts, resentment, and uncertainty. Yet had he not made his revocation a prerogative matter he might have got somewhere, for there was some will to recover the teinds (tithes) for the ministers; the covenanters revived the idea in 1641. It is a measure of Charles's folly, and the problems he posed for his Scottish subjects, that he should have the right idea and carry it out in so comprehensively wrong a way.

In these years of uncertainty, heavy-handed interference was combined with visible and insulting indifference. In 1633 he came to Scotland for his coronation, eight years late. His presence was no more reassuring than his absence. Cold, remote, and formal, he had no understanding of how to deal with his Scottish subjects. But because of the presence of Scottish courtiers at the English court—men like James marquess of Hamilton, James duke of Lennox, and others—he made the mistake of thinking that he did. The extent to which these 'London-Scots' had become thoroughly Anglicized has certainly been exaggerated. Nevertheless, they were undoubtedly affected by their experience, not least in having learned to treat the king with the expected level of deference and flattery. Scottish court life had been traditionally much less formal. The casual and blunt approach of his courtiers in Scotland, with which James had been at ease, outraged Charles—just as his attempts to snub them alienated them. The London-Scots were also inclined to be more favourable to English religious practices. In 1633, these practices were forcibly imposed in Edinburgh, when Charles forced the bishops into rochets and surplices for his coronation, the bishops themselves causing huge offence by genuflecting to the large crucifix installed for the occasion. He had already raised a storm when he unsuccessfully tried to persuade the chancellor, George Hay, earl of Kinnoul—'that old cankered gouty man', he called him—to cede precedence to Archbishop Spottiswoode. And the parliament held during his visit was no better. For the first time, voting on individual Acts was prohibited: 168 bills were voted on as a single whole. It did not prevent opposition; and Charles was there to make a list of those who voted against. It was a futile and silly gesture.

In the next four years, Charles made the situation in Scotland steadily worse. Edinburgh was badly hit financially, not only by the expense of his visit, but by his demands for—ironically—a new parliament house and the reconstruction of St Giles, then divided up to provide for three congregations, now to become one large cathedral church. This was part of the process whereby religion became a central and threatening issue. Charles and Archbishop Laud made no secret of their intention to Anglicize the Kirk; for the first time, it was what London wanted which almost exclusively directed ecclesiastical policy. The Five Articles were pushed with renewed vigour. The episcopacy began to be transformed, as men of Arminian leanings, like Thomas Sydserf, John Maxwell, and James Wedderburn, a Scot in Anglican orders, were intruded onto the bench of bishops; and bishops had a much more prominent place on the council than under James. The king survived the introduction of the canons of 1636, closely modelled on those of England. The breakdown came on 23 July 1637, when the new prayer book, issued by royal proclamation and again closely following the English book with only a few changes as a nod to Scottish practice, was ordered to be read in Edinburgh. If Jenny Geddes and her famous stool never existed, there were plenty of rioters, with stools to hurl, who did—as had been planned in advance. The prayer book—'Laud's Liturgy'—was a religious and political disaster. Charles's government in Scotland collapsed.

As the nickname shows, Laud was the convenient scapegoat. Briefly, therefore, the Scots adopted the normal English fiction of the king's evil councillors. It was a departure from the much more direct political tradition of dealing with problematic kings, a tradition free of the English need to provide ideological justification when they removed unacceptable monarchs. This was not because there was no earlier ideology of kingship and the right to resist. It was simply not given much prominence at times of immediate political crisis. The deposition of Mary queen of Scots had produced, with the political theory of George Buchanan, such justification, but that was for Elizabeth's consumption. In James's reign, Buchanan's ideas about contractual kingship and, even more importantly, the anti-Erastian stance of the Melvillians, had given the contemporary European debate about the nature of kingship—contractual or by divine right—direct relevance to Scottish secular and ecclesiastical politics. James himself, in 1598–9, had made his own contribution to that debate; and the heir to Buchanan and Andrew Melville was David Hume of Godscroft, whose remarkable *De unione insulae Britannicae* argued that the way to preserve Scottish civic society and the rights of the king's Scottish subjects was to create an integrated kingdom of Britain, whose emblem would be, in effect, the Scottish lion rampant, and whose Church would be established by reforming the English Church on Scottish lines. But after the ideological flurry of the late sixteenth and early seventeenth centuries, the debate went quiet. It flared into life again after 1637. Political tradition and political theory came together, to challenge the king directly and to produce more radical arguments about kingship than had ever been expressed before. The onslaught on the king's authority between 1637 and 1640 was underpinned by ideas developed by the lawyer and fanatic Archibald Johnston of Wariston, and the ministers Samuel Rutherford and Alexander Henderson, which drew on the contractual theory of Johann Althaus, the great defender of the Dutch revolt.

With remarkable speed and efficiency, Charles's opponents seized control of events. Petitions flooded into Edinburgh, to be united into a national petition. Charles's dismissal of it led to further rioting in October, during which his councillors had to be protected from the mob by his opponents. It led also to a national supplication, drawn up by David Dickson, minister of Irvine, which explicitly put the covenant with God above the duty of obedience to the king. In 1596, James had successfully undermined Edinburgh's support for the Melvillians by threatening to remove council and law court from the capital. Charles tried the same tactic—and failed. Moving his council away from Edinburgh simply left the opposition a clear field to create an alternative government, the Tables, in existence by November and formally constituted in December. Scotland was now ruled by four Tables, of nobles, lairds, burgesses, and ministers, with a fifth, containing representatives of the other four, as the executive body.

Opposition was certainly led by the nobles. Yet Charles was not, now or later, without aristocratic friends, not only his London-Scots but also members of the resident nobility. The problem in 1637–8 was the absence of too many of these friends. Not until the spring of 1638 did Hamilton persuade the king to send them north, where they could hopefully use their own local influence to offset that of his aristocratic enemies; it was too late, and their intermittent appearances in Scotland had in any case made that influence weaker. Neither they nor the councillors who remained loyal had any answer to the impetus for revolution spearheaded by the councillor who did not remain loyal, Archibald earl of Argyll, along with that long-standing critic of Charles, John earl of Rothes.

Revolution had begun in 1637. The first of its three great milestones came with the justly famous and excessively turgid and lengthy National Covenant—or 'Nobles' Covenant'—signed in Edinburgh on 28 February 1638 and the three succeeding days, after which copies were circulated for signatures throughout the country. It was an astonishing document, with a constitutional flavour, thanks to Johnston, exceptional in Scotland; it rehearsed the Negative Confession of 1581 with its violently anti-Catholic flavour, and then launched into a list of Acts from 1560 made in support of the true Church and against popery, and finally demanded that a 'general band' be made and subscribed by all Charles's subjects, for defence of the true religion and maintenance of the king's majesty. Johnston described its signing in Edinburgh as 'the glorious marriage day of the kingdom with God'. Not all joined so joyfully in its celebration. The earl of Huntly, along with the burghs of Aberdeen and Crail, and the town council of St Andrews, though not the majority of the burgesses, refused to sign. The principal of the University of Glasgow signed belatedly and reluctantly. In Aberdeenshire—the conservative north-east—there was certainly coercion, as there may have been in the Lowlands, despite the general enthusiasm there. Nevertheless, it deserves its title of 'national'. Despite the tedious text, it signalled, perhaps even created, that most heady moment when God's covenanted people appeared to speak with a united and passionate voice.

Charles's attempt to regain the initiative by issuing the 'King's Covenant'— the Negative Confession—failed; few subscribed it. Meeting the covenanters' demand for a general assembly, the first for twenty years, only led to the second revolutionary milestone, the Glasgow assembly of November–

December 1638. Henderson was its moderator, Johnston its clerk. Hamilton, the king's commissioner, was powerless. His attempt to dissolve the assembly failed; it sat on after he had withdrawn, and banned episcopacy, as well as abjuring the Five Articles and secular offices being held by churchmen. Although in the minority, it was the covenanting nobles and lairds who were now in control. Chief amongst them was Argyll.

There was no hope of accommodation, and Charles, king of Scots, used his position as king of England to bring an English army against his Scottish subjects in 1639. Unusually, the Scots won, and in June 1640 came the third milestone. Parliament met, defying the king's order for prorogation, and the dismantling of the king's civil powers began; a Triennial Act was passed, the clerical estate in parliament abolished, the committee of the Articles put into abeyance, the Acts of the Glasgow assembly, already confirmed in the Edinburgh assembly of 1639, ratified, and the government of the country put into the hands of a committee of the estates. The revolution was complete. It provided a model for the king's English opponents if they wanted to follow it. And the covenanting army invaded northern England—and again won. Charles, in desperate need of money, was forced to end his personal rule in England, calling the Short Parliament after the first Bishops' War and the Long Parliament after the second, giving the English a forum which, unlike the Scots, they had lacked since 1629. The king, having failed in his attempt to use Englishmen to crush the covenanters, now had to sue for English money to pay off the covenanting army and persuade it to go home.

It had been an astonishing three years. And covenanting success appeared to continue for a further three, interrupted only in 1641 when there was a minor backlash, inspired by a reaction in favour of the hounded king as well as by family rivalry within Scotland: fear of the power of the earl of Argyll, head of the mighty Campbell kindred. Led by James earl of Montrose a small group of nobles and gentry tried to oppose Argyll, and failed miserably. When Charles came to Scotland in the autumn of 1641, therefore, it was his enemies who were rewarded with office, title, and money, his friends left empty-handed. And so the triumph continued until 1643, when the covenanters of the smaller nation dictated their terms to the parliamentarians of the greater as their price for military support in the English Civil War; the Solemn League and Covenant laid down that the English Church would be reformed on Scottish presbyterian lines, thus bringing briefly into the realm of practical politics Hume of Godscroft's vision of the British Church almost half a century earlier. It was, of course, illusory. Sending a covenanting army south to take part in the first great English parliamentarian victory at Marston Moor in 1644—and get little credit by Oliver Cromwell for it—opened the way for the remarkable year of victories in Scotland by Montrose, now a declared royalist, and the Irish Catholics under Alastair McColla who fought with him; the five victories were humiliating for Argyll and the covenanting troops in Scotland, but achieved no political settlement, whereas it took only one defeat of Montrose at Philiphaugh in 1645 to destroy any hope of a royalist settlement.

What would now determine events was what was happening in England. No longer the dominant players, the Scots became the junior partners in the union, and as they did so the remarkable unity of the covenanting movement was broken. A sizeable body of covenanters made an Engagement with the defeated king that he should be restored to power, the price being a trial three years of Presbyterianism in England. This desperate attempt to recapture the initiative for the Scots was a total failure. The Engager army suffered a stunning defeat at Preston in August 1648, and between them Cromwell, who came to Scotland in October, and Argyll and the hard-line covenanters then wiped them out as a political force, banning them from office-holding and depriving ministers who had supported them. Ironically, the extent of the opposition to those who now governed Scotland was such that they were forced to make concessions to the ministers: lay patronage was abolished in March 1649. Such was the lack of touch with reality that this was remembered as the moment when the purity of the Kirk was at last achieved.

The marginalized kingdom

Reality was very different. On 30 January 1649 Charles I was executed in London. The Scots, who had begun the challenge to his rule, reacted with horror and fury, just as the Scots got rid of Mary queen of Scots and then complained when the English killed her. Their solution was to accept his son as their king, in conditions which made kingship impossible. His father's great servant Montrose tried to fight for the royalist cause, was defeated at Corbisdale in April 1650, brought to Edinburgh, and hanged. Charles I's other supporters, the Engagers, were denied political influence. Charles II himself was to sign both the National Covenant and the Solemn League and Covenant. Had Cromwell's solution been adopted, something might have been salvaged, because what Cromwell was prepared to countenance was the breaking of the union; England would be a republic, the Scots could have their Stuart monarchy. The Scots, still living in their dream world, joined Charles

THE CORONATION OF CHARLES II, 1651: the king who insisted on retaining the union. Charles and the Scots refused to accept kingship only of Scotland, thus forcing Cromwell to invade Scotland and impose the republican regime. The coronation itself was a travesty; the king was crowned by the marquis of Argyll, and forced to take the covenants of 1638 and 1643. His Scottish experience was such that, after the Restoration of 1660, he never came back.

II in insisting that he was the British, not just the Scottish king. His coronation, on 1 January 1651, was a travesty; harangued about his sins, obliged to state his adherence to the covenants and promise to extend them to his other kingdoms, he was crowned not by a churchman but by Argyll. Already, in September 1650, David Leslie had managed to have his army, more than twice the size of Cromwell's, defeated at Dunbar. The covenanting movement further split, into the hard-line remonstrants and the more moderate resolutioners. The resulting political chaos was of little relevance. Cromwell was steadily taking over southern Scotland; and the Scottish army which went south to be wiped out at Worcester in September 1651 was the last and most dismal failure of that great enterprise begun in 1637. At that point, the place of Scotland within the union changed decisively. Charles II was the last king to be crowned in Scotland. After he left in 1651, the only personal contact which the Scots had with the house of Stuart was with James duke of York, sent north in 1679 to get him out of the way of the Exclusion Crisis raging in London.

From 1651, military rule was imposed from England, the country being kept under control by General Munck's armies and a series of forts set up throughout the country, notably at Inverlochy and Inverness, but also in the Lowlands and as far north as Orkney. It was certainly effective—more effective, it seems, than the much-vaunted discipline of the Kirk. Also imposed was a 'happy union' whereby the Scottish parliament was suppressed. Thirty Scottish commissioners, half of them English army officers, the rest drawn from the minority still allowed to hold office, were allowed to attend the Westminster parliaments, themselves a shambles as the English republic struggled and failed to find a workable constitutional answer to the problem of survival. Neither policy was appreciated, despite the carrot of free trade. Cromwell himself would have ditched Scotland had he been able to, and intensely disliked the ministers of the Kirk; 'I beseech ye in the bowels of Christ', he wrote to them memorably, 'think it possible that ye might be mistaken.' Covenanting failure did not create the climate in which the now divided but, on both sides, intransigent ministry might do so; more generally, military oppression, the economic distress resulting from war, the disruption of trade, and, in the 1650s, the high taxation through which the Scots had the privilege of paying for a repressive regime, made Scotland and its Kirk a harsh and stagnant place. Some efforts were made to mitigate it, and to balance military with civil rule. After the rising of the earl of Glencairn in 1653–4, a new Scottish council was established, under the presidency of the Irishman Lord Broghill. JPs were reintroduced in 1656. It is a measure of what Cromwellian Scotland was like that their main achievement was to spark off witchhunting on a large scale between 1657 and 1659.

It was Munck's army which went south from Scotland as the first move to restore Charles II in 1660; and Munck seems to have had some idea for improving the terms of union for the Scots. There was no interest. The chill wind of neglect was now fully felt. Under Cromwell, there had been a measure of order in the way in which Scotland was ruled. For the rest of the century, it became very clear that it was English, not Scottish, interests which were paramount. Political life was now chaotic. Aristocratic feuds might be less bloodless than in the past, but they were probably more virulent and certainly more purposeless. Charles II initially tried to establish a balance, giving offices to the royalist Glencairn and the earl of Middleton along with the covenanting Rothes, the plum job of secretary going to the earl of Lauderdale. A reaction against the covenanters made life easier for Charles himself. But the royalists were split between Lauderdale at court in London and Middleton in Scotland and assailed by intrigue and faction in both locations; and an early idea of having five Scottish privy councillors in London was quickly dropped. After Middleton's fall in 1663, Charles in effect ruled Scotland until 1680 through his commissioner Lauderdale, while the new earl of Argyll, son of the convenanting marquess who was executed in 1661, continued the dominance of the Highlands, and the resentment, created by his father. Scotland was left to turn in on itself, and fail to find a political *modus vivendi*. There were repeated complaints that freedom of speech was now denied to parliament; repeatedly Lord Advocate Mackenzie of Rosehaugh and, in 1669, William duke of Hamilton forcefully expressed their opposition to royal intimidation. It is perhaps symbolic of the lamentable state it was now in that rejoicing at the Restoration was accompanied by the biggest outbreak of witchhunting, in this sporadically witch-persecuting kingdom, when some 300 witches were executed in 1661–2. Confusion reigned, as erstwhile Presbyterian and covenanting nobility supported the restoration of episcopacy, ironically with more enthusiasm than Lauderdale himself. In 1662 a widespread attack on dissenting ministers, including revolutioners as well as protesters, began. Its upshot, the Pentland Rising of 1666, led to a more moderate policy, but that was reversed in 1674. It did not help that the new bench of bishops was itself utterly split between moderates like Robert Leighton, archbishop of Glasgow, and Alexander Burnet, his predecessor and then successor at Glasgow—a procession which aptly sums up the violent swings of policy in the period.

This was the backdrop to the most notorious aspect of Charles's rule, the 'killing times' of the early 1680s. Throughout his reign, hard-line covenanters driven out of the Kirk, or choosing to leave it, met in conventicles, notably in south-west Scotland. A group of them murdered Archbishop Sharpe of St Andrews, with his daughter present, just outside St Andrews; there was then an armed rising in the west, which was put down by a government army led by Charles's son James duke of Monmouth; and for the next few years, conventiclers were hunted down and executed or transported. A terrible blot

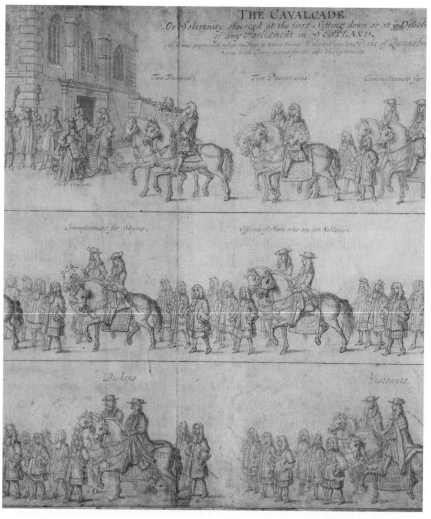

THE RIDING OF PARLIAMENT (detail), 1685, a drawing possibly by Roderick
Chalmers, appointed a Herald Painter in 1724, based on a contemporary set of drawings.

on the history of a country not known for repression of nonconformity on this
scale? So it has long seemed; the Cameronions, followers of the preacher
Richard Cameron, but actually the smallest and most extreme but least influential group of conventiclers, themselves a divided movement, are still commemorated in parts of Ayrshire today. If the picture of the early Kirk is a
distorted one, because of the dominance of the Presbyterian historians, so the
myth of the killing times is distorted, brought into being in the early eighteenth century by the antiquary Robert Wodrow. Far from Scotland being a

nation of devout covenanters oppressed by a ruthless government, the conventiclers were a very small group, which included men all too willing to resort to murder and force; and even so, the numbers who suffered were not especially large. Given all the uncertainties of a nervous government, its reputation deserves to be rescued from this particular myth.

Lauderdale died in 1680. Faction and uncertainty survived him, complicated by the presence of James duke of York in Scotland 1679–81, in which year he pushed through parliament an Act enforcing the acknowledgement of royal supremacy in all matters, secular and ecclesiastical. It is surely a measure of the divisions and weakness of the political nation that he could persuade it to do this for its future Catholic king. His own reign, beginning in 1685, created further divisions. Argyll, his opponent from 1681, tried to join with the Monmouth rising of 1685, failed dismally, and was executed. In 1687, two indulgences granting complete religious toleration were issued, with minimal opposition. There were some conversions to Catholicism from those seeking political power, most notably the chancellor James earl of Perth in 1686, but fewer than in England. Scotland sat on the sidelines while in 1688 William of Orange and a small group of James's English opponents got rid of the king, whose own pathetic lack of resistance helped them immeasurably; he failed to fight, because of a nose-bleed, and then ran away.

The end of the independent kingdom?

For the first time since 1651, the Scots acted decisively in 1688–9, at both popular and elite level. There was a sudden upsurge of anti-popery, leading to the sacking of Holyrood Abbey and the desecration of the tombs of the Stewart kings—an apparently dramatic departure from the traditional loyalty to and enthusiasm for the Stewart monarchy, but one which reflected the fact that not since 1625 had there been a monarch who commanded such loyalty. Among the elite, another old tradition surfaced, that of contractual monarchy: while the English insisted that James had abdicated, the Scots were equally adamant that they had removed him. The Scottish parallel to the English Bill of Rights was the Claim of Right. But as in England, what happened was neither particularly glorious nor revolutionary. Events in both kingdoms were basically determined by the fact that William was not exclusively interested in being king of England, let alone Scotland, something which, given their different seventeenth-century experiences, was much less palatable in England. An indifferent king gave way in 1690 to what was supposed to be the final triumph of Presbyterianism, when episcopacy was abolished from the Kirk. In fact, episcopacy was never eradicated in Scotland, nor was the unity of the Kirk assured. Breakaway movements, some short-lived, some long-lasting, continued to make nonsense of yet another myth. William's only concern with Scotland was to acquire men and money to pursue his real interest, war with the long-standing enemy of the prince of Orange, Louis XIV. Thus decisive politics reverted to muddle; the 1690s became memorable not for political impetus, but because of two notorious episodes, the Massacre of Glencoe, the notorious product of Highland support for the Jacobites, and the Darien Disaster. Yet more than anything else, they were to catapult Scotland out of its languishing state.

What is remarkable about the Massacre of February 1692 is the reaction. A botched effort to eradicate a small clan, the Macdonalds of Glencoe, on the excuse that its chief had been five days late in taking the oath of allegiance to William, might have passed, on previous experience, relatively unremarked. Indeed, the astonishing tactlessness of the English, who listened to Purcell's Birthday Ode for Queen Mary some six weeks after the Massacre, an ode which incorporated the Scottish ballad 'Cold and raw'—all too reminiscent of the fate of Macdonalds dying of exposure—suggests that this was what was expected. In fact, it became headline news not only in Britain but abroad; it appeared in the Paris newspapers as well as those in London, and it even gave its name to a Latin verb, 'glencoabitur'—murdered under trust. A highpowered scapegoat had to be found, and was, in the person of the lord advocate, Dalrymple of Stair. What had its origins in internal Highland rivalries became a matter of national politics.

Worse was to follow. Once again Scottish trade was disrupted because the king of England was at war with France. It was a too familiar pattern. Back in 1672, the Scots had tried some self-help with their foreign trade, when an Act of parliament removed the stranglehold of the royal burghs and opened it up to the barony and regality burghs. It had not been enough to offset the damaging effects of English foreign policy. In 1695, the Scots again tried to seize an economic initiative, establishing a Company of Scotland for trade with Africa and the West Indies. The mastermind was the impressive and forward-looking William Paterson, founder of the Banks of England and then Scotland. In the aftermath of Glencoe, William and the English parliament first offered support, and then offensively withdrew it because of the purely English interests of the East India Company and William's fear that the Scots might antagonize the Spanish, his allies against Louis XIV. The Scots pressed

(Page 3.)

A LIST, &c.

	lib.
A.	
William Arbuckle Merchant in *Glasgow*	2000
Archibald Earl of ARGYLE	1500
Michael Allan Merchant in *Edinburgh*	1000
William Farl of ANNANDALE	1000
Mr. William Areskine Governour of *Blackness*	1000
The FACULTY OF ADVOCATS	1000
Sir Patrick Aikenhead Commissary-Clerk of *Edinburgh*	1000
John Anderson of *Dovehill* and Provost of *Glasgow*	1000
James Auchinleck Chirurgion-Apothecary in *Edinburgh*	600
John Marquis of ATHOL	500
Alexander Anstruther of *New-wark*	500
William Ainslie of *Blackhill*	500
Mr. Walter Atchison of *Rochfolloch*	500
Sir William Anstruther of *Anstruther* one of the Senators of the Colledge of Justice	400
Captain Alexander Anderson in Sir John Hills Regiment	400
Sir John Areskine of *Alva*	300
Sir James Abercrombie of *Birkenbog*	300
Captain John Areskine Brother to the Laird of *Alva*	300
Lady *Alva*	300
Robert Anstruther of *Wrea*	300
James Allan of *Sauchnell*	300
John Allardes younger Merchant in *Aberdeen*	200
Mr. William Aikman of *Cairny* Advocat	200
Sir Alexander Areskine of *Cambo* Lyon King at Arms	200
Sir John Aioun of that *Ilk*	200
The TOWN OF AIR	200
John Alexander of *Blackhouse* for himself and Lady *Grange*	200
Mrs. Veronica Areskine Daughter to the deceas'd David Lord CARDROSS	200
Thomas Anderson Son to Baillie Anderson	200
William Alves Writer in *Edinburgh*	200
John Angus Brewer there	200
James Adam Merchant in *Glasgow*	200
John Armour Taylor there	200
John Alexander Merchant in *Glasgow*	125
Penelope Areskine Sister to *Cambo*	100
Mr. Thomas Aikman Writer to the Signet	100
Claud Alexander of *Newton*	100
Matthew Atcheson Merchant in *Glasgow*	100
John Aird Dean of Guild there	100
John Anderson *junior* Merchant there	100
Carry forward - -	17825

Transported from A. - - 17825

John Allan Merchant in *Hamilton*	100
John Adam *senior* merchant in *Glasgow*	100
Alexander Adam Taylor there	100
William Arthur Taylor in *Cannongate*	100
Thomas Alstoun Shoe-maker in *Glasgow*	100
Mr. Alexander Auchterlony Indweller in *Dundee*	100
Archibald Arnot Apothecary there	100
Thomas Abercrombie Skipper there	100
James Alison late Baillie there	100
George Anderson merchant in *Haddington*	100
Colin Alison Sub-Collector of His Majesties Excise	100
William Allan Taylor in *Stirling*	100
John Archibald Writer in *Edinburgh*	100
William Allan Portioner of *Dudingston*	100
George Anderson Son to Mr. John Anderson Minister at *Leslie*	100
Gabriel Alison of *Dunjop*	100
Margaret Adamson Daughter to the deceas'd Patrick Adamson merchant in *Kello*	100
Robert Arbuthnot Servit. to E. MARSHALL	100
Michael Arideison of *Tushallow*	100
Jean Arthut Daughter to John Arthur of *Newton*	100
The TOWN OF SAINT-ANDREWS.	100
B.	
John Lord BELHAVEN	3000
The ROYAL BURROWS	3000
Mr. Robert Blackwood Merchant in *Edinb.*	2000
James Balfour Merchant there	2000
Sir Thomas Burnet of *Lees*	1000
William Baillie of *Lamington*	1000
George Baillie of *Jervifwood*	1000
Alexander Brand Merchant in *Edinburgh*	1000
John Baillie Chyrurgion there	1000
Robert Blackwood Merchant there	1000
Alexander Baird Merchant there	1000
James Byers Merchant there	700
The TOWN OF BRICHEN	700
Sir John Baird of *Newbyth*	500
John Bruce of *Kinrofs*	500
Sir William Baird younger of *Newbyth*	500
Sir William Binning of *Walsford*	500
William Biggar of *Woolmet*	500
Lieutenant Colonel James Bruce of *Kennet*	500
Hugh Blair Merchant in *Edinburgh*	500
Thomas Burnet Merchant in *Aberdeen*	500
John Broun Skipper in *Leith*	400
Elizabeth Lady *Borthwick*	400
Thomas Baxter Taylor in *Glasgow*	400
Carry forward - -	44025

A 2

SUBSCRIPTION LIST for the Company of Scotland, 1696. £400,000 was raised from contributions ranging from £3,000 to £100. This was the minimum amount, so townspeople were allowed to subscribe communally. It was a heavy proportion of Scotland's available capital, raised for and lost in the appalling Darien disaster.

on, getting huge investment at home. There were two expeditions sent to establish New Caledonia in Darien. Both were utter failures, partly because of English and Spanish hostility, partly because bibles and woollen hats were not the most obvious trading commodities to take to Darien. It was English hostility which was remembered. Once again, and monumentally, Scotland had suffered grievously because of being tied to England. What made it worse was that it happened at a time of severe economic distress, with 'King William's Seven Ill Years' of the 1690s, years of poor or failed harvests and a high rate of death from starvation, between 5 per cent and 15 per cent generally and in Aberdeenshire possibly as high as 25 per cent. Their impact was all the greater because these dreadful years of suffering came after a relatively stable economic state since 1660. Resentful and embittered Scots were caught as never before in the trap of economic as well as political stagnation—and worse. Anglo-Scottish relations were fast collapsing.

Seven years after the second Darien expedition the parliaments of England and Scotland were united under a British monarchy, and Scotland sent a rather fairer number of representatives than in the 1650s to the House of Lords and House of Commons at Westminster. These seven years saw pressure and counter-pressure, as politicians on both sides of the Border acknowledged that the Union of the Crowns could not be sustained, but struggled to find an alternative. The English Act of Succession of 1701, ignoring the Scottish parliament's right claimed in 1689 to determine the succession, announced that both England and Scotland would be ruled by Sophia, electress of Hanover, granddaughter of James VI and I, after the death of the childless Anne. The Scots answered in 1703 with the Act of Security, which said that they would not necessarily accept Sophia, and the Act anent War and Peace, which prevented them being embroiled in English foreign wars. In 1705 the English raised the stakes with their Alien Act, threatening Anglo-Scottish trade. This legislative war cannot simply be seen as bluff and counter-bluff, although the Scottish Act of Security was shorn of much of its force by the difficulty of finding an alternative successor to Anne, given that the senior Stuart line was cut out because of its Catholicism, as laid down in the Claim of Right. There was no clear answer to the problem. The influential Andrew Fletcher of Saltoun urged a federal union, on a regional rather than national basis; others thought in terms of a treaty. The Scottish political nation was once again fundamentally split. Union became the solution only from April 1705, when Argyll threw his weight behind it, the duke of Hamilton was bribed, or blackmailed, into supporting it, and the marquess of Tweeddale and his thirty followers, known as the *Squadrone Volante*, made up their minds in 1706 to follow the union route. As the run-up to the constitutional redefinition of the Anglo-Scottish union, it could hardly have been less impressive.

Indeed the constitutional underpinning of the union of 1707 defies definition. It was not federal, for there was now one parliament as well as one monarchy. Nor was it incorporating, because Scotland retained its own Church, law, and educational system. That was perhaps its saving grace, and the reason why eighteenth-century Scotland regained the confidence of the pre-1603 past, so grimly lost in the later seventeenth century. Constitutionally and to an extent politically, it was no longer an independent kingdom. But culturally and socially, it retained its independence, most impressively exemplified in the flowering of the Scottish Enlightenment.

The other side of the coin

Seventeenth-century Scotland, especially after 1625, was a disturbed and sometimes horrible place. What happened to it was determined by the Union of the Crowns, and the loss of freedom of manoeuvre. The political map was redrawn. Gaelic culture was increasingly under attack, because it did not fit well with the need to find accommodation with the new ties with England, and because the Campbells of Argyll transformed themselves from leading Scottish magnates heavily involved in Highland society into British politicians, using their new dominance of the Highlands as the springboard for their dominance of Scottish politics in the eighteenth century. Moreover, whereas before 1603 genuine achievements had been bolstered by propaganda which might exaggerate but was grounded in success, the seventeenth century became the breeding ground for myth, in order to conceal failure, and that myth tended to focus on God's covenanted people, whether portrayed as militant in his cause or suffering for it. What Scotland aspired to seems to be encapsulated in its recurrent bouts of witch persecution, and in the terrifying Act of 1649 which would impose death instead of remissions, respites, or fines as the penalty for crimes in this 'whole Land polluted with sin'; and the death penalty would be used for blasphemy and abuse of parents. In 1682, in another godly spasm, there were burnings of homosexuals, although—like witches—they were probably strangled first. And there was the gruesome execution of the student Thomas Aitkenhead for blasphemy in Edinburgh in 1697, pushed through despite the modified Act of 1695 and the illegality of having only one witness. The heavy pall of sin, the presumptuous dispensing of God's law, and the devil stalking the land hangs over much of the religious and legal language of the seventeenth century.

Nevertheless, it would be wrong to portray Scotland only in these terms. Under the political and religious strife and confusion there were still many signs of cultural and intellectual vibrancy. In terms of the law, there were huge developments to set against the culture of sin. At the beginning of the century a small group of academic lawyers, Thomas Craig of Riccarton, John Skene of Curriehill, and others, were setting out to codify and rationalize Scots law, and what they began would reach fruition in the magnificent *Insti-*

tutions of the Law of Scotland by James Dalrymple, Viscount Stair, published in 1681, when civil law was given a comprehensive philosophical underpinning and firmly based on Roman law which therefore preserved it from royal and political interference. In criminal law, Lord Advocate George Mackenzie did something similar in his work of the same name in 1684, although his approach was more royalist. In the 1680s he presided over the creation of the Advocates' Library, the core of what is now the National Library of Scotland. And already, in 1672, the high court of justiciary, the first central criminal court in Scotland, was founded, by giving the judges of the court of session dual civil and criminal roles, distinguished by the colours of their robes 'for the splendour of that court'; was 'godly' Scotland so very godly, when its judges dressed in flamboyant colours, contrasting sharply with the black worn by English judges?

These developments in the law were part of a remarkable period of an intellectual surge in Edinburgh, helped on by the patronage of James duke of York, the one saving grace in his dealings with Scotland. James succeeded, where his father and grandfather had failed, in establishing the Royal College of Physicians of Edinburgh, something eagerly sought by the physician and geographer Robert Sibbald and others but hitherto frustrated by the powerful opposition of the guild of surgeons, backed by the city magistrates. Sibbald himself had founded the Physic Garden in 1667 which became the Royal Botanic Garden, but which in its early years was specifically intended to provide the materials for medical research. The 'tounis college' was given a new charter in 1688 as 'King James's university', a direct and conscious linking of James VII to the original founder James VI; and in the same year—and therefore for the moment too late—Edinburgh got its own royal charter which envisaged the building of new streets and bridges. Further emphasis on the Scottish monarchy was seen in the commissioning of 111 portraits of the Scottish kings to hang in Holyrood House, the palace restored and extended under Charles II by the great Scottish architect William Bruce, but used—apart from James's brief sojourn in Edinburgh—by government officials rather than kings. It was a heady period, one which shows the advantage, though not the necessity, of having a royal patron personally present in Scotland. But equally it was undermined by James's own divisive policies. It was Episcopalians who enjoyed his patronage as duke of York, and Catholicism which went public when he was king; his revival of the Order of the Thistle in 1687 was designed to recreate the Order of the pre-Reformation past. It was therefore interrupted by the events of 1688–9 and their aftermath.

THE UNIVERSITY OF GLASGOW, 1630–60, from John Slezer's *Theatrum Scotiae* (1693). The burgh's gifts to the university, for buildings and the library, were very much more generous than Edinburgh's. Indeed, more than enough money was raised in Scotland for Glasgow University, which must surely be almost unique in the annals of academic fundraising.

Nevertheless, the combination of aspiration and achievement was the first step towards the achievements of the eighteenth century. But it did not come from nowhere. It was also a landmark on the road which could be traced from the sixteenth century. The ever-growing use of the printing press to produce late medieval and sixteenth-century literature and histories of Scotland, as well as bibles, religious works, and school books, does not support any idea that godly Scotland was uncultured Scotland. True, much of intellectual life during the mid-seventeenth crisis was channelled into the godly and political. But the cartographer Timothy Pont in the 1590s, lawyers like Craig and Skene, the great poet William Drummond of Hawthornden, and his contemporaries Robert Aytoun and William Alexander, the herald and antiquary James Balfour of Denmilne, the development of the professions, were impressive in their own time and all foreshadow the 1670s and 1680s and beyond. And the basis of so much of it, that vision of universal school education first set out in the *First Book of Discipline* in 1560, though far from being realized by 1700, was never lost; advances in English education went into reverse after the mid-seventeenth century, but in Scotland they continued, to the extent that by then most Lowland parishes had grammar or at least parish schools. Moreover, if the first known secular music book to be printed in Scotland did not appear until 1662, in music as in education the Kirk did make a distinguished contribution, in its encouragement of what was already becoming one of its most noted and impressive cultural aspects, congregational psalm-singing. On the other hand, it was despite the opposition of the Kirk that drama revived in Scotland, which got its first theatre in the 1660s, run by Thomas Sydserf. Here at least Anglo-Scottish relations had their positive side: plays by Dryden and Sydserf were performed in both London and Edinburgh. More generally, what the post-Restoration period witnessed was the throwing off of godly shackles and a renewed balance between the sacred and the profane.

What men built in this century again takes us far from the archetypal world of the godly. This applies even to ecclesiastical architecture. There was not a sudden switch from ornate Catholic churches to austere and simple Protestant ones; many pre-Reformation parish churches, for economic reasons, were themselves exceedingly small and plain. Archbishop Spottiswoode's church at Dairsie might be a deliberate reaction against puritanical attitudes. But it is something of a revelation to find that the new and imposing church at Burntisland, built in the 1590s, followed the plan of San Geminiano in Venice. And the stark little St Mary's, Grandtully, was built in 1533. It was in 1626 that its interior was adorned with a splendid painted ceiling. Moreover, if all men were equal in the sight of God, they were certainly not equal in the sight of the Kirk. Seating was by rank; and hierarchical considerations produced further embellishments, as coats of arms were duly attached to relevant pews.

Secular architecture exemplifies the same thing. That great, if erratic, Catholic magnate George earl of Huntly openly defied the Kirk with his magnificent doorway at Huntly Castle, completed in 1602 and displaying, in ascending order, the arms of the marquess and his wife, the royal arms, the papal arms, the five wounds of Christ, and above them all St Michael. The crypto-Catholic Alexander earl of Dunfermline undoubtedly nailed his political colours to the Anglo-Scottish union, but he was much more enthusiastic

ST MARY'S CHURCH,
Grandtully, Perthshire.
Religious architectural
expression the wrong way
round? The exterior shows
a very simple pre-
Reformation building
(1533). The riotous painted
ceiling of 1626 hardly bears
out ideas of presbyterian
austerity.

SECULAR RIOTOUSNESS: the great hall of Craigievar Castle, Aberdeenshire, 1612–26.

about Catholic-French rather than Protestant English architectural styles, when he remodelled Fyvie Castle at the beginning of the seventeenth century, and put in a splendid staircase reminiscent of the stairways of the great Loire chateaux of Chambord and Amboise. But it was not only the Catholics. The need for defensive castles was obviously on the wane, but Scottish taste determined that the castellated style of architecture would be continued, gloriously embellished by large oriel windows, delightfully painted ceilings and plasterwork, and impressive statements of lineage in publicly displayed coats of arms. Glamis, in Angus, built in the early seventeenth century and remodelled in the late 1660s, stands as the most glorious example of Scottish baronial architecture. In Aberdeenshire in the 1610s and 1620s, William Forbes—'Willie the Merchant'—created a marvellous and lovely tower-house and constructed in his great hall a spectacular plaster ceiling and plaster royal coat of arms over the fireplace. No doubt because of financial restraints, Robert earl of Nithsdale retained his medieval castle of Caerlaverock, but incorporated into it a Renaissance wing in the 1630s; David Lindsay of Edzell was one of those who constructed fine Renaissance gardens, in his case running himself out of money to do so. Style, elegance, and luxury were what determined the buildings of the aristocracy and lairds, in the country and in their town houses, such as 'Argyll's Lodging' in Stirling, rebuilt in 1632, and the earlier Moray House in Edinburgh. Merchants and burgesses followed suit. It was the covenanting Andrew Lumsden who in the 1620s made the improvements to his Aberdeen town house, which included another impressive painted ceiling showing scenes from the life of Christ and the Greek symbols for Christ's name; and Provost Skene, who took over the house, and gave it its current name, continued its decoration. After the Restoration, there were further developments, as those who could afford it sought out the fashionable and innovative architect William Bruce to build them more palatial houses, as at Hopetoun and Thirlestane. In its architecture, therefore, as in its literary and intellectual culture, we get a quite different picture of Calvinist Scotland.

Conclusion

The myth of the godly society of seventeenth-century Scotland has had a long and dominant life. It is now beginning to be unpicked. There were always those who resisted the godly, and those who recognized the tension between the devastating logic of predestinarian theology and the scriptural insistence that Christ died for all men. Moreover, many of the leading covenanters, lay and ecclesiastical, at the height of their powers in the mid-century, were not just grim and dour men. They were men of lofty vision, whose religious experience encompassed a level of emotional and sexual imagery which is only now coming to be fully recognized. There were indeed godly excesses, seen to the full in Johnston of Wariston's diary which has an unpleasant tendency to hector the Lord, and they have tended to obscure the appeal of the simplicity and dignity of the Kirk's form of worship and its practices, an appeal perhaps made more likely by the comparative lack of lavish pre-Reformation church-building and ceremonial; pilgrimages and processions may rouse less enthusiasm in a cold and wet climate. Possibly Burns's *Cottar's Saturday Night*, which brings this out so well, should be required reading for students of the seventeenth century—along with *Holy Wullie's Prayer* for the pharasaical godly, and, of course, *Tam O'Shanter*, for witchcraft. We need to see the Kirk as less unique, more typical of other reformed churches, struggling to establish their identities at a time of division and uncertainty. What determined the particular form this took in Scotland was the fluctuating fortunes of the kingdom, as it wrestled with the problems of union with England, and the follies of the intransigent Charles I, who allowed the covenanters a dramatic and rapid success which, coupled with centuries-old and ingrained belief in the importance of Scotland, led them to overstate their power and freedom of manoeuvre. The problem for seventeenth-century Scotland was that the defining landmarks with which its history was punctuated never turned out to be quite defining enough. What should not surprise us is that its inhabitants were much more human than the myth sometimes suggests, and that, given the legacy of their past, they muddled through and survived, not as the marginalized people of an inferior nation but as the Scots of the Enlightenment, who, in sharp distinction to the English, who wanted to make England and Britain interchangeable, leaving everyone else out, had the confidence to be North Britons.

6 Scotland Transformed:
The Eighteenth Century

Richard B. Sher

'Is it not strange . . .?'

Really it is admirable how many Men of Genius this Country produces at present. Is it not strange that, at a time when we have lost our Princes, our Parliaments, our independent Government, even the Presence of our chief Nobility, are unhappy, in our Accent & Pronunciation, speak a very corrupt Dialect of the Tongue which we make use of; is it not strange, I say, that, in these Circumstances, we shou'd really be the People most distinguish'd for Literature in Europe?

The paradox of the Scottish Enlightenment that David Hume articulated in this private letter of 1757 may be extended to other aspects of eighteenth-century Scottish life and culture. Hume's litany of Scottish national losses—of king and court following the Union of Crowns in 1603, of an independent Scottish parliament following the parliamentary union of 1707, and of many of the higher nobility who set up residences in London during the eighteenth century, rarely if ever returning to their native land—might well have spelled disaster for a small, relatively poor nation situated along the northern periphery of Europe. Yet the eighteenth century in Scotland was the era not only of the brilliant efflorescence of literature and learning to which Hume referred but also of remarkable developments in agriculture and urban life, commerce and industry, religion and society, and much more. In the age when Scotland lost its sovereignty, its people asserted themselves with renewed vigour and acquired an unprecedented degree of international recognition for their achievements. If that accomplishment seemed 'strange' to contemporaries, it appears no less extraordinary two and half centuries later.

The paradox should not be overstated. Not every region and group in the nation benefited from Scotland's so-called 'awakening' in the eighteenth century: many were marginally affected or, like those displaced from the land in both the Lowlands and Highlands, adversely affected by events of the age. Moreover, the transformation was not always abrupt. Scotland in the seventeenth century was not the stagnant and isolated backwater that it has sometimes been made out to be by careless or patronizing scholars, and several decades would pass before the nation would begin to reap significant advantages from the union of 1707.

It nevertheless remains true that Scotland underwent a dramatic transformation during the eighteenth century, especially after 1746. Perhaps the union's most productive effect was to stimulate a dynamic new mind-set among many Scots, a psychological drive to succeed rooted partly in traditional Scottish attitudes, partly in new opportunities. An enduring tradition of national self-doubt and uncertainty became a creative force, as Scots struggled to overcome real and imagined shortcomings by demonstrating their own worth to themselves and others. The sense of inferiority about the Scots language that appears in Hume's letter, for example, was often translated into a passion for gaining mastery of the English language. Hume's exaggerated claim about the literary reputation of Scotland in 1757 was another way of handling feelings of uncertainty about national identity; such boasting sometimes functioned as a self-fulfilling prophecy by encouraging positive developments already under way. Similarly, traditional Scottish religious values, such as a strong Calvinist work ethic and a belief in Scotland's special status as a covenanted nation, were increasingly adapted to secular pursuits, with impressive results.

As for opportunities, the union eventually had a profound impact by opening up England and its empire to Scottish trade and migration. Scholars are more likely now than formerly to emphasize global implications: the union was for empire, from Asia to the Americas, and Scots had more than their fair chance to participate. They dominated the tobacco trade with America, served in vast numbers in the imperial army, and were conspicuously over-represented in the East Indian administration and West Indian sugar plantations. It has been plausibly argued that 'Britishness' was grounded less in assimilation to England or in fundamental similarities among England, Scotland, and Wales than in a growing sense of imperial solidarity and common cause against France, Spain, and other continental rivals with whom Britain was frequently at war during the second half of the century. The fact that those rivals tended to be predominantly Roman Catholic added to the sense of cohesion among British Protestant denominations which otherwise differed substantially among themselves.

The Godly commonwealth transformed

In Scotland, where religion exercised a powerful hold on the people and few Roman Catholics were to be found until the advent of extensive Irish Catholic immigration in the nineteenth century, conflicts among Protestants were endemic. For most of the eighteenth century Scottish Episcopalians were led by bishops whose Jacobite sympathies ensured the continued presence of disabilities. Presbyterians opened the century in control of the Church of Scotland, the universities, and the rest of the national Establishment, but schism and internal division would soon be their lot. Within the Kirk, there was by mid-century a well-defined opposition between an Evangelical, Popular, or Orthodox party and a Moderate party whose outlook was theologically and culturally liberal but socially and politically conservative. The primary issue over which they clashed concerned the proper mode of selecting parish ministers. The Moderates accepted a law of 1712 which vested that power in the patron of the parish, who was usually either the most powerful local landowner or the crown. Their opponents were uniformly hostile towards patronage and usually favoured some version of the complex procedure contained in the 1690 Act establishing Presbyterian government, which placed the power of selection chiefly in the hands of the parish heritors (landowners) and lay elders. They also tended to be stricter and more evangelical in their Calvinism, more stridently whiggish, and less tolerant of Roman Catholics and Episcopalians. Numerically, the two ecclesiastical parties were well matched, but the Moderates usually controlled the annual general assembly, and the Church itself, by means of superior political management.

The hegemony of the Moderates was aided by the growing tendency towards secession and schism among those Presbyterians most hostile to Moderate policies. Small pockets of radical Presbyterians, such as the Cameronians, had never accepted the 'Erastian' revolution settlement of 1690. In the 1730s Revd Ebenezer Erskine of Stirling spearheaded the first true secession from the Church of Scotland, ostensibly over opposition to the law of patronage but more generally on behalf of a stricter interpretation of

Calvinist piety and church polity. Although more democratic in regard to the selection of parish ministers, Erskine and his followers were more intolerant in other respects. Not long after the famed English preacher George White-field answered their invitation to visit Scotland in 1742, they denounced him for taking part in the great religious revival that occurred at Cambuslang near Glasgow under the auspices of the evangelical wing of the established Church. The seceders were 'the Lord's people', Ebenezer Erskine's brother Ralph told the astonished Whitefield. The same sectarian spirit soon led to a major split among the seceders themselves over the anti-Jacobite burgess oath: the Erskines' faction of 'Burghers' was willing to sign, but an 'Anti-Burgher' faction was adamantly opposed and excommunicated the Erskines in 1747. The Anti-Burghers took their opposition to Erastianism so far that in 1788 one of their leading spokesmen, Archibald Bruce, published a work condemning the centenary celebration of the revolution. Both groups of seceders tapped a rich source of discontent within the established Church among pious merchants and tradesmen seeking a measure of autonomy, and they grew to have hundreds of congregations by the end of the century. Meanwhile, other groups of Presbyterians continued to fall away from the Church of Scotland, such as the Relief Church, established in 1761 by sever-al evangelical clergymen who refused to accept the strict enforcement of the law of patronage by the Moderate majority. Still others gave up Presbyterian-ism entirely to become Independents or Anabaptists or Methodists.

The massive *Statistical Account of Scotland* that Sir John Sinclair compiled from the accounts of parish ministers illustrates the extent of religious diver-sity by the last decade of the eighteenth century. In the royal burgh of Stirling, 2,795 individuals were said to be members of the established Church, but there were also 1,415 Burghers, 172 Anti-Burghers, 120 Cameronians, 89 Episcopalians, 74 adherents of the Relief Church, and 33 Berean Indepen-dents. There was still more diversity in Glasgow, Edinburgh, and other sizeable towns. For example, Perth, with a population under 15,000, was reported to contain one congregation of each of the following dissenting groups: Scots Episcopalians, English Episcopalians, Cameronians, Anabap-tists, Burghers, Anti-Burghers, 'Relief people', Balchristy Independents and Glassite or Sandemanian Independents. In the little parish of Buittle in the south-west, Cameronians and Roman Catholics, surprisingly, constituted the two largest religious groups outside the Kirk. In Aberdeenshire and the north-east, Episcopalians continued to have much greater representation than elsewhere.

The General Assembly of the Kirk of Scotland 1787.

THE GENERAL ASSEMBLY OF THE KIRK, 1787. Scottish advocates like James Boswell often pled patronage cases at the bar of the Church of Scotland's general assembly, which met each spring in Edinburgh. In a magazine article of 1772 Boswell called it 'an excellent school for eloquence', though in a private journal entry on 26 May 1777 it was termed 'that vulgar and rascally court'.

The ramifications of the pluralist religious configuration emerging in Scotland were enormous. The very existence of so much diversity fostered a kind of *de facto* toleration, first among Presbyterians and then among all varieties of Christians. During the last quarter of the eighteenth century, and especially after the death of Charles Edward Stuart in 1788, Scottish Episcopalians renounced their Jacobite tendencies and became respectable Hanoverians, obtaining relief in 1792 from the worst disabilities to which they had been subjected. Roman Catholics had a similar experience. In 1779 the prospect of even a modest Catholic relief bill provoked national hysteria and urban rioting in Scotland, preparing the way for the much larger Gordon Riots in London the following year. By 1793, however, the attack on the Roman Catholic Church by the French Revolution made it possible for Henry Dundas to enact similar relief legislation for Scottish Catholics with scarcely a murmur of protest.

In this environment, church discipline—traditionally maintained at the parish level by the minister and church elders sitting as the kirk session, and beyond that by presbyteries, synods, and the general assembly, working closely with local magistrates in the burghs—could not have the same bite as formerly. The puritanical Scotch sabbath could no longer be strictly policed, especially in the larger towns. A pious pamphlet of 1787 entitled *The Former and Present State of Glasgow Contrasted* complained of military bands, loud celebrations by journeymen barbers, and 'parties of pleasure' held by the 'better sort of folks' on Sundays. A pamphlet on changes occurring in Edinburgh around the same time voiced similar concerns and illustrated the shift by observing that Sunday was now the busiest day of the week for hairdressers.

Within the established Church in particular, a general softening of manners and attitudes occurred, causing the Welsh traveller Thomas Pennant to remark in his *Tour of Scotland* in 1769 that 'the clergy of *Scotland*, the most decent and consistent in their conduct of any set of men I ever met with of their order, are at present much changed from the furious, illiterate, and enthusiastic teachers of the old times'. The Moderate clergy aggressively advocated toleration, and in 1766 their leader, the historian William Robertson, went so far as to compare the diversity of religious sects and denominations in Scotland to the multiplicity of flowers enhancing the beauty of the natural world. To Calvinist adherents of the seventeenth-century vision of a godly commonwealth, united and covenanted in the service of the Lord, Robertson's outlook was anathema; yet it corresponded to the reality of growing religious diversity during the second half of the eighteenth century. Sectarianism was increasingly relegated to the intolerant past or associated with the narrow outlook of the seceders.

Even the evangelical clergy within the Church of Scotland, who strenuously opposed relief for Roman Catholics and joined the chorus of complaints against the backsliding character of the Moderate majority, became increasingly broad-minded. John Witherspoon's mid-century satire of Robertson and his clerical friends, *Ecclesiastical Characteristics*, mocked the younger Moderates' concern with secular learning and politeness. Yet Witherspoon respected those attributes as long as they were kept within a properly Christian perspective, such as he tried to establish in the colonies after becoming president of the College of New Jersey (Princeton) in 1768. Another leading minister in the Popular party, John Erskine, demonstrated an openness to pious evangelicals of all nations and denominations and in 1793 preached and published an admiring elegy at the funeral of Robertson himself, for many years his colleague at Old Greyfriars Church in Edinburgh.

The change in Scotland's religious climate during the course of the eighteenth century was vital to the nation's transformation. Religious differences which had formerly produced hostility and bloodshed became less confrontational, and were therefore a less destructive force in social, economic, and political life. Under these circumstances, those for whom religious faith remained a matter of intense concern were more likely to channel their energies into socially creative activities. In 1761 the minister preaching the anniversary sermon before the Society in Scotland for Propagating Christian Knowledge explained that true religion 'is a powerful and continual prompter to a good man to be diligent and industrious in that calling to which he hath betaken himself' and 'is so far from interfering with a just and reasonable concern for our temporal interests, for our own wants and necessities, and those of others, that, on the contrary, it teacheth us to consider this as an indispensable duty, and a necessary qualification for our enjoying the love and favour of God'. The life of the industrialist David Dale illustrates this teaching. After some years as a member of the evangelical wing of the established Church, Dale broke from the Kirk and from Presbyterianism generally in the 1760s and eventually became a strict member of the sect later known as the Old Scotch Independents. Business and religion operated as the twin motors of Dale's life, and both as a lay preacher and an industrialist he exemplified the view that making money and serving the Lord were not only equally necessary but intrinsically related to each other. In industrial enterprises like the famous cotton-spinning mill that he co-founded at New Lanark in 1785, capitalist acquisition and public service, motivated and justified by religious belief, often seemed inseparable. Was it the profit motive or Christian philanthropy that lay behind Dale's willingness to import orphans from the Edinburgh workhouse to solve a labour shortage at New Lanark and then to provide his pauper apprentices with secular and religious instruction? Either way, Dale's version of the Calvinist work ethic left no room for religious bickering or persecution of other denominations. There was simply too much work to be done.

From the age of Ilay to the Dundas dynasty

The union of 1707 stipulated that in place of an independent parliament in Edinburgh there would be forty-five Scottish representatives in the House of Commons, and sixteen Scottish peers in the House of Lords, in the new 'Parliament of Great Britain' at Westminster, which looked suspiciously like the old parliament at Westminster, slightly augmented. Judged by modern principles of demographic democracy, the arrangement was patently unfair: Scotland, with a population of about one million, as against about five million in England and Wales, would have well under 10 per cent of the representatives in each house of parliament. But the union had less to do with the attainment of equal representation for all British subjects than with economic and political power, and according to that criterion Scotland was entitled to considerably less representation at Westminster than it actually received.

Numbers do not tell the whole story. Because only sixteen out of more than 150 Scottish peers acquired the right to sit in the House of Lords, the Scottish nobility was immediately relegated to second-class status. English peers sat in the British House of Lords by virtue of their titles alone, but Scots peers were in fact selected by the government; any display of political independence or challenge to the rigged procedure for 'electing' the sixteen peers could result in their exclusion from the political process. In regard to the Commons, where the new arrangement created thirty Scottish constituencies in the shires and half that number in the royal burghs, it is difficult to say whether elections were more corrupt and less representative in the counties or towns. County elections carried the practice of fictitious votes to new heights, while in the burghs bribery of self-propagating town councils, drawn from the towns' merchants and incorporated tradesmen, was a fact of political life. With the exception of Edinburgh, which had its own member of parliament, clusters of royal burghs were made to share representatives whose loyalties were divided, and fast-growing towns that were not royal burghs, such as the western textile centre of Paisley, had no representation at all. In short, Scotland combined archaic elements from its pre-union days, notably an obsolete property qualification that severely restricted the number of legitimate voters, with some of the worst abuses of the unreformed English political system. No one has ever claimed that Scottish electoral politics experienced an 'awakening' in the aftermath of the parliamentary union with England.

For these reasons among others, the union was initially so unpopular that it barely squeaked through its first decade. To many Scots, the nation appeared to have surrendered its national integrity and political independence for an unproven, and unwarranted, dream of economic prosperity. The Articles of Union and an accompanying Act for Security of the Church of Scotland had specified that the established Presbyterian Church and the legal system would remain unaltered in Scotland, in effect providing some assurance of institutional stability despite the loss of the Scottish parliament.

To some degree these assurances had the desired effect. The Scottish courts took over the parliamentary buildings in Edinburgh, and the judges of the court of session (who were expected to assume honorific titles of nobility, such as Lord Kames and Lord Monboddo) assumed a social status that in some respects resembled the French *noblesse de robe* more than their judicial counterparts in England. At the same time, the general assembly of the Church of Scotland, meeting annually in Edinburgh, became the closest thing in Scotland to a national forum for public speaking. Yet the Patronage Act of 1712 demonstrated that English ministers and members of parliament were quite willing to tamper with Scottish church polity in spite of assurances to the contrary, and the rulings of the Scottish court of session were to be subject to appeal, and therefore to possible reversal, by the House of Lords. When parliament abolished the Scottish privy council in 1708, it not only disbanded yet another Scottish institution but brought to the fore a question that has remained problematic since the union: how and by whom would Scotland be governed and administered in a 'united kingdom'? A new export duty on linen in 1711, an increase in the salt tax in 1712, and a particularly hateful new tax on malt in 1713 (revived in 1725, when it set off major urban riots) bred further resentment. The extent of discontent can be gauged by the fact that in 1713 all the Scottish peers supported a motion—narrowly defeated in the House of Lords—to repeal the Act of Union.

Others resorted to extraparliamentary action. The union was immediately greeted with riots in Edinburgh and Glasgow, and the year after it went into effect a French fleet nearly landed an army in Scotland in an attempt to place on the throne the only surviving son of James VII and II. In 1715 a full-fledged Jacobite uprising, led by the earl of Mar, tried to attain the same end and enjoyed some short-lived success, until brought down by a combination of poor leadership and French apathy. Jacobitism drew its support principally from Highland clans and the Episcopalian north-east, but it played upon the pervasive feelings of national discontent that permeated Scottish society for some time after the union. It produced a rich culture of art, music, and political symbolism which centred around vague notions of lost national glory. After it ceased to be a serious threat to the Hanoverian order, that culture was sentimentalized and homogenized as a general expression of Scottish national feeling, most appealingly in Walter Scott's popular novel *Waverley* (1814). Throughout the first half of the eighteenth century, however, Jacobitism was a matter of more than sentimental interest. Mar was able to raise an army of 12,000 men on short notice and with little foreign support, and thirty years later a still more powerful army would rally to the standard of James's 25-year-old grandson Charles Edward Stuart, popularly known as Bonnie Prince Charlie. On that occasion, Jacobite armies commanded brilliantly by Lord George Murray won impressive victories over Hanoverian regulars, occupied Edinburgh, and marched as far south as Derby before retreating to the Highlands and suffering a brutal defeat at the battle of Culloden in April 1746.

Political stability developed slowly in the post-union period. The Hanoverian establishment in Scotland had its most enthusiastic backing in larger towns and Presbyterian strongholds, especially in the west and south-west. It also enjoyed the wholehearted support of the largest and most powerful of the Highland clans, the Campbells of Argyll. It was the military-minded second duke of Argyll who outmanoeuvred Mar's Jacobite army and defeated it decisively at Sheriffmuir near Dunblane in 1715. Yet it was the second duke's younger brother Archibald—who obtained the ducal succession in 1743 but is best known by a lesser title, earl of Ilay—who did the most to build up his family's political interest and to erect a stable, if not always admirable, system of Scottish political administration. For nearly forty years, from the mid-1720s until his death in 1761, Ilay was the leading dispenser of the relatively few choice plums that grew in Scottish soil. His authority derived from a unique combination of factors, including his enormous Highland power-base and the wealth (and soldiers for the British army) that it generated, his family's demonstrated Hanoverian loyalty, his thoroughly political nature, his cosmopolitan education (at Eton, the University of Glasgow, and Utrecht) and considerable learning in the arts and sciences and the law, and his close friendship with early eighteenth-century Britain's dominant prime minister, Sir Robert Walpole. The only non-Jacobite challengers to the Argathelian interest, the Squadrone faction, enjoyed none of these gifts to the degree Ilay did, and their one brief flirtation with political power, in the period following Walpole's fall in 1742, had the misfortune to coincide with the largest Jacobite uprising. Throughout the second quarter of the century, the close association of the Argathelian interest with the government served to encourage Jacobite sentiments among rival Highland clans who resented the growing power of Clan Campbell.

Scotland in the age of Ilay was not so much governed as managed. That is, political authority derived less from a formal system of accountable political officials and institutions than from an informal network of patronage dispensation. The key to the system was the indifference of English ministers: so

THE HIGHLAND MILI-
TARY TRADITION.
Lord George Murray is
generally credited with
masterminding the early
victories of the Jacobite
army during the 1745
uprising. He advised
against engaging the
Duke of Cumberland's
forces at Culloden Moor
in April 1746 but was
overruled by his young
sovereign, Charles
Edward Stuart, whose
poor judgement brought
his cause to an abrupt
end.

long as Scotland stayed quiet, produced loyal votes in parliament, and contributed manpower to the army, what else happened there was of little interest. Exceptions to this pattern, such as the interventionist ministry of the
duke of Newcastle in the 1750s, usually had less to do with concern for managing Scottish affairs than with preventing Ilay from doing so. Ilay's genius lay
in keeping himself well informed about the political views and abilities of
large numbers of Scottish candidates for the various legal, medical, ecclesiastical, and political offices available, and in skilfully manipulating the appointments in his care in order to achieve his political ends while at the same time
rewarding merit to a substantial degree.

From his primary residence in London, Ilay carried on his Scottish business through a vast correspondence (some of it coded) with his Edinburgh
'sous-ministre' Andrew Fletcher, whom he had raised to the bench as Lord
Milton in 1724. Milton, in turn, employed a network of Argathelian agents to

INVERARY IMPROVEMENTS. Archibald Campbell, earl of Ilay and third duke of Argyll, rebuilt Inverary Castle and founded Inverary New Town, a pioneering effort in town planning that was largely implemented by the architect Robert Mylne during the era of the fifth duke. Both appear in this picturesque early nineteenth-century print showing views of Loch Fyne from the north.

manage local town councils, the Church, and other Scottish institutions. At its best, the system stimulated various kinds of social and economic improvement, rewarded deserving individuals when politically possible, encouraged political and religious moderation, and maintained political order and stability. Thus, serious, patriotic efforts were made to bolster the linen and fishing industries and to support improvement-minded local magistrates, such as six-times Edinburgh lord provost George Drummond; Scotland's most desirable academic and judicial appointments went increasingly to men of the highest calibre; the process of softening the manners and moderating the tenets of the Presbyterian clergy was accelerated; and a conciliatory attitude was adopted within Scotland towards those who had taken up arms in the Jacobite risings. At its worst, on the other hand, the system functioned as a form of institutionalized corruption, in which interest and influence mattered more than principle. Milton's own promotions to a judgeship on the court of session, and subsequently to lord justice clerk, solely because of his political usefulness to Ilay, constitute an obvious example. So does the fact that Drummond's improving schemes generally took a back seat to his role as the Argathelian interest's chief political agent on the Edinburgh town council. The system was particularly corrupt in regard to the Church of Scotland, which Ilay treated less as a fellowship of believers than as a political body, to be managed and manipulated for the sake of order and interest.

Each autumn during his ducal tenure, Ilay travelled to his Highland estate at Inverary in order to shore up his political interest in Scotland. Two of his local projects say much about the man and his age. Almost immediately after obtaining the dukedom, Ilay began building a new town on his own land at Inverary, the first of many such planned communities in Scotland and one still worth visiting for the insight it provides into eighteenth-century conceptions of the rational utilization of small-scale urban space. Although relatively little work was completed during Ilay's lifetime, the new town took shape during the 1770s and 1780s, under the architectural direction of Robert Mylne and the patronage of the fifth duke. More grandly, Ilay rebuilt the family residence as a storybook castle, translating his role as a Highland chief into a Gothic fairy tale. Once the fortresses of a warlike people, Scottish castles could now be recast in stone to fulfil Georgian fantasies of grandeur and elegance, much as Robert Adam, who had worked briefly on Inverary Castle with his older brother John, would later do with majestic Culzean Castle on the Ayrshire coast.

After Ilay's death, the management of Scotland fell to his nephew, the third earl of Bute, who assigned the job to his own brother, James Stuart Mackenzie, retaining Lord Milton as Edinburgh *sous-ministre*. Like his uncle, Bute had been raised mainly in England and educated at Eton and in Holland, and in dispensing patronage he too tried to balance a genuine concern for merit (particularly noticeable in some of the academic appointments he made or approved during the early 1760s) with the advancement of his political interest. Although he lived some years on the island in the Firth of Clyde that bears the name of his title, Bute was more of a stranger to mainland Scotland than Ilay. More importantly, he lacked Ilay's political savvy, and his conspicuous role as the favourite of the prince of Wales, who ascended to the throne in 1760 as George III, made him the target of virulent anti-Scottish feeling in England. That feeling ran deep, as young James Boswell discovered in 1762 when two Highland officers who entered Covent Garden Theatre were pelted with apples amid the cry of 'No Scots! No Scots! Out with them!' A host of Englishmen, among them Horace Walpole, John Wilkes, Charles Churchill, and Samuel Johnson, charged that the Scots were clannish, chauvinistic, and overly acquisitive, and every instance of Scottish patronage or of bad conduct by an individual Scot was cited as additional supporting evidence for their ethnic prejudice. In reality, widespread English antipathy towards Scotland during the 1760s was a function of the union's belated success, or rather of the inability of some Englishmen to accept the idea of a political association that enabled Scots to participate fully in the economic, cultural, and political life of a truly united kingdom—blemishes and all. We are apt to forget that the union necessitated a psychological adjustment on the part of England no less than Scotland.

With the fall of Bute and his brother, Scotland entered a period of unstable political leadership, lasting from 1765 to 1780. The situation was largely the result of ministerial instability at Westminster, along with the lack of any figure in Scottish public life with the right combination of influence, skill, and charisma to take advantage of the existing political vacuum. When such a figure finally appeared, he came from an unlikely quarter. Rather than a high-born peer like Ilay or Bute, Henry Dundas was an Edinburgh advocate from a respectable family of East Lothian judges and politicians. His rise to political power began with his appointments as solicitor general in 1766 and lord advocate in 1775, but those offices alone do not account for his unprecedented ascent. Working closely with the third duke of Buccleuch, who provided the necessary funding and status, Dundas built an interest that gained control of Edinburgh and other Scottish localities. His stranglehold over Scottish affairs from 1780 to 1806 derived not only from that power-base but also from his close friendship with the younger William Pitt and his usefulness to that powerful prime minister as a parliamentary debater and manager both of Scotland's parliamentary constituencies and of the government's India interest.

Dundas had his share of ups and downs, ranging from his reincarnation as Viscount Melville in 1802 to his impeachment in 1805 for irregularities concerning funds earmarked for the navy (he was acquitted). By and large, however, 'King Harry' had little competition for control of Scottish patronage. With nephew Robert on the scene as his Edinburgh manager, Scottish positions in parliament, the Church, the courts, the universities, and all commissions and boards were usually his for the picking. The 'Dundas despotism' naturally bred resentment, much of it justified. The regime was at its harshest during the era of the French Revolution, when a small radical movement in Scotland was brutally suppressed. On the other hand, Dundas often used his vast powers in the service of what might be called the Scottish national interest, by enabling large numbers of Scots to reap the rewards of empire, for example; and on certain issues, such as Roman Catholic relief, he was progressive. For these reasons among others, it has recently been argued that he deserves more respect as a national leader than he has traditionally received.

Some of the similarities and contrasts between eighteenth-century Scotland's two greatest political managers can be gleaned from a comparison of Allan Ramsay's portrait of Ilay in 1758 with Sir Henry Raeburn's early nineteenth-century portrait of Dundas—a comparison which also shows off the skills of two of the eighteenth century's greatest portrait painters, both Scots. Ilay is captured in a seated position, perhaps to hide his diminutive size. Dundas, however, was a giant of a man, and his immense stature and commanding presence are powerfully communicated in Raeburn's representation. Both men are pictured in formal attire, including wigs and robes. Ilay is dressed in the scarlet robes of the lord justice general of Scotland, and his appearance is that of an eminent legal lord consulting a learned tome. Dundas, wearing the robes of a viscount over a business suit, appears to be a man of business and affairs; from his picture, one would not be surprised to learn that he was wholly educated in Edinburgh and spoke English with a strong, unaffected Scottish accent rather than in the well-cultivated Eton accent of Ilay. Yet for all their differences, Ilay and Dundas both strike the viewer of their portraits as intelligent, well-informed, imposing men who were not to be trifled with, and it was ultimately this similarity that mattered most. Whatever their shortcomings, both men were unquestionably master politicians who employed skilful management to solidify the system of Scottish 'semi-independence' that prevailed in their day.

The improving spirit

'Improvement' permeated Scotland during the second half of the eighteenth century, affecting country folk and townspeople alike. In the countryside, the common problems of poor, rural countries with traditional farming methods were frequently exacerbated by a difficult climate and inhospitable terrain. Throughout much of the country, a system of cooperative strip farming, called runrig, practised by a group of families who constituted a 'ferm toun', ensured that innovation would be kept to a minimum. Cultivation patterns were characterized by the standard problems besetting pre-industrial nations in Europe: too little fodder for extensive animal husbandry, too little manure

SCOTLAND'S POLITICAL BOSSES. The third duke of Argyll (*above*) was the chief of Clan Campbell and the most powerful political figure in Scotland in the decades preceding his death in 1761. He is shown here at age seventy-five, in a painting by Allan Ramsay that was commissioned for the duke's nephew, the third earl of Bute. Henry Dundas, Viscount Melville (*right*), aged sixty in this portrait by Sir Henry Raeburn, managed Scotland so absolutely during the last quarter of the eighteenth century and opening years of the nineteenth century that he was popularly known as King Harry the 9th.

for extensive fertilizing of fields, rudimentary ploughs and other agricultural equipment, inability or unwillingness of landlords and farmers to deviate from time-honoured traditions—hence small yields, little if any surplus to generate capital, and the necessity of leaving fields fallow for long periods to replenish themselves. The Scottish variation on this traditional pattern was the division of each farm into a constantly cultivated 'infield' adjacent to the farmhouse, comprising only about 20 per cent of the arable land but receiving almost all the available dung, and a surrounding 'outfield' where most of

the land at any given time was not cultivated. Oats and barley were the staples, with inferior strains (black oats and bere) often used because they fared better under adverse conditions.

Although the traditional system of Scottish agriculture did not disappear overnight, the spirit of improvement rapidly gained ground. Especially in regions with hard, rocky soil, the food supply was increased by the durable potato. Elsewhere more comprehensive methods were promoted. Agricultural improvement societies, such as Edinburgh's pioneering The Honourable the Society of Improvers (1723–45), focused attention on the problem of rational farming methods. Enlightened landowners such as Lord Kames set the example on their own estates, and a new industry of agricultural improvement literature sprang up. The title of one book from the mid-1770s, written by Kames himself, reveals the agenda: *The Gentleman Farmer: Being an Attempt to Improve Agriculture, by Subjecting It to the Test of Rational Principles*. 'Rational principles' dictated the use of modern equipment, such as a new plough developed by James Small in the 1760s, and modern patterns of crop rotation, such as a Scottish version of the Norfolk System (turnips, barley, clover, oats), which not only put more land under the plough by replenishing the soil but also provided more fodder for animals and, therefore, more fertilizer for the land. Abolition of runrig, ferm touns, and the infield–outfield system of cultivation was also part of the process, as were larger, enclosed farms with longer leases, granted to tenants willing to embrace innovation. Topics covered in the various chapters of Kames's book set out the main themes: using new farm implements, rotating crops, planting trees, building fences, fertilizing. The appendix, entitled 'Imperfection of Scotch Husbandry', defined the problem to be solved, and in Scotland's most fortunate and progressive regions, the challenge was fully accepted. In Ayrshire, for example, new farming techniques made it possible to sustain a better breed of dairy cattle fed on a combination of grass and fodder crops (hay, oats, and turnips), and by the early 1790s improvements from enclosures and subdivisions, crop rotations, and the application of lime were so well advanced that the minister of the little parish of Kirkoswald called it 'a total and happy revolution'.

Of course, the revolution was not happy for everyone. Agricultural modernization was disastrous for many small farmers and landless labourers who experienced dislocation, and in the Highlands it was rarely compatible with the traditional clan structure. The clan system was weakened by a variety of factors, including the steady decline of Gaelic, the unsuccessful Jacobite uprisings, and government attempts to break up Highland culture in the aftermath of the Forty-Five by abolishing heritable jurisdictions and military land tenures and by forbidding Highland dress to be worn and bagpipes to be played. Ultimately, however, the adoption of commercial practices by the Highland chiefs did the most damage by undercutting the traditional economy, squeezing out the intermediary tacksmen who held the system together, reducing the labour force required for certain kinds of economic activity (notably sheep-farming), and replacing the traditional concept of heritage as a paternalistic trusteeship (*duthchas*) with an impersonal, legalist concept of heritage as ownership without social obligation (*oighreachd*).

By the last third of the eighteenth century, both seasonal and permanent varieties of migration from the Highlands to the Lowlands were commonplace, giving rise to the new phenomenon of 'urban Highlanders', who carried aspects of Gaelic culture to Lowland towns. Emigration to North America by Lowlanders and Highlanders alike was so widespread that contemporaries worried about depopulation. Yet the population of Scotland continued to rise dramatically—from 1 million people in 1700 to 1.25 million in 1750 to 1.6 million in 1800—and for all its problems, the Highlands shared in the general trend. One Lowlander touring Scotland in the 1790s, Robert Heron, argued that complaints about Highland depopulation as a result of incursions by new economic practices such as sheep-farming were 'unreasonable', not only because they were exaggerated but also because 'by those modes of managing the lands, which are complained of as depopulating, maintenance is obtained from them for a much greater number of mankind, than they could before maintain'. In the long run, Heron reasoned, the most commercially viable mode of subsistence would be the most desirable. Most economists would agree, although such calculations do not take into account the amount of human suffering entailed by the dissolution of a traditional social and economic system.

More significant than the sheer quantity of demographic growth was the pattern of distribution. Using the number of people living in towns of 10,000 or more as a standard, late eighteenth-century Scotland appears to have been urbanizing at a faster rate than almost any place in Europe. By 1800 more than 17 per cent of the Scottish population lived in towns of at least 10,000; only the Low Countries and England had higher percentages of their populations living in towns of that size, even though Scotland had only seven such towns (in demographic order: Glasgow, Edinburgh, Paisley, Aberdeen, Dundee, Greenock, and Perth) as against forty-four in England. Urbanization was accompanied by a related demographic development: an increasing percentage of the people living in the central Lowland belt that includes Edinburgh and Glasgow. Comprising less than 15 per cent of the land in Scotland, the Central Lowlands already contained nearly 40 per cent of the population by mid-century, and that proportion would continue to rise in subsequent decades and centuries.

Urbanization and demographic concentration in the central Lowlands both stimulated and benefited from economic growth, which was consider-

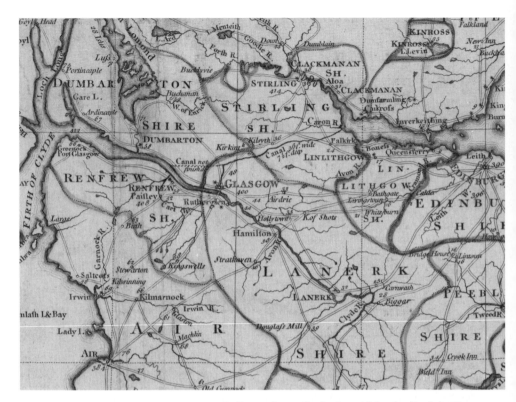

A REVOLUTION IN COMMERCE. In September 1782 the Scottish bookseller John Knox of London published A Commercial Map of Scotland to advocate the formation of a 'Commercial Parliament' that would promote Scottish trade and manufacturing. This section of the map shows the central belt from Glasgow's port cities of Greenock and Port Glasgow on the Firth of Clyde to Edinburgh's port city of Leith on the Firth of Forth, including the new canal network that linked east and west.

able, sometimes spectacular, during the second half of the century. The most remarkable case was Glasgow, which expanded in less than a hundred years from the cosy little commercial town that Daniel Defoe visited during the 1720s into a sprawling industrial city of over 80,000 inhabitants in 1800 and nearly twice that number two decades later. The tobacco trade with America led the way between the 1740s and the mid-1770s, infusing the city with large amounts of capital and spawning a new species of wealthy merchants, the 'tobacco lords'. Although the War of American Independence ended Glasgow's tobacco era, the city recovered splendidly after the war by redirecting its economic energy into other sectors of the economy, cotton manufacturing above all. In 1783 Glasgow founded the first Chamber of Commerce to promote its economic life, and John Mayne observed in *Glasgow. A Poem*:

In ilka house, frae man to boy,
A' hands in GLASGOW find employ.

'A' hands' also included women and girls, whose absorption into the formal labour market was crucial.

Of several reasons that may be cited to explain Glasgow's boom in industrial employment, perhaps the most important was the regional, interactive character of the economy. Glasgow itself was not an Atlantic port, but it had access (further improved after the River Clyde was dredged and widened) to excellent deep-water ports at Greenock and Port Glasgow. With the opening of a portion of the Forth and Clyde Canal in the 1770s, followed after a delay of some years by completion of the entire project in 1790, products moved relatively easily and cheaply from one side of the country to the other. The Monkland Canal, also completed in 1790, improved Glasgow's supply of cheap coal from Lanarkshire. Large-scale industrial sites were frequently situated in rural areas within the broader industrial region: the famed Carron

INDUSTRIAL COMMUNITIES IN THE COUNTRYSIDE. Large-scale manufacturing began in rural settings, particularly where fast-flowing water was available to drive the mill machinery. The cotton-spinning complex at New Lanark (shown here as engraved by Robert Scott in 1799), founded in 1785 by David Dale and John Arkwright, was typical of this trend, although the scale of operations and the experimental social policies initiated by Dale, and expanded by his famous son-in-law, Robert Owen, were unique at the time.

Iron Works, for example, was founded in 1759 scarcely 20 miles to the east of Glasgow, near the Forth and Clyde Canal, and the large cotton-spinning complex that was built at New Lanark to take advantage of the power generated by the Falls of Clyde was the same distance to the south-east. To the west and south-west, in Renfrewshire and Ayrshire, the textile industries flourished in towns such as Paisley, Ayr, and Kilmarnock. Glasgow merchants and industrialists were at the hub of all these operations, importing raw cotton, overseeing and coordinating the various stages of production, raising capital for investment, developing industrial processes such as bleaching and calico printing, and exporting finished products.

The career of James Watt illustrates the strengths and weaknesses of the early Industrial Revolution in the Glasgow region. A mathematical instrument-maker from Greenock, Watt gravitated to the University of Glasgow during its heyday. There he participated in the cultivation of applied science which was one of the distinguishing features of the Glasgow Enlightenment, associating with natural philosophers and chemists such as John Anderson, Joseph Black, and John Robison. He moved easily between the roles of 'mechanick' and man of science, and employed both kinds of knowledge to devise his famous solution to the problem of energy waste in Newcomen's atmospheric engine: the separate condenser. What is usually forgotten is the fact that Watt needed a dozen years, from 1764 to 1776, to translate that idea into a successful production model, built in Birmingham with capital provided by his second English partner, Matthew Boulton, and a cylinder bored by John Wilkinson. For all but two of those difficult years, Watt continued to live in the west of Scotland, supporting himself chiefly by working as a land surveyor and engineer on the Monkland Canal, the harbour at Port Glasgow, and other regional projects. He was typical of the early Industrial Revolution in Glasgow in his wide range of technological expertise and his smooth integration of academic science and mechanical technology, and his Scottish career also demonstrates the high degree of geographical, technical, and economic interaction that characterized the greater Glasgow region at this time. But Scotland could provide neither the substantial working capital and acute entrepreneurial and political skill that Boulton brought to their partnership nor the technical expertise needed to bore a cylinder with sufficient precision—the iron workers at Carron being incapable of doing so. These shortcomings determined that the double-acting, self-regulating, machine-driving steam engine developed by Watt and Boulton during the late 1770s and 1780s would be a British rather than a purely Scottish innovation.

As Glasgow became wealthier and more populous, it expanded ever westward: dozens of new streets were constructed in a gridlike pattern during the late eighteenth and early nineteenth centuries. Rival Edinburgh had a more difficult time of it, for until the coming of the New Town a much larger population (almost twice that of Glasgow at mid-century, though roughly the same by 1800) was crammed into a small, often dilapidated physical space. The old town stank and smoked, earning the affectionate nickname 'Auld Reekie' on account of the latter trait, and its distinctive multi-storey tenements or 'lands', built along the High Street and in a maze of closes and wynds running off it, made it one of the most congested towns in Europe. Yet old Edinburgh had its charm. If it lacked Glasgow's commercial ethos and industrial development, it had as fine a university as Glasgow's (buildings aside) and was still the undisputed legal, administrative, ecclesiastical, medical, and financial capital of Scotland. It also boasted a richer cultural life than Glasgow, with more bookshops, more theatrical productions (though technically illegal until the 1760s), regular dancing assemblies, enticing oyster cellars, a fencing and riding academy, a botanical garden that an English visitor in 1775 pronounced 'one of the best in Europe', and a thriving musical society. In 1784 the English dissenter Samuel Rose rejoiced at having been educated at Glasgow rather than Edinburgh because he had encountered none of the 'many Amusements, and avocations from Business' which made it difficult for an Edinburgh student to perform 'his college-Business without stumbling'. The stereotypical distinction between mercantile, industrial Glasgow and professional, cultural Edinburgh was a product of the eighteenth century.

By the middle of the century prominent Edinburgh citizens were insisting upon a programme for 'enlarging, beautifying, and improving the capital', as Lord Minto of the court of session put it in an influential pamphlet of 1752. The first reaction was to erect more imposing buildings in the old city, such as the royal exchange that was completed in 1760 though never used for the commercial purpose intended (it eventually became the city chambers). A more ambitious response was the construction of the New Town, a neoclassical project of large straight streets and crescents, squares and handsome stone residences that would be linked to the Old Town by bridges. From the outset the New Town was an exercise in gentrification. In Minto's pamphlet, urban improvement was meant to enable Edinburgh to compete with country estates and the 'superior pleasures of LONDON' in the eyes of highborn Scots who were put off by the squalor and crowded quarters of the

EDINBURGH FROM CALTON HILL. This image of Edinburgh in 1789 by Robert Barker shows the Old Town at the left and the emerging New Town at the top right, linked by the handsome new North Bridge. Robert Adam's Register House, with its distinctive dome, sits along Princes Street, on the New Town side of the bridge.

Old Town, and the same parliamentary Act of 1767 which authorized the extension of the royalty 'over certain adjoining lands' permitted the construction of a theatre there. New Town living was strictly for the cultured élite.

The New Town provided rich opportunities for Scottish architects, such as James Craig, who submitted the winning (though eventually somewhat modified) plan in response to a civic competition. New Town projects lured Robert Adam, Scotland's greatest architect, back to Scotland after a career spent mainly in England. In 1774 work began at the eastern end of Princes Street on Adam's design for a repository of Scottish public records, Register House, a brilliant example of patriotic, public architecture in the neoclassical style. Yet the fact that neither Register House nor the new university buildings that Adam designed at South Bridge were completed until well after the architect's death in 1792 demonstrates the financial strain imposed by Edinburgh's massive public building project of the late eighteenth century. A year before his death, Adam designed Charlotte Square, often considered the epitome of New Town elegance, although it too underwent modification and delay before construction was complete.

The sense of improvement experienced by Edinburgh residents during the second half of the eighteenth century was vividly conveyed in a short work that William Creech originally published in 1783 and reissued in revised form ten years later with the significant title *Letters, Addressed to Sir John Sinclair, Bart. Respecting the Mode of Living, Arts, Commerce, Literature, Manners, etc. of Edinburgh, in 1763, and since that Period. Illustrating the Statistical Progress of the Capital of Scotland*. Creech, a wealthy bookseller who would become Edinburgh's lord provost in 1811, particularly wanted to show off the city's rapid development over the twenty-year period following the conclusion of the Seven Years War. Beginning with the building of the New Town, he proceeded to present detailed evidence to support his thesis. In 1763, he noted, Edinburgh had only one stagecoach to London every month, and the journey took twelve to sixteen days; in 1783 there were sixty trips a month, each just four days long. In 1763 Edinburgh had six printing houses, and three paper mills in the vicinity, manufacturing 6,400 reams; in 1783 there were sixteen printing houses and twelve paper mills, manufacturing 100,000 reams. In 1763 there were no hotels in Edinburgh ('the word indeed was not known'); twenty years later 'a stranger might have been accommodated, not only comfortably, but most elegantly, at many public Hotels'. And so on. 'So remarkable a change is not perhaps to be equalled, in so short a period, in any city of Europe', Creech boasted; 'nor in the same city for two centuries, taking all the alterations together. When the plans at present in contemplation are completed, Edinburgh will be the most beautiful and picturesque city in the world.'

Edinburgh's growth was certainly impressive, but was it all for the better? Creech had his doubts. Contrasting 'the decency, dignity, and delicacy' of manners in 1763 with the 'looseness, dissipation, and licentiousness' that he believed was prevalent twenty years later, he remarked that 'many people ceased to blush at what would formerly have been reckoned a crime'. He claimed a 'twenty fold' increase in brothels, a 'hundred fold' increase in 'women of the town', and a large increase in various kinds of theft, necessitating the locking of doors at night. He worried that female infidelity had ceased to be a permanent mark on a woman's social standing, and that 'separations and divorces were become frequent, and have since increased'. He expressed displeasure that frivolous activities and immoral diversions, such as cockfighting, had recently become commonplace, and that the meaning and connotations of certain terms had been altered in disturbing ways. In 1763, he explained, a 'fine fellow' was a well-informed, accomplished individual with elegant manners and principled conduct; in 1783 the same term signified a slave to fashion who could 'drink three bottles', avoided paying his debts, 'swore immoderately, and before ladies', 'ridiculed religion and morality as folly and hypocrisy', and 'disregarded the interests of society, or the good of mankind, if they interfered with his own vicious selfish pursuits and pleasures'. In short, the growth of Edinburgh revealed the ambivalence of 'statistical progress'. 'Improvement' did not come cheap, and Creech wondered if the price of modernity were not too high—a central concern of the intellectual and cultural phenomenon known as the Scottish Enlightenment.

The Scottish Enlightenment

When David Hume boasted in 1757 that the Scots had become 'the People most distinguish'd for Literature in Europe', he exaggerated to make a point: Scotland's literary reputation was increasing significantly. Within a few years, Europeans were publicly acknowledging that tiny Scotland was now a major force in the republic of letters. Writing in Italian in 1763, Carlo Denina credited Francis Hutcheson, the Irish-born Glasgow University professor of moral philosophy from 1730 until his death in 1746, with having 'diffused through the whole country, by his lectures and discourses, as well as by his excellent printed works, a lively taste for the studies of philosophy and learning'. By the end of the century the catalogue of internationally known Scottish men of literature and learning who had flourished in their various fields during the intervening decades was formidable: Hume himself, Adam Smith, Adam Ferguson, Lord Kames, Lord Monboddo, David Fordyce, Thomas Reid, Dugald Stewart, John Millar, Robert Wallace, and Sir James Steuart in philosophy, political economy, and social and legal thought; Hume, Ferguson, Millar, William Robertson, Tobias Smollett, Gilbert Stuart, and Robert Henry in history; William Cullen, Joseph Black, James Ferguson, John Gregory, James Hutton, Alexander Monro, and William Buchan in science and medicine; Kames, Hugh Blair, Alexander Gerard, George Campbell, James Beattie, and Archibald Alison in literary criticism and aesthetics; Blair and James Fordyce in sermonizing; Smollett, Henry Mackenzie, and John Moore in prose fiction; Beattie, Robert Burns, John Home, and James Macpherson in poetry and drama; James Boswell in literary biography; Smollett, Moore, and Boswell in travel literature—to name only a few. The works of these and other Scottish authors were frequently reprinted in Britain and abroad and often translated into other European languages, and they included quite a

THE URBAN LANDSCAPE is conveyed in J. Q. Pringle's portrayal of Bridgeton, the working-class area in Glasgow's East End, one of the few paintings by a nineteenth-century Scottish artist of a city.

THE INTER-WAR PERIOD witnessed a revival of Scottish culture which has become more appreciated by Scottish society today than it was at the time. In the centre of Alexander Moffat's painting, *The Poets' Pub*, is Hugh MacDiarmid, widely regarded as the finest Scottish poet of the twentieth century.

Facing, above: LORD FORTROSE (with his back to the viewer) hosts a gilded musical party at his Neapolitan apartment in 1770: on the violin is the Scots-born Sir William Hamilton; on the keyboards are Leopold Mozart and his fourteen-year-old son, Wolfgang Amadeus.

Facing, below: VOYAGE OF SCOTA AND GATHELUS. The Greek Prince Gathelus and his Egyptian spouse Scota, key figures in the Scottish origin myth, are shown sailing to the West in a mid-fifteenth-century manuscript of Walter Bower's *Scotichronicon*.

nu voir dire et a
parler par rayso
les anglois estoient
plus foulles et pꝛy
trauaillies que ne furet les
escochois car ilz estoient œ io²
venus iusques la du neuf
chastean sur thyn ou bien y
avoit sieues antresches chau
dement et secretement po²
trouuer les escochois ainsy œe
ilz furent. Dont le plus pouꝛe
se trauail du chemyn quoy
que sa voulente y fust bonne

et grande seur affection hoꝛs
estoient de seur alame et les
escochois estoient fres; non
ueaulx et reposes et tout ce se²
uault grandement et bui se
moustrerent au plus fort de
la besoingne Car sur celle
darreniere empainte sicome
cy dessus est contenu ilz recusse
rent les anglois tellement
que depuis ilz ne peurent re
culler sur leur premier pas
et passerent ses batailles tout
oultre ce conte de dougras qui

THE SCOTTISH VICTORY over English forces at the Battle of Otterburn (1388) was commemorated in great detail by the chronicler Jean Froissart. The triumph was marred by the death of the Scottish commander, James, 2nd earl of Douglas. Nevertheless, like the even more famous and crucial Battle of Bannockburn, a Scottish defeat of an English army was a matter of high morale and pride.

few of the most popular books of the age, such as Blair's *Sermons*, Hume's *History of England*, and Robertson's histories of Scotland, Charles V, and America. Behind these well-known figures stood dozens of other men of letters whose fame was less extensive, sometimes because their greatest strength lay in teaching rather than in writing for publication.

Still others distinguished themselves for their accomplishments in the arts, such as Allan Ramsay and Sir Henry Raeburn in portrait painting, David Allan in genre painting, and Robert, James, and John Adam and Robert Mylne in architecture. The brothers Robert and Andrew Foulis became famous all over Europe for their handsome editions of the Greek and Roman classics—books as works of art—and from the mid-1750s to the mid-1770s supplemented their printing with a fine arts academy in Glasgow to train painters, engravers, and other artists. The *Encyclopaedia Britannica*, which first appeared in Edinburgh in 1768–71 and passed through three increasingly popular editions before the end of the century, featured scientific and technical engravings by the co-publisher, Andrew Bell, who also provided the engravings for a nine-volume translation of Buffon's *Natural History* by William Smellie, the original printer and editor of the *Britannica*.

Accounting for this explosion of Scottish intellectual and cultural activity is not easy. Religious, political, economic, and social factors discussed earlier in this chapter all contributed. Religious pluralism, toleration, and control of the Kirk by the Moderate party created an environment conducive to free enquiry and secular culture. Theatre, for example, was widely condemned as immoral by orthodox Calvinists during the days of the elder Allan Ramsay, author of the Scots 'pastoral comedy' *The Gentle Shepherd* (1725), and an Edinburgh production of John Home's tragedy of *Douglas* stirred up a similar controversy in 1756–7 because the author was a Presbyterian clergyman. By 1784, however, the general assembly could not conduct important business on the days that the renowned Mrs Siddons was performing in *Douglas* because so many of the lay and clerical members of the assembly were at the playhouse.

Enlightened patronage by Scotland's political managers ensured that many talented Scots obtained appropriate positions in Scotland's leading academic, legal, ecclesiastical, and medical institutions. A particularly important example was the Edinburgh town council's election of William Robertson as principal of the 'tounis college' in 1762 on the express orders of Lord Bute, transmitted via Lord Milton and George Drummond. Robertson then used his academic office to guide the University of Edinburgh into its greatest

La. Ran. Eternal providence ! What is thy name ?
My name is Norval : and my name he bears.

Douglas

'DOUGLAS' ON THE EDINBURGH STAGE. The tragedy of *Douglas*, by John Home, a Church of Scotland clergyman who became Lord Bute's personal secretary, was a national triumph when first produced in Edinburgh in December 1756, and its fame grew after David Garrick produced it in London the following March. In May 1784 Sarah Siddons performed the sentimental role of Lady Randolph before sobbing, sold-out audiences in Edinburgh, an event captured by the contemporary Edinburgh caricaturist John Kay.

period as well as to strengthen his position as leader of the Moderate party in the Church. Most of the other leading lights of the Scottish Enlightenment were also members of the liberal professions who occupied positions within the Scottish institutional establishment, especially the universities. Few did not owe a position or a pension to Ilay, Bute, or Dundas. In a country as poor as Scotland, learning proved to be one of the few paths to security and success.

Learning could also be a path to prosperity, even wealth. As Adam Smith understood, because professors in the Scottish universities were usually paid fees by their students, in addition to a fixed salary, they had incentives for exerting themselves in the classroom far beyond those of their lacklustre counterparts at Oxford and Cambridge. Exceptionally popular classes, such as the ones taught at the University of Edinburgh by Alexander Monro in anatomy and Dugald Stewart in moral philosophy, could earn professors hundreds of additional pounds each term. The effect was to raise the standard of competition for Scottish chairs and to guard against the English tendency to treat professorships as sinecures.

Another form of financial incentive came from the book trade. In 1783 William Creech observed that 'the value of literary property was carried higher by the Scots than ever was known among any people'. William Robertson was then receiving thousands of pounds for his historical works (equivalent to hundreds of thousands today), and Blair's *Sermons* had not only 'obtained the highest price that ever was given for any work of the kind' but also secured their author a pension worth £200 per annum, through the intervention of Henry Dundas. Although Creech himself was among the booksellers responsible for the enormous rise in the value of literary property, the key players were his associates in London, the printer William Strahan (born Strachan in Edinburgh) and the bookseller Thomas Cadell. Both had been schooled in the publishing craft by Andrew Millar, the London-based Scot who stimulated his countrymen to take up their pens by paying them well for it and by collaborating with Edinburgh booksellers in the production of new work by Scottish authors. In 1759, for example, Millar co-published with Kincaid & Bell of Edinburgh the first book written by Adam Smith, the *Theory of Moral Sentiments*, and in 1776 Millar's successor Cadell co-published with Strahan Smith's second work, the *Wealth of Nations*, in association with Kincaid's successor in Edinburgh, Creech. The book soon became a best-seller and earned its author at least £1,500 in just fourteen years.

The Scottish Enlightenment benefited from and encouraged the prevalent spirit of agricultural and economic improvement. The development of political economy among the Scots, culminating in the *Wealth of Nations*, was rooted in their concern with the workings of the Scottish economy, just as Kames's *Gentleman Farmer*, which also bore a 1776 imprint, reflected a passion for agrarian improvement. The flowering of the Scottish Enlightenment occurred chiefly within the growing economies of Scotland's three largest cities—Edinburgh, Glasgow, and Aberdeen—whose universities attracted students from all over Britain and abroad. Politicians were well aware that students constituted a boon to local economies, estimated by Robert Heron to be of the order of £30,000 per academic term for Edinburgh in the 1790s. Decisions about the construction of new academic lecture halls and buildings, or the creation of new chairs and the filling of old ones, were increasingly made with an eye for enhancing a college's academic reputation and for attracting more students. Once again, financial incentives stimulated the quality of intellectual and cultural life.

The presence of the court of session, the Royal College of Physicians, the Advocates' Library, and other prominent institutions gave Edinburgh a particularly distinguished air during the eighteenth century. Yet Edinburgh remained manageable in size, without the impersonal character of London and Paris. To James Boswell, a Londoner by inclination, that very trait made the environment of Edinburgh appear stifling and dull, but most of the 'literati', as they were sometimes called, felt differently. 'In London, Paris and all other great cities of Europe, though they contain many literary men, the access to them is difficult; and even after that is obtained, the conversation, for some time, is shy and constrained,' said William Smellie. 'In Edinburgh, the access to men of parts is not only easy, but their conversation and the communication of their knowledge are at once imparted to intelligent strangers with the utmost liberality.' The lively depiction of Edinburgh's intellectual life in Smollett's 1771 novel *Humphry Clinker* conveys the same impression, climaxing in its famous assertion that 'Edinburgh is a hot-bed of genius'.

Because of the manageable scale of urban life, Scottish men of letters could easily associate with each other on a regular basis, particularly in the many clubs and societies that flourished in the larger towns. Intellectual or academic clubs, such as the Glasgow Literary Society and the Aberdeen Philosophical Society (or Wise Club), mixed conviviality with serious scholarly purpose: members read and discussed original discourses, which often developed into major treatises. In Edinburgh, intellectual clubs were more varied: the Select Society and the student-run Speculative Society were debating bodies; the Edinburgh Philosophical Society, which evolved into the Royal Society of Edinburgh in 1783, had a scientific focus; the Society of Antiquaries in Scotland was chiefly concerned with the nation's material heritage. Other clubs and societies were strictly convivial or, like the Edinburgh Poker Club, which campaigned for a Scots militia, mixed conviviality with ideology. Besides clubs, which often met in taverns, the urban literati of Scotland congregated at bookshops. Creech's centrally located shop in the middle of the High Street constituted, in Lord Cockburn's words, a 'convenient hive' about which 'lawyers, authors, and all sorts of literary idlers . . . were always buzzing'.

These references to clubs and societies, taverns and bookshops, remind us that the Scottish Enlightenment was not simply about formal learning, published in books and taught in Scotland's five universities. A second, closely connected component was sociability. The dynamic nature of the movement, its special character, derived from the constant interaction that occurred among the literati in informal as well as formal settings. A sense of camaraderie arose among the Scottish literati, complementing their purely intellectual connections as members of identifiable 'schools' of historical thought, rhetoric, medical science, common-sense philosophy, and the like. It is in part the lack of this kind of sociability, or bonding among men of letters, that makes the concept of an English Enlightenment more problematic. In the French Enlightenment, this social dimension was present, but it assumed different forms. Often it centred on salons, which were similar to Scottish intellectual and academic clubs in their regularity (meeting in the same place on a fixed evening each week) but differed in that they met in private homes and were usually conducted by female *salonnières*, who had no equivalent in the predominantly male world of the Scots literati.

A third feature of the Scottish Enlightenment was its shared value system. Despite differences among themselves, the Scottish literati maintained similar ideals and concerns which went well beyond their common interest in philosophy, science, and literature. Freedom of expression, religious toleration, polite but unaffected manners, private and public virtue, patriotism (Scottish and British), faith in improvement, and opposition to all forms of inhumanity (such as slavery) were almost universal tenets among them. Moral philosophy, indeed most forms of scholarship, were thought to have a didactic, moral function. It is important to remember that the word 'enlightenment' is not merely a synonym for 'knowledge'. The contrast with England is once again instructive: eighteenth-century English men of letters did not possess this sense of common values and common purpose to anything like the degree of the Scottish literati and French *philosophes*, and this is another reason why the term 'English Enlightenment' lacks resonance. In Scotland, as in France, men of letters had a tendency to join forces and to fight against what they perceived as unenlightened policies and prejudices. The battle for a Scots militia that many of the Scottish literati waged unsuccessfully during the 1760s and 1770s was one such issue, for in their view the militia cause represented public virtue, Scottish national pride, and the need to ward off the corrupting effects of modern economic life.

The values shared by the Scottish literati included fears and uncertainties rooted in their circumstances. Concerned that Scots sometimes appeared to be barbarous in foreign and especially English eyes, they were particularly sensitive to questions of national development, from 'rude' to 'cultivated' or 'polished' states of refinement. Having seen their country undergo rapid social and economic change, they worried about the adverse effects of the new economic order on human relationships. Adam Smith, Adam Ferguson, and John Millar, for example, recognized the economic efficiency inherent in the concept of the division of labour, but each expressed reservations about its consequences for the mental health of workers and the social health of the nation. This belief in the ambivalent nature of progress, already noted in regard to Creech's account of Edinburgh, gives Scottish political economy and social thought a distinctly modern feel.

Although the Scottish Enlightenment is justly famous for scholarship and teaching in the arts and sciences, eighteenth-century Scotland also produced a number of major figures in imaginative literature. Some, such as the Gaelic poet Alasdair Mac Mhaighstir Alasdair (Alexander MacDonald) and the Scots poet Robert Fergusson, laboured in relative obscurity. Others, such as Tobias Smollett and John Moore, found fame as novelists in London. In Edinburgh, Henry Mackenzie popularized the cult of sentimental moralizing in novels such as *The Man of Feeling* and in the popular periodicals *The Mirror* and *The Lounger*. Mackenzie, Blair, and other Edinburgh literary men patronized a young farmer from Ayrshire whose vibrant poetry would revitalize Scots as a literary language: Robert Burns. In 'Address to Edinburgh', an English poem published by Creech in the 1787 Edinburgh edition of *Poems, Chiefly in the Scottish Dialect*, Burns returned the compliment:

> Thy Sons, *Edina*, social, kind,
>   With open arms the Stranger hail;
> Their views enlarg'd, their lib'ral mind,
>   Above the narrow, rural vale:

In another stanza, Burns paid homage to the transformation of Edinburgh, and by implication the nation generally, by praising its 'Wealth', 'Trade', 'Architecture', 'Justice' (i.e. the law), 'Learning', and 'Science'. It was while being fêted at this time at the home of one of the literati, Adam Ferguson, that Burns had his only known encounter with a fifteen-year-old boy who would take Scottish imaginative literature in new, largely uncharted directions. By the end of the eighteenth century, Burns was dead and Ferguson, Mackenzie, and Blair in retirement, but the age of Walter Scott was about to begin.

7 Workshop of Empire: The Nineteenth Century

I. G. C. HUTCHISON

Introductory

The nineteenth century produced radical changes in Scotland, which can perhaps be measured most strikingly by the movement, literal and metaphorical, of population, which grew faster than in any other century. In 1801, the population was 1,608,420; in 1901 it was 278 per cent higher at 4,472,103. Additionally, the spatial distribution of the population was drastically re-formed. At the outset, the balance between core and periphery was reasonably equitable: 30.3 per cent of the population lived in the most northerly and southerly regions, and 38.9 per cent in the industrializing central belt (the rest were in the more agricultural central areas). But by 1901, only 13.8 per cent were in the outlying parts, and 65.6 per cent in the industrial midlands.* The size of settlements had also changed. In 1801, four out of five people lived in communities of under 5,000, but a hundred years later about three out of every five lived in towns of over 5,000; among European states only England and Wales were more urbanized. Glasgow in particular experienced spectacular expansion, rising nearly four times as fast as total population increase, from just over 75,000 in 1801 to upwards of three-quarters of a million in 1901.

---

* The counties in each grouping are: northern and southern fringes—Argyll, Berwick, Caithness, Dumfries, Inverness, Kirkcudbright, Orkney, Peebles, Ross & Cromarty, Roxburgh, Selkirk, Shetland, Sutherland, Wigtown; central industrial belt—Ayr, Clackmannan, Dumbarton, Fife, Lanark, Mid-Lothian, Renfrew, Stirling, West Lothian. The other, generally less industrialized, Lowland counties are—Aberdeen, Angus, Banff, Bute, East Lothian, Kincardine, Kinross, Moray, Nairn, Perth. Their share of the total population was 30.8% in 1801, and 20.6% in 1901.

Lastly, the composition of the population was different. By 1901, there were many non-natives living in Scotland: the Irish-born, for example, numbered over 200,000, and the Irish community as a whole was perhaps over 10 per cent of the population. In addition, there were English and Welsh incomers—above a quarter of a million settled in Scotland over the century—as well as a smaller (mostly East) European presence.

The causes of these seismic shifts were primarily economic: industrialization and sweeping agrarian changes were crucial. In their tow came drastic social changes: the social structure and class relations were transfigured, while living conditions were profoundly affected. Key elements inherent in the older Scottish value system were equally modified: religious, educational, and political systems and attitudes were affected. By 1900 the concept of Scottish identity was significantly removed from that obtaining in 1801.

Industrial achievement

The performance of Scottish industry was remarkable. By 1900, it is arguable that the Scottish economy, by some criteria, outpaced the rest of Britain, and its pre-eminence in heavy engineering, one of the frontiers of skill and technology, was unquestioned. For a country which had hitherto been viewed condescendingly by its southern neighbour as economically backward, this was a source of great pride within Scotland.

Textiles stimulated and led Scottish industrialization in the first half of the century. Cotton production was initially highly successful, with conditions similar to Lancashire: a damp climate, plenty of natural energy resources, and easy access to world trade routes. Hence the sector surged from 39 mills and 312,000 spindles in 1793 to 168 mills and 1,363,000 spindles in 1850. Skills transferred from the pre-existing linen industry, and close links with English cotton-masters, exemplified by Robert Owen's move north to Lanarkshire as a mill manager in 1800, also facilitated growth. By the 1830s production had switched from the original water-powered rural sites to Glasgow and its environs, as the application of steam power meant that large, urban-based factories could be built. Then the city vied with Manchester for the title of 'Cottonopolis', but within twenty-five years the latter decisively won the contest. Scottish cotton was unable to match its English competitors in quality and productivity. In the second half of the century, only specialist cotton products remained afloat; Paisley's thread manufacture was the prime example. Other textile sectors, however, fared better. In Dundee, jute ousted linen

BAIRD'S GARTSHERRIE IRONWORKS, the most important in Scotland, represented the first phase of Scottish industrialization, transforming the landscape and economy of North Lanarkshire.

as the core activity in the 1850s, and by 1900 was the centre of world production, employing some 35,000 workers.

The expanding textiles sector generated the impetus for the speedy development of coal and iron. Iron production was transformed from a small-scale industry, primarily Highland based (for proximity to charcoal supplies), by J. B. Neilson's innovation in 1828 of a new technique—hot-blasting. This permitted the profitable exploitation of the Lanarkshire and Ayrshire deposits of black-band ore. It enabled Scottish iron producers to undercut English rivals, reducing costs by 40 per cent. By 1852, 750,000 tons (28 per cent of total UK output) were produced, against 23,000 tons (9 per cent) in 1806. Coal production, in the wake of iron's trajectory, mushroomed. Lanarkshire and Ayrshire coalfields yielded splint coal, necessary for smelting iron, while the eastern area—notably the Lothians and Fife—catered for domestic and export markets, growing because of, respectively, urbanization and international transport needs. By 1900, coal output had risen to 33 million tons from 2 million in 1800, and the workforce expanded from 9,000 to 103,000. Scotland's share of overall UK output grew over the period from 15 to 27 per cent.

SHIPBUILDING was Scotland's premier industry from the late nineteenth century until well into the twentieth. Here at Clydebank the *City of New York* is being built in 1889.

The mainspring of Scottish economic success after the eclipse of cotton was shipbuilding. An impressive stream of technical innovations was initiated on the Clyde. New materials—iron, then steel—were readily embraced. Major engineering improvements, yielding greater speed and significant fuel economies, were pioneered. The river specialized in top of the range products: most of the great transatlantic liners were Clyde-built, a notable exception being the *Titanic*. The Admiralty also placed many of its warship-building contracts there. By 1900 the Clyde had secured pole position in world shipbuilding, producing about half a million tons of shipping annually, approximately a third of world output, sometimes exceeding the combined German and US totals.

The Glasgow region rapidly became a lodestar for ancillary and cognate heavy engineering specialisms. Marine engineering naturally bulked large, while locomotive-building became a second Glasgow strength. Scottish-built rolling stock was to be found throughout the world. Bridge-building also enjoyed an international reputation, confirmed by the erection of the Forth Bridge in 1890, when it immediately became a testimony to Scottish engineering skills. Scottish steel expanded hugely from the 1870s, so that by 1900, with nearly 1 million tons produced, it contributed one-fifth of UK output. In 1880, Scotland had made a mere 85,000 tons, 7 per cent of the UK total.

Part of the reason for this success lies in the infrastructure and support systems. The long-established trading activities of Scots, particularly eighteenth-century colonial merchants, gave knowledge of overseas markets. Shipping facilities and transport networks had accordingly been well developed. Scottish banks were more forward-looking than English ones, being sensitive to the needs of business by applying a generous lending policy.

At the time, much emphasis was placed on the sterling entrepreneurial attributes of Scottish businessmen. Astuteness in spotting new techniques and adroitness in penetrating new markets were singled out for praise. Some ascribed these strengths to Presbyterianism: hard work, self-analysis, sturdy independence, and a willingness to take risks, fortified by belief in divine support for the elect, were seen as fostered by Calvinism. Education, too, was highlighted: the universal availability of instruction, and the esteem given to intelligence, it was felt, gave the Scots the edge in an age of technical expertise. But too rosy a picture of Scottish genius should be tempered. For a start, while some like the Baird family of ironmasters were devout Presbyterians, religion was not omnipresent among the capitalist class.

Other, more material, factors also mightily assisted Scottish industrial prowess. The highly favourable geographical propinquity of ironstone and splint coal, both adjacent to the Clyde, gave a distinct cost advantage over competitors. A significant part was played by cheap labour, caused by the steady movement of work-seekers from rural Scotland and Ireland to growth points. Wage levels in Scotland lagged behind England by about 20 per cent in the 1840s, narrowing somewhat to about 10 per cent in the 1880s.

The acumen of the industrialists was sometimes rather defective. By the 1890s, Clyde shipbuilding was beginning to lose its position at the technical forefront: diesel fuel and the steam turbine engine, two major breakthroughs, were pioneered elsewhere. There was a profitability crisis: the greatest liner built on the river, the *Lusitania*, yielded a derisory, but not atypical, 3 per cent return. From the mid-1880s, serious financial difficulties occurred, with Govan's mighty Fairfield yard almost capsizing.

By 1900, depletion of natural resources was apparent in the western iron and coalfields. Pit closures in Lanarkshire had begun, while iron output peaked in the 1870s, and thereafter the industry was heavily reliant on imported ore. Steel also showed inherent weaknesses; the units of production were too small to be competitive, and most produced nothing but the particular form of steel used exclusively in shipbuilding. Hence, to a considerable extent, many of the problems which were to plague the Scottish economy after 1918 had their origins in the nineteenth century, the era to which subsequent generations looked back fondly as an untarnished golden age.

The rural Lowlands

Lowland agriculture was fundamentally reshaped. By about 1830, the last vestiges of the old modes of working and thinking were extinct. Joint farming had been replaced by single tenants; fields formerly divided into strips ('runrig') were now consolidated. Long leases of up to nineteen years, instead of the previous annual lets, were standard. These changes promoted experimentation in crops and livestock-rearing, and the reward for improvements to buildings and soil could now be recouped. Hitherto intractable land was drained by new methods, cleared of stones, and manured with an exotic range of fertilizers from seashells to South American seabird droppings, by way of industrial and human waste. New crop rotations were introduced, restoring the land to optimum fertility. The use of root crops and hay permitted overwintering of animals, so encouraging stockbreeding. Farmsteadings were constructed with better materials and grouped in an accessible and efficient layout, no longer spread higgledy-piggledy across the holding. New technology was readily embraced. The iron plough ousted the wooden one; horses supplanted oxen as beasts of burden. The threshing machine and the scythe dramatically reduced the time and labour involved in harvesting.

As in heavy engineering, so in farming Scotland became the exemplar for the whole kingdom, although in the previous century Scottish agricultural productivity was half that of England. Agriculturalists now streamed north to inspect the feats of the Scots, and Scottish farmers were imported into England to serve as initiators of change. Hardy's Donald Carfrae, the estate manager in *The Mayor of Casterbridge*, indicated how widespread and normal such an occurrence had become.

Regional specialization evolved. Beef cattle was the main north-east product, dairy cattle that of the south-west—both assisted by the advent of the railway and the steamboat, opening up access to mass urban markets. The Lothians concentrated on grain crops, the eastern borders on sheep-rearing. But most farms were essentially mixed, so sheltering them from the vicissitudes of over-concentration on one product. This gave Scottish agriculture greater resilience in periods of crisis, such as the so-called 'great depression' from 1873 to 1896.

The tenant farmers who pioneered the new system were an impressive force. Hard-working, intelligent, educated, and with a keen eye for business opportunities, they exuded confidence and determination. Someone like William McCombie of Tillyfourie, acclaimed as the first to rear Aberdeen-Angus cattle, was merely the most illustrious of a broad army of farming innovators. The tenant farmers were rural capitalists with the assurance and identity of a middle class. They did not subscribe to the romantic rural myths which were more prevalent in England, and showed scant deference to the landowning class. The English rural bonding agents of hunting and cricket did not apply in Scotland; indeed the excessive application of game rights by landowners triggered a farmers' political revolt in the 1860s and 1870s. This ended with legislative victory for the farmers, after pro-tenant candidates had swept the field in successive county elections by defeating lairdly incumbents.

There were profound social consequences of this wholesale reconfiguration of Lowland agriculture. The casualties of the changes—cottars, subtenants, and local craftsmen-labourers—had no place in the new rural order. Unlike England, the Scottish poor law gave no relief to able-bodied unemployed. Almost all of these marginalized people were accordingly obliged to remove, either to Lowland towns, there to seek work in the burgeoning industries, or abroad. These Lowland clearances affected many rural communities—only one-quarter of parishes in the south-west had a population growth in line with the national rate between 1851 and 1901. The population of several counties remained virtually static; e.g. Berwickshire: 1801: 30,206; 1901: 30,824.

The new labour force was organized in very sharply etched strata. The horseman was the key to farmwork—to a greater degree than in England—and was therefore given special status as an indispensable skilled worker. Moreover, the custom of half-yearly hiring gave farmworkers a high degree of independence, as they could swiftly move on if dissatisfied with their conditions. This lack of deference to laird and farmer alike shown by ploughmen was in marked contrast to England. Again unlike England, there was no resident Scottish army of casual agricultural labourers—the poor Hodges described by Richard Jeffries. Instead, additional labour was provided at peak pressure points, notable harvesting, mainly by Highland and Irish itinerant workers. But once their work in the locality was finished, this rural proletariat moved on. Thus, the Scottish countryside was less densely populated, with English-style estate villages full of day labourers something of a rarity.

The Highlands

The Highland problem of the early nineteenth century was created by a blend of incompetent landowners, severe demographic pressure, and profound economic weakness. The consequence was a drastic reduction in and redistribution of population. The intensity of the crisis and the extreme solutions applied were not, however, universal throughout the region. Generally, in those districts abutting the Lowlands, changes took a more controlled course. While they did indeed lose population, it was a gradual occurrence, mostly a response to opportunities for a higher standard of living in the nearby Lowlands. For those who remained, an ordered adjustment to the economic circumstances of the nineteenth century was more viable.

The starkest resolution of the problem occurred in the more remote western mainland and islands. The quarter-century of war with Europe after 1790 initially offered an economic lifeline to these impoverished areas. Kelp, a form of seaweed, became an indispensable provider of alkali to the chemical industry after an embargo on trade with Europe excluded the previous Spanish product, and the price rose tenfold to £20 a ton in 1810. By then 7,000 tons were produced annually, and Highland landowners reaped the benefits of this maritime harvest—Clanranald's Uist estate yielded as much revenue from kelping as from rental. To provide adequate labour supply, tenants were encouraged to subdivide their holdings, while simultaneously rents were hoisted to levels which obliged them to eke out their income by kelping. Emigration was made more expensive in 1803 to discourage the flight of Highlanders.

Other factors conspired to ease the pressure of hardship. Cattle prices, the main cash product of the tenantry, rose sharply under favourable war conditions. Crucially, the potato was, as in Ireland, a crop custom-built for the poor soil and wet, cool climate of the region, and its yield was about four times

A REAL "SCOTTISH GRIEVANCE."

THE HIGHLAND CLEARANCES in popular radical perception. The factor of Lord Mac-
Donald expels Skye crofters from their homesteads to the waiting ship and transportation
to Canada—or Glasgow.

greater than the previous staple, oats. The shackles normally imposed on
population growth by food supply and cash in times of failure were doubly
unlocked. In the early decades of the century, the demographic trajectory of
the Highlands altered; it grew more rapidly than before—although still more
slowly than the rest of Scotland.

The collapse of kelping after peace in 1815 was precipitate, and by 1828, at £5
per ton—against a peak of £20—labour costs were not covered. Landowners
faced financial ruin; their income was depleted, while the costs of maintaining
the poverty-stricken peasantry intensified their predicament. Some did nothing,
and when inertia bankrupted them, new owners, mostly non-Highlanders,
frequently businessmen, took over—two-thirds of Highland estates changed
hands between 1800 and 1850. This new ownership class pursued broadly the
same strategy as the surviving traditional owners, maximizing estate revenue
by assigning land to the only profitable commodity: sheep. The demand for
wool offered vast profits, well beyond the rental income from smallholders.
By 1825 Scotland supplied 40 per cent of British wool, up from 25 per cent in
1810, pulling people from the interior to the seaboard to work on kelp, while
leaving the interior deserted for sheep. Hence, the population of the Highlands deemed surplus to the new priorities of the estates was systematically
removed. The failure of the potato crop in the 1840s intensified the landlords'

resolve to effect clearance. The poorest class was affected by the dearth of their staple, and landowners targeted these for wholesale eviction. Most of the cleared population went overseas, others to Lowland cities.

Thirty years of relative stasis, if not stability, obtained after the mid-1850s: the crofters clung precariously to their marginal patches on the littoral, while the big capitalist sheepmen operated inland. The 1880s saw a second stage in the Highland question. Australasian competition made sheep-farming unprofitable (no doubt to the mordant satisfaction of the many Highlanders who had emigrated there), aided by soil exhaustion in the Highlands through over-exploitation. Now the key to survival for the landowners was the rise of sporting activities. The plutocracy was attracted to the Highlands, thanks in part to Queen Victoria's love affair with the region. As sporting estate rentals soared, large tracts of the Highlands were converted to deer forests. By 1885 105 deer forests covered 1,700,000 acres, one-sixth of the Highlands. These developments posed a major menace to the small tenants. The economy of the crofting townships depended on upland summer grazing for livestock; now these areas were being appropriated for deer stalking.

The significant change from the previous phase was that now crofter resistance was successful. There had been protests at eviction then, but these had been ineffectual, partly because they were isolated and uncoordinated. This time, various elements altered the equation. The Gaelic diaspora gave sustenance to the embattled crofters. Émigré Highlanders, in Britain and overseas, sent money, mobilized opinion, and acted as a liaison between Highland communities. The sense, too, of the threat to Gaelic language and culture was important; Celtic societies had been growing from the 1860s to champion these, and the 1872 Education Act seemed to imperil Gaelic by granting it no standing in schools. Radical politicians in Lowland Scotland campaigned vociferously on behalf of the crofters. Irish nationalism provided a model for tenant resistance. The Free Church, omnipresent in the Highlands, now offered local leadership, as clergymen and teachers possessed the eloquence and correspondence skills to unite and enthuse crofters. Lastly, the granting of the vote in 1884–5 to rural workers bestowed a vital tool on the crofters. In the 1885 election, five Crofters' Party MPs were elected. Legislation was in place within six months of the election.

The 1886 Act gave crofters security of tenure, compensation for improvements, and a fair rent tribunal. Evictions became a thing of the past. While this was a distinct triumph for one of the poorest and most remote groups in Victorian Britain, it was not the complete solution. The numerous cottars and landless squatters were explicitly excluded from the provisions of the Act. Landowners, for their part, had little interest in developing estates, since the Land Court fixed rents at low levels. The last fifteen years of the century accordingly saw a continuing ebbing of people from the poorer, overcrowded districts, such as the Outer Hebrides.

Social structure

The severe economic and social upheavals of this century naturally produced profound reverberations in class structure and relations. Many landowners benefited greatly from industrialization: those sitting on mineral rights boosted their income quite handsomely. Yet there was considerable instability as estates regularly changed hands throughout the century. Incompetence or profligacy took their toll. A steady incursion of wealthy businessmen, as discussed below, also had its effect in diluting the aristocratic nature of landed proprietorship.

Landowners were not accorded the automatic deference they enjoyed in England. They were identified with the corrupt unreformed political system. Many refused to allow the emergent Free Church to build on vacant sites, so appearing simultaneously anti-democratic and anti-religious. The conflict with tenant farmers in the 1860s and 1870s portrayed them as arrogant and greedy. The Highland clearances confirmed the negative stereotype. The main avenue for restoring their prestige lay in military and imperial service. National pride in the role of the Scottish regiments added esteem to the aristocratic officer class. Colonial governors-general were frequently drawn from the ranks of Scottish noblemen, such as Lord Linlithgow in Australia.

At the top of the middle class there existed a highly dynamic business cadre. By 1900, there were proportionately more millionaires in west central Scotland than in any other British provincial region. Many of this super-rich class merged with the landowning aristocracy by marriage or by purchase of large estates. The great chemical manufacturer Sir Charles Tennant bought a splendid estate in Peeblesshire and married most of his daughters into the peerage, while Margot made do with the future prime minister, Asquith.

Below this narrow strip of extreme wealth lay a solid core of middle-class individuals—perhaps numbering a quarter to a fifth of all occupied males—living on more modest means. Approximately four-fifths of the middle class were small to middling business people, and the rest were professionals and white collar employees.

This class, self-confident and assertive, tended to be critical of privilege and inherited rights. They assailed entrenched customs and perquisites—the Corn Laws, a bastion of landownership and an affront to the doctrine of free trade, were roundly denounced. Hence much of the tension, especially in the first half of the century, was as much between the upper and middle classes as between the working and middle classes.

In place of patronage, they adopted *laissez-faire* and self-help as guiding precepts. This was typified by the extreme harshness of the Scottish poor law, with its insistence that no relief be given to the able-bodied unemployed. The middle class dominated town life and stamped the century with their values. They ran charitable agencies which reinforced their doctrines of self-help, ensuring no feckless claimant benefited. They dominated all layers of local government, helped by franchises which favoured them. It was only in the very last years of the century that a handful of working men won any local government seats.

The working class manifested only a slow and intermittent self-consciousness. Dogged by internal divisions, they failed to mount any very serious challenge to the existing order. Some of the schism was religious in origin: the hostility between native Scots and Irish Roman Catholic workers scarred many districts and areas, as is discussed below.

Otherwise, the gap was much more between skilled workers and the rest. The 'aristocrats of labour' saw themselves as closer to the lower middle class than to the less skilled workers below them. The artisan elite lived in distinct residential areas and identified with the middle-class values of churchgoing, temperance, education, and purposeful leisure. Intermarriage with the *petite bourgeoisie* was usual for skilled workers. They occupied an ambiguous place in the social scale. Many nurtured prospects of moving upwards, and so felt little solidarity with the proletarian mass. Journeyman tradesmen might become small masters themselves, and in larger works the enticement of a foreman's job was hard to resist.

Above all, the skilled men were organized into trade unions, from which by and large the unskilled were excluded until the very last decade of the century. The artisans, with their cooperative societies, friendly organizations, and trade unions, were independent free-standing individuals beholden to nobody. The economic success, the ethos of self-help, and the rhetoric of Scottish egalitarianism all served to inculcate these values. They shared many of the anti-aristocracy views held by the middle class, and were prone to regard most employers as reasonable men. When conflict arose at work, they were ready to use industrial action, but believed it to be a regrettable last resort. In an expanding economy, with demand for skilled workers high, they did not need to remain with difficult employers, and instead simply changed to another workplace.

For the less skilled, or those displaced by technological change, conditions could be very bleak. Handloom weavers, numbering perhaps 85,000 in 1840, either faced starvation or, like Andrew Carnegie's family, opted for emigration. By 1850, their numbers had been reduced to 25,000. In the second half of the century, around a quarter of the urban workforce held casual unskilled jobs. These were paid well below the skilled rates, and employment was sporadic—probably work could be found for only about three-quarters of the year. Unorganized, physically exhausted by hard work and poverty, the unskilled had few effective champions, and rarely achieved any impact on society. Thus, an abortive rising in 1820 spearheaded by weavers was easily dispersed by the authorities. There was no major success in the trade unionization of the unskilled until the 1890s.

Irish immigrants

The Irish immigrants were mainly concentrated in the industrial western Lowlands. However, Dundee, a magnet for Irish textile workers from the 1820s, had the highest percentage of Irish-born of any town at mid-century. Irish Roman Catholics stayed in distinct, separate communities, not assimilating to any great extent with the indigenous population. They seldom married native Scots—certainly less so than other incomers to the urban Lowlands. They tended to be concentrated in certain parts of towns. Irish Catholics came to work in unskilled occupations with low pay and inferior status, and most remained there from one generation to another.

This segregation had two sides: on the one, the host community repulsed the Irish, but on the other, the immigrants resisted wholesale assimilation. Part of the native hostility stemmed from religious factors. Scotland was in the grip of an evangelical mood for much of the century, and Calvinism of all the main varieties of Protestantism was perhaps the most antipathetic to Catholicism. Many Irish had been brought over by iron- and coal-masters to break strikes, and antagonism towards the Irish as 'blacklegs', although unjustified, persisted long in the western coalfields, where the Scots defined themselves as 'honourable men', as distinct from the Irish 'degraded slaves'. Being overwhelmingly in low-paid occupations, the Irish tended to live in the poorest areas of towns which were associated with the worst health and living conditions, as the Glasgow MOH regularly noted. Crime, too, was often identified as a concomitant of the Irish presence. While these problems might nowadays be ascribed to social factors, at the time they were often interpreted by Scots as proof of the dangers of mixing too closely with the Irish. Politically, too, the Irish Catholic community was isolated from mainstream politics. They were overwhelmingly committed to Irish nationalist movements from the later 1860s, and to a proportionately greater degree than in England. The unwillingness of the Irish to follow the rest of the Scottish electorate enraged many of the latter. While they were mostly prepared to vote Liberal, Irish Nationalists could switch. In 1900 they helped return Bonar Law to parliament in place of a Liberal lukewarm to Home Rule—a nice irony, as Law became the greatest paladin of Ulster Unionism.

On the other hand, Irish Catholics often did not wish to merge with the host society, for fear of losing their religious and ethnic identity, so instead they created a separate society, centred on the Church. Self-help bodies mir-

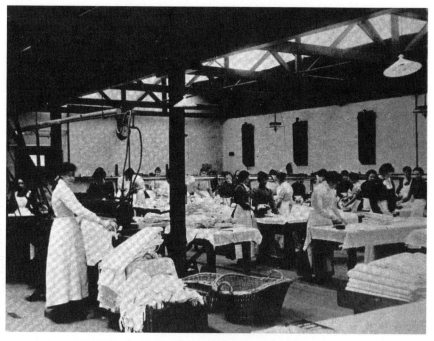

WOMEN'S WORK: a laundry in Aberdeen about 1890. Laundrywork was a fairly unskilled occupation for young women, who would quit work immediately upon marriage.

rored the existing institutions, but control of policy was retained by co-religionists; poor relief, orphanages, temperance societies, literary and saving
associations all existed in a parallel world. The two most prominent instances
were education and leisure. Catholics, although mainly in poorly paid jobs,
nevertheless declined to send their children to the state schools after 1872,
because in most instruction was still conducted within a Protestant framework. Instead they financed their own schools, so underlining their segregation. In sport, the formation of Celtic Football Club highlighted the intimate
link between religion and ethnicity.

The problems for Irish Catholics were compounded by the significant
presence in Scotland of Ulster Protestant immigrants, who integrated more
easily into the host society, economically, religiously, culturally, and even
politically. Their arrival also meant the spread of Orange lodges across
central Scotland. By 1900, there were more lodges in Scotland than anywhere outside of Ireland. Native Scots, of course, were also well to the fore
in the movement. By dint of the Orange Order and, more discreetly,
Masonic lodges, the standing of Catholics as second-class citizens was reinforced. Here again was a problem bequeathed to the next century to
attempt a solution.

Women

The position of women in Scotland was always likely to be subordinate. The
dominant heavy industries were exclusively male in employment, reinforcing
the idea of masculine superiority. Women's role in this culture was supportive: preparing meals, raising children, and keeping the house clean were the
limits of their world. John Knox's philippic against Mary queen of Scots had
set the tone for the Presbyterian Church's evaluation of women's place in the
general scheme of things. This attitude prevailed even among critics of
the existing order: the Scottish socialists were almost without exception male.
So it is no surprise that the percentage of married women in paid employment in 1901 was half the English level.

But there was rather more to women's role in the nineteenth century than
this epiphany to male chauvinism suggests. Many women did paid work:
about one-third of the labour force was female, and about one-third of all
women worked. In textiles, especially after 1850, they formed the bulk of the
workforce—three-quarters of Dundee's jute workers were female. The other
main occupations were domestic service, agriculture, and clothing. There

was a sizeable female presence in Edinburgh printing works. However, women factory workers invariably left employment after marriage, and the jobs they held were mostly less skilled. Women were barely unionized until the end of the century, and their rates of pay were usually half the male level. Lower-middle-class women also frequently worked. Many ran shops while their husbands operated in kindred trades, such as bakers. Some, however, ran independent businesses, notably boarding houses or restaurants. These were careers often opted for by those widowed early.

Yet there were signs of growing independence for women. Middle-class women began to play a greater public role, initially in philanthropic endeavour. Many charities, most notably the temperance movement, had a large women's wing. Added impetus to this trend came in the last third of the century with the enfranchisement of some women at the local government level. In particular, the creation of elected school boards in 1873 gave scope for women to undertake public office, and they also sat as town councillors.

This enhanced public profile coincided with the entry of middle-class women into employment. Schoolteaching became a favoured job for women, as the 1872 Education Act opened additional opportunities for intelligent women. By 1900, there were 17,000 female teachers—60 per cent of the total—whereas in 1851, there had been only 4,500, or 35 per cent. The universities allowed females to matriculate in the 1890s, with the first graduates being capped in 1893, some thirty years before the ancient English universities. Many then entered teaching, but a smattering of doctors also emerged.

While most of these widening opportunities appealed primarily to middle-class women, working-class women also began to find a non-domestic forum for social activities. The Cooperative Women's Guild, formed in 1892, soon became a resounding success, clearly tapping into long suppressed aspirations among working-class women. They had rarely been involved in charitable or church organizations, and had limited educational experience. But the guilds, with a mixture of companionship and instructional work, opened up wider horizons. The twentieth century was to see the fruits of this experiment.

The urban environment

While it was possible to point to the glittering spoils of economic success in the palatial residences of the triumphant capitalists, there was a darker angle on Scottish achievements. In urban areas, social conditions for the vast majority were extremely harsh for most of the century, and this degree of deprivation far exceeded English levels.

Housing standards were especially low, with the one- or two-roomed house the norm for the vast majority of working-class families. A one-roomed house would be about 12 feet in both length and breadth, with no kitchen or internal WC, and a two-roomed house would have a small annexe of about 8 feet square. In 1901, one-half of the urban population was living at more than two to a room.

Not surprisingly, health conditions were dire. The death rate in Glasgow rose in the mid-1820s to 24.8 per 1000 living, and did not fall below that level for seventy years. One in eight Scottish children died before reaching one year, a statistic that remained pretty constant throughout the second half of the century. The rate for large cities, notably Glasgow, was far worse. Inside the congested houses, contagious and infectious diseases were rife; respiratory and chest ailments were common and tuberculosis ever-present. Outside the house, environmental standards were defective. With communal toilets and washing facilities, the lowest common denominator of sanitary standards prevailed. The backyards of tenements were full of rubbish; farmers collected human ordure on an occasional basis well into the second half of the century.

These conditions, embracing almost the entire working class, produced varying responses. For the ultra-sensitive, life and spirit were crushed: young Edwin Muir, arriving in Glasgow from Orkney, suffered a breakdown. Others, following the adage that the fastest way out of the city was through the bottle, took to drink: visitors to Scottish towns commented on the prevalence of drunkenness on display in the streets.

Reforms were slow, sometimes imperceptible. In many towns, the infrastructure creaked under the mass inflow and struggled to respond. Hospital and health services could scarcely cope with the pressures. Adequate clean water was not available in most towns until mid-century: Loch Katrine supplied Glasgow only from 1859. The reason for this tardy addressing of problems was only partly a question of better technical knowledge becoming accessible. The prevailing ideology blamed the problem on the people. It was frequently pointed out that there were many unoccupied houses in cities, even while families were crammed into tiny houses, often taking in lodgers. Moreover, the evidence of huge expenditure on drink suggested that the Scots opted for self-indulgence rather than decent housing, especially as

A GLASGOW SLUM, *c*.1870. Each window represents a household. The size of the interiors can be gauged from the two men standing beside the demolished building in the centre, in which probably five or six families would have lived.

English working men paid higher rents. However, in terms of real wages, the proportion spent on rent in Scotland was less than in England, because of lower wages and also because the Scottish cost of living was some 10 per cent higher.

On the supply side, facets peculiar to Scottish law and local government practice increased costs. Feudal dues exigible by the superior could add up to 10 per cent to land purchase costs, compared to England. From mid-century Scottish burghs imposed tight controls on building standards. Aimed at preventing jerry-built structures, the quality criteria laid down effectively pushed building costs above those in England. Therefore, the total cost of construction in Scotland could be anything up to 30 per cent higher, so the builder had to squeeze in more units of accommodation.

Houses—except the very lowest stock—were leased on a yearly basis, with the missives signed three months in advance of entry. Breach of the agreement could mean eviction, confiscation of goods and chattels, and blacklisting by property factors (letting agents). A family thus deprived of its home would have to settle for the gruesome indignity of living in unspeakable slums, or submission to the rigours of the poor law. Yet skilled men in the west of Scotland could not foresee the fortunes of their industry over a year ahead, since activity in the heavy industries was unpredictably cyclical. For the unskilled, a quarter of the year was likely to be spent out of work. Hence cautious working men were loath to move to superior flats lest they be caught out by the long lease, instead choosing to stay in the substandard housing which was always affordable. It is no coincidence that Edinburgh, where employment was relatively stable, had one of the best housing conditions of Scottish towns.

Power in local government also impeded a satisfactory resolution of the housing crisis. Great energy was indeed put into improvements, accelerated by the frightening aptitude of diseases like cholera to strike regardless of social standing. The provision of municipal water supplies was one testimony to this mood, as was Glasgow council's ambitious scheme in the 1860s to clear the worst slum districts for redevelopment. Yet there were profound obstacles to radical treatment. While ratepayers accepted municipal amelioration of the broader environmental infrastructures—for example, street lighting, water supply, public wash-houses—they vehemently objected to the application of their taxes to helping individuals in poor housing who were, as noted above, perceived to be feckless. The municipal electorate was heavily geared towards the middle class, with only just over one-half of working-

class men enfranchised around 1914. Accordingly, the voters threw out reforming councillors, like Glasgow's Lord Provost Blackie in the 1860s. Hence
a major social problem was left to fester throughout the second half of the
nineteenth century, leaving a legacy which the next century struggled to eradicate.

Politics

After the First Reform Act of 1832, Scottish politics remained resolutely anti-
Tory for the rest of the century. This stood in contrast to England, where the
Conservatives made a reasonably rapid recovery, and from 1874 onwards
enjoyed a clear majority. By contrast, they won a majority of seats in only one
Scottish election—1900—and even then they did not get the most votes.

The unreformed electoral system was in itself a major recruiting officer for
Liberalism. The grand total of 4,500 voters in Scotland represented just less
than one in a hundred adult males, against one in eight in England. The
narrowness of the electorate meant that far more sections of society were
excluded in Scotland, so giving the reform party a broad base. The franchise
qualifications were anachronistic in the extreme. The county vote was based
not on actual physical ownership of land, but on possession of the feudal
superiority, which in Scots law was quite separate. Hence many substantial
estate owners not holding feudal rights were excluded from the political
nation. Electorates were extremely small—Bute had twelve voters in all—so
landlord dominance was the norm. Where feudal superiors felt politically
insecure, it was easy to manufacture votes, for instance by dividing the feudal
superiority into qualifying titles. Several counties were accordingly quite
swamped by fictitious, often non-resident, voters. Burgh MPs were elected
by the town councils, themselves a self-perpetuating oligarchy immune from
any democratic electoral process.

Added to this antediluvian set-up, pre-1832 Scottish government was seen
as irredeemably corrupt. The imprint of Henry Dundas, Lord Melville, lay
heavily on the first third of the century. The use of patronage and place
enabled the Tories to wield political power to the great benefit of their partisans and the virtually total exclusion of opponents, whether in Church, law, or
civil government. Free trade carried deep resonance in Scotland, to the detri-
ment of Toryism. Indeed, the organized campaign against the Corn Laws
began in Scotland, but subsequently was fully developed in Manchester.
Agricultural interests in Scotland were far less committed to the protection of

wheat, and Scottish business was very heavily dependent on international free trade. Religion, a major politicizing influence, worked against the Tories. For the Voluntaries, the key issue was disestablishment of the state Church, so placing them firmly in the anti-Conservative camp. After 1843, the newly formed Free Church aligned itself with the Liberals. The Tories, in office at the time of the Disruption, were anathema to Free Churchmen, for having failed to avert the schism. The adherents of these two churches comfortably outnumbered the Church of Scotland.

Working-class enfranchisement in 1868 and 1884–5 did little to challenge the Liberals' ascendancy. The Liberal ethos, in both its political form (democracy, anti-landlordism, and support for national self-determination in Europe) and its socio-economic form (free trade, self-help, moral improvement through temperance and education) received virtually unquestioned sanction from the enfranchised skilled workers endowed with the vote. Even the establishment of the Scottish Labour Party in 1888, the first avowedly working-class party in Britain, did little to shake the Liberals' predominance. The new party, an alliance of trade unionists, socialists and Irish Nationalists, had limited electoral success before 1900. As well as the solid identification with Liberal precepts, the lack of a strong trade union movement in Scotland militated against independent labour politics.

The Tories therefore faced formidable barriers to embarking on the sort of road to recovery achieved in England. The breakthrough came for the Tories with the Liberal split over Irish Home Rule in 1886. Many Scottish Liberals supported Liberal Unionism—mostly for economic, religious, or imperialist reasons. The sole Unionist electoral success of 1900 owed a great deal to the victories logged up by Liberal Unionists. But many of the latter still kept aloof from their Tory allies; whereas in England the merger of the two parties moved forward apace in the 1890s, serious rifts persisted in Scotland. Even in schism, the Liberal legacy proved hard to dissolve.

Presbyterianism

Presbyterianism was intensely important for Scots. It was, until the arrival of a substantial Irish Catholic immigration, the religion of the overwhelming majority—probably about 90 per cent. It was also seen as bestowing on Scots great strengths of national character, such as logic, adherence to principle, democracy, and self-analysis. But besides confronting an external challenge from a growing Catholicism, Presbyterianism faced severe internal difficul-

ties of an intellectual, social, and organizational nature. As a result, by 1900 its position was less secure.

The Disruption of 1843 was the major incident in the century for Presbyterianism. About one-third of the Church of Scotland clergy and laity seceded to form the Free Church. Their leader, Thomas Chalmers, had been exercised by the failure of the established Church to tackle the problems of urban-industrial society, which he encountered in stark reality as a minister in Glasgow from 1815 to 1823. Poverty, godlessness, and revolution seemed to him to be growing in an interlinked menace. For Chalmers, the rise of the Voluntary Presbyterian churches was a dangerous tendency, since by stressing the need to be free of any state connection, they would sever the vital ties between Church and state, so jeopardizing his ideal of the Christian community. The Voluntaries were particularly strong in Lowland urban areas, where the Church of Scotland had faltered in responding

THIS EARLY EXAMPLE OF PHOTOGRAPHY portrays the scene at the 1843 General Assembly of the Church of Scotland, when the Disruption, the most momentous event in nineteenth-century Scottish religion, took place. But the photograph is not a true depiction of the episode, for it is a montage incorporating portraits of many of the leading figures of the time, most of whom were not actually present at the assembly proceedings.

to rapid social and demographic change. Chalmers ascribed the state Church's failings to the lack of an evangelical ministry, and strove to counter the attractions of Voluntaryism. A key prop in his strategy was attained in 1834, when the General Assembly of the Church of Scotland heavily diluted the principle of lay patronage in the appointment of ministers, allowing congregations greater say in the process. The secular courts, however, rejected the doctrine that the Church's lawmaking took precedence over parliament's, and reinstated the full rights of patrons. Unable to persuade the Tory government to accede to their demands, Chalmers and his supporters duly quit to form the Free Church.

At one level this precipitated a flourishing of Presbyterian achievement. As the three sects vied with each other to establish a superior claim to be the authentic Presbyterian vessel, churches were built and home missionary work undertaken on an unprecedented scale. For instance, in 1895 there were some 50,000 Presbyterian Sunday school teachers.

The churches nevertheless also encountered, by their high standards, areas of failure. Efforts to win the working classes back to Christianity were at best a partial success. It was the 'lapsed masses' who had so concerned Chalmers, and whom his Free Church was supposed to reach. Ironically, in the 1850s, it appears that the rump Church of Scotland had a higher proportion of its congregation drawn from the working class, especially the less skilled section. Even though the working class composed a majority of city centre churches' membership, the majority of that class did not attend church.

By the 1880s, the evangelical impulse itself was waning. New theological currents, and the impact of Darwin, tended to make old-fashioned fundamentalism less credible. The middle class retreated to suburbia, and became less involved in home missionary endeavours. Socialism and trade unionism offered the working class alternative interpretations of social and economic relationships. The churches were frequently seen as vehicles of status advancement, by promotion to elderships, for the aspiring middle class. Middle-class leadership could make the churches appear inimical to working-class interests, for instance in periods of industrial unrest.

Yet while Presbyterianism was perhaps issuing a less certain call by the end of the century, it still had an impact on a broad swathe of Scottish society. Many early socialists retained much of their Presbyterian upbringing—for example, they often portrayed themselves as following in the tradition of the covenanters, suffering for their beliefs. The well-known teetotalism of the Scottish ILP activists mostly stemmed in good measure from their religious backgrounds, and godless Marxist socialism had little impact in Scotland.

Schools and universities

The Scots took inordinate pride in their educational system. It was one field in which England seemed inferior; a survey in 1855 indicated the Scottish

MASS SCHOOLING, 1887: a large class, with patriotic propaganda on the walls, and female teachers in charge.

female literacy rates were higher than English male levels. By an Act of 1696, every parish had to have a school, maintained by local landowners. This nationwide arrangement stood in sharp contrast to England. University provision was equally advanced; in 1865 there were proportionately six times more university students in Scotland than in England.

But the positive features of Scottish education were not simply quantitative. The special strengths of the Scottish system were held to be a most potent shaping force in the national character. Schooling was seen to be open to anyone to proceed as far as his ability—and not, as in England, money or status—would permit. Two crucial concepts, the parochial school tradition and the 'lad (never the lass) o' pairts' gripped the imagination of Scots.

The universities provided the link between a democratic egalitarian schooling, where children from all backgrounds shared the same experience, so counterpoising wealth and position with an elite of intellectual attainment, and social mobility. Parish schoolmasters would talent spot promising young boys, coach them, and then pass them on to the university which they themselves had attended. Poor but able students were assisted by a proliferation of

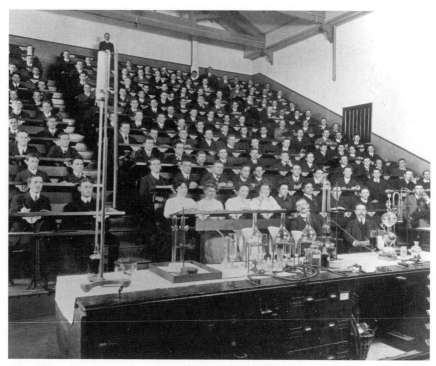

MASS UNIVERSITY TEACHING, mid-1890s. The female students attending this Glasgow University chemistry lecture are clustered together in the front row.

bursaries—about one-third of Aberdeen students usually held these. Being non-residential, universities were not expensive to attend, so, unlike England, where rank determined admission to higher education, the 'lad o' pairts' was feasible.

Much of this rather self-congratulatory portrait is valid. Scottish universities were less socially exclusive; in the 1860s, about one-fifth of students were working class. Yet, as the century advanced, the gap between ideal and reality widened. The much-vaunted parochial network was, even in its heyday, inadequate. Many children attended only fitfully, with labour in the fields taking priority in rural parts, while in industrial areas, poor parents put their offspring to paid work at a very early age. Those who did attend school mostly went to institutions outwith the parochial system, where the quality of instruction offered was variable, but frequently of very low standard.

The 1872 Education Act marked a watershed by abolishing the bewildering plethora of schools, but it only provided a uniform system of education at elementary level, with a leaving age of 13. This confirmed the polarizing aspects of Scottish education. The 'Higher Grade' schools, numbering around 200 and nearly all in burghs, became exclusively middle class in composition, through charging high fees, and served as the natural conduit for university entry. They could afford to hire top-quality teachers, and thus produced children better equipped for university standards than the parochial schoolmaster. By the 1870s, a minister's son was nearly 300 times more likely to go to university than an unskilled labourer's child.

The *coup de grâce* to the old democratic vision came with the introduction of the Scottish Leaving Certificate examinations in 1888. Universities quickly demanded passes in these as a prerequisite for admission. But as these examinations were normally taken at about the age of 17, only the Higher Grade schools could offer that quality of teaching. By 1900 most universities had abandoned the junior classes which had existed to train up students from a parochial school to adequate competency. So Hardy's Jude the Obscure was as likely to be an anomaly in Scotland as in England. When working-class students did go to university, they frequently went as mature students, and seldom graduated; instead they studied a few courses and then moved on.

Culture

While in the economic sphere nineteenth-century Scotland was eminently successful, its performance in arts and culture was distinctly inferior—indeed in some areas there were almost no noteworthy achievements, for example, drama and sculpture. Instead of engaging with the paradoxes and predicaments of the new civilization, virtually every sector of Scottish creative culture seemed to retreat into an idealized sentimental world.

The first thirty years of the century were the most significant for most artistic fields. In literature, Scott, Galt, and Hogg produced works of real merit which critically confronted a range of contemporary concerns—notably, the impact of profound economic and social change; the incubus of religious tradition; political reform and the changing nature of national identity. Wilkie and Raeburn created paintings of high order, while in architecture the last phase of neoclassical design flourished under Playfair and Hamilton with the completion of Edinburgh's New Town, along with other large public buildings.

Subsequently there was a general and sharp decline in quality. Fiction and poetry alike averted their eyes from urbanized society, instead degenerating into the maudlin kailyard school, which was firmly grounded in a saccharine depiction of Lowland rural and small town life as the norm: not only was there no Scottish Dickens, Eliot, or Gaskell, there was emphatically no Hardy. Painting likewise drifted into commercial prettified productions of landscape and countryside scenes, while in architecture, Gothic churches and neo-baronial domestic houses—a trend influenced by Scott's Abbotsford and Queen Victoria's Balmoral—prevailed. The euphoniously named Hamish McCunn specialized in the musical equivalent of these trends.

The occasional emergence of the talented individual only underscored the general prevailing mediocrity: Stevenson and Mackintosh both showed that it was possible to blend modernity with the best in the Scottish tradition. Some painters, including the Glasgow Boys, MacTaggart and Peploe, similarly sought to relate developments in French Impressionism to the Scottish context.

The reasons for this weak performance are much contested. Evangelicalism is one popular culprit: frivolous pastimes distracted from religious activity, while the austere Presbyterian liturgy suppressed all artistic expression, musical or decorative, in worship. Yet by the last quarter of the era, church services had become more aesthetic, without any concomitant rise in creative output.

In Victorian Scotland, preoccupied with making money and material gain, interest in things cultural was always somewhat suspect. There were collectors and patrons of art, but often they were more interested in the works of the past, and others lacked discernment, buying large pictures of Highland scenery simply to fill the expansive walls in their mansions. Possibly most businessmen were like the inordinately wealthy ironmaster James Baird. It is related that on a cultural tour of Egypt, he was spotted open-mouthed in wonder at a pyramid. Asked what he was thinking as he looked at one of the seven wonders of the ancient world, he is reported to have said: 'Jings, I wish I'd had the contract to supply the bricks for that job.'

Perhaps the impact of industrialization, occurring with greater speed and dislocation than in England, was so traumatic that Scots could not address it directly. This rapid transition meant that most Scots still had immediate rural roots, so the escape to a sentimentalized non-urban image, epitomized by the education myths, was viable. Some have argued that artistic expression was sublimated into engineering precision, so that an elegant and effective construction yielded both aesthetic and commercial rewards, with the Forth Bridge as the apotheosis of this approach.

There were, however, fruitful areas of intellectual creativity, and some central concerns of the Enlightenment era persisted. Scientific enquiry continued: Clerk Maxwell's mathematical work was of international importance, as were the achievements of Lord Kelvin. In medicine, Lister and Simpson maintained the country's pre-eminent reputation. J. G. Fraser, W. Robertson Smith, and Patrick Geddes produced pioneering work in the social sciences. The characteristic nineteenth-century strain of critical social and moral commentary was deeply imbued with Scottish influences, from the two earliest and greatest quarterlies, the *Edinburgh Review* and *Blackwood's Magazine*, to Carlyle.

Scots or Britons?

Nineteenth-century Scotland presented an unusual picture of a people who were intensely conscious of their distinct national characteristics, but were uninterested in any outright form of separatism or independence. This was primarily because most Scots felt no serious grievance against England, believed that their prosperity was intimately bound up with the union of the two countries, and encountered no barriers to advancement because of their ethnic identity.

Scots felt that they were not subject to a colonial regime, nor that their national institutions were in peril. Westminster and Whitehall mostly ignored Scotland until the very end of the century, leaving the running of the country to administrative boards peopled by Scots. Scottish legislation was dealt with by Scottish politicians—from 1832 to 1885 by the lord advocate, subsequently by the Scottish secretary. There was little serious attempt to assimilate the cherished pillars of Scottish civil society—the law, the Presbyterian Church, and education—to English practice. Indeed, some in Scotland argued that greater integration would prove highly beneficial. In the universities, the impetus to emulate England by introducing honours degree programmes came from Scots who felt that they were missing job opportunities with the less specialist traditional ordinary degree. When a brief flurry of quasi-nationalist agitation arose in the mid-1850s, it was emphasized by its leaders that all that was sought was a fair share for Scotland within the union, rather than secession. Even the campaign for Scottish Home Rule, initiated in 1886, did not reflect an upsurge of separatist feeling. Rather, efficiency was sought: the Westminster parliament could not deal competently with Scottish measures and also devote enough time to imperial matters.

The union was seen as highly beneficial to the Scots, since economic growth was ascribed to the merger of the two nations. Scotland, then, was never a colony taken over by an imperialist power, nor did it have settlers imposed. The wars with France, which ended in 1815, helped bind Scotland closely into the idea of Britishness, as the menace of invasion unified opinion and identity. The prominent part played by Scots in acquiring and running the Empire cemented wholehearted identification with Britain. Missionaries like Livingstone, traders like Jardine & Matheson, explorers like Park, colonial governors like Elgin, soldiers like Dalhousie—all focused the attention of their compatriots on the centrality of Scots in the imperial construct. The presence in the settler colonies of hundreds of thousands of people with Scottish origins further underlined the identification. It was no coincidence that opposition among Liberals to Irish Home Rule was especially strong in Scotland, for it was regarded as presaging the break-up of the Empire.

There was, then, no difficulty in working within the British framework, economically, politically, or otherwise. Scots sat for English constituencies, and there were likewise Englishmen, notably Asquith and Morley, who held Scottish seats. The top political office was open to Scots: Aberdeen, Gladstone (of Scottish origin, and, from 1880, a Scottish MP), and Rosebery all served as prime minister, while by 1900 Balfour was the premier in waiting.

The Scottish character was defined mostly by religion and education. Presbyterianism had given the race its independence, egalitarianism, and democratic tendencies. The educational system had provided a higher standard of teaching than in England, had offered a broad curriculum, and had emphasized the practical applications of learning. It had not discriminated on grounds of money or class, only on intellectual capacity, so tapping into a broad wealth of talent. All of these explained the remarkable success of the Scot in the nineteenth century—in the eyes of Scots and non-Scots alike.

But the picture of the earnest achieving Scot became increasingly overlaid with a kitschier image: that of tartanry. The influences of Scott and Queen Victoria were influential here, and fused with the military element in Scottish identification with Britain. It also reflected a sense of Scottishness that teetered on the comic, as Harry Lauder was later to exploit, while also signifying the merging of Highland and Lowland identities, which in the previous century had been quite distinct and not always harmonious. Yet the Scots were content with the existing constitutional arrangements; there was no desire to launch a revival of Scottish culture as an integral stage in resurrecting a suppressed nationality, as happened in much of Europe. But if the props to this British identity were to buckle, there would be a sufficient persisting sense of a separate Scottish identity to return to.

Epilogue, 1901–1914

The years from the end of the nineteenth century to the outbreak of the First World War seemed to confirm Scottish success and esteem on the world stage. A huge international trade exhibition held in Glasgow in 1901 paid tribute to the city's world economic standing, while in 1911 a world missionary conference which met in Edinburgh acknowledged the country's religious contribution. The economy looked ever more secure: 1913 was a record year for Clyde shipbuilding, with over 750,000 tons of shipping—one-fifth of world output—launched. Yet beneath these headlines, disquieting trends were evident: a freeze on warship-building in the mid-1900s pushed several Clyde yards to the verge of bankruptcy, underlining the precarious profitability of the sector. Scottish steel's share of UK output fell from 20 per cent to 18 per cent between 1901 and 1914, and pit closures in the western coalfields continued apace. Politically, the Liberals had regained their pre-eminence after losing the 1900 election to the Tories, so that after the last pre-war election, there were fifty-eight Liberal and only nine Tory MPs. Yet the Labour

THE SMITHS AT THE COWLAIRS LOCOMOTIVE WORKS in the later nineteenth century typify the independence and self-confidence of the industrial artisan class.

Party, while advancing more slowly than in England, seemed to be gaining footholds—albeit less at the parliamentary level than in local government. In the Highlands, people were still leaving the region; between one in ten and one in five of the population in western parishes moved away between 1901 and 1911. Urban social problems remained intractable: despite the steady growth in the population of towns and cities, house-building for the working class in the immediate pre-war period was at its lowest level for over thirty years. Sectarian feelings were heightened by the revival of Irish Home Rule after 1910, but Presbyterian union was set on an irreversible track when the Free and United Presbyterian churches merged in 1900. In turn, this brought the fusion of the new church with the Church of Scotland much closer, and by 1914 this process was well in train, although formal union was not achieved until 1929. Working-class women still worked in menial jobs, earning far less than men and quitting employment upon marriage. In contrast, middle-class women were entering careers to a small, but marked, degree, and more were attending university. Scottish support for the British state was highlighted when war broke out in August 1914, as the proportion of Scots volunteering was higher than in any other component nation of the United Kingdom. But the war would either begin or accelerate the dissolution of many of the landmarks of nineteenth-century Scotland.

8 The Turbulent Century: Scotland since 1900

RICHARD FINLAY

The opening of the twentieth century shook a number of common Scottish assumptions. The belief that the nation was natural bedrock of Liberalism was dispelled when, for the first time since 1832, the Conservatives won a majority of Scottish parliamentary seats as a result of the patriotism engendered by the Boer War. Queen Victoria, who had always held Scotland and the Scots in great affection, died in 1901 and was replaced by her son Edward, who immediately incurred the wrath of the nation by using the numeral VII; her love affair with her northern kingdom made the Scots sensitive about the proper numeral. The period between 1900 and 1914 was marred by a number of crises, all of which affected Scotland. The Boer War had highlighted social, economic, and military weakness which threatened the integrity of the Empire. The issue of protectionism split the Conservative Party in 1903 with about half the Scottish Unionist MPs unable to support the policy. Normality seemed to return to the nation when it rallied behind the issue of free trade in the general election of 1906 and restored the Liberal Party to its position as undisputed champions of Scottish politics. This sense of equilibrium was soon challenged as an economic downturn triggered a period of increasingly bitter industrial disputes. Ideas of social reform came to the fore as the best way to deal with mounting working-class discontent. Political acrimony intensified as the issues of House of Lords Reform and Irish Home Rule polarized Liberals and Tories into 'radical' and 'diehard' camps. Women entered the arena of political warfare by stealth attacks on golf-playing members of the Cabinet at St Andrews in order to publicize their demand for the vote. On the shipyards, workers were kept busy building warships in anticipa-

UP-HELLY AA. Scotland has a rich and varied cultural heritage; people in the Northern Isles continue to look back to Viking times in this annual celebration.

tion of the conflict with Germany which was looming on the horizon. For all these difficulties, there was no sense of panic. Businessmen believed the economy would maintain its position as a leading exporter of ships, engineering, and machinery. Liberals had held back the challenge of socialism and the Labour Party. While things may have seemed normal on the surface, the new century opened with powerful undercurrents of ideological, economic, and social discontent. The war would bring them to the surface.

When the lights went out, 1914–1924

The outbreak of war in August 1914 was greeted with relief by many in Scotland. Patriotic unity was the perfect antidote to the divisions which had plagued society in the Edwardian era. Catholics and Protestants, employers and employees, men and women could put behind them what seemed petty squabbling about sectarianism, higher wages, and votes, now that they had to defend their liberties from the 'heathen Huns' who were menacing the peace of Europe. This wave of unity manifested itself immediately in the surge to join the colours and see some action before it was all over by Christmas. The Liberals and Tories suspended normal political activity and turned over their offices and staff for the recruiting drive. The appeal to young men to come forward and 'do their bit' did not go unheeded and, in the first few months of war, the recruiting offices were overwhelmed by the rush. Accommodation, uniforms, food, and even signing-on forms all ran out. As most Scottish regiments had a local base, considerable civic pride was invested in turning out a good show for the colours. Such was the demand to join up that the physical standard of entry was raised on 11 September in a bid to ease the pressure by taking only the fittest and best. Although the first few months of the war would witness the greatest enthusiasm for signing up, by 1915 standards of entry were lowered to accommodate the insatiable demand for recruits. Of the 157 battalions which made up the British Expeditionary Force, 22 were Scottish.

The reasons why so many young Scottish men flocked to do their duty are as varied and as different as the soldiers themselves. Many grew up on a diet of popular militarism in which the soldier was the embodiment of masculinity. The fulfilment of a childhood fantasy of derring-do and adventure attracted many, as did the belief that it would be a short war after which the combatants would be stocked up with stories of chivalry, bravery, and romance, enough to set any young lady's heart a-flutter. For those trapped in a boring and tedious job, the war was an escape from a dreary existence. Undoubtedly, some were patriotic, but for many, especially the one in four miners who joined up, there was a fear that the war would lead to unemployment and so it was thought that enlisting was the best way to ensure a steady income. The peer pressure to enlist was intense. The young man who failed to do his bit had his masculinity assailed by young women handing out white feathers. His family and friends would be tarred with the social stigma of having a 'shirker' in their midst and most employers would not employ a man who refused to enlist. Recruitment was based on the locality and workplace so that neighbours, friends, family, and workmates all joined up together and were deliberately kept together to maintain morale and ensure maximum peer pressure to join up. Tramwaymen, engineers, miners, and other workers served together and 'pals' battalions were formed from local communities. In spite of massive social pressure, ever-decreasing physical entry standards, and the growing professionalism of the recruiting offices, voluntary enlistment could not satisfy the demands of the killing fields of France and conscription was introduced in 1917.

The naive and wildly optimistic hope that business would carry on as usual was cruelly swept aside as the casualty figures began to mount up and reveal the true extent of tragedy on the Western Front. It is estimated that Scotland lost about 100,000 servicemen out of the British total of 745,000, although the official figure of 75,000 Scottish dead was based on the crude assumption that as Scotland had a tenth of the population it followed that it must have contributed a similar proportion of the dead; a sort of Barnett Formula of slaughter. The loss of such a large section of Scottish male youth was traumatic in itself, but the patterns of recruitment and service conspired to add an extra twist of cruelty for the loved ones of the fallen. The pals who joined up together, usually died together. Whole communities, villages, and streets were affected by mass grief. The death of a husband was likely to be accompanied by the news of the deaths of brothers and friends. An unlucky shell could wipe out a third of the male population of a small village. The reports of casualties were read with fear and trepidation by local communities. For the wounded and those who survived, the world would never be the same again. Guilt-ridden at having escaped the fate of one's comrades, having suffered horrors which were incommunicable and inexpressible, many men retreated into their own inner world. Inter-war Scotland must have been populated by tens of thousands suffering from the as yet undiagnosed post-traumatic syndrome.

As the casualties began to mount in 1915, so too did the class tensions which had been temporarily mollified by patriotism. The war greatly strengthened the bargaining position of the industrial working class. The paramount importance of munitions production meant that there was an abundance of work. Labour shortage meant that workers could demand higher wages without fear of being undercut, and readily available overtime helped to push up earnings. Thousands of workers gravitated into the Clyde basin, which became the most important centre of armament production in the United Kingdom. With increasing wages and abundant overtime, trade unionism expanded because more workers were able to pay the levy and sought to defend their new-found improvements. Inflation, however, ate away most of these gains, with engineers, for example, experiencing a 50 per cent rise in the cost of living. Furthermore, the fact that the government was intent on maximizing output and had appointed Lord Weir, a believer in Tay-lorist ideas on streamlining and rationalizing production, meant that skilled workers were threatened with 'dilution' as women and unskilled apprentices were able to perform tasks preserved for the industrial elite. In spite of gov-ernment assurances that this was simply a short-term measure to overcome the shortage of skilled labour and it would be removed once the war was over, it cut little ice with the mainstay of Clyde workers. Believing their trade and craft skills to be under threat, the workers engaged in wildcat strikes towards the end of 1915 and articulated their grievances through their shop stewards who formed the Clyde Workers Committee. Alarmingly for the authorities, many of those leading the agitation were socialists, and the spectre of Red Clydeside became lodged in the middle-class imagination.

The Red Clyde was able to emerge as a mass movement because griev-ances were not just confined to the workplace. Within the first year of war, some 20,000 people drifted into the area in search of work in the booming armaments industry. Housing was in short supply and overcrowding became endemic. Landlords, adhering to the notion of business as usual, made the most of the laws of supply and demand and hiked rents up by a quarter in some areas to capitalize on rising wages and overtime payments. Compounded by the 'Shell Scandal' when it became known that armament manufacturers were guilty of holding back production to keep prices high, workers were rightly indignant at the naked profiteering of capital whose appeals to the 'patriotic duty' of employees not to strike demonstrated clearly the argument of the socialists that there was one rule for the bosses and another for the workers. The moral indignation of the movement was also fuelled by the fact that it was often the most vulnerable who were hit hardest by unscrupulous rent-rack-ing. The wives and dependants of soldiers at the front, for example, could not rely on rising wages or overtime to keep up with spiralling rent increases. Their victimization exposed the patriotism of the landlords as nothing more than a hollow sham. These growing grievances culminated in the Rent Strike of 1915 when payment was withheld for overpriced housing. Factors who attempted to collect the rent were subject to ritual humiliation, led by women, aid was dispatched to neighbours in need, demonstrations were held outside the court where defaulters were supposed to appear, and the commu-nal sense of protest was reinforced when the men downed tools in November. Within a couple of weeks, the government was forced to intervene and rents were pegged for the duration of the war. Although members of the Indepen-dent Labour Party and the Cooperative Movement played a leading part in the agitation, the movement was fuelled more by a sense of pre-war fair play than a belief in socialist principles. Yet, that said, the success of the Rent Strike did demonstrate to the working class that they could achieve a political victory on their own without relying on middle-class intermediaries. Also, the claims of socialism seemed to match their aspirations better than the pre-war Liberalism which had once been their political mainstay.

The Rent Strike established the credibility of the labour movement as a vehicle for promoting the political interests of the working class, as trade unionists and members of the cooperative movement and the Independent Labour Party were the leaders in the orchestration and organization of demonstrations. Labour also did well in the workplace as socialist activists were given unprecedented access to the workers through the auspices of the trade unions. The ability to talk directly to the working class in trade union meeting places and call upon their organizational and financial muscle in the pursuit of political ends was essential in transforming Labour from a fringe movement into a mass political party. Furthermore, just as Labour was flexing its muscles, the Liberal Party appeared to be doing everything in its power to alienate its former working-class adherents. After all, it was a Liberal government which had introduced dilution and arrested and locked up working-class activists. The Liberals had supported the interests of capital in the early stages of the Rent Strike and only acquiesced due to people power. The Liberal government was denounced for its incompetence in the war effort and in April 1916 the Irish community, arguably the most loyal of pre-war Liberals because of support for Home Rule, turned away in revulsion as the 'misguided' patriots of the Easter Rising were executed for treason. The subsequent political wrangling which followed the collapse of the Liberal government, the formation of a coalition, and the split between Lloyd George and Asquith into rival Liberal factions in 1917 did little to enhance the party's credibility. Also, the fact that the darling of the pre-war radicals, Lloyd George, was now reliant on Tory support made it difficult to claim that Liberalism was in the best interests of the working class. On the ground, Labour, buoyed up by success and capitalizing on growing working-class discontent, was able to push its reform message into the community, whereas the Liberals, divided, confused, and with a dilapidated organization, found their message falling on deaf ears.

Just as a new dynamic working-class politics was emerging, the changes induced by war reshaped the politics of the middle class. While it is possible to dismiss Red Clydeside as a myth in the sense that it was not a mass socialist movement intent on effecting a revolution, it was no myth as far as the middle class and Establishment were concerned. While the workers may have simply been demanding better pay and social conditions without much thought as to how to achieve this, the middle class took their socialist leaders' claims at face value and believed a Bolshevik revolution was in the offing. Evidence of this appeared to be confirmed on 31 January 1919 when more than 100,000 protesters demonstrated and hoisted the Red Flag in George's Square in Glasgow. The demonstration was driven by the Forty Hours strike, which was fuelled by the Scottish Trade Union Congress demand that the working week be limited to prevent mass unemployment in the wake of rapid demobilization. Further discontent was caused by anxieties about the impact of the end of the war on rent restrictions, wage regulations, and dilution of labour. Many were worried that the outbreak of peace would mark the beginning of employer hostilities on the limited gains achieved by the working class during the war. Although the protest was largely inspired by bread and butter issues, the authorities detected more sinister motives behind the unrest. Following revolution in Europe and the appointment of John Maclean as a Soviet consul in Glasgow, Sir Basil Thomson, head of Special Branch, and Robert Munro, the Scottish secretary, believed that the events in Glasgow were being orchestrated by socialist revolutionaries. Troops and tanks were dispatched to put down the impending revolution. The so-called 'riot' which took place in George Square had little to do with Soviet insurgency, but rather was the result of police insensitivity and poor crowd control. The protest ebbed when the government gave assurances that the regulations covering wages and rents would not be lifted in the meantime. The demonstrations of November 1919 marked the high-water mark of working-class protest and arguably the best chance for revolution. They also made a physical reality of middle-class fears about the Red Spectre.

The social and economic turbulence which followed the war changed Scottish politics by promoting the rise of the Labour Party. Although initially divided between a gradualist right which believed that socialism would evolve naturally and a revolutionary left which advocated immediate action to achieve the socialist state, electoral success was enough to keep everyone happy. The biggest factor in accounting for the rise of Labour was the franchise reform of 1918 which almost tripled the size of the electorate from 779,000 in 1910 to 2,205,000 in 1918. Although women over the age of 30 were added to the electoral register, the bulk of the new voters were drawn from the working class. Given that the war had heightened class tensions and had improved the credibility of the trade unions and the labour movement, it might be reasonable to expect this to be translated into political change in the 1918 election. Yet, it was the Unionist (Conservative) Party which did best by improving the number of parliamentary seats it won from seven in 1910 to thirty-two. The Liberals, although winning the largest number of seats (thirty-four), were divided between those who supported the Coalition government of Lloyd George and were dependent on Tory support and those who were loyal to Asquith. Labour with 23 per cent of the vote could only take seven seats. The Unionists and their Coalition Liberal allies benefited from the almost hysterical 'hang the Kaiser' fervour which dominated the election campaign. Also, the threat of Red Clyde had mobilized middle-class anxieties, and anti-socialist organizations such as the Middle Class Union and the People's League gave support to candidates who were in the best position to defeat the Labour candidate. Yet, the numbers were on Labour's side. The extension of the franchise took time to work, as new electors had to be added to the register. In the local elections of 1919 Labour made significant gains and in the general election of 1922 emerged as the largest party in Scotland, winning twenty-nine seats. Further evidence of the importance of franchise reform to Labour's fortunes can be shown by the increased turnout between the 1918 and 1922 general elections.

The failure of the Forty Hours strike and the fact that Labour was making significant advances through the ballot box strengthened the moderate wing of the party. Also, the trade unions, which were essential to Labour's financial and organizational well-being, were more interested in bread and butter issues and had little time for socialist rhetoric. Indeed, in spite of their reputation as firebrands, the Clydesiders who were elected in 1922 had little understanding of Marxist ideology, and for them socialism was more an ethical creed which promoted the interests of their working-class constituents than a political ideology. The reformist wing of the Labour Party was also strengthened by an influx of former radical Liberals who would have no truck with revolution. The fact that Labour emerged as the party of opposition in 1922 demonstrated that power through the ballot box was not only feasible but, as many argued, imminent. By this time, however, many of the leading revolutionaries, such as John Maclean and William Gallagher, had isolated themselves from the mainstream labour movement by forming their own parties or joining the Communist Party. The advent of a minority Labour government in 1924, which embarked on a limited and pragmatic programme of social reform, vindicated the gradualist approach to socialism.

The other side of the coin of Scotland's post-war political development was a realignment on the right. In many ways, this was more protracted and complex than the rise of Labour as there were two parties in Scotland which claimed to be the champions of anti-socialism, the Unionists and the divided Liberals. The war had been good to the Unionist Party. Before 1914, it was expected that the Tories would never win another general election and that the party was facing extinction. By 1918, however, they formed the backbone of the Coalition government, had a capable organization, and found a ready listener to their bellicose, no compromise, hard-line anti-socialist message in the traumatized middle class. The reasonable Liberals were thought by many to be too soft to stop Bolshevism. Yet, the Liberal Party had one main advantage. Given that anti-socialism was the dominant theme of the right in the early 1920s, the Unionists faced the conundrum of challenging a sitting Liberal and letting in the Labour candidate. The Coalition government put off this choice in the election of 1918 as Liberals with the 'coupon' were to be endorsed by both parties. Even when the Coalition ended in 1922, there was a reluctance among many local Unionist organizations to challenge a sitting Liberal for fear of splitting the anti-socialist vote. Indeed, when the Liberal Party united under the leadership of Asquith in 1923, it was able to do quite well in that general election because of the number of sitting MPs it had. With just under a third of the vote, the Liberals won twenty-three seats and demonstrated quite clearly that talk of the death of the Liberal Party was premature. Echoes of pre-1914 politics also emerged when the Tories endorsed protectionism only to find that it received short shrift in a Scotland which had historically rallied to the free trade battle cry. The decline of the Liberal Party was, however, self-inflicted. Asquith had made great play of the fact that his party was the best able to halt the advance of socialism. Indeed, keeping out Labour was the most significant contribution to his own by-election victory in Paisley in 1923. Asquith's decision to support the minority Labour government in 1924 brought howls of derision from the Unionists who claimed that the Liberal Party's anti-socialist credentials were discredited. Also, the fact that the minority Labour government acted very moderately and its leaders behaved like statesmen meant that the party proved itself fit for government. There was no revolution, no anarchy, and no chaos. Yet this moderate Labour government was eventually brought down by the Liberal Party, which was now cast as the enemy of the working class by its former Labour allies. Caught between a moderate Labour Party and an increasingly moderate, but firmly anti-socialist Tory Party, the Liberals were squeezed out of British and Scottish politics. A two-party system based on class interests had been established.

Dislocation 1924–1939

Hopes that Scotland would return to those halcyon days before August 1914 were forlorn, although the pre-war era was the measure against which the standards of normality were measured. The war and its consequences had unleashed powerful forces which brought the Scottish economy to its knees. In addition to the old social problems of poverty, poor housing, and bad health was the new one of long-term mass unemployment. The political and cultural values which dominated Edwardian society had been swept away in an avalanche of class conflict and national self-doubt. By the end of the 1920s, it seemed to most cultural commentators that the nation was locked into a spiral of terminal decline. 'The end of Scotland', 'North Britain; that dis-

THE CARRON IRONWORKS. Although Scotland in the twentieth century is characterized as being predominantly industrial and urban, much of Scottish industry was located in semi-rural surroundings.

tressed area', 'the slum problem', 'the southward drift of industry', and 'provincialization' leapt out at Scottish newspaper readers in the early 1930s, while the accompanying text told of another factory closure or relayed another statistic to show that the nation was falling behind the rest of the United Kingdom. This pessimism was best captured by a memo written by the Scottish secretary of state, Walter Elliot, in 1936 when he complained that there was a 'dissatisfaction in every book written on Scotland now for several years'.

The most serious and far-reaching problem facing the Scots in the inter-war era was the structural imbalance in the economy. Nineteenth-century prosperity was based on heavy industry which was reliant on international markets in capital investment goods such as ships, heavy engineering, railway locomotives, and the like. Even before the First World War, though not apparent to contemporaries, the Scottish economy was over-reliant on too narrow a base of industries which were tightly interconnected and interdependent. The drive for munitions after 1914 killed off the limited diversification which had taken place. Car manufacture, chemicals, light engineering, and machine tools were abandoned in favour of the good profits which could be made in the heavy industries by producing armaments. The war had the effect of finally tipping the Scottish economy off balance and into over-dependence on a narrow range of industries whose success was conditioned only by the war. But the war could not go on for ever.

During the conflict, export markets, particularly in textiles, were lost as indigenous industries sprang up to meet the demands of the home market. The jute industry of Dundee found not only that it had lost its pre-war market in India, but also that native industry was now challenging it in other parts of the world. Although there was a short restocking boom in 1919, confidence in the international market evaporated. German reparations, Communist revolution, war debt, and financial uncertainty hit the demand for capital investment goods. In the shipyards, the restoration of old working practices reduced competitiveness in a market which was already suffering constraints as the building of warships ceased. A glut of cheaply produced American ships and confiscated German boats dried up orders for Scottish ships. With shipbuilding in decline, steel lost orders from its largest customer. Markets for coal in Eastern Europe were lost and the reduction in the price of raw materials meant that former imperial customers in Australia, India, and Canada were unable to raise the cash for new engineering and instead made do with old machines. The industries which had characterized the power of the nineteenth-century economy gave way to the petrol engine, light engineering, chemicals, and consumer goods, none of which were produced to any great extent in Scotland.

The key failing of the Scottish economy in the inter-war period was its inability to diversify into the new 'sunshine' industries which were leading the way in the revitalization of the southern English economy. New industries would not come north because it made little sense to manufacture cars, washing machines, vacuum cleaners, and radios in a place where there was little purchasing power. Instead, they gravitated to the more prosperous southern market. The longer unemployment remained high, the less incentive to come to Scotland. The political reputation of Red Clyde helped to frighten off potential investors, and Scottish industrialists pursued a 'wait and see' policy, reluctant to believe that the old staples would not revive. To survive the lean times, Scottish industries formed defensive amalgamations which further reduced productive capacity and employment. Many fell victim to competitive takeovers and were moved south, while others left of their own accord. Scotland lost four of its main banks, control of railways, and substantial parts of the steel industry.

The frailty of the Scottish economy was cruelly exposed with the onset of the Great Depression in 1929. The statistics of economic failure speak for themselves. In 1932 400,000 or 26.2 per cent of the insured workforce was idle; twenty new factories opened while thirty-six shut; in 1933 fourteen opened while fifty-eight closed and in 1934–5 thirty-eight opened only to be offset by the fifty-eight which shut. The west central belt, where most of the traditional heavy industries were located, bore the brunt of the economic onslaught. Fishing and agriculture, likewise, faced decline as output and employment fell as prices collapsed and markets dried up. Rationalization and the 'southward drift of industry' gathered increasing momentum in the 1930s as companies and headquarters relocated to the more stable and prosperous markets of England. The growing north–south divide confirmed to many contemporaries that the Scottish economy was locked into a spiral of terminal decline. As traditional industries declined and unemployment grew, the prospects for attracting new industry diminished. The prosperity of the south was sucking the blood out of the Scottish economy, claimed the president of the Edinburgh Chamber of Commerce in 1932, and soon, he warned, 'Scotland will drop to a position of industrial insignificance.'

The impact of the depression was selective and savage. The most immediate consequence was a rise in unemployment, from 14 per cent in the period 1923–30 to nearly 22 per cent for the remainder of the 1930s. The number of

THE BLACKSMITH was a central figure in the life of rural Scotland and it was only in the period after the Second World War with the advent of motor transportation that the craft began to disappear.

destitute seeking poor relief rose from 192,000 in 1929 to 341,000 in 1936. Such bald statistics, however, fail to convey the grim reality of life on the dole. Unemployment was confined to industrial areas where whole communities were crippled by mass unemployment. Chances were that if you were on the dole, so too would be your neighbours. Places such as Airdrie and Motherwell had more than a third of adult males out of work. The statistics also hide the fact that the lower middle class, who did not pay unemployment insurance and as such did not make it onto the register, also suffered as demand for their goods and services dried up. It was reckoned that there were some 100,000 men who were 'permanently surplus to requirements' in the west of Scotland. Psychologically, unemployment scarred the skilled, industrial, male ego. Pride, self-respect, and manliness were bound up with work and for many men the impact of unemployment was a form of social emasculation. For the skilled worker helping out with the housework or taking a part-time or unskilled job was considered demeaning. In communities with little money and a crumbling social infrastructure, women did most to shore it up by doing part-time work, managing the house, and making sacrifices. In a patriarchal society, it was what was expected of them.

The faltering economy meant that the long-standing problems of bad health and poor housing received little attention. In 1917 it was reckoned that a quarter of a million new houses would have to be built if there was to be any chance of realizing the 'homes for heroes' aspiration. Instead, there were continuing public expenditure cutbacks and lower housing targets. Although over 300,000 new houses were built during the inter-war years (two-thirds in the public sector), this failed to keep pace with demand as old stock was constantly falling into disrepair. Indeed, given that most of the worse housing was concentrated in the unemployment blackspots where there was little money for rent, landlords maintained profit margins by cutting back on repairs and improvements. In the countryside, legislation for the improvement of rural dwellings went unheeded, as it would have meant bankruptcy for farmers and eviction for tenants. While the foray into public sector housing created good homes, they were beyond the financial reach of those who needed them most. The need to keep rents low meant that in the 1930s municipal authorities were constructing two-roomed housing on the edge of town with the cheapest of materials. By any reckoning the majority of Scottish housing was substandard and in 1935 overcrowding in Scotland was six times greater than in England.

Unemployment, poverty, and poor housing took its toll on the nation's health. Although in decline, the rates for maternal and infant mortality did not decrease to the same extent as for England and Wales. In the 1920s, Glaswegians were 25 per cent more likely to die than their rural neighbours. Time and time again, experts testified that in terms of height, weight, diet, and life expectancy the average Scot was worse off than his English counterpart. Although the industrial structure had collapsed, the patriarchal values which had been part and parcel of the Scottish working man's culture did not. Women were hounded out of the workplace to make way for men to resume their traditional breadwinning role. The limited gains of the war were pushed back in the search to restore the Edwardian equilibrium. Films, magazines, and education reinforced the gender apartheid at a time when family values were thought to be in decline because of the depression. Maternity and childcare provisions were constantly pruned back with cuts in public expenditure. Bad mothers were blamed for a perceived rise in juvenile delinquency and 'problem' children were dispatched out into the Empire as cheap labour for Canadian farmers where it was believed that the rustic life would lead to moral improvement.

One dismal testament to the failure of Scottish society to provide adequate economic and social opportunities for its people was the extent of emigration and migration to other parts of the United Kingdom. For the first time since records began, the 1931 census showed that the Scottish population was declining. Even though the Scottish birth rate was higher than that of England and Wales, the population north of the Border fell by 40,000 while it increased by two million in the south. For many contemporaries this was clear evidence that the nation was in decline as the best and most able people left to find pastures new. In tandem with fears that the lifeblood of Scotland was being drained away by emigration, a state of near hysteria broke out about the supposed threat of uncontrolled Irish immigration. Although official figures showed that Irish immigration to Scotland in the inter-war era had reached minuscule proportions, the Presbyterian churches, sections of the intelligentsia, and many politicians fuelled racist scaremongering by spreading lurid tales of an Irish 'invasion'. It was claimed that native jobs were being stolen, poor relief abused, and the future of the Scottish race was threatened. Although the Kirk reunited in 1929, it was believed that it was losing its central position within Scottish society. The growth of state powers and the rise of socialism were seen to undermine the Church's moral authority. The appeal to sectarianism by many Scottish churchmen, often orchestrated in secret, was a desperate effort to justify their existence. The outbreak of sectarian violence on the streets of Glasgow and, in particular, Edinburgh was further evidence of the disintegration of Scottish society. Yet, in spite of their pessimism, church attendance in Scotland did not dwindle away, but rather remained fairly constant until the 1960s when the upwardly mobile deserted the faith. Catholic Scotland, on the other hand, was better able to keep a tighter grip on its flock. The influence of the Kirk remained particularly pervasive in small-town Scotland and it was only in the 1950s that Christmas and Easter became public holidays.

Although inter-war Scotland was plagued by social problems, it must be remembered that they were confined to a minority of the population, albeit a substantial one. For those fortunate enough to be in work, the 1930s was a period of rising real wages and increasing standards of living. Cheap credit and hire purchase brought a wide range of consumer durables within the financial reach of many families. An increasing number of Scots became homeowners thanks to cheap mortgages and affordable bungalows. Domestic technology such as washing machines and vacuum cleaners eased the burden of housework for many women and the motor car enabled the family to travel the length and breadth of the country. Yet, in spite of all these improvements, the mood of economic pessimism did not lift. Most were aware that the fragility of the economy was such that today's good fortune could easily become tomorrow's misfortune. As late as 1937, the economy experienced a sharp downturn. Also, the casualties of the depression were everywhere and a constant reminder to the fortunate that their security was not guaranteed in a world of chaotic market forces.

SCOTLAND for most of the twentieth century was a place where there were more children than pensioners—a reversal of the situation today.

The problems of the economy dominated Scottish politics in the 1930s. As far as the Labour Party was concerned, the magnitude of social and economic dislocation was such that salvation would only come from harnessing the superior resources of the British state. Consequently, there was little point in promoting home rule. Labour's ambivalent stance on the Scottish parliament was instrumental in the creation of the National Party of Scotland (NPS) in 1928 which sought to promote the cause of self-government by contesting elections. The NPS made little impact electorally and succeeded only in confirming Labour suspicions of nationalism by its campaign of spoiling tactics at by-elections. The failure to make an electoral impact led the nationalist leadership to purge the party of its more radical elements and in 1934 the NPS joined with the right-wing Scottish Party to form the Scottish National Party (SNP). Like its predecessors, the SNP failed to make any impression on the Scottish voter, largely because it did not have any credible solutions to the problems of the economy. They were not the only ones. Labour found itself in power with a minority government when the depression struck in 1929. Ideologically it was ill equipped to deal with the magnitude of the problem. Committed on the one hand to the protection and promotion of its working-class constituents' interests and to economic orthodoxy on the other, the government found that the two could not be reconciled, as social security spending rose with mounting unemployment to create a financial deficit. Balancing the budget meant that savings would have to come from those areas of government expenditure which helped the working class. Things came to a head in 1931 when the trade unions and the majority of the party's MPs refused to endorse cuts in social security and led the prime minister, Ramsay MacDonald, to form a 'government of national emergency' which effectively wiped out the Labour Party in the 1931 general election. Dominated by the Conservative Party, the National Government was able to secure an electoral hegemony throughout the 1930s.

With most of its energies spent on rebuilding the party organization and deprived of its most articulate spokesmen in parliament, Labour also suffered from the secession of James Maxton's Independent Labour Party in 1932. The Unionists, on the other hand, were free to get on with the business of governing Scotland with little challenge from the opposition. Yet, it was not plain sailing for the Scottish Tories. The party faced a barrage of criticism from its traditional middle-class supporters on the contrast between Scottish economic fortunes and those in the south. Fearful of unemployment, they highlighted the fact that government policies of low interest rates, tariff protection on consumer goods, and farming subsidies worked best for the south of England but did little to deal with the problems of Scotland. Also, the government was committed to a fiscal policy which stressed non-intervention in the case of Scotland and was fuelled by the hope that things would somehow pick up. The fact that things did not confirmed suspicions that the government was pursuing a policy which was not fair to Scotland. It was in order to counteract these claims that a programme of administrative devolution was proposed which would increase the profile of government in Scotland, acknowledge Scotland's status as a nation within the union, and hopefully abate criticism. The Scottish Office was relocated to Edinburgh in 1939 and it was claimed that decisions about Scotland would now be taken in Scotland by Scots. Administrative devolution, however, was nothing more than a public relations exercise as power remained firmly in the hands of the Scottish secretary of state, who, in turn, took his orders from the Cabinet in London.

A very British consensus, 1939–1979

For the second time in the century, the Scottish people faced global war. There was no rejoicing or euphoria, only a dark realization that a long, hard struggle lay ahead. The war initiated a revolution in Scottish society. The first victims of the upheaval were working-class children. The fear of the bomber and the mass destruction that could be wrought by the use of poison gas meant that children had to be evacuated from the inner cities to the countryside. Families were broken up and it was expected that some 176,000 mothers and children would have to be dispatched to areas of safety. For many it was a journey into a strange and unforgiving environment, and the fact that nothing happened in the first months of war, coupled with the heartbreak of separation, meant that many drifted back. As the war progressed from bad to worse with the fall of France in 1940, it became apparent that the full resources of the state would have to be mobilized in life or death struggle. Military and industrial conscription, rationing, the command economy, and emergency social and welfare provision meant that the state was omnipresent in every aspect of Scottish life. The Churchill coalition appointed Labour's Thomas Johnston as secretary of state for Scotland in 1941 to oversee the Scottish war effort. The choice was inspired because Johnston was a gifted and practical politician who soon grasped the opportunities which were opened up by the use of state power. Previous claims that the state could not regulate the economy or society in the best interests of its citizens were

ON THE OUTBREAK of the Second World War about one in three schoolchildren were evacuated from their homes to safer areas, causing considerable heartache for both parents and children.

proven wrong. The publication of the Beveridge Report in 1942 which committed the government to the implementation of a Welfare State was greeted with great enthusiasm in Scotland because there was a lot to do north of the Border. Johnston also capitalized on the new thinking which emphasized the role of experts and planners and applied them to post-war reconstruction. If it was possible to achieve great things during war to combat the evil of fascism, surely, the argument went, then it was possible with political will to tackle the evil of poverty, unemployment, and inequality?

The managed economy would free Scotland from the haphazard swings of the free market, and state planning would enable society to adapt more quickly and effectively to new challenges and changes. Evidence of this new type of approach is to be found in the publication of the *Clyde Valley Plan* of 1947 which advocated a programme of industrial diversification that would loosen the grip of the traditional industries on the Scottish economy. Finally, Scottish politicians had the solution to the problems which had caused so much damage during the inter-war era.

THOMAS JOHNSTON was arguably the most significant Scottish politician of the twentieth century.

It was impossible to underestimate the extent of the problems which faced Scottish society in the aftermath of the Second World War. War damage was added to the dismal catalogue of social problems that had been inherited from the 1930s. The power of the state had been well and truly demonstrated in the fight against fascism, but was now exhausted and financially bankrupt. Furthermore, the people expected that their efforts during the war would be rewarded with a more just and caring society regulated by the state. The plans for post-war reconstruction, therefore, would be implemented on the basis of limited resources. The first casualty was the plan for industrial diversification. Heavy industry was a valuable export earner, as the American-funded reconstruction of Europe meant that orders piled into Scotland for coal, steel, ships, and engineering. Few expressed concern at this development, because the main objective of diversification was to ensure full employment. But as the traditional industries were still booming, everybody had a job. Scottish industry had a major advantage at this time because there was little competition from the war-ravaged economies of Europe. Yet it was a situation that would not last for ever. By 1958, major difficulties were becoming apparent. Indeed, Scotland was now more dependent on heavy industry than it had been at any time during the 1930s and, worse still, it suffered from poor rates of productivity and an annual growth rate that was half that of the United Kingdom. Wages and the standard of living were falling behind the rest of Britain, while deflation and public expenditure cuts, together with the ending of national service, brought the jobless total to 116,000. The Toothill Report of 1961 recommended that there was a greater need for more planning and targeted regional assistance. A consensus was formed that economic salvation was dependent on government intervention.

Social reconstruction was a major expectation of the post-war generation. Wartime bombing, poor and makeshift repair work, and the decline of privately rented accommodation added to the problems of Scottish housing. As with most things, the state was expected to tackle this problem and this meant a focus on municipal housing. The high standards insisted on by the Labour governments of 1945–51, together with a shortage of cash and building material, meant that construction was painfully slow. In 1951, a quarter of the Scottish population still lived in one- or two-roomed houses and a third had to share a toilet. The Conservative administrations after 1951 called in the experts to tackle the problem and 'pre-fabs', tower blocks, and new towns were deemed to be the best solutions. These schemes meant that the problems of cost and raw material shortage could be overcome and impressive

government housing targets could be realized. The experts' theoretical plans did not quite translate into reality. Housing was subject to competing political pressures and various agencies did battle to consolidate their own interests. The Scottish Special Housing Association, for example, was kept at arm's length by Glasgow District Council which regarded local housing as its own political fiefdom. Local councillors and MPs put in their own tuppenceworth which meant that some housing estates had no shops or pubs in order to keep the capitalists at bay. Slum clearance meant that whole families and communities were uprooted and dispatched to the bland and uniform new towns or 'overspill' towns. This massive social transformation was ameliorated by the fact of full employment and rising standards of living. By the early 1960s the impact of the national health service and increased purchasing power was making a substantial improvement on the nation's health. Infant and maternal mortality rates were decreasing, average heights and weights of children were increasing, and people were living longer.

Not surprisingly, Scottish politics were dominated by the role of the British state in social and economic welfare. Given that these issues were determined at a British level, Scottish politics in the period between 1950 and 1964 tended to follow the trends of British elections. Indeed, in this period, there was very little to separate the Labour and Conservative parties in terms of their share of the popular vote. Labour tended to win more seats, but this was due to the vagaries of the first past the post electoral system. In 1955, the Unionists won just over half the vote, an achievement unsurpassed in twentieth-century Scottish politics, and the more remarkable because the social structure of Scotland with its heavy representation of the working class should have been more favourable to Labour. One reason for Conservative success can be explained by the fact that the party adopted a high Scottish profile and denounced Labour's policy of nationalization which, it was claimed, meant that control of industry moved from Scotland to England. Also, the Conservatives came to power at the end of a period of extreme austerity and rationing. As the economy was picking up, they were able to take advantage of greater financial flexibility and preside over a period of growth. Significantly, it was when the problems of the economy became more acute in the early 1960s that a visible swing to Labour can be detected.

The Labour governments of Harold Wilson (1964–70) embarked on an ambitious project of state-sponsored economic expansion north of the Bor-

Facing: THE GORBALS. Post-war dreams that tower blocks were the way of the future turned sour as people found them badly planned and constructed. Most were eventually destroyed.

der. The Highlands and Islands development board and regional economic boards were set up to facilitate a massive public expenditure programme that was designed to improve the social infrastructure by concentrating on housing, health, transport, and education. It was believed that this would have important economic spin-offs by creating employment in the construction industry and local government. These jobs would offset losses in the traditional industries, it was hoped, and with full employment and money to spend, new industries would be attracted to Scotland to cash in on a vibrant consumer market. The new industries would then provide employment as the social infrastructure construction came to an end. The theory sounded fine, but its practical implementation was more or less handicapped from the outset. Periodic financial crisis militated against long-term strategy as budget deficits had to be clawed back. Wild optimism, short-term political calculations, poor and inexperienced planning, and inter-agency rivalry helped to produce a catalogue of failure. Extra pressure was brought to bear on the government's plans by the fact that its majority was small and could be jeopardized by Scottish disaffection, especially as Labour did proportionately better in Scotland than the rest of the United Kingdom. This was ruthlessly exploited by the secretary of state, William Ross, especially after 1967 when the SNP won a by-election in Hamilton, to make the case for high-prestige projects such as a car factory in Linwood, Bathgate. While politically popular, it made little economic sense as components had to be transported from the Midlands, which made unit costs higher. In spite of full pay packets, consumer industries did not come to Scotland as the nation had a reputation among multinationals for poor industrial relations and bad productivity. Scots bought their washing machines, fridges, TVs, and cars from abroad. The more traditional industries were in slow decline and the Scottish economy failed to diversify, the more people expected government intervention to maintain their social and economic aspirations. By the late 1960s, government favour in Scotland was being purchased by a public expenditure rate which was 20 per cent higher than the United Kingdom average.

The rise of nationalism and the faltering Scottish economy seemed to go hand in hand. The SNP capture of the safe Labour seat of Hamilton in 1967 occurred at a time of mounting unemployment, devaluation of sterling, and trailing standards of living. The Nationalists were also ably assisted by an ossified Scottish Labour Party whose political horizon on the ground stretched no further than the local council. With a vibrant youth counter-culture that sought to tackle issues such as the war in Vietnam, the stationing of nuclear

LAUNCH OF THE QE2. Ships were one-off creations and those who built them often invested a considerable emotional attachment in them.

submarines at Faslane on the Clyde, and women's liberation, Labour recruitment dried up. The Nationalists, on the other hand, seemed better able to tap into this movement and contrasted their youthful dynamic image with Labour, which came across as old and tired. The ebb and flow of the Nationalist vote between 1967 and 1974 suggests that it was largely a protest vote against London government, rather than a demand for independence. Voting for the Nationalists, however, did have one advantage over the British parties: it helped to get more attention for Scotland. In 1967, in response to the advance of the SNP, Harold Wilson ordered a Royal Commission on the

Constitution, and in 1968, Ted Heath, the leader of the Conservatives, came out in favour of devolution at the party conference in Perth. As the Nationalist vote faded in the general election of 1970, so too did the new prime minister, Ted Heath's, commitment to devolution.

The respite from the rise of nationalism was only temporary. The publication of the Kilbrandon Report on the Constitution came at the same time as the SNP won the Govan by-election in 1973 and was out just in time for the two general elections of 1974. The rise in oil prices and a miners' strike added to the growing problems of spiralling inflation and mounting unemployment. Although the SNP won almost a third of the vote in the second election of 1974, opinion poll evidence from the time seems to suggest that the party's rise was fuelled by mounting discontent at the government's handling of the economy. Only 12 per cent of respondents were in favour of the Nationalist flagship policy of independence, and it can reasonably be concluded that the SNP was supported as an effective way to make the British government take notice of Scottish problems. The threat of Nationalist secession was given an added impetus by the discovery of North Sea oil, which held out the prospect of economic salvation or the choice of, as Nationalist propaganda put it at the time, 'Rich Scots or Poor Britons'. Faced with mounting problems in the economy, Northern Ireland, and a slender majority which was reduced to a minority in 1976, the difficulty of Scotland was added to a catalogue of crises faced by the Labour government that was threatening to get out of control.

Although devolution had its enthusiasts in the Labour Party, it did not command universal support in the mid-1970s and, indeed, there were a number of high-profile members who were exceptionally hostile to the idea of a Scottish parliament. The need to go cap in hand to the International Monetary Fund for a loan to bale Britain out of its financial predicament had a number of bearings on Scotland. First, along with the rest of the United Kingdom, the IMF's insistence that public expenditure be cut meant rising unemployment and growing industrial tensions, all of which added to Labour's unpopularity. Secondly, it meant that Scottish discontent could not be bought off with extra government-funded economic assistance. If nationalism was being fuelled by economic grievance, as most thought, how could it be stopped? Devolution seemed the best solution. After much internal debate and dissension, Labour finally endorsed the creation of a Scottish assembly as the best political solution to the rise of nationalism. Devolution would give the Scots a form of national recognition and a means of limited self-government which it was believed would take the steam out of the Nationalist juggernaut. As with the

SCOTTISH FOOTBALL FANS had a terrible reputation in the south during the 1970s. Bravado following victory over England in 1977 turned to tears the following year when Scotland was 'hammered' in the World Cup in Argentina.

best-laid plans, the Government of Scotland Act was more or less doomed from the outset. The minority government was at the mercy of its back-benchers who ambushed the bill at its various stages through the House of Commons. Devolution would require popular endorsement from the Scottish electorate in the form of a referendum. Furthermore, the Cunning-hamme amendment stipulated that more than 40 per cent of the total electorate would have to vote yes for the Act to become law. It was a huge hurdle to overcome, especially when it is remembered that few governments have been elected in Britain by over 40 per cent of the electorate. A campaign to mobilize support suffered from internal divisions as the Nationalists and Labour refused to cooperate. In contrast to the deeply divided Yes campaign, the No campaign was united and well funded by business. Taking place during the aftermath of the winter of discontent when public sector strikes brought much of normal living to a standstill, the government-sponsored assembly undoubtedly suffered from Labour unpopularity. Although the Yes campaign won by a narrow margin (1.6 per cent), it failed to break the 40 per cent barrier. Put crudely, what the referendum showed was that a third of Scots wanted the assembly, a third did not, and a third did not care. Devolution was not the settled will of the Scottish people in 1979 and, if anything, it was a major source of division. At the subsequent general election in the same year, the Nationalist vote evaporated back to Labour, showing that it had largely been fuelled by protest.

A nation again? 1979–2000

The last twenty years of the twentieth century witnessed a degree of political, social, economic, and cultural change in Scotland that has perhaps been unprecedented since the Industrial Revolution. The 1960s and the 1970s witnessed the end of an old Scotland which probably had more in common with the nineteenth century than the early twenty-first. The rapidity and totality of change has been such that contemporaries, let alone historians, have difficulty in offering a clear explanation of how and why it happened. The best way to demonstrate this is to outline the most dramatic changes. In politics the Conservative Party declined at a time of ascendancy in England and the campaign for home rule led to the creation of a Scottish parliament. Scottish political behaviour diverged violently from the British (i.e. mainly English) norm. The economy moved away from its traditional heavy industries to one which was dependent on services and electronics. Also, the centre of economic gravity moved eastwards towards Edinburgh. Socially, Scotland became more middle class as the proportion of homeowners grew, more were employed in middle management, and average per capita income rose. The gap in wealth increased greatly in this period, leading to large isolated areas of social deprivation whose inhabitants were labelled as the 'underclass'. The 1980s and 1990s witnessed a cultural renaissance with an outpouring of artistic achievements in music, poetry, literature, film, drama, and art. Cultural self-confidence had not been as high since the nineteenth century and was reflected by the fact that Scotland and Scottishness tended to be incidental rather than the main focus of artistic endeavour. This was in marked contrast to the 'renaissance' of the 1920s and 1930s where national angst was the predominant theme. Finally, the British state has become less important as the global economy and the European Union have emerged as major determinants of Scottish social and economic trends. Inward investment by multinationals, the triumph of free market economic ideology, the scourge of drugs, pockets of urban deprivation, and an increasingly global popular culture, all of which affect Scotland, are features common to most modern societies.

Casting an omni-present shadow over this dramatic period of change in Scottish history is the figure of Margaret Thatcher. The victory of the Conservative Party in Britain in 1979 coincided with a downturn in the international economy which was coupled with an ideological commitment to free market economics. Thatcherite rhetoric denounced the pervasive influence of the 'nanny state' which had led to Britain's economic decline. State socialism, it was argued, meant that competition was stifled under bureaucracy and that the only way Britain could compete in the international market was to cut the chains of state support to failing industries. The policy of 'modernize or die', coming as it did with a downturn in the global market, unleashed a massive wave of de-industrialization in Scotland in the early 1980s as shipbuilding, steel, engineering, and manufacturing reeled under 'year zero' rules of competition. Privatization of public corporations added to the calamity as British Steel, British Gas, and British Telecom shed labour in order to make themselves fit for sale. High interest rates were used to curb inflation and strengthen the international value of sterling, which further undermined the capacity of manufacturing to compete. Caterpillar at Uddingstone, Linwood at Bathgate, the aluminium smelter at Invergordon, and the Gartcosh steel works, together with many smaller factories throughout Scotland, all withered away under the chill winds of free market competition. The defeat of the miners in the strike of 1984 paved the way for restructuring and closure, with mining towns in Fife, Lanarkshire, and Stirlingshire losing their biggest source of employment. In 1985, unemployment peaked at 15.6 per cent. Paradoxically, the high cost of social security was paid for by North Sea oil receipts. The expected salvation of the 'black gold' never came, as Scottish business proved incapable of responding to these new opportunities. The discovery of oil off Scottish shores did more for the economy of Texas in the 1980s than for Scotland.

It is difficult to assess the precise impact of de-industrialization on the course of Scottish politics. In the national psyche, manufacturing was part and parcel of Scottish identity, and although the economy underwent a successful process of diversification in the period after 1985 in which electronics, petro-chemicals, financial services, light engineering, and tourism led the way, the electorate was not prepared to forgive Thatcher for the massive upheaval and uncertainty of the early 1980s when it seemed that no one was safe from unemployment. In the elections of 1983 and 1987, the Tory vote declined and collapsed. Tactical voting was used to punish the Conservatives and the most marked feature of Scottish political behaviour in the period after 1987 was its almost pathological anti-Toryism, which left the party with less than a quarter of the vote and only ten MPs. This was in marked contradistinction to England, where Thatcher seemed invincible. Rejection at the ballot box did little to cool Conservative reforming ardour. The introduction of the Poll Tax a year ahead of the rest of the United Kingdom in 1988 helped to provide a graphic illustration of the two new phrases on the lips of political commentators; the democratic deficit and the Doomsday Scenario. The seeming inability of Labour to win a British election gave rise to a widespread fear that Scotland would continue to suffer the imposition of unpopular Conservative policies. The fact that Conservative support had withered away in Scotland counted for little and inevitably such grievances took on a Nationalist air. The creation of a devolved Scottish parliament was mooted as a defensive mechanism which would balance the democratic deficit and counter the effects of the Doomsday Scenario. The SNP had another solution which was independence. It was in an effort to tackle the twin problems of unpopular Tory rule and the drift towards nationalism that Labour and the Democrats signed up to the cross-party Scottish Constitutional Convention (SCC) in 1988 which would provide an umbrella organization that would bring together the churches, local government, and the trade unions as a representative forum of the people in order to press for a Scottish parliament. The Nationalist victory at the Govan by-election in November 1988 added urgency to their endeavours.

The recovery of Labour in the late 1980s, a near miss in the general election in 1992, the departure of Margaret Thatcher, and a consensus voiced by the new Labour leader, John Smith, that devolution was the 'settled will of the Scottish people', helped to stave off further Nationalist gains. Although the politics of Scotland and Britain took divergent paths, the same could not be said about social and economic trends. From the late 1980s and throughout the 1990s, Scotland became more similar in its social composition to England. For all the Scots may have despised Tory policy, they took advantage of it to buy council houses. For all the problems of the decline of manufacturing, they took to employment in white collar occupations. By the mid-1990s, Scotland had attained the European Union average on a whole range of socio-economic indicators. All of this suggests that the rejection of Thatcherism was not motivated by poverty or economic disadvantage. Put plainly, if voting was determined by socio-economic factors, the Conservatives should have done well in Scotland. The fact that they did not can be explained by reference to Scottish political culture. The Scots kept faith with the social democratic vision which dominated British politics in the era before the advent of Thatcherism. After all, it had served the nation well by providing full employment, made for greater distribution of wealth, and had rewarded a great many Scots. It was the reluctance to abandon these values which led to the collapse of the Tory Party and the demand for home rule. The return of a Labour government in 1997 and the successful outcome of a referendum on devolution in the same year secured the establishment of a Scottish parliament. Opened in 1999, it completed the transformation of the nation at the end of a turbulent century.

9 The Scottish Diaspora

DAVID ARMITAGE

'The ubiquitous Scots'

'Rats, lice, and Scotsmen: you find them the whole world over,' ran the medieval French proverb. Half a millennium and half a world away from France in the Middle Ages, an observer in the 1850s of Highlanders on the Australian goldfields agreed: 'Poor as rats at home, they are as rapacious as rats abroad.' The abiding reputation of the Scots for mobility and ubiquity has been well deserved; Scots emigrants' reputation for poverty much less so. By the late twentieth century, there were an estimated 25 million people of Scottish descent living outside Scotland. Their ancestors could have left Scotland at any point since the thirteenth century, and they fetched up on almost every imaginable foreign shore. It is notable that so many of those who claim Scottish ancestry retain an attachment to their homeland, even as they and their forebears assimilated so successfully to the new societies in which they found themselves. The distinctiveness of the Scottish experience outside Scotland lies in this apparently paradoxical ability of Scots to blend in so completely with their background yet still to maintain sympathetic connections with Scotland itself. Scotland's history is a transnational history because the Scots have been such a prominently international people. In their far-flung wanderings, their diverse settlements, and their well-tended nostalgia, the Scots are a diasporic people. Scottish history is thus not just the history of a nation and its citizens; it is no less the history of Scottish migration, and of Scottish migrants, wherever they may be found. No history of Scotland could be complete without an account of the Scottish diaspora.

The Scots are, of course, not unique in laying claim to the title of diaspora.

THE 'ARAB PRINCESS' (on the left, with her 'black maid') allegedly fell in love with the young Sir John Henderson of Fordel in Zanzibar in the 1620s and saved him from 'Barbarian' captivity: an African Pocahontas to his Scottish John Smith?

Indeed, as historians, sociologists, and anthropologists have increasingly argued, dispersal, resettlement, and intermingling have been abiding characteristics of human history over many thousands of years. The phase of history which associates peoples with nations, and nations with states, now seems a rather fleeting one. States with fixed borders, settled governments, and legally defined citizenship have existed only since the fifteenth or sixteenth centuries. They began to look increasingly embattled in the late twentieth century, when the globalization of the world economy challenged the sovereignty of states and when the creation of large supranational organizations, from the United Nations to the European Union, created political entities larger than the classic nation-states which flourished in the nineteenth century. In this perspective, communities whose histories have overflowed the boundaries of states appear more interesting, even exemplary. Diasporic peoples like the Jews, sub-Saharan Africans, Chinese, Indians, Irish, Armenians, or Palestinians may be the harbingers of twenty-first-century rootlessness and forced migration. Moreover, the history of peoples like the Scots, whose dispersals were, for the most part, voluntary, may show the advantages of mobility, ingenuity, and assimilability in the new century.

The Scots have long been known for the supposed talents they took with them into their temporary or permanent exile. When John Macky, the notorious English journalist, traveller, and spy, toured Scotland in the 1720s, he admired Scottish wanderlust, and wondered about its causes. 'The *Scots* have made a greater Figure Abroad than any other nation in *Europe*,' he asserted; 'this hath been generally ascribed to the Barrenness of their Country, as not being able to maintain its Inhabitants: But this is a vulgar Error, for it's entirely owing to the Fineness of their Education.' In support of his first observation, he catalogued the achievements of the Scots in Europe. They had formed the bodyguard of the king of France (the famous *Garde Écossaise*) since the fifteenth century; they had commanded the armies of Gustavus Adolphus of Sweden in the early seventeenth century; as Macky noted, even the field-marshal of the Holy Roman Empire was General Ogilvy, the grandson of a Scot. Quite apart from this military diaspora, Scots could be found in more peaceful occupations across Europe. There were Bruces, Gordons, and Douglases in Muscovy, a Count Hamilton in the Palatinate, and one could hardly travel anywhere in Italy without bumping into Scottish families, such as the Wemysses whom Macky had met on Lake Garda. Though anecdotal, Macky's evidence was at least indicative of the fact that, even a generation after the Anglo-Scottish union of 1707, the Scots were still primarily a European people, as they had been since at least the thirteenth century.

Macky witnessed the beginnings of a transformation in the Scottish economy and Scottish attitudes. He wrote at a turning point in Scotland's relations with the outside world, when admission to the English Atlantic empire promised new—or at least newly legitimate—outlets for Scottish ingenuity. The most famous provision of the Treaty of Union in 1707 had admitted Scots to 'full Freedom and Intercourse of Trade and Navigation to and from . . . the Dominions and Plantations' of what now became a fully *British* Empire. Foreign connections still shaped the manners and began to pad the wallets of those who stayed at home. Macky found that the better-bred young men of Stirling adopted a polite Gallic disdain for commercial employment; meanwhile, he saw that the merchants of Glasgow, now legally supplied by shipping from the Atlantic colonies, were waxing fat on the profits of tobacco and sugar. He speculated that eventually these colonial superprofits would inspire even the Frenchified gentry to hitch their fortunes to the wagon of empire by engaging in trade. That might demand that Scots turn their back on centuries of cultural ties with Europe, but the gains would surely compensate them.

Macky may have been right to observe that the Scots stood at a crossroads in their international connections, but his explanations for Scottish migration have not stood the test of time. The anecdotal and biographical approach to the Scottish diaspora predominated in the most impotently self-mythologizing periods of Scottish history, particularly in the nineteenth century, and may have compensated for the failure of Scottish historians to provide themselves with the comforting sustenance of convincing national myths. Like Macky, later historians of the Scots abroad looked to the achievements of exemplary Scottish men (rarely women), but paid little attention to what their exploits betokened. Above all, they took no interest in the wider currents of migration that had carried these Scots to foreign shores. Displaced pride in martial prowess or a social Darwinist attachment to ideas of racial peculiarity did little to provide a clearer picture of Scots' diasporic tendencies. The explanations for the Scottish diaspora necessarily made little advance beyond Macky: a barren country, chilling to its inhabitants' bodies, did nothing to dampen their ardent and ingenious spirits, encouraged by a notably advanced educational system. What else could these canny, but overeducated, Scots do but take their talents abroad, for the use of others but to the enduring glory of an unwelcoming, if not ungrateful, mother country?

Mobility and migration

The biographical-anecdotal approach to the Scottish diaspora is far from dead: a recent author attributes to Scots the discovery of America, traces the ingenuity that led Marconi to invent the radio to his Scottish ancestry, and finds it significant that there are more Scottish-Americans in the Baseball Hall of Fame than among the ranks of US presidents. Yet every achievement (or indeed every crime) of every Scot abroad should not be attributed solely to their Scottishness: as the duke of Wellington put it in another context, 'Just because one is born in a stable does not make one a horse.' In the attempt to get beyond these unhistorical pieties, scholars have shown much more clearly the dimensions, the diversity, and the varying causes of Scottish migration over time. Scotland seems to have produced a surplus of population ready and willing to migrate since at least the thirteenth century. David I had imported 'Scots, French and Flemish burgesses' to people his new burghs in the twelfth century, but Scotland neither needed nor experienced any major inward migration before the Irish came to the Lowland belt during the Victorian industrial boom. Even New Commonwealth immigration after the 1950s was relatively light compared with that into England. Instead, Scots in varying numbers have chosen to move, either within Scotland, across the North Channel to Ireland, over the Border into England, or more broadly into Europe and the extra-European world.

Emigration from Scotland, as from most European countries, was often continuous with internal mobility. Scots law imposed few legal or institutional constraints on movement within the country though, at least until the seventeenth century, the Highland divide formed a natural barrier. The increasing permeability of that boundary has been called 'the most important single change in Scottish migration patterns during the eighteenth century', and this in turn contributed to the higher incidence of Highlanders emigrating from Scotland, especially after mid-century. Before the seventeenth century, most migration within Scotland took place within rural areas, migrants rarely travelled more than 6 miles, and women were generally less mobile than men. Need propelled some of this mobility. Temporary migration frequently followed the subsistence crises of the 1620s, 1690s, 1741, 1782, and 1799 or the bubonic plague in the 1640s; the potato famine in Ireland later drove Irish immigrants into Scotland, but the parallel blight in the Highlands in 1848–56 also compelled Scots to move, both within the United Kingdom and further abroad. By and large, such subsistence migration declined in the eighteenth century, when rapidly increasing urbanization in Scotland encouraged migration from the countryside to the burgeoning cities as Glasgow, Aberdeen, and Dumfries joined Edinburgh as major centres of urban immigration. This set a pattern of migration-cum-urbanization that would be reproduced in the nineteenth century when many migrants went directly from the cities of Scotland to the cities of the Empire, in Canada, Australia, and South Africa.

Scottish participation in the British imperial diaspora of the eighteenth, nineteenth, and early twentieth centuries certainly bulks largest in the popular historical imagination, inside and outside Scotland, and may have taken the largest accumulation of migrants out of Scotland. Yet, in the perspective of the last 700 years, that two-century-long movement to the anglophone Empire was a historical aberration. For at least four centuries before 1707, and increasingly again since the Second World War, the main destinations for Scottish migrants have been European. In this perspective, the true crossroads for Scottish emigration may not have been the generations after the union, but rather the last quarter of the seventeenth century, when Scots first successfully turned their attention to the Caribbean and the mainland of North America. Before the mid-seventeenth century, Scots had exploited three escape routes above all: across the channel to Ireland; over the North

THIS STRIKING POSTER, printed in red and black, appeared in post-offices around Britain in 1888 to direct emigrants to North America, Australasia, and (with less success, among Scots at least) to Southern Africa.

Sea to Scandinavia, northern Europe, France, and beyond; and over the Border to England. A century and a half after Columbus had established a repeatable oceanic path from Europe to the Americas, Scots still overwhelmingly preferred European destinations.

The contrasts among patterns of migration in the early seventeenth century are striking. Before 1650, by far the greatest number of Scots—an estimated 30,000–40,000—made their way to Poland, as pedlars, petty tradesmen, or soldiers: the poet-traveller William Lithgow in the 1630s called Poland 'a mother and nurse for the youth and younglings of Scotland who are yearly sent hither in great numbers' and estimated that 'thirty thousand Scots families . . . live incorporate in her bowels'. The estimated 20,000–30,000 Scots who travelled to settle in Ireland, especially between the opening of the Anglo-Scottish Ulster plantation in 1609 and the uprising of 1641, were matched only by the 25,000 or so who went to Scandinavia, many as soldiers rather than settlers in the armies of the Thirty Years War. By comparison, the number of Scots who left for the Caribbean and North America in the same period has been estimated at 250—fewer than the crew of James IV's huge warship, the 'Great' *Michael*, and barely half the number of Fife Adventurers who twice attempted to colonize the Isle of Lewis between 1599 and 1607.

The traditional European patterns of Scottish migration before the late seventeenth century gave little inkling of the shift in horizons to come. If the seventeenth century was England's century for migration to the western hemisphere, then the eighteenth century would be Scotland's. By the end of the seventeenth century, some 6,000 Scots had left for the Americas, a trivial number compared to the estimated 380,000 English people who had migrated between 1630 and 1700. Scottish emigration only began to excite widespread notice in the 1770s, when James Boswell and Samuel Johnson, along with the government in Westminster, remarked the 'rage for emigration' which seemed to be depopulating the Highlands and Islands. The eighteenth century saw the conquest of subsistence crises in Scotland but, as mortality declined, so opportunity knocked in the new territories in North America acquired after the Seven Years War. For four decades, the ups-and-downs of Britain's worldwide wars dictated patterns of Scottish emigration. The conquests in British North America and, to a lesser extent, the Ceded Islands of the Caribbean pulled ever larger numbers of migrants, often as families, westward across the Atlantic. Governmental fears of depopulation formally closed the door for voyagers to the west in 1775, but not before officials had compiled the most revealing demographic snapshot of early British migration. The flow only resumed after the end of the American War in 1783; thereafter it boomed for another decade until halted by the French Revolutionary Wars with their unprecedented demands for British military muscle. The Peace of Amiens in 1802 opened the door to migration once again, and foreshadowed the great migrations of the nineteenth century, which increasingly turned away from North America to newer parts of the Empire.

The eighteenth century was Scotland's North American century; the nineteenth would be the century of Australasia and, to a lesser extent, South Africa. The Scottish population doubled between 1801 and 1870, more than doubled again between 1850 and 1900, then slowed to increase by only a tenth between 1900 and 1940. Yet, despite these enormous demographic surges, only Ireland in the period 1850–1930 lost a greater proportion of its natural increase to emigration than Scotland, nor did Scotland have any single population movement to match the Irish diaspora after the Famine of 1848. Scottish migration proceeded by briefer bursts, with 1831–3, 1842–3, and 1869–74 the peaks of a century of emigration which saw more protracted, but no less populous, movements throughout the 1850s (when Australasia definitively replaced North America as Scots emigrants' primary destination), and the 1880s and 1900s (in each of which some quarter of a million Scots emigrated). A greater proportion of the Scottish male population fought in the Great War than of the English or the Welsh (an estimated 26.9 per cent, compared to some 24.2 per cent of English or Welsh men), though that war did once again prevent conventional forms of emigration. The 1920s saw another migrant boom which collapsed during the harsher times of the 1930s.

The pattern of Scottish mobility in the nineteenth and early twentieth centuries reveals what one historian has called 'the paradox of Scottish migration'. Though temporary hardship, such as plague, famine, or clearance, could drive Scots to move, the greatest movements of population in the modern period coincided with Scotland's broad upswing in industrial prosperity and a secular increase in the standard of living. Most Scottish emigrants after 1860 came from the new manufacturing and urban economy. Like their predecessors since the thirteenth century, these Scots were generally better educated and better off than contemporary migrants from other European countries. As the English conservative Josiah Tucker had noted in the 1770s, 'it was not Poverty or Necessity which compelled, but Ambition which enticed them to forsake their native soil'. This ambitiousness cannot be attributed to the general 'Fineness of [Scottish] education', however, *pace* Macky, only to the greater likelihood among Scots of all periods that the most skilled would migrate. Scottish literacy levels before the nineteenth century were lower than those of Sweden or New England: Iceland, not Scotland, would be the first European country to achieve universal adult literacy, in the eighteenth century. Education did not fuel the Scottish exodus of the nineteenth century. Population increase, rapid industrialization, and a shift from rural to urban society spurred movement at home; they also inspired mobility abroad. Much of that mobility coincided with industrial depression in Scotland, in the later 1840s and early 1850s, the mid-1880s, and 1906–13. Industrialization and urbanization therefore offered new reasons for emigration, rather than new remedies for the causes of mobility.

Scots often travelled on paths beaten by their forebears, but the shift away from Europe and outward to the Empire in the mid-eighteenth century snapped the chains along which migration had traditionally run. Across that divide, some broad characteristics of the Scottish diaspora remained stable. Scots were generally more likely than their English counterparts (save for those who travelled to New England in the Great Migration of the 1640s) to leave as families, or in parties, like the fifty who went from Glenorchy to North Carolina on 4 September 1775, in company with seventy-seven more from Appin in Argyll. Such group migration offered Scots ready-made communities on landing and aided settlement even as it reinforced Scottish separatism. Scots were likely to be better educated than other European migrants because they frequently went as skilled professionals, dogging the footsteps of fellow ministers, merchants, soldiers, educators, or doctors. Such migrants followed the institutional channels of the Kirk, the army, the navy, the civil service, and the East India Company to new arenas for their skill and enterprise. Scottish patronage often smoothed their way. In this way, John Witherspoon and John Pagan tried to bring their countrymen to settle in Nova Scotia; Dundas packed the ranks of the East India Company with deserving Scots, as Ilay had done even more successfully before him; the Highland and Island Emigration Society attracted 4,000 Scots to Australia in the 1850s; and the countess of Aberdeen encouraged the departure of more than 330 female emigrants from north-east Scotland in the late nineteenth century. Most famously, David Livingstone found his way both to Africa and to worldwide fame by the inspiration afforded by the self-improving homilies of the Scot Samuel Smiles, the patronage of a Scottish president of the Royal Geographical Society, Sir Roderick Murchison, and the promotion of his Scottish publisher, John Murray. Necessity, nepotism, and cronyism together

account for much of the legendary clannishness of the Scots. This was no ethnic trait, but rather the fruit of centuries of experience in exploiting professional opportunities: like the Jews, the Huguenots, or the Irish, the Scots held
their diaspora together by vigorous global networking.

Not all Scottish emigration was voluntary, even in the broadest sense of following from choices made in the face of overwhelming circumstance. After
Cromwell's defeat of Scottish armies at Dunbar and Worcester in 1650–1,
many more Scots went to North America and the Caribbean in chains than
went of their own free will. No less recalcitrant royalist regimes transported
Scots to the colonies after Bothwell Brig and Argyll's rising, offering precedents for the wider transportation movement of the eighteenth century, like
the two fathoms of rope bought by the burgh of Stirling in 1700 to restrain the
unfortunate 'Laurence M'Lairen quhen sent to America'. In general Scottish
felons were less likely to be transported than their English compeers, but
only because Scots law reserved transportation as the punishment for its most
fearsome criminals. (This accounts for the relatively tiny proportion of
Scots—only 3 per cent—among British convicts in Australia.) When the
American War closed off the British colonies of the western hemisphere as
sinks for felons, the potential of the newly discovered lands of the southern
hemisphere was soon realized. Among the most prominent early trans-
portees to Australia were the 'Political Martyrs', prosecuted and condemned
during in the 1790s for agitating in favour of a Scottish convention. Their
obelisk stands in the Old Calton Burying Ground in Edinburgh, close to
Robert Adam's monument to that great cosmopolitan francophile David
Hume (who had lived on four separate occasions in Paris), and near to the
memorial to the Scots-Americans who died fighting for the Union in the
American Civil War. All three are evidence of the diversity of the Scottish
diaspora, both free and forced.

It would be a mistake to think that all forms of Scottish migration were permanent, or that all migrants, even the most notorious, were necessarily lost to
Scotland forever. Temporary migration had characterized the seasonal passage from Highlands to Lowlands from the sixteenth century, and had been a
feature of Scottish mobility since Irish kings had imported Hebridean-Norse
mercenaries from the Western Isles in the eleventh and twelfth centuries.
Throughout the late medieval and early modern period, substantial numbers
of Scottish pedlars traversed the Border into England or the sea to northern
Europe, but many would have returned at the end of their selling stints.
Though military service often led to settlement abroad—in France during

the fifteenth century, Sweden, Poland, and Prussia in the early seventeenth century, or North America in the late eighteenth century—the bulk of later survivors of Britain's global wars, Scots among them, returned to their homelands. Other temporary migrant groups punctuate the history of the Scottish diaspora, from the 'sojourners in the sun' who made up half of the white population of Jamaica in the 1740s (most of whom remigrated) to the Scottish writers to the East India Company in Bengal, the Orcadians employed by the Hudson's Bay Company, or the Aberdeenshire granite workers who journeyed seasonally to build the state capitol in Austin, Texas, in the mid-nineteenth century. Less conspicuously, but more importantly for Scottish demographic history, an estimated 27 per cent of the 1,667,300 Scots who migrated between 1853 and 1938 subsequently returned to Scotland. It is, of course, impossible to chart the effect of these remigrations on Scotland, but the experience of these returnees from the Scottish diaspora must have nurtured the cosmopolitanism of metropolitan Scots.

The twentieth century has seen one of the greatest, most continuous, though least-heralded periods of Scottish migration. The 1981 census of the United Kingdom showed that the Scottish population was only 5 per cent higher than it had been six decades earlier. (By contrast, the English figures showed an increase of 30 per cent, some of whom must have been Scots.) Decreased fertility since the 1920s contributed to this decline, but outmigration must have accounted for a good part of it. Though it has hardly been as often remarked as in earlier periods (such as the 1770s), the almost flat population statistics reveal a quiet rage for Scottish emigration in the latter half of the twentieth century. Just under 200,000 Scots left Scotland—and the United Kingdom—between 1984 and 1994 in what have been called 'The Lowland Clearances'. Even that figure must still mask the numbers of Scots who have moved within the United Kingdom, mostly south to England. There is no sign that this movement will be halted, even with the revival of a measure of Scottish political autonomy under its devolved assembly since 1999. The borderless labour market within the European Union will surely accelerate professional mobility, to return Scots to familiar migratory paths, albeit within a new Europe.

Scots as Europeans

Geography, opportunity, and necessity together conspired to make Scotland the most lastingly European and cosmopolitan of the Three Kingdoms' four nations. The common bonds of Roman Catholicism before the Reformation, like the increasingly strong ties of Protestantism after it, involved Scots in the concerns of Catholic Christendom and the later confessional divisions of Europe. The pan-European Latinate culture bequeathed by medieval clerics, nourished in the universities, and maintained by the republic of letters of the seventeenth and eighteenth centuries allowed Scots access to an ample Europe of the mind. Continental warfare, from the Hundred Years War to the Second World War, drew Scottish manpower into European conflicts, while the Scottish mercenary tradition bled into the lands and populations of France, Sweden, Poland, and Russia. Scottish merchants planted themselves around commercial Europe to create small but self-contained Scottish communities in Danzig, Rotterdam, Veere, Bordeaux, and Copenhagen by the seventeenth century. Over time, demand for skills surplus to requirements in Scotland pulled Scottish migrants towards the armies of French kings, the mercantile towns of northern Europe, the construction projects of imperial Russia, and the factories of industrial England.

European contacts brought with them knowledge of a wider world, knowledge which may in turn have encouraged further movement, especially among the literate. Manuscripts of guidebooks for pilgrims such as *De passagio ad terram sanctam* ('On the Journey to the Holy Land') and *De mirabilibus mundi* ('On the Wonders of the World') could be found in Aberdeen Cathedral library in 1464. By the 1680s, the 'Bibliotheck' of Kirkwall, in the Orkneys—the most northerly library in seventeenth-century Britain—contained books from (among other places) Danzig, Freistadt, Frankfurt, Amsterdam, Leipzig, Middelburg, Paris, Brussels, Wittenberg, Rostock, and Cracow. Orcadians had access to a 1509 Paris edition of Pope Pius II's Latin *Cosmographia*, a folio history of the Dutch Revolt (in Dutch), and *Bloudy News from Ireland* (one of thirteen pamphlets on the 1641 Irish uprising in the library); they could also follow the terrifying advance of Islam on the fringes of Europe in such pamphlets as *The Whiggs Lamentation for the Loss of Buda* (1686). Such bibliographic resources provide evidence not only of the expansive intellectual panorama available even to the most distant subjects of the Scottish crown but also of the trading currents which carried books across the North Sea to the Orkneys from the major coastal towns and publishing centres of northern Europe. Even in the seventeenth century, the ocean was Scotland's road to a wider world, and intellectual links became inseparable from mercantile connections.

Pilgrims and crusaders introduced Europe to Scotland. Medieval Scotland was a consumer, rather than an exporter, of human resources, and the best-travelled Scots of the thirteenth and fourteenth centuries had religious purposes. The largest traffic from Scotland led to the shrines of Europe and the Levant, to Canterbury, Compostela, Rome, and the Holy Land, where the Scottish pilgrim could see the sacred sites described in Abbot Adomnán of Iona's guide, *De locis sanctis* ('On the Holy Places'). John, bishop of Glasgow, is recorded as being in Rome and Jerusalem in 1122, and more Scots became noticeable in Palestine after the First Crusade when, according to the English chronicler William of Malmesbury, 'the Welshman abandoned his poaching, the Scot his familiarity with fleas' to answer the call of defending Christendom. Scots took part in all of the major crusades of the eleventh, twelfth, and thirteenth centuries, though in lesser numbers than the English, the Germans, or the French. No Scottish king ever went on crusade, though one of the more grandiose schemes of James IV was to build a great crusading battle fleet in the early sixteenth century that would create European unity in the face of the Turkish threat. The more general decline of the crusading spirit had encouraged a rise in peaceful pilgrimage since the fourteenth century. The road to Jerusalem would be trodden by Scots until the traffic faded in the seventeenth century, but not before the heart of James I had been carried there on posthumous pilgrimage, as Robert Bruce's heart had earlier been transported to Spain during the crusade against the Saracens. The Loretto hermitage in Musselburgh, built in 1533 by the latter-day crusader Thomas Doughty, who had fought the Turks in the eastern Mediterranean, was perhaps the last concrete evidence of the pilgrim spirit in pre-Reformation Scotland.

Hard on the heels of the pilgrims came the scholars: a Scottish brain-drain was no modern phenomenon, though most of these early intellectual migrants returned to Scotland. Macky's theory that Scottish wanderlust derived from Scottish education may have been more true for the three centuries before the early 1600s than for any other period. An estimated 1,000 Scots went to universities outside Scotland in the two centuries before the foundation of the University of St Andrews in 1410, the bulk of them to Paris, Oxford, and Bologna in the thirteenth century; after 1296, all went anywhere other than England. Even once Scotland had acquired institutions of higher learning comparable in number and stature to those on the continent (even as England went comparatively underendowed), Scots still travelled abroad for their higher education. Symptomatic of the Scottish literati's European contacts is the fact that all five principals of Marischal

College, Aberdeen, between 1593 and 1649 had studied abroad, at the universities of Rostock, Herborn, Helmstedt, Sedan, La Rochelle, Leiden, and Basle.

By the seventeenth century, the bulk of Scottish students travelled to France and, increasingly, Holland to study law at Paris, Louvain, and Leiden and medicine at the scientifically more advanced Dutch universities, where the great Herman Boerhaave taught 244 students from Scotland, including most of the founders of the Edinburgh Faculty of Medicine. Though James Boswell (a student of pipe-smoking, if little else, at Utrecht) was a member of almost the last generation who could expect to pursue their legal education in Holland, his eighteenth-century forebears would have gained from such schooling a grounding in the proto-Enlightenment values of liberal Dutch intellectual culture, as well as the theoretical broadening which came from exposure to the natural law tradition of Hugo Grotius and Samuel Pufendorf. The same could hardly be said for Adam Smith, whose experience as a Snell Exhibitioner at Balliol College, Oxford, in the early 1740s at least did nothing to damage the first-rate education he had received at Glasgow under Francis Hutcheson and his peers. (Smith, like Edward Gibbon, acknowledged no obligation to the University of Oxford.) Scots' preference for continental universities undoubtedly contributed to the cosmopolitanism of Scottish legal, medical, and professorial culture, and thereby shaped the distinctive tenor of the Scottish Enlightenment of the eighteenth century.

Ideas, like books, were commodities: the paths of Scottish learning were frequently also the paths of Scottish earning. Scots scholars in the Low Countries frequently trod where merchants had gone before in the thirteenth, fourteenth, and fifteenth centuries, when Scotland's greatest trading post in Europe for the sale of wool was Flanders. Bruges had its 'Schottendyc' from the fifteenth century, but the greater Scottish presence would later be found in Holland, when the Scots settled on Veere (Campvere) as their entrepôt for national exports, home to the Schotse Huizen on the quay of the staple port. In the later seventeenth century, Rotterdam took over as the Scots' major port of entry, and from there Scottish merchants had access to the whole of northern Europe; from there, too, a merchant like Andrew Russell traded with New England, Surinam, and Sweden. The presence of such contacts softened the blow of exile for those ministers, nobles, and lairds who left Scotland during the turbulent times of the late seventeenth century. The Scottish population in these commercial centres was fluid and variable; the presence of merchants and ministers, trading houses and meeting houses, could make exiles into immigrants and channel support from home to Scots who had gone unwillingly abroad.

Despite the prominence of Scottish commercial and intellectual links with the Low Countries, Scotland reached its greatest mercantile hinterland on the continent by way of the Baltic ports. The origins of Scottish trade with the Baltic lay in the thirteenth century, after which Aberdeen, Dundee, St Andrews, and Leith established regular commercial ties with Copenhagen, Stockholm, Rostock, Hamburg, Bremen, Danzig, Elbing, and Königsberg. These ports provided entryways for Scottish migrants, especially into Poland during the late sixteenth and early seventeenth centuries. William Lithgow's estimate of 30,000 Scots families in Poland by the 1630s must be an exaggeration, but it does capture both the scale of the Scottish diaspora in Poland and the fact that many Scots who came as itinerants stayed to leave behind descendants with recognizably Scottish names, like the Tomas Czamer (Thomas Chalmers) who was four times mayor of Warsaw before his death in 1709. These expatriates assimilated readily to Polish society, but retained their ties to Scottish institutions. When Charles II appealed for funds from Polish Scots in 1651, £10,000 was promised, even if only £800 was remitted; more successful was Marischal College's 1699 alumni appeal for building repairs, to which sixteen Polish Scots sent donations. The scale of the Scottish migrant stream to Poland caused concern until at least the 1650s. Though by the late seventeenth century it had dwindled to a trickle, settlers on Jamaica were still petitioning the Scots privy council in the 1670s 'that all prudential means be found to encourage Scots to come hither . . . and prevent them going to Poland and other foreign nations'. By this time, the Scots in Poland had settled and assimilated. Few new migrants joined them. Descendants of those earlier settlers still dimly recalled their roots when the Lithuanian general Ludwik Pac recruited eighty families to settle his estates after the Napoleonic Wars: even then, there were Hays, Dicksons, Stuarts, and Broomfields in Poland to settle corners of a foreign land that are forever Scotland, on farms called Govenlock, Linton, and Berwik, and in the village of New Scotland itself.

These peaceful migrants—the clerics, scholars, and merchants—may not have been entirely representative of the European face of the Scottish diaspora, which more often expanded under the sign of war. For five centuries, the common ties of Gaeldom between south-west Scotland and Ireland sustained a Hiberno-Scottish military tradition that endured until the last force of west Highland warriors was defeated at Knockanauss in November 1647.

An estimated 2,000 armoured, axe-wielding galloglasses (*gallóglaigh*) 'for-eign warriors') were in Ireland in 1539, far fewer even than the 35,000 red-shanks (many from the Hebrides) who helped to combat the English recon-quests of Ireland in the late sixteenth century. Scots mercenaries made their most notable, and frequently enduring, contributions on the battlefields of early modern Europe. The Hundred Years War drew them in unprecedent-ed numbers into French service against English armies, so much so that by 1419–24 *c*.2 per cent of the entire population of Scotland could be found in the French armies. The *Garde Écossaise* remained behind as the French royal bodyguard from 1419 until the eighteenth century, and the Franco-Scottish military families produced such warrior notables as Sir Bernard Stu-art, seigneur d'Aubigny, who commanded French troops at Bosworth, was the captain of the *Garde* for fifteen years, became governor of Calabria, viceroy of Naples, and ruler of Milan, and composed a notable *Traité sur l'art de guerre* before his death in 1508.

By the late sixteenth and early seventeenth centuries, Scottish soldiers were, according to that wordy worthy Sir Thomas Urquhart, 'like Ishmael, whose hand was against every man, and every man's hand against him'. Scots were willing students in the universities of war, as the Low Countries were known during the Dutch wars of independence from Spain, and they fought as mer-cenaries on both sides of the conflicts. As in France, so in Holland they left an enduring legacy: the three regiments of the Scots Brigade, which had been founded in 1579 at the start of the Dutch Revolt, lasted until 1781. The post-Reformation Protestantism of the Scots drew them increasingly into the European wars of religion; for example, an estimated 25,000–30,000 Scottish troops fought in Scandinavian armies in the period of the Thirty Years War. Scottish troops had been first recorded in Sweden in 1502, in the service of Denmark, but their numbers only became appreciable when Sweden and Denmark fell to war in 1563, and the Swedish King Eric IV attempted to enlist 1,200 Scots for his army.

Scottish migration to Sweden reached its zenith between 1626 and 1632, partly because of commercial expansion, but also due to the personnel demands of the Scandinavian armies. As in any such conflict, military service could be the path to stability, as for the Scots cavalrymen who settled in Swedish towns, or to yet greater success, as for Patrick Ruthven, who had served in Sweden for almost thirty years before becoming the commandant of Edinburgh Castle in 1639; his successor as castle governor in 1641, Alexan-der Leslie, had himself spent three decades in Swedish service. Both had returned home during the British Civil Wars, along with a great many other battle-hardened Scots whose modern skills were now needed on Britain's wargrounds. Though there were further waves of Scottish migrants after 1715–16 and 1745, the Wars of Religion marked the zenith of Scots' involvement in Sweden. A sizeable community of Scottish merchants could be found in Gothenburg throughout the eighteenth century, but by the early nineteenth century, they had become all but Swedish—combatants in the commercial battles of Europe and Asia, perhaps, but only distant cousins to their fighting forebears.

Scotland's relations with France have always overshadowed its links with the Baltic states and Scandinavia in the national memory. The Auld Alliance begun in 1295 reached its height when the Scottish and French crowns were joined in 1558, yet was broken by the Scottish Reformation in 1560. It was maintained sympathetically well into the nineteenth century, and as a result has been the most mythologized of all Scotland's European connections. In part the myth of Franco-Scottish amity has been a means for Scots to distinguish themselves from the English, whose antagonism with France dominated foreign relations and national ideology from the fourteenth century to 1815, with only relatively brief periods of rapprochement in the late sixteenth and seventeenth centuries. For all that, the ties of dynasty, sympathy, and culture between Scotland and France were lasting, even if France took in relatively few Scottish immigrants, at least after the fifteenth century.

The Scots (and even at times the French) believed that their alliance stretched back to the reign of Charlemagne in the eighth century, just as they backdated the origins of the *Garde Écossaise* to the thirteenth century. Nonetheless, most French kings between Charles VII and Louis XIV offered Scots the unique privilege of naturalization, partly in recognition of the signal part played by Scots in France's victories over England. This offer usually rested on the guarantee of Scottish reciprocity, a privilege only granted in 1558, but not formally repealed until 1906; even then, during the negotiations for the Franco-British *Entente Cordiale*, France refused to consider retrospective abrogation: any Scot alive in 1906 therefore retained—and, indeed, retains—rights of naturalization under French law. However, France remained, by and large, the destination of the well connected, the well educated, and the extraordinary rather than the ordinary Scot, from John Mair and George Buchanan to the exiled Jacobite court at Saint-Germain and the various visits of David Hume. Its importance as an outpost of the wider Scottish dispersal has been greatly exaggerated, though as a source of Scottish cosmopolitanism, queens, and claret, the Franco-Scottish nexus—if not exactly the Auld Alliance—cannot be overlooked.

Italy shared with France the dubious distinction of harbouring the most prominent members of the Jacobite diaspora in the eighteenth century, as the Stuart court-in-exile took refuge in Italy and was more or less permanently resident at the Palazzo Muti in Rome from 1719 until the death of Henry, cardinal of York, in 1807. Though some Scots (like Sir John Clerk of Penicuik) in

THE SCOTTISH KING David II and his wife, Joan, arrive in France in 1333 for safe-keeping during the Wars of Independence; their regal splendour obscures the fact that the king was nine and his queen twelve at the time.

the late seventeenth century had extended their Grand Tours to include Italy, most came after the union, following in the footsteps of English Italophiles. The Scottish presence in Italian universities had declined even before the Reformation. The Scots College in Rome, founded in 1600 near the Trevi fountain, continued to attract Scottish Catholics well into the seventeenth century, but by the eighteenth century most Scots came to Italy as political untouchables, as fashionable tourists, or as apprentices in the arts. Between roughly 1730 and 1780, over fifty Scottish painters and architects—among them William Aikman, Gavin Hamilton, Robert Adam, and Allan Ramsay (who made four visits, in 1736–8, 1754–7, 1775–7, and 1782–4)—travelled to Italy to paint, to be painted, to derive inspiration, or to make connections with cicerones and antiquaries like James Byres in Rome or the Scots-born Sir William Hamilton in Naples. Their influence, like their fame, would be disproportionate to their numbers, but few of them settled or assimilated, save, perforce, for the Jacobites. Their legacy was architectural and artistic, both in the stimulus they derived from Italian originals, and for the traces they left, in the swagger portraits of Pompeo Batoni and the salon-pieces of Pietro Fabris.

Europe in the eighteenth century encompassed Russia, and the reigns of Peter the Great and Catherine the Great opened windows on the west through which Scots, among others, looked and even climbed. Scots came to Russia as soldiers, doctors, architects, artisans, and industrialists. There had been Scots in the imperial service since the reign of Ivan the Terrible, while in the seventeenth century General Tam Dalyell had earned a fearsome reputation as 'a Muscovia beast who has roasted men'. Rewards for Scots' valour came in the form of lands and titles: by the eighteenth century, Prince Barclay, Counts Balmaine, Bruce, Fermour, and Graham, and Barons Ramsay, Rutherford, Stewart, and Sutherland could be found calendared among the Russian nobility. Scots admirals dominated Catherine's navy as they found new imperial service, often after distinction in Britain's wars. Between 1704 and 1854, some thirteen Scottish doctors transformed the Russian medical system: as an armchair traveller commented in 1778, Russia's 'doctors are scarce and commonly Scotch'. Peter and Catherine both had Scottish doctors. In 1714, Thomas Erskine, Peter's chief physician, planted Russia's first physic garden; in 1776, John Rogerson, Catherine's personal physician, became the first Briton elected to the Russian Academy of Sciences. Three Scottish architects worked over thirty years on the imperial palace of Tsarskoe Selo: the great Charles Cameron, the innovative iron-caster William Hastie, and the mason-architect Adam Menelaws. Cameron hired seventy-three Scots craftsmen to work on Tsarskoe Selo between 1784 and 1790, some of whom stayed in Russia after the end of their contracts. These Scots would often have found their countrymen representing Britain in Russia: indeed, in 1760, Scots diplomats headed British missions not only in Russia but also in Prussia, Portugal, Sardinia, and Saxony-Poland. Like their forebears who had helped to mould a united Christendom, and to create the ideals that underpinned post-classical Europe, Scottish diplomats, doctors, industrialists, and architects shaped eighteenth-century Europe into a single great republic, even as they reminded Enlightened Europeans that the borders of their community extended eastward to the Urals and beyond.

The imperial diaspora

In due course, Scots would be bearers of industrial modernity to the world, just as they were participants in its rise in England. Nevertheless, their connections with England were neither inevitable nor particularly deep rooted. Scotland's common land border with England often provided a greater barrier to migration than the seas around Scotland. Before the opening of the Wars of Independence, aspiring Scots might have looked to the then new Universities of Oxford and Cambridge for their education, and would have seen England as a natural arena of opportunity. Anglo-Scottish antagonism diverted those energies into new channels. Scots only found themselves fighting alongside English soldiers in the mercenary armies of early modern Europe. The common Protestant cause after the Scottish Reformation exacerbated, rather than calmed, mutual distrust between the new co-religionists. Nonetheless, small communities of Scots could be found in the Durham coalfields and among the keelmen of Newcastle, half of whom were Scots by the early seventeenth century. An enterprising entourage followed James VI south to his new English throne in 1603, but the British nobility created fitfully during the course of the Union of the Crowns was hardly conspicuous. By the last third of the eighteenth century, however, Scottish migrants were becoming more noticeable in the blossoming English centres of commerce and manufactures. Skilled Scottish artisans began increasingly to populate the mills, glassworks, soapworks, and bakeries of Lancashire, Liverpool, and Manchester. The premier peers of this labour aristocracy were those Scottish heroes of invention and ingenuity, James Watt, Thomas Telford, and John Macadam. They were however less remarked for their Scottishness than the Caledonian crew that came to London on the coat-tails of Lord Bute. Anti-

Scottish satire under Bute, like that a generation later under Dundas, testified to the success of Scots professionals in colonizing the power centres of post-union Britain. Scotland supplied Britain with prime ministers, with publishers (from Andrew Millar to the various John Murrays), and even, in Harold Macmillan, with a publisher-prime minister. The estimates of Scottish migrants to England are what statisticians would call a dark number. These prominent Anglo-Scots were the bright lights in that statistical gloom.

The Scottish reputation for mobility and ubiquity stems from their even more conspicuous success in colonizing the Empire and from the mythologization of that success by their descendants. As the Glasgow merchant John Spreull asked in 1705: 'Although [the English] gain more lands and islands, where have they the people to inhabit them and defend them without Scotland to assist them?' Spreull's words were as pragmatic as they were prophetic. The Scots had not been short of overseas opportunities before 1707, nor were they lacking in the skills and experience—or, rather, the patronage and recruiting networks and the cosmopolitan education—to make the most of such opportunities. Their participation in the British imperial diaspora, in the Americas, India, Australasia, Asia, and Africa, was as much an extension of their previous history of migration as it was a response to the novelty of Anglo-Scottish union and the access to the formerly English empire it afforded. Nevertheless, union did put Scots soldiers, merchants, and administrators on an equal footing with their English (and Protestant Irish) counterparts, to create a pan-British imperial elite.

The realm of Scotland was an empire even before the English crown first claimed that status under Henry VIII in the 1530s. The Scottish parliament asserted James III's 'ful Jurisdictioune and fre Impire within his Realme' in 1469, and this assertion may have been linked to the crown's acquisition of the Orkneys and the Shetlands after James's marriage to Margaret of Denmark the year before. With the acquisition of these islands from Norway, Scotland had shown itself to be a territorially acquisitive power; later, by the crown's attempts to 'civilize' the Highlands and Islands by settlement, evangelization, and legal reform, it had also shown that Scotland was capable of acting as a colonial power, even within its own borders. The term 'Empire of Great Britain' first appeared during Anglo-Scottish antagonism in the 1540s, as a sign that the origins of the British Empire lay within Britain itself, and not solely in Anglo-Irish relations. The settlement of Ulster after 1609 continued the history of Scottish imperial and colonial activity by the creation of the first equally and conjointly 'British' settlements in the Atlantic world, thereby offering precedents for later British imperial ventures involving Scots and other Britons, as well as a later launch-pad for so-called 'Scots-Irish' migrants in their progress across the Atlantic.

Scots planted their first independent and lasting colony in North America in the 1680s, in East New Jersey, and in the same decade sent colonists to Charlestown in what is now South Carolina. Even earlier Scottish settlements had been attempted after 1603—in Cape Breton and Nova Scotia, especially—but none had provided a successful base for Scottish plantation, or a permanent extension of the Scottish realm outside the Three Kingdoms. The promoter of Nova Scotia, Sir William Alexander, had warned in 1623 that 'my Countrimen would never adventure in such an Enterprize, unless it were as there was a *New France*, a *New Spaine*, and a *New England*, that they might likewise have a *New Scotland*', but such a reproduction of Scotland abroad was not to be. When Scots did plant a viable transatlantic colony, in East New Jersey, it was originally a Quaker-led settlement under the umbrella of England, rather than a dependency of the Scottish crown. The sole attempt before 1707 to create a colony that could become the entrepôt for a transoceanic trading empire—the New Caledonia settlement on the Isthmus of Darien—was a conspicuous and costly failure; even the 2,000 settlers who moved (and mostly died) there between 1698 and 1700 were dwarfed numerically by the estimated 40,000–70,000 Scots whom famine propelled to Ireland in the 1690s.

Once Scots were admitted, legally, to the trade and settlement of a newly 'British' Empire, they exploited their opportunities as vigorously as they once had in Europe, and in ways that were familiar from their European diaspora. The myth of the Highland clearances notwithstanding, most eighteenth-century Scottish migrants to North America departed voluntarily. Colonial governments, especially in southern colonies like North Carolina, actively encouraged the skilled, relatively well-off migrants whom Scotland could supply. Back in Scotland, the initiative for emigration often came from above, with tacksmen helping their tenants to move in family groups, most of whom needed some resources to pay for their initial passage. This meant that Scots migrants tended to be wealthier than their neighbours: it is telling that Scots were more likely than any other national group to hold slaves in eighteenth-century North Carolina. They were also better educated. Scots went to North America (and to the Caribbean) in distinct professional groups, as doctors, educators, preachers, colonial officials, and soldiers. They traded and travelled, ministered and administered, taught and fought among and alongside fellow Scots who rapidly created professional networks in the western hemisphere similar to those that had sustained their ancestors in medieval and early modern Europe. Indeed, these new networks—especially when extended throughout the imperial diaspora, to South Asia and Australasia—effectively diverted Scottish professional migration out of its traditional European channels by the mid-eighteenth century.

Yet, in eighteenth-century North America, Highlanders for the first time became a substantial tributary to the migrant stream as they travelled to the Cape Fear Valley in North Carolina, to the Mohawk and upper Hudson valleys in New York, to the Altamaha Valley in Georgia, to Pictou in Nova Scotia, and to Prince Edward Island. In these far-flung settings, those who had resisted the Hanoverian government in Britain became its greatest supporters in North America as Jacobite clansmen turned loyalist in the face of American rebellion. The presence of Highland regiments in the British armies sent to crush the Revolution only enhanced their reputation for untempered authoritarianism: George Washington complained of 'those universal instruments of tyranny, the Scotch', and Thomas Jefferson's rough draft of the Declaration of Independence likewise execrated the 'Scotch & foreign mercenaries' sent by George III 'to invade & destroy us'. This was also in part the result of experience during the Seven Years War, when colonial auxiliaries' encounters with their fellow provincials had done little to inspire a common identification of one another as imperial Britons. Even less did the settled Scots loyalists sympathize with the rebellious Scots-Irish. The supposed Celtic affinity between Scots and Scots-Irish is, in large part, a later invention. Political and religious identities, not indefinable ties of ethnicity, determined the allegiances of different groups, both before and after the American Revolution created two nations in North America.

Until the second half of the twentieth century, descendants of Scots still formed the third largest ethnic groups in both Canada and Australia. The availability of free land in British North America rapidly transformed soldiers into settlers after the Seven Years War and provided precedents for later migrants to Canada. Later, in the early nineteenth century, Scottish Catholics settled in eastern Ontario, on Prince Edward Island and in eastern Nova Scotia, and showed their neighbours that it was quite possible to be both Catholic and British, especially in the colonial context. Between 1838 and 1905, the United States provided the focus of Scottish emigration to North America; after 1905, the migrant stream diverted again to Canada, as 170,000 Scots moved there in the four years before the First World War. Canada benefited

'THE UNITED STATES would have been a poor show had it not been for the Scotch', argued Andrew Carnegie: here, three of his young compatriots look their best for the camera on arrival at Ellis Island, c.1910.

especially from the emigration of skilled Scottish workers during the nineteenth century, and profited further from the wave of Scottish investment that accompanied them. Canada's cities drew urban Scots in disproportionate numbers, leaving a permanent mark on the cultural landscape of Ontario and Upper Canada as earlier Scots had left legacies in Quebec and, more distantly, in Nova Scotia.

In the middle of the nineteenth century, Scottish emigration gradually began to shift from North America to Australia and, to a lesser extent, New Zealand. Over half a million Scots emigrated to Australia between 1788 and 1987. Before 1831, free emigration to Australia had been strictly limited to those with capital, though after the abolition of this restriction European migration mounted, especially after the gold rush of the 1850s. Scots governors like Lachlan Macquarie and Sir Thomas Brisbane had encouraged their countrymen to settle in New South Wales, and Scots clustered there, in Victoria and in Queensland. The proportion of Australians born in Scotland gradually declined throughout the twentieth century, though the number of descendants of former Scottish immigrants naturally increased. The influ-

DUN-SHAW, by James Gillray, 1788. Henry Dundas, Viscount Melville, bestrides the world like a colossus from Leadenhall Street (the East India Company's offices in London) to Bengal: according to the earl of Rosebery, Dundas 'Scotticised India, and Orientalised Scotland'.

ence of Scots on Australian politics, professions, and commerce was disproportionate to their numbers, as Scots were overrepresented among graziers,
businessmen, bankers, and investors, and supplied 42 per cent of all foreign-
born MPs before 1901.

Scots were 'invisible ethnics' in North America and Australasia, the stal-
wart supporters of Empire, predominantly Protestant and eager to assimilate. White settlers in India were always in a tiny minority, and the Scots were
always especially visible among them. Like the Scottish sojourners in the
Caribbean, those who went to India hoped to make their fortune and then to
return home: 'The great object in coming out to this country', wrote James
Balfour in 1780, 'is to make a Genteel Independency in as few years as possible and endeavour to return home before the constitution is broke'. Unlike
the Scots fortune-hunters of the Caribbean, many failed to return. The predominantly well-born Scots who did survive their stints in India became key
members of the British imperial elite. The more responsible the position, the
more likely it was to be staffed by Scots: in 1772, only one-eleventh of rank-
and-file soldiers were Scots (a fair representation of the relative populations
of England and Scotland), but one-ninth of civil servants and a remarkable
one-third of all army officers came from Scotland. Their way had been
smoothed since the 1720s by patronage, first by Sir Robert Walpole, through
his Scottish political managers, Argyll and Ilay, later by Bute, Warren Hastings, and, most notoriously, Henry Dundas—who, according to the earl of
Rosebery, 'Scotticised India, and Orientalised Scotland'—though Scottish
patronage in India may actually have declined under his ministry. Scots ministers, educationalists, governors, and ethnographers, such as Mountstuart
Elphinstone, Charles Grant, Thomas Munro, and Alexander Duff, spearheaded the Anglicization of British India in the early nineteenth century;
they pioneered conservationist practices in the botanical gardens of Calcutta
and Bombay, as they also did in southern Africa: from Sir John Macpherson
in the 1780s to the marquess of Linlithgow in 1936–43, Scots regularly occupied the highest echelons of British imperial power in India.

The ties that bound Scots to Scotland and to one another in the imperial
diaspora prevented them from wholly assimilating to Anglo-British norms,
and fostered that attachment to a homeland which is so characteristic of diasporic peoples. 'We are scattered over the face of the earth, and are united only
by hope and a tender remembrance,' wrote the East India company employ-
ee George Bogle to his sister in 1774 from Bhutan. 'While you are passing
your cheerful evenings with friends and relations at Daldowie; while Robin,

THE DEATH OF MUNROW. In 1793 the *Gentleman's Magazine* reported that an 'immense royal tiger' had killed the son of the Scottish commander Sir Hector Munro in West Bengal: two decades later, this version of the gory scene, in Staffordshire pottery, graced fashionable British mantlepieces.

with his negroes (and happy they are that are under him), is planting the sugar cane; while I am climbing these rugged mountains, there is a secret virtue, like the magnet, which attracts us together, and cheers and solaces us.' Bogle was a client of Warren Hastings, and the first European to visit Tibet since the Jesuits of the seventeenth century. One of his brothers, Robert ('Robin'), became a sugar-planter in Grenada; another, John, was a merchant on the Rappahannock river in Virginia. All saw themselves as part of a far-flung family group that was also consciously part of a diaspora sentimentally linked through Scotland. The ability simultaneously to remain attached to Scotland yet to be detached when dealing with the outside world had distinguished Scots migrants since the medieval period, especially in their encounters with the extra-European world. Descendants of Scots in Poland and Sweden had assimilated completely by the eighteenth century while those in France and Russia found their ties to Scotland frayed and broken. Only in the former colonies of white settlement would Scots sustain their common attachments through social clubs, Caledonian associations, St Andrews societies, pipe-bands, and Highland Games, as they carried the cult of the kilt from Canada to New Zealand.

Post-imperial Scotland?

The reputation of the Scots in the imperial diaspora is ambivalent. From the mid-eighteenth century to the mid-twentieth century, they represented both the hard face of military imperialism and the exploitative force of capital extraction within the Empire. Conversely, the Scots have been praised for the ameliorating effect they had upon the British Empire. The Scottish legacy of education throughout the anglophone settlements, as well as in Africa, has been held to be as positive as the worldwide force of missionary Presbyterianism in softening the after effects of conquest and acculturation. Similarly, Scottish traditions of communitarian politics, scientific environmentalism, and espousal of provincial nationalism have been seen as forces which counteracted imperial impulses towards uniformity, expropriation of natural resources, or permanence in the face of national self-determination. These positive legacies of the imperial diaspora cannot be underestimated, but they do need to be balanced against the harsher side of Scottish expansion, the legacy of militarism, authoritarianism, and capitalism. The highest incarnation of the literary school of snobbery with violence remains that fictional Scot James Bond, whose ancestry lies in the novels of John Buchan. That buccaneering spirit was caught in the self-congratulation of *Greenmantle* (1912): 'We call ourselves insular, but the truth is we are the only race on earth that can produce men capable of getting inside the skins of remote peoples. Perhaps the Scots are better than the English, but we're all a thousand per cent better than anybody else.' Here, once again, is that paradoxical combination of empathy and aggression, assimilability and impregnability, that characterized the Scottish diaspora, especially in its imperial phase.

Male Scots had frequently seen the world at the point of a sword or down the barrel of a gun, though this was in itself not a novel development in Scotland's diasporic history. Nor was Scottish investment in overseas commerce unprecedented, though the scale of that involvement, like the size of Scottish profits, overshadowed anything that could ever have been dreamed of by the merchants of Veere, Gothenburg, or Virginia. The financial benefits to Scot-

'THE TRUTH IS', wrote John Buchan in 1912, 'we are the only race on earth that can produce men capable of getting inside the skins of remote peoples'. Here Buchan, the 'teller
of tales', tries to get inside the skin of a Native American.

land were remarkable, though surprisingly little remarked, even in the nineteenth century. The *faux*-Venetian palazzi constructed by Glasgow's merchant princes to conceal their warehouses signified an attachment to European civilization even on the part of the most aggressive profiteers of Empire; however, their attempt to hide the workings of capital formation behind those elegant façades was also an emblem of the willed amnesia which distinguished so much of the British imperial enterprise.

'All over the Highlands of Scotland may be observed, here and there, the effects of the little stream of East or West Indian gold, running side by side with the mountain torrent, spreading cultivation, fertility, and plenty along its narrow valley,' noted a Scottish commentator in 1835. Yet only fifty years later, an article in *Blackwood's* magazine argued that myths of Scottish poverty, such as those that plagued Scots in their travels across the world, were now entirely redundant: 'Scotland herself is but dimly conscious of the revolution she has undergone in this respect,' not least as a result of the spoils of empire and the profitable export of capital abroad (over £40 million, at the author's count). Railways, ranches, forests, mines, mortgages, and banks across the world, from Canada to New Zealand, rested on Scottish capital and brought profits back to Scotland, just as John Macky had predicted they would. The Empire clearly paid, though it paid largely in intangible assets; nonetheless, these invisible earnings and the far-flung investments which generated them were as much a part of the Scottish diaspora's global impact as were the soldiers, settlers, and professionals whose presence has more often, because more easily, been portrayed. Andrew Carnegie's libraries across Scotland remain among the most visible tributes paid by Scottish capital abroad to the homeland of the diaspora itself.

The overall effect of emigration on Scotland itself is unknowable. The loss of so many young men to the armies of Europe and the Empire over the centuries clearly depressed Scottish fertility, though whether it deprived Scotland of talent which it otherwise so badly needed is more debatable. The advantages of Empire were spread unevenly within Scottish society. Those who had the ability to remigrate to Scotland with their spoils, or to manipulate foreign capital from Scotland, clearly had most to gain from their connections with the wider diaspora. It has often been argued that Scotland exchanged national independence in 1707 for the profits of Empire; once those profits ebbed, Scottish enthusiasm for British union was bound to ebb too. Yet, seen from the perspective of over six centuries of the Scottish diaspora, this view is bound to seem incomplete, whether as an explanation for

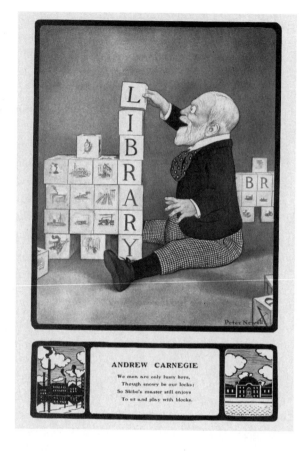

ANDREW CARNEGIE'S PHILANTHROPY (especially endowing the Carnegie Libraries) was satirized in 1903 by *Harper's Weekly* as only the amusement of an overgrown child: 'We men are only lusty boys,/ Though snowy be our locks;/ So Skibo's master still enjoys/ To sit and play with blocks.'

the union or as an account of Scotland's place in post imperial Britain or the wider world.

Scots were the pall-bearers of Empire: the British army in India made its retreat in 1947 to the sound of 'Auld Lang Syne', while the band of the Black Watch piped Hong Kong over to Chinese rule in July 1997. Sixty years earlier, Andrew Dewar Gibb, in his *Scottish Empire* (1937), had speculated that '[i]t may be that with her imperial task ended, [Scotland] will seek to form and justify a new conception of her function in the framework of European civilization'. In the aftermath of Empire, this seems prophetic. Scots are now poised to profit from their heritage of cosmopolitanism, from their professional traditions in finance, banking, law, and technology, from their long series of connections with the Commonwealth and their abiding kinship with continental Europeans. With this dual attachment, to the bonds of Empire and the spirit of Europe, the future for Scots and for Scotland in the new century looks especially bright. Britain may have lost the Empire but, while the English have floundered in their attempt to find a role, Scots have been quietly rediscovering theirs as a diasporic and European people.

THE SCOTS bring down the curtain on the last major outpost of the British Empire: a piper of the Black Watch plays in the rain at the handover of Hong Kong to China in July 1997.

10 Scotland's Stories

SALLY MAPSTONE

Notions of nation

From the start, storytelling has formed a dynamic part of the imagining of Scottish identity. One of the earliest Older Scots poems, John Barbour's *Bruce* (*c*.1375), commences by yoking narrative to the investiture of what are seen as truths with a fundamental national resonance:

> Storys to rede ar delitabill
> Suppos that thai be nocht bot fabill,
> Than suld storys that suthfast wer
> And thai war said on gud maner
> Hawe doubill plesance in heryng . . .
> For auld storys that men redys
> Representis to thaim the dedys
> Of stalwart folk that lywyt ar . . .
> As wes king Robert off Scotland
> That hardy wes off hart and hand . . . (I. 1–5, 17–19, 27–8)

This impulse to make the Scottish past speak meaningfully through a tale-telling form is a markedly persistent one in Scottish literary history. It moves from the poetry of the medieval period, most famously *The Bruce* and Hary's *Wallace* (*c*.1475–9), into the novels of Hogg, Galt, and Scott, and continues into the contemporary novel in the storytelling of Kenneth McHoan in Iain Banks's *The Crow Road* (1992). Mr McHoan speaks of the furthest past imaginable in the potent nationalistic terms of separatism and union:

Within the oceanic depths of time that lay beneath the surface of the present, there had been an age, when, appropriately, an entire ocean had separated the rocks that would one day be called Scotland from the rocks that would one day be called England and Wales. That first union came half a billion years ago.

These two literary examples point up the key elements which have accompanied the retelling of Scotland's past from the Middle Ages to the present: the identification of a perspective which gives a quintessentially Scottish inflection to the 'truth' told; and the preoccupation with Scottish independence, the country's association with or severance from its English neighbour. These issues have received especially urgent inspection at signal historical junctures. Equally importantly, however, viewpoints on them have not been uniform across the centuries, or indeed within the medieval to Renaissance ambit that is this essay's main concern. Scotland has stories rather than one story, and both the contents and the perspectives of those different stories do not always accord. Ideas of national identity must likewise be understood in pluralistic terms; what it meant to be a Scot had competing interpretations throughout this period.

That the reconstruction of the past could depend on a sense of national origin was well known in the Middle Ages. But the Scottish Wars of Independence (1296–1328) focused the matter acutely. The period in which the kingship of the country was both contested by rival native claimants, Balliol and Bruce, and laid claim to by the English ruler Edward I and his successors, was one which also saw the production of a number of documents and texts, the best known of which is the Declaration of Arbroath of 1320, which give forceful statement to ideas and ideals of nationhood and community. Moreover, following the conclusion of the wars, and their aftermath, and the beginning of Stewart rule under Robert II in 1371, the first literary work in Scots to emerge from that dynasty, Barbour's *Bruce*, focuses back on the Wars of Independence. Barbour's use of the Scots vernacular began the process whereby the national tongue entered into an association with the literary expression of nationalistic sentiments, which has remained a charged issue up to the present day.

Literature in languages other than Scots had been composed in the area we now think of as Scotland and about people we now call Scots from long before *The Bruce* was written, of course. From at least the sixth century onwards there is a growing corpus in poetry and prose which gradually embraces a wide range of languages: Latin, Gaelic, Welsh, Old English, Norse, and French (Anglo-Norman). Quantities of these works, such as the sixth-century series of poems known as *The Gododdin* and the poems attributed to the

THE DECLARATION OF ARBROATH, the famous defence of Scottish independence from England, sent by the barons of Scotland to Pope John XXII, and dated 6 April 1320. This parchment copy has the seals of its baronial signatories attached to it.

poet Taliesin, commemorate battles and skirmishes in a tenor that can antic-ipate the Scots and Latin verse about military encounters in the Wars of Independence over half a millennium later.

However, many of these works also differ from those principally discussed in this chapter in two major ways. First, they were not necessarily composed by Scots writers. *The Gododdin* and Taliesin's poems survive only in later

Welsh copies, and much Gaelic literature treating Scottish subjects is of Irish origin. But, more significantly, they are concerned with a 'Scotland' not identical with the country that takes territorial and political shape as a kingdom later in the medieval period. *The Gododdin* and Taliesin's poetry deal with a number of kingdoms that overlap areas now in both present-day Scotland and northern England. Near-contemporary historians of Scotland and their later medieval successors responded enthusiastically to the idea that Kenneth mac Alpin (Kenneth I) had 'united' the kingdoms of the Picts and the Scots in the mid-ninth century, and the idea of the early establishment of the kingdom of the Scots continues to be reiterated in some modern histories of Scotland; but this is a form of shorthand that does not do justice to the political complexities of the situation. Kenneth's reign certainly saw the construction of a type of kingship that contained both political and symbolic elements that were crucial in later definitions of Scotland. It is likely, for instance, that the establishment of the kingly inauguration stone at Scone occurred during his rule. It is better to see Kenneth's reign as giving significant transitional shape to the formation of influential notions of kingship and nationhood.

It is demonstrable, moreover, that between the tenth and thirteenth centuries contemporary perceptions of Scotland were very much of a variety of areas and divisions, rarely encompassing the whole of the area that we now think of as Scotland. 'Scotland' as a term describing the whole of the country is not in regular use until the thirteenth century, and the notion of the Scots as a separate people is a feature that primarily emerges in the rhetoric of the Wars of Independence. This chapter therefore concentrates on the literature produced during and after the period in which the kingdom and people of the Scots takes shape as an idea that carries through to today's Scotland. The primary languages used in these works are Scots and Latin.

Kingship and national identity are closely intertwined throughout the history of medieval and early modern Scotland. But while Scottish kings had a strongly vested interest in their formulations, from early on such definitions are not the sole prerogative of the monarch. The Declaration of Arbroath presents itself (in Latin) as an epistle to Pope John XXII on behalf of a series of named 'barons and freeholders' as well as 'the whole community of the kingdom of Scotland'. Kingship is at the heart of this document. This is focused first through an account of the unjust acts of Edward I in laying claim to the kingdom and then attacking it. This is contrasted with the liberating actions of Robert I, which together with 'divine providence, his succession to his right according to our laws and customs... [and] the due consent and assent of us all, have made him our prince and king'. This conjunction of arguments is carried through into the Declaration's most quoted assertion: 'But if he should give up what he has begun, seeking to subject us or our kingdom to the king of the English or the English, we would immediately strive to expel him as our enemy and a subverter of his right and ours, and we would make someone else our king, who is capable of seeing to our defence.'

These statements present a view of a realm predicated on kingship, but assert with equal force the view that, where the kingdom's independence is concerned, kingly rule is predicated on the congruence of its interests with those of the political community. They also mark a defining moment in establishing Scottish national identity as something that constitutes itself in opposition to the English. Present-day perspectives on the forming of that identity often ignore the closeness of the relationship between Scotland and England before the divisive years of the Wars of Independence. In a related way these statements in the Declaration also ignore the fact that for tracts of the previous thirty years sections of magnate society, including Bruce himself, had at best connived with and at worst collaborated with the English king or the English interest. They respond to a situation in which the dominant political constituency in the country now saw their interests as strongly identified with a patriotism founded on a hostility to their English neighbour. While Robert I probably broadly supported these sentiments, a couple of years earlier in 1318 he had established an entail designed to ensure the continuing succession to the kingdom after his death of the nearest direct blood member of his kin, with guardianships in the interim should a minority come about. This document puts the Declaration of Arbroath's assertions from another point of view. It states that a full parliament has agreed in the presence of the king that all his subjects will 'assist him faithfully with all their strength in the protection and defence of the right and liberties of the said kingdom against all mortals however mighty'. And it goes on, in terms that will find striking parallels with the syntactical and argumentative formulations of the Declaration's own hypothesizing, 'And that if anyone in future (may it not be so!) proves to be a violator of that ordinance, he by that act is to be regarded for ever as a traitor to the kingdom and guilty of the crime of lese-majesty.' These sentiments both identify the king with the defence of the realm and posit opposition to those interests as a crime of treachery to king and kingdom. They are the mirror-image of the Declaration's identification of a king figure as one potentially acting in a manner alien to the kingdom's good. Their inclusion in a document designed to provide for the continuation of the Bruceian dynasty reinforces how closely the ideological and the locally political were connected in the forging of statements of Scottish national identity.

For the next several hundred years Scottish kings and their empowered subjects engage in the making of further statements on kingship and nationalism, in texts both of record and of literary exposition. They often share the same forms of discourse, and their views are often closely allied, but there are also decisive moments of punctuating political and textual difference in the period between the establishing of the Stewart dynasty in 1371 and the union of the Scottish and English crowns in 1603.

The country's conscience: William Wallace

In the first century of Stewart rule this is nowhere better illustrated than in the different poetic narratives of the Wars of Independence in Barbour's *Bruce* and Hary's *Wallace*. Written in the early years of the new Stewart dynasty, under Robert II, by an Aberdeen cleric who had also worked for his monarch in diplomacy and administration, Barbour's long poem is concerned with both the civil wars and the wars against England that had concluded half a century earlier. Good, unifying kingship, as personified in the career and character of Robert the Bruce, is a dominant motif in the poem, and one designed to speak to a cultural elite recently emerged from further periods of political uncertainty during the reign of David II and during that of Robert II himself. The 'political correctness' detectable in Barbour's narrative thus manifests itself in proclaimed support for Robert II's celebrated grandfather Robert I, but also in a reading of history which affirms the important connection between male succession and the kingdom's stability, a policy also promulgated by Robert II's entailing of the crown early in his reign in a fashion that explicitly recalled Robert I's entailing of 1318. It also leads Barbour to merge two historically separate personages, Robert Bruce, lord of Annandale, the 'Competitor' for the throne in the Bruce–Balliol dispute, and his grandson Robert earl of Carrick, who did indeed become Robert I. This does not make *The Bruce* unusable as a 'historical' text: it has much information which is confirmed by other sources, and it is employed in some of the most authoritative historical reassessments of the Wars. It does, though, necessarily also remind us that Barbour presents his work as a 'romans', rather than a chronicle—but chronicles too in the Middle Ages could be more than economical with the 'truth', and the near-contemporary Latin chronicle of John of Fordun was equally a purveyor of what has been termed 'Bruceian ideology'.

Barbour's poem well illustrates the way in which the narration of the Scottish historical past always carries the stamp of the concerns of the present in which it is composed.

This manifests itself too in *The Bruce* in a significant absence. William Wallace, so fêted in much subsequent Scottish writing, and a major icon of Scottish nationalism in the 1990s, receives not a single mention in Barbour's poem. The suppression of reference to Wallace's early championing of the cause of Scottish independence permits Barbour to gloss over the Bruce family's compromised role in the 1290s, when Wallace was indeed acting as representative of King John (Balliol) and 'the Community of the Realm of Scotland'. It also enables the smoother identification of Bruceian kingship with the defence of the realm. Bruce does have a co-star throughout the poem, but this is the *echt* aristocratic James Douglas rather than William Wallace, the second son of an undistinguished knight. Douglas's strongly supportive role towards his leader may itself have been intended to provide an instructive model to the contemporary magnate community. Thus, although much of *The Bruce* is concerned with strife between Bruce and his supporters and other Scots opposed to them and/or complicit with the English, the identification of Robert Bruce as 'the king' early on in the poem secures a way of reading it which allies the vantage points of author and ruler with little divergence. The most memorable example of Barbour's criticism of Bruce is in relation to the Bruce's murder of John Comyn early in the poem, which Barbour cannot condone but which he treats relatively leniently. While in its insistent attention to magnate–crown friction, *The Bruce* may hold a subtext of anxiety about the harmony of king–magnate relations at the time of its composition, the dominant political standpoint it communicates is that the world-views of the virtuous king and those of his well-intentioned subjects are complementary. The similarities in diction and content between Barbour's own encomium on national freedom close to the poem's start and the hortatory speech he later gives to Bruce in front of his troops at Bannockburn (I. 225–75, XII. 172–327) signify the degree to which Barbour's own loyalties are bound up with the Bruceian cause. It cannot be demonstrated that *The Bruce* was written under direct Stewart patronage, but the fact that Barbour is said to have composed another work, now lost but known as *The Stewartis Originall*, which was a genealogical account of the king's house, reinforces his closeness to the concerns of the ruling family.

Hary's *Wallace*, by contrast, was composed outwith the immediate royal circle. His lengthy twelve-book poem was written about a century after *The

Bruce, in the late 1470s, mid-way through the reign of James III. In the last parts of his poem Hary claims that two lowland lairds, Sir William Wallace of Craigie and Sir James Liddale of Halkerston, oversaw at least parts of its composition. These men were minor aristocracy, but they had connections: Wallace was married to the countess of Crawford, and Liddale was steward of the earldom of March, and was linked to the king's brother, the duke of Albany—to the point whereby, after the spectacular fallings-out between Albany and James III in the early 1480s, Liddale was forfeited as a traitor with Albany in 1483, and executed in 1485. Wallace and Liddale had neighbouring properties in north-west Fife, but they also both had estates in the south (Ayrshire and Edinburgh). Their views, as men with something to lose from a climate in which Border raiding was frowned upon, and as, strongly in Liddale's case, Albany supporters, underscore the poem's virulently anti-English posturing and its highly equivocal reading of Bruceian kingship. The context for this was James III's policy of rapprochement with the English during the 1470s, which was marked in 1474 in a marriage alliance between the king's son James and Edward IV's daughter Cecilia, and which was indeed to be pursued throughout James's reign. Albany was opposed to this alliance. While there is little to substantiate the argument that Hary's representation of Wallace is created to bring to mind Albany's person and qualities, the way in which *The Wallace* entertains so dramatically the image of William Wallace as a form of alternative king-figure does have a meaningful link to Hary and his sponsors' doubts about James III.

However, a crucial qualification here is that the opposition to James III's pacific policies towards England was not uniform in the Scottish political community. Substantial sectors of it, including many powerful northern magnates, appear either not to have resisted or indeed to have endorsed James's strategies in this area. *The Wallace* cannot be taken as a text whose underlying tenets would be shared by the majority of those on whose political support the king relied. It rather reflects the vested interests of a section of the aristocracy. One of the reasons for the longevity the Stewart dynasty achieved in Scotland was that it took a lot to bring the magnate community into collective opposition to it.

The Wallace, moreover, is a poem riven by ideological contradictions. On one level it offers a determined recasting of events and individuals in Barbour's *Bruce*. It borrows scenes from it, alludes to it explicitly in places, and shares key dramatis personae with it. These borrowings, however, are never straightforward, and often point up differences between the two works, in which the issue of kingship is pivotal. About a third of the way through *The Bruce* the Bruce is being pursued by a troop led by John of Lorne, who is employing a bloodhound said to have been formerly Bruce's own. The bloodhound's unwavering pursuit of its former master's scent acts as a confirmation of Bruce's kingly status: 'The hund folowyt alwayis the king And changyt for na departing' (VI. 583–4). In book V of *The Wallace* Hary's hero is similarly pursued by Sir John Butler and a bloodhound, but the narrative is not explicitly charged with associations of kingship. Hary's passage brings Barbour's to mind, but it invites a comparison between the two men which at this stage suggests that Wallace's career shadows that of Bruce but does not yet merit a 'kingly' identification. However, towards the conclusion of his poem Hary achieves a different kind of emphasis in a comparison with another section of *The Bruce*. Wallace is finally captured by the English through the treachery of a Scottish noble, Sir John Menteith, to whose family he has been close. Contemplation of the dastardly nature of this act prompts Hary to release a catalogue of comparisons of great leaders similarly brought down by covetousness: Hector, Alexander, Arthur, Julius Caesar (XII. 835–42). He inherits this from the early part of *The Bruce* where Barbour is commenting on John Comyn's treacherous role in the pact he establishes with Bruce to promote Bruce's claim to the throne (I. 521–60). The intertextuality here is a fascinatingly layered one. Hary uses the recollection of Barbour's passage to promote Wallace into the category of the famous 'nine worthies', several of whom feature in Barbour's catalogue, and with whom Barbour is also associating Bruce. But Barbour's reference comes within the difficult section of his poem dealing not only with Comyn's treachery towards Bruce but with Bruce's eventual killing of Comyn in the Franciscan friary at Dumfries. Hary indeed imitates Barbour in investing his protagonist with associated worth in the face of treacherous acts against him, but then employs the association to diminish Bruce as he inflates Wallace. For shortly after this part of *The Wallace*, Hary makes one of his most critical allusions to Bruce in relation indeed to the Comyn killing itself: 'That hapnys wrang, our great haist in a king' (XII. 1188). Bruce's kingliness is profoundly problematic in Hary's poem and exists in a tense dynamic with the positive representation of Wallace.

This shows through more strongly still in the multiple additions that Hary makes to the narrative of the Wars of Independence. The most major is, of course, the central role assumed by Wallace, but Hary also contrives a radical revision of the role of the Bruce. For much of Hary's poem Bruce is a prisoner of the English, a stratagem that usefully restrains the number of his appearances in *The Wallace*, but which also has its own metaphorical valence in the poem's relentless Anglophobic culture. Bruce's situation compels him to be the advocate of 'gud pes' with the English—of which both Wallace and *The Wallace* are deeply distrustful. *The Wallace* thus admits outspoken criticism of Bruce in a manner unimaginable in Barbour's work. And it puts it into the mouth of Wallace who, in a celebrated encounter with Bruce before the battle of Falkirk, accuses him of being a 'renygat deuorar off thi blud' (XI. 492). The scene is decisive in effecting a regeneration in Bruce which the poem indicates will lead him to assume the kingly government of the realm, but this rehabilitation is incomplete by the time *The Wallace* ends. The figure whose qualities and practice most embody those values traditionally associated with good kingship is thus far more Wallace than Bruce in Hary's poem.

But, as the Menteith episode memorably indicates, *The Wallace* must also continually address the fact that Wallace is opposed and ultimately brought down by fellow Scots as well as by his English enemies. This was in Hary's sources, most prominently in Walter Bower's Latin *Scotichronicon* of the 1440s, but it is enhanced by Hary's long narrative and its insistent focus on Wallace. To a degree, his treatment of this aspect of Wallace's history creates another parallel with *The Bruce*, which takes its point of origin and much of its succeeding action from conflicts between the main protagonist and parts of the Scottish political community. But in Barbour's poem this is always perceived as a struggle between king and wrong-thinking opposition, and it is one that works out entirely in Bruce's favour. In *The Wallace* the conflict is between a right-thinking protagonist of comparatively low birth and an opposition that involves not only portions of the Scottish nobility but the rightful king himself, and the poem ends with Wallace's death at the hands of the English.

Hary is as identified with Wallace's viewpoints as is Barbour with Bruce's. But a form of divisiveness emerges at the very end of Hary's poem which speaks to a level of discord between Hary and his aristocratic patrons over the central matter of Wallace and kingship. In an extraordinary passage in book XII, Hary looks back to his account in book VIII of the battle of Northallerton and claims that his patrons, Wallace of Craigie and Liddale, made him 'mak wrang record' of it (XII. 1445). The truth, he claims, is that Wallace did take the Scottish crown for a day in order for this battle to take place—the English having declared they would only fight against the king of Scotland. In book VIII Hary had shown Wallace turning that proposal down, while still contriving to give the English the impression that he had been crowned.

In now rejecting the accuracy of that account, Hary puts himself in the contradictory position of having first denied and then belatedly confirmed that Wallace was king for a day.

It would be hard to find a more telling illustration of the extent to which Scottish definitions of the national interest were centred on their identification with kingship. Hary's doubts about James III's ancestor Robert Bruce—which themselves manifest his own anxieties about James—lead him to evoke an alternative king figure in Wallace, but one who can never be totally endorsed. And this interpretative crux moves him virtually to part company with the Wallace's descendant, Wallace of Craigie, and with Liddale, who seem, when it came to it, to have been greater political trimmers than Hary was prepared to be.

The Bruce's and *The Wallace*'s stories are thus vitally connected to Barbour's and Hary's positions on the practice of kingship in their own day. Barbour's account takes a Stewart party line; Hary's contests that. In implicit challenge to Barbour's version of 'suthfastnes', he asserts the truth of what he is saying, even, he adds, if hearing the reality of Wallace's activities may not be too easy: 'Thocht this mater be nocht till all plesance, His suthfast deid was worthi till awance' (XII. 1428–9). But, even on Hary's part, the challenge goes only so far, and it would have its counterpart in the conclusion of the reign of the king during whose rule *The Wallace* was written. James III's reign ended in 1488 with a serious noble rebellion against the king, in which—typically—many but by no means all of the Scots nobility were involved. However, although James III died during the rebellion, and was replaced by the young man at the head of the opposition, that man was his own son James. Finding a true alternative to a Stewart ruler was never an easy thing. The reasons for this go back to the very events with which Barbour's and Hary's poems concern themselves. A recurrence of the lacerating effects on their society of the Bruce–Balliol dispute was something to be avoided at all costs. This expressed itself both in nationalism and in the endorsement of a dynasty that had the capacity to bring political stability. Kings might be unpopular, as Stewart kings—and queens—often were, but it took really major crises to produce their permanent replacement.

Both *The Bruce* and *The Wallace* were popular texts in the sixteenth and seventeenth centuries, but the popularity of Hary's poem greatly exceeded that of Barbour's. It was one of the earliest works to be printed in Scotland. *c*.1509 by Andrew Myllar and Walter Chepman. The length of *The Wallace* made its printing a far more ambitious undertaking than that required for their other literary productions, and the fact that they carried it out at all is probably indicative of public demand. Between its next printing in 1570 and the publication of a modernized version by William Hamilton of Gilbertfield in 1722, *The Wallace* had gone through over twenty-five editions. It is often said that Hamilton's rendition became the book most commonly owned in Scotland after the Bible. But the popularity of the 'old-style' version of Hary's poem, which had been progressively Anglicized in spelling by successive printers, held up well and it continued to be printed after the publication of Hamilton's; that version was not in fact reprinted until fifty years after it first came out.

That Scottish culture has persistently favoured the narrative of events in *The Wallace* ahead of that in *The Bruce* draws attention to formative elements in the complex phenomenon that is a sense of national identity. Many of these elements are also dependent upon conventions that have grown up around *The Wallace*. The sense of Hary as identified with his hero, and distanced from his noble sponsors, has surely fed into the afterlife of the poem. From John Mair's description in his 1521 history of Britain of the poem's author as one 'blind from his birth', the idea of *The Wallace* as a poem by a man of the people about a man of the people has taken a powerful hold. The image of Hary is erroneous: *The Wallace* amply demonstrates that he was learned in both Latin and English literature and probably had a clerical background. But nonetheless, the much purveyed notion of Hary as a blind, inspired minstrel figure in touch with folk tradition, along with—crucially—the much projected image of his hero as alienated from the aristocratic political establishment, but championed by the common people, all speak to a sense of Scottishness in which 'popular', non-elitist elements play major defining parts. The reactions of Robert Burns, a great enthusiast for the Wallace, sum this up: 'The story of Wallace poured a Scottish prejudice in my veins which will boil along there till the flood-gates of life shut in eternal rest.' The 1994 film *Braveheart* draws on similar sentiments.

Of chronicles and kings

The early emergence of Wallace as a hero of literature in the Scots vernacular was also an important shaping aspect of his cultural identity. But his literary history had actually turned from its inception on a creative dialogue between texts in Scots and in Latin. Hary's poem drew on material not only from *Bruce* but from another massive vernacular work, this time in chronicle form, the Augustinian canon Andrew of Wyntoun's *Original Chronicle* composed in the first half of the 1420s for a minor laird, Sir John Wemyss of

ANDREW OF WYNTOUN'S
Original Chronicle of Scotland. This
vernacular poetic chronicle attracted
a wide readership. In this fifteenth-
century manuscript, the rubricated
heading gives an injunction to readers: 'The proloug of the auchtande
[eighteenth] buk/ In to this chapter
now 3he luk'.

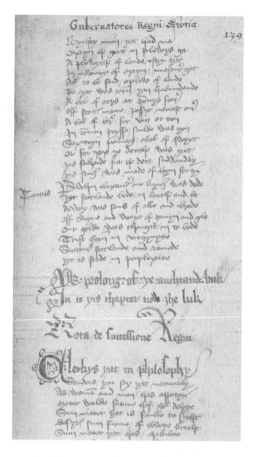

Leuchars and Kincaldrum, places not far from St Andrews, where Wyntoun
had been a canon, and Loch Leven, where he was prior when he wrote his
chronicle. Wyntoun is the earliest source for a number of episodes concerning Wallace, especially in the opening parts of Wallace's career, and the lively
way in which he relates them undoubtedly inspired Hary. Wyntoun may have
provided even more of a trigger than this. Commenting on the quantity of stories about Wallace in circulation, he states, 'Qwha all his dedis and prysse
walde wryt, Hym worthit a gret buk to dyt' (VIII. xv. 2304).

As we have seen, another chronicle, but this time a Latin one, Bower's
Scotichronicon, was another vital source for Hary's poem. Like Wyntoun,
Bower was also an Augustinian, and like Wyntoun too he was writing in the
neighbourhood of Fife, in the abbey of Inchcolm, an island on the Firth of
Forth, of which he was abbot. He also had a lay patron, Sir David Stewart of
Rosyth. Bower and Wyntoun drew on some of the same sources, but their
chronicles are conspicuously different in tenor and construction, pointing up

the variant roles of the vernacular and the learned language in this period. Wyntoun has more of the feel of Barbour, Bower of Fordun. Bower's chronicle was indeed a substantial extension of Fordun's chronicle, and it increased that work's propensity for interspersing its historical narrative with sections of documentation. One of the most important texts of the Declaration of Arbroath, for example, is included in *Scotichronicon*. Wyntoun's Scots chronicle has little of this kind of thing, preferring anecdote to document, and narrative to analysis.

Another facet of Fordun's chronicle that Bower intensifies is its fiercely anti-English and Scot-centred perspective. Like his predecessor, Bower prefers the terms *regnum* (kingdom) and *gens* (people) for Scotland and the Scottish people; *nacio* is an occasionally used synonym for *patria* (homeland), which is itself employed as an emotive alternative to *regnum*. Indeed, the word *nacio* does not assume a dominant force in Scottish historiographical writing until Hector Boece's *Scotorum historia* (1527). But Bower's insistent use of *regnum* also speaks to a decisive element in his chronicling enterprise. It reinforces the close connection between *rex* and *regnum* which is at the heart of Bower's conception of Scottish best interests, and which picks up on a major facet of the ideological programme of many Scottish rulers. Bower was writing during the minority of James II, when different magnate factions were vying for control of the government of the kingdom; his sense of kingship as a unifying fundamental in Scottish politics, and of noble power as too often self-serving and disruptive, defines much of his narrative of Scottish history from the origins until the reign of James I with which his chronicle concludes. Admittedly, Bower will acknowledge the worth, in certain circumstances, of good noble guardians, such as Thomas Randolph; he also had his own doubts about inadequate or exploitative kingship, the latter showing through even in his encomia of James I. But the murder of that king in 1437 by a small group of his disaffected relations and associates created, as Bower saw it, a 'tyranny', in the form of the factions disputing the exercise of power, that was more dangerous still. At the end of his work Bower declares that he has written it 'pro solacio regis et regni', for the comfort of the king and of the kingdom. That the *Scotichronicon* was intended in part as an advice to princes work for the young Prince James may also be borne out by the nature of the illustrations in its principal manuscript, Corpus Christi College, Cambridge 171, all of which take episodes involving kingship as their subject.

Bower's presentation of Wallace exemplifies the near and often tense contacts between nationalism, kingship, and the role of the magnate class in his

DURING THE TYRANNOUS REIGN OF MACBETH Malcolm (later Malcolm III) and Macduff, thane of Fife, meet in England. This celebrated encounter is transmitted in the historiographical tradition, eventually reaching Shakespeare's *Macbeth*.

political way of seeing. The paradox of Wallace's position is that he embodies nationalistic values without being either king or noble. For Bower, as later for Hary, Wallace encapsulates the qualities essential to a successful king. The portrait of Wallace Bower gives in book XI draws on one he had deployed in books III and VI in depicting the quintessential monarch, Charlemagne. But there are, tragically, limitations to his role, as Bower's adaptation of the traditional body politic metaphor illustrates. Without a king, the body politic of Scotland is 'headless and unable to defend' itself; but Wallace 'appeared as a mighty arm' to save it in time of trouble (XI. XXXI). Wallace thus assumes the metaphorical bodily role more commonly bestowed upon the nobility. While this makes his achievements all the more impressive, the fact that he cannot supply the head the kingdom lacks also fosters the destructive envy towards him amongst members of the nobility that Bower condemns as a lamentable national characteristic: 'Why is covetous envy so much in control in Scotland? How sad that it is natural for Scots to detest not only the happiness of other people, but also the happiness of their own countrymen' (XI. XXXI).

As with Barbour and Hary, nationalistic assertions of independence are in Bower's eyes almost inseparable from accusations of national enviousness and divisiveness. But Bower and Hary differ in that the former places a far greater belief in the power of kingship to heal such rifts. Hary may wish to believe in this; he is less willing actually to demonstrate it.

The next generation of Scottish historical writing owes more to Bower and to Hary than to Wyntoun, despite the evident popularity of the latter in the fifteenth and early sixteenth centuries. Latin is in fact the major medium of Scottish historical writing in the sixteenth century, but the vernacular continues to play a vital complementary role.

Origin-myth wars

In 1512 the vernacular 'epic' tradition in Scots moves from dealing with the Wars of Independence to dealing with the great wars of Roman history, in Gavin Douglas's *Eneados*, the first full poetic translation of Virgil's *Aeneid* in Scots or English. That Douglas focuses on the history of Rome is indicative of the humanist leavening to his project, but a nationalist impetus is hardly absent from the *Eneados*. Douglas makes much of the fact that he is translating into the 'langage of Scottis natioun' (Prologue, I. 103). Douglas is one of the earliest Scottish writers consciously to describe himself as writing in 'Scottis' as a distinct, national tongue. His predecessors, including Hary himself, had referred to their language as 'Inglis', drawing attention to its linguistic, as well as literary, associations with their English neighbour. As his paralleling phrasing shows, Douglas's keenness to dissociate himself from that terminology may owe something to his contempt for the William Caxton 'of Inglis natioun' (Prologue, I. 138), of whose prose version of the *Aeneid* Douglas was deeply critical. But his reference to Scotland as a 'natioun' may also reflect a sense of the political importance of that statement. Douglas had good contacts with the Scottish court and would have been aware of the extent to which James IV had during his reign broadened his range of counsellors so that, as James's biographer has noted, 'individuals from every locality might find a patron at court'. A sense of nationhood could be generated not just by inspirational texts like *The Wallace*, but by the actual experience of daily political life. Nationhood was also very prominently on James's political agenda when Douglas was finishing his epic. The *Eneados* was completed only months before the Scots campaign against the English which culminated in the disastrous battle at Flodden in 1513. The phrase 'Scottis natioun', and its Latin equivalent, were at this date still not so commonly used in contexts of a strongly patriotic (as opposed to nationally identifying) kind, but Douglas may have known it from vernacular works dealing with the defence of Scotland against the English (e.g. Wyntoun, IX. ix. 1401). And again, the wide geographical range to the death-roll of those members of the aristocracy who fell at Flodden is indicative of the magnate support for this particular Scottish king across his kingdom. The sense Douglas's poem offers of a burgeoning national identity communicated in a language that translates the poem with bravura and style catches something of the cultural progressiveness of the last decade of James IV's reign. But if Douglas hoped for a Scottish, or possibly a continental, printing of his *Eneados*, such aspirations were swept away in the political chaos and cultural abatements that followed 1513, and in the difficulties of his own career. The *Eneados* was not printed until 1553, and then in London.

Bower's *Scotichronicon* was of course produced before printing came to Scotland, but its continuing appeal in the sixteenth century was dependent on manuscript circulation; it did not appear complete in print until 1759. By contrast, its sixteenth-century successors, the chronicles of John Mair and Hector Boece, went immediately into print. Both used the same Flemish Parisian-based scholar and printer, J. Badius Ascencius, who in 1521 published Mair's *Historia Majoris Brittaniae tam Angliae quam Scotiae* ('A History of Greater Britain, both England and Scotland') and in 1527 Boece's

Scotorum historia a prima gentis origine ('A History of the Scots from the First Origins of the People'). Ascencius was certainly known to Gavin Douglas too, and it is tempting to wonder if Douglas considered him as a publisher. But Ascencius was essentially a printer in the learned language; while he was clearly not averse to printing works with a strong Scottish political resonance a strong Scottish linguistic resonance would have appealed to him less.

The waning of the nascent Scottish printing industry in the wake of Flodden was probably one of the reasons why Mair and Boece had their works printed on the continent, but the choice also reflected their own European ambits. Like many Scots before them, both had completed their education in

Ad Iacobum Quintum Scotorum Regem,Magnæ spei ac
spectatæ indolis puerum
Iodocus Badius Ascensius.
REX Iacobe,puer fatis melioribus orte,
    Cui moderanda dedit Scotica sceptra Deus,
Perlege maiorum regalia gesta tuorum,
    Et libertatis protege iura tuæ.

JOHN MAIR'S HISTORY of 1521 is notable for its support for union between Scotland and England. James V, to whom the work is here dedicated, was the son of James IV of Scotland and Margaret Tudor, daughter of Henry VII of England.

¶ Heir beginnis the first buke of the croniklis of Scotland,

¶ Hovv Gathelus our first progenitour left the land of Grece, and come in Egipt, & maryit Scora dochter to king Pharo, and of his cumyng to Spanze, Capitulo. Primo.

 fter the maner of othir peppl ß Scottis despzand to schaw thair begin ning richt anciant schawis thame be this present histoze discendit of the Grekis & Egiptianis. Foz as auld croniclis beris,thair wes ane Greik nampt Gathelus sonne of Cecrops kyng of Athenes,otherwayis sonne of Argus kyng of Argiues. Gathe= lus be his insolence maid mony heit= schippis in Macedone and Achaia/ quhilkis war certane landis of Gre= ce. And becaus he couth not suffer ß cozrectioun of freindis,he left his na tiue cuntre of Grece & come in Egipt with ane cumpany of siclik zoung men fugitiuis as he wes fra thair cuntre. In this tyme rang in Egipt Pharo the scurge of the peppl of Is= rael:quhais son followand his fade= ris iniquite wes dzownit eftir wt all his army in ß reid seis be punitioun of god. Gathelus wes the moze ple= sandly resauit in Egipt that he appe= rit be his cumpany to suppozt kyng Pharo aganis ye mozis and peppil of Jnd,quhilkis be vnpzouisit and hastly incursionis wastit all the lan= dis and townis of Egipt to Mem= phis the principall ciete of his real= me,thus had Pharo sene ane mise=

rabyll rewyne of all his realme war nocht he changit the gouernance of the empyze of Egipt be industry of Moyses,to quhome be command of god the army of Pharo wes comit= tit. Pharo be supple of Gathelus wan ane maist dangerus battall a= gane the mozis, and bzocht thame to sa hie rewyne,that he tuk thair pzin= cipall ciete callit Merop. Gathelus eftir this happy victozy returnit in Egipt,and becaus he wes ane lusty persone strang of body, with greit spzeit, he conquest baith the fauour of ye kyng and his familiaris.This plesand victozy generit mait inuy thā gloze to Moyses. Foz the Egip= tianis hatit all the blud of Israell, and thairfoze Moyses knawing the hatrent of Egyptianis persewyng hym plk day to the deith fled out of Egipt in vnde to saif his lyfe. Ga= thelus foz his victozius and vailze= and dedis wes maid generall lieute= nand to all kyng Pharois army. And becaus he wes ane lusty pson, semely,& of the blud riall of Gzece, with pzudent ingyne, he gat kyng Pharois dochter nampt Scota in mariage, with part of thay landis in heritage,quhilk laitlie war tane be fozce of battall fra the peppll of Israel. Foz thir causis ye Grekis be= gan to reios,seand thair capitane in sic familiarite with the pzince trai= styng thairthzow sumtyme to haue ane sicker dwellyng place in Egipt, Schozt zeris eftir Pharo deceissit, eftir quhome succedit to the croun of Egipt his sonne Bochozis Pha=

THE OPENING OF THE FIRST BOOK of the printed edition of John Bellenden's *Croniklis of Scotland*, produced in Edinburgh c.1540 by Thomas Davidson. The volume makes prominent the historical longevity of the Scottish nation by beginning with the account of the story of Gathelus, 'our first progenitour', and Scota.

Paris. They were colleagues in the 1490s at the college of Montaigu, but whereas Mair remained teaching there until 1518 before returning to the universities of first Glasgow and then St Andrews, Boece went back to Scotland in 1497 to teach at the new University of Aberdeen, of which he became the first principal. While both writers clearly envisaged a Scottish audience for their histories, most immediately by dedicating them to the boy James V—like the *Scotichronicon*, these chronicles were produced during another period of kingly minority—they were also looking to a wider continental reception.

And an English one too. This is especially apparent in Mair's case since his chronicle is predicated on what in 1521 would have seemed as contentious an assumption as it does in 2005, the union of Scotland and England. To Mair this is the eminently logical solution to generations of enmity between the two countries, but it is a union he envisages as achieved more in terms of matrimonial alliance than by any detailed inspection of the constitutional implications of such an initiative. But Mair's discriminating attitude to his country's history extended beyond the saga of its relations with England. One of the most incisive challenges it posed was to an origin myth, the story of Scota and Gathelus and their descendants, held dear by previous generations of Scots.

This story, extant in various versions (Wyntoun cites three), had Irish origins but was given its impetus in Scotland by Fordun and was developed by his successors. In essence it states that Scotland owed its origins to the eponymous Scota, a daughter of the Egyptian Pharaoh, and her husband Gathelus, a Greek prince, who after a series of hardships and exile, travel to Spain; their descendants eventually settle first in Ireland and then, under Fergus I, in Scotland in 330 BC. The emotive nature of this sequence of episodes for Scots is indicated by the fact that one of them is chosen as a key illustration in the Corpus Manuscript of Bower's *Scotichronicon*, which features Scota and Gathelus (picked out by name in the picture) on board ship travelling to find their new home.

The Scota story provides a classic example of how Scottish historical writing declared its independence from England not only in focusing on its struggles against the old enemy but also in freeing itself from oppressive textual traditions. The manifest purpose of the Scota material was to quell one of the staples of the English origin myth tradition, which had been launched in the late-twelfth century by Geoffrey of Monmouth. His *Historia Regum Britanniae* had asserted that the British Isles had been colonized by the Trojan Brutus, great-grandson of Aeneas, after whose death his three sons divided up the constituent parts of the island between them. To the youngest one, Albanactus, Scotland was given and called Albany, but when he died childless the realm was absorbed into that of his elder brother Locrinus, king of England. This created, it was argued, English overlordship of Scotland, which Scottish kings had periodically acknowledged. This tradition was still valent in English histories when Mair was writing. He notes that 'Caxton's history' (in fact Caxton's printed editions of Higden and *The Brut*) holds that 'from the days of Brutus the Scots had been vassals'. The Scota story was designed to quash this account by providing a narrative that accredited the Scottish kingdom with a longevity that made the Brutus story implausible, and made the Trojans look like *parvenus* in comparison to the ancient Greeks and Egyptians.

But until Mair no Scottish historian was remotely willing to acknowledge this; rather, the story's validity was strenuously declaimed. Mair's account, however, shows a canny understanding of the functions of ideology on both sides of the Border. He saw the Scota narrative as 'a fable', created by the Scots because 'their English enemies had learned to boast of an origin from the Trojans so the Scots claimed an original decent from the Greeks who had subdued the Trojans, and then bettered it with this about the illustrious kingdom of Egypt'. But Mair was equally dismissive of the credibility of the English Brutus myth; Caxton, he wrote, vented as many lies as words in asserting it. He refers Caxton to another Englishman's history, Bede's, where 'he will find that not only were the Scots at no time subject to the Britons, but that many times they boldly attacked the Britons'.

Mair's enthusiasm for union thus has no basis in any diminishing of Scottish independence. Mair is as vociferous an exponent of the longevity and centrality of that notion as any of his foregoers. And though his book may differ from those before it in deliberately setting out to write a combined history of both countries, its overall emphasis is unequivocally on Scotland.

Mair takes further Bower's deep-set suspicion of the divisive activities of the Scottish nobility. In Mair's rewriting, the celebrated conversation between Wallace and Bruce at Falkirk becomes one in which Wallace warns Bruce against the dangers of over-mighty nobles, especially the Comyns. And Mair has an especially devastating analysis of the treachery of the aristocracy who opposed Wallace:

It may be that the nobility looked upon William as aiming at the royal power, and that they preferred English rule to William's. That is a feature of nobles generally—to prefer the yoke of a superior to that of an inferior. I fancy, too, that they aimed thereby at weakening the power at once of Edward and of William—which done, the government of the kingdom would revert to them.

The complexity of Mair's ideological position is such, though, that while he follows Bower in embracing strong unifying kingship as the solution to the persistent problem of over-mighty magnates, his analysis of the kingly role is yet accompanied by more far-reaching prescriptions than the earlier chronicler would have contemplated. A quarter-century in a European climate, and especially a French one, had exerted a distinct influence on Mair. His arguments on accountable kingship build on those expounded *c*.1490 in *The Meroure of Wyssdome* by John Ireland, another Scottish theologian trained in Paris and influenced, as Mair was, by the conciliarist writings of Jean Gerson.

Mair's fundamental points are that the king is 'a public person' empowered by the people: 'For he holds of his people no other right within his kingdom but as its governor.' Mair acknowledges that the necessary implication of this is that 'at the will and pleasure of the people kings might be deposed'. But he immediately qualifies the statement: 'if kings are any way corrigible they are not to be dismissed for what fault you will; but then, and only then, when their deposition shall make more for the advantage of the state than their continuance.'

Mair introduces his discussion of rights to kingship within the context of the disputes over the Balliol and Bruce claims to the throne. It is often noted that one of his arguments is that John Balliol was rightly deprived of the throne because of his quisling-like attitudes to the English. It is also often observed that Mair is thus supportive of Bruce as the successor chosen by the community of the realm (this does not deny his hereditary right, but makes it less of an issue). Mair will indeed eventually assert that Bruce should be placed 'even before William Wallace', but the terms in which he states this are revealing: 'after a beginning of disaster, when he had lost all that he had, when he had not a friend to stand by him, he remained ever of the same unconquered spirit, and drove, in the end, out of Scotland the Scots who favoured English rule and the nobles of England.' Mair's account of Bruce's compromised role in the struggle against the English thus plays down the degree of his fellow-travelling, but it is still acknowledged. Mair is juggling ideological priorities here. But what emerges from his treatment of these events is that the quality of Bruce's kingship is worth waiting for, particularly in the face of the magnate menace. Thus Mair's acceptance that kingly deposition can be conceived of in the face of prodigious kingly error is always strongly qualified by his estimation of the political value of forceful kingship over a disruptive political community. The case of Bruce shows how it is wise to give kings the benefit of the doubt.

The received view of Mair's *Historia* is that as history it had relatively little impact, but that its arguments on kingly deposition fuelled those of George Buchanan. It was not reprinted until 1724. But there is more evidence than is admitted that Mair's history was responded to. John Bellenden and William Stewart cite material from Mair at different points in their 'translations' of Boece's history, as does the chronicler Adam Abell in his *Roit or Quheill of Time*, also written in the 1530s. The antiquarian William Sinclair of Roslin marked up his copy of the *Extracta e variis cronicis Scocie* ('Extracts from the Various Scottish Chronicles'; Bower's is the most important) with cross-references to Mair's chronicle, among others. And in the preface he wrote for his 1594 edition of Hary's *Wallace* the Edinburgh printer Henry Charteris takes issue with Mair over the question of Wallace's retreat to France after Falkirk, for which Mair had claimed that there was no evidence in the Scots Latin chronicles. Interestingly, given that he could only have seen it in manuscript, Charteris quotes and translates from the *Scotichronicon* (in fact a revised version of it known as the Book of Cupar) to demonstrate that there is evidence in the Latin tradition for this sojourn of Wallace's.

However, the even greater challenge that Mair had posed to another of the central elements of the Scottish national image exercised other readers still more. One of his earliest readers was in fact Gavin Douglas. Douglas may have shared Mair's dim views of the reliability of Caxton's publications, but he also took exception to this particular work of Mair's. An exiled Scot in London, his family having fallen foul of the regent Albany during the minority of James V, Douglas yet adhered firmly to the nationalistic origin myths of his homeland. He urged Polydore Vergil, who was composing his own history of England, to take no account of the views in 'an historie of an certaine contriman of his', clearly Mair, and went to the trouble of providing Vergil with a statement of the traditional Gathelus and Scota account—perhaps a copy of the *Brevis chronica*, a highly abbreviated abstract of the *Scotichronicon*, which was in circulation in Latin and in Scots in the early sixteenth century. Douglas died in London shortly after this; the tablet which marks his burial place describes him as 'natione Scotus', 'a scot by nation'.

Douglas focused precisely on that aspect of Mair's history, the Scots origin myth, which was to be contested in Hector Boece's *Scotorum historia*, which was in part intended as a response to Mair's work. But Boece did not only reinstate the Gathelus and Scota story, he extended it in an unprecedented manner by naming the forty kings from Fergus I onwards, who established, as J. H. Burns has memorably put it, 'an unbroken line of kings of Scots which, with James V, was well into its nineteenth century'. Visitors to the Gallery of Holyrood House will find their 'portraits' in a sequence extended to James VII as painted by de Witt in 1684. The antiquity and independence of the Scottish kingdom was thus established, in comparison to those of England and other European countries which had been subject to periods of invasion and submission. But Boece's sense of Scotland also differed from Mair's in another decisive respect. While Mair looked southward to England, Boece looked north to the Highlands. While Mair censored the uncivilized manners and divisive political practice of the Highlanders, Boece held the austerity of the lifestyle of the Gaels as a model of the kind of virtues that Lowlanders would do well to imitate. Boece also makes more use of the term *nacio*—because he wishes, far more than does Mair, to see a greater unity of kingdom and people in terms primarily of the Scots, rather than the Scots and the English.

Kingly reigns are the dominant organizing principle of Boece's history. Like his medieval predecessors, Boece invests much value in the unifying relationship of king and kingdom. But there are qualifications to this which create, in this instance, a significant degree of alignment between Boece and Mair. Boece's innovatory catalogue of the forty kings between Fergus I and Fergus II includes quantities of bad rulers, several of whom are eventually formally deposed. There was precedent for this in Bower, the majority of whose corrupt kings are located in the early part of his history. But Boece and Bower differ revealingly over their treatment of a much later episode, the deposition of John Balliol. Whereas Bower declares that King John was deprived of his kingdom, albeit unlawfully, by Edward I, Boece asserts that Balliol, having effectively proved himself inadequate, was deprived of his title by the people of Scotland, who rightly installed the Bruce in his place. This was also Mair's argument, and it is possible that Boece's treatment of this issue approvingly recalls Mair. These sixteenth-century chroniclers edge, albeit almost despite themselves and against the grain of the bulk of their presentations of kingship, towards the countenancing of deposition in crisis circumstances.

Boece indeed enhances Mair's equivocal but finally vindicating reading of Bruce. Like Bower, he uses the encounter between Wallace and Bruce at

Erettyll chyff he mary his son or doghter with ony follis dwelland within his boundis/ he sall tyne his office/ and It sall no be lefull to his son nor his middis to brouk that office/ this and suchlyk lawis war thir he lang makketh/ thaeth quhille he hondint the realme xx zeris in syde/ nychor honheads the sanny wes contrar his naturall Inclinatioun mar geving to conquest the fauo of the peple/ and to stable the realme to him/ than to ony set of the comon weall xij

Hott banquho wes slewe be makbeth and his son fleance slewe in wale/ hoth walter the son of fleance come in scotland/ and of the genolochy of stewartis/

Short tyme efter se makketh returnit to his Innatibe conttis/ and become furyus (as the nature of all tyrandis Is) quhilkis conquessit realmes be violence/ mens/ trusting all peple to do their consellers to him/ as he did afor to vij/ fary remembring the wordis geven to him (as Is rehearsit) that banquhois posterite suld reios the colby be lang progressioun/ he callit banquho and his son fleance to ane supper/ quhilkis suspecet na thing les than his tresoun/ makbeth (quhen the bankat wes done) thot/ that he wald not sla thame oppinlye for ennos of peple/ bot bad ane band of armyt men to sla thame at thare returnyng hame/ this me (quhilkis war laid in way to this effect) slew banquho/ not theles fleance (ifthappin be consent of vij) and (this parfist as appeirs) be singular fauo of god to ane bett fortoun/ fleance escaping in this nycht and senit nocht weching laid for his slauchte All day/ fledd in wale/ quhair he wes plesindlye ressavit be the prince vij/ and maid sa familiar/ that he lay with the princes dochte/ and mad hir with child/ the prince of wale fiinding his dochte desflovt/ prout this fleance with sic hatrent/ that he finally slew him/ and helde his dochter becaus scho consentit to his pleisure in maist schamefull plentude/ at last scho wes delivrit of ane son namyt walt/ quhilk feeb finalye quhill he wes vij zeris sa lusty of feebs curage and spreit than ony man that wes almost in Landhart/ as he wes/ and yocht he wes halding with the prince of wale his gudfather in sall estat/ zit he had ane his mynd/ and abill to na thing mar than to attempt feeb charge/ It happenit at last that he fell at contentioun with his cusinzoun quhilkis obiectit to him/ that he wes not gottin of lauchfull bode/ thaeth quhill he wes sa Impacient/ that he slew his cusinzoun/ sone fledd in scotland to seik support of frendis/ at his cuming he happenit in cumpany with thay Inglishmen/ quhilkis come In scotland with sanct asofewhit and had him sa plesand he in ony sort/ that he conquest benivolence of all the quenis familiaris/ ifp this he wes send with feeb

Falkirk to focus this, having Wallace angrily accuse Bruce of being a traitor. But there is much less sense in Boece's account, as in Mair's, of Wallace
as a potential king figure. Rather, these later writers use Wallace as a value-
carrying figure, whose embodiment of patriotism is contrasted with the less
clear-cut representation of a key kingly personality in the ancestry to the
Stewart dynasty. Their treatments bespeak an awareness of the capacity in
kingship for corruption which comes further and further to the surface as the
sixteenth century goes on; that it is articulated through anxiety over relations
with the English is also an insistent feature.

It is thus not really surprising that John Bellenden's translation of Boece,
the *Croniklis of Scotland*, printed *c*.1540, and dedicated to a king, James V,
who was now a mature ruler, does a considerable amount to soften the harsher edges of Boece's representation of Bruce. It is indicative of the greater
immediate popular appeal of Boece's history, as opposed to Mair's, that no
fewer than three translations of it were produced in the decade following its
publication, two in prose and one in verse. The translations by Bellenden and
William Stewart in particular respond to Boece with a freedom that conveys
their translators' live sense of the political issues his work raised. Bellenden
indeed made revisions not only to Boece but between the manuscript and
printed versions of his translation. Bellenden's translation, the only one which
was printed, was a high-quality production, by Thomas Davidson, the king's
printer; copies still survive, probably produced for the monarch himself,
printed not on paper but on vellum—an unusually lavish method. A strong
identification of king and chronicle was also encouraged by the extremely
elaborate title page which featured the king's coat of arms; Davidson used the
same illustration for his edition of *The New Actis and Constitutionis of
Parliament*.

Kirk, queen, and constitution

But with the Scottish Reformation of 1560 came a major severance of king, or
queen, and chronicle or history. This period also sees a notable return of the
fertile connection between documentation and historical writing. The rheto-

Facing: JOHN BELLENDEN'S *'Croniklis of Scotland'* (*c*.1533) translated Hector Boece's
Latin *Scotorum Historia* into Scots, and divided its books into chapters. This chapter, in a
contemporary manuscript, begins with Macbeth's killing of Banquo and the escape of
Banquo's son Fleance, and concludes with an account of the genealogy of the Stewarts,
who descended from Fleance's son, Walter.

THE TITLE PAGE of
The New Actis and Con-
stitutionis of Parliament,
printed by the King's printer, Thomas Davidson, in
Edinburgh in 1541–2. The
dramatic version of James
V's royal coat of arms may
have been designed by the
poet Sir David Lyndsay, in
his capacity as Lyon King
of Arms.

ric of the Protestant Congregation's statements in the late 1550s and 1560s, in
which John Knox played a salient part, finds ready parallels in that of his
History of the Reformation of Religion within the Realm of Scotland. What
was at issue during these years was not only a wholesale change in the nation's
religious identification but opposition to two successive Catholic rulers, the
regent Mary of Guise and Mary queen of Scots. The majority of Knox's
History was written in between the establishment of the Protestant Church
in Scotland and the deposition of Mary queen of Scots in 1567; he continued
revising parts of it up to his death in 1572.

Knox's *History* is not in the model of those Scottish histories which had
preceded it. Its focus is the recent history of the Reformation rather than the
past history of the country. But on key occasions its rhetoric yet evokes an
emotive historical lineage. The preface to book II of the *History*, in fact the
earliest part of the work to be written, and composed as a propagandistic jus-

tification for the opposition to the regent, concludes by asserting that 'The Protestants of the Realm' have sought 'the liberty of this our native country to remain free from the bondage and tyranny of strangers'. Similar claims were expressed in the proclamation issued in August 1559 by the Congregation and addressed 'To the Nobilitie, Burghis and Communitie of the Realme of Scotland', which Knox indeed incorporates in book III of the *History*. The recollections of the Declaration of Arbroath may be coincidental, but that pre-Reformation nationalistic sentiments are being restyled in a radical political context is unmistakable.

The identification of the national interest with a section of the political community that does not include the monarch was of a piece with the moves towards the deposition of Mary of Guise that were taking shape in the Scottish parliament, but which were eventually rendered unnecessary by her death in 1560. However, with Mary queen of Scots matters went several steps further, and in book IV of the *History* her deposition is called for. Crucial to the justification for this in Knox's thought was the notion of the covenant, the league between God and his people, which bound those people to forms of obedience, the penalty for the infringement of which—such as tolerating an idolatrous queen—was eternal damnation.

As we have seen, in the previous histories of Scotland dialogue between subject and king, Wallace and Bruce, formed a major means of highlighting issues of where the national and royal interest should lie. It is also the dialogues of subject and monarch that give book IV of the *History* its compulsive narrative vividness, but these episodes are even more highly charged for the subject is Knox himself. In a sequence of encounters with Mary, and latterly with Maitland of Lethington, her secretary, Knox dramatizes their polarized positions on matters of religion and royal accountability. But Mary is not Bruce; she may be amazed and distressed (as Knox claims) by Knox's arguments, but she shows little sign of agreeing with them, indeed at times sets forth an acerbically perceptive view of how their positions might be interpreted: 'Well then, I perceive that my subjects shall obey you, and not me; and shall do what they list, and not what I command: and so must I be subject to them, and not they to me.'

Mary was, of course, removed on the grounds of her claimed adultery rather than her idolatry. As with the Congregation's attacks on Mary of Guise, book IV of Knox's *History* charts a series of arguments towards the justification of deposition, rather than dealing directly with its actuality. Nonetheless, royal deposition had now become a contemporary reality.

Knox wrote his history in the vernacular, a Scots showing varying degrees of Anglicization—Knox had spent considerable amounts of time in England and also wrote partly with an eye to an English audience. *The History* (books I–III) was indeed first printed in London by Thomas Vautrollier in 1587 but it was suppressed, and a complete edition was not issued until 1644. The Scots vernacular was also used by a chronicler more in the traditional mode, Robert Lindsay of Pitscottie, whose *Historie and Chronicles of Scotland* was composed during the 1570s during yet another minority, that of James VI. Pitscottie is really the Wyntoun of the sixteenth century, his colourful chronicle being full of anecdote. This is not to say that Pitscottie is without political bias—his reading of James III, for example, did much to blight the reputation of that monarch until the late twentieth century. But the continuing importance of Latin as an international medium for statements on nationalism is nicely brought out by the productions of John Leslie, bishop of Ross, and a passionate supporter of Mary queen of Scots. Having originally composed a vernacular history of Scotland at the end of the 1560s, he rewrote it in Latin and published it in 1578 as *De origine, moribus et gestis Scotorum*. In the wake of the Reformation and of an awareness of Knox's writings, Leslie's project is powerfully influenced by his determination to defend both the Catholic religion and Mary; thus although he makes much use of Boece, his chronicle is designed to work against any notion that Scotland had a tradition of deposing its rulers.

But less than five years after Leslie's history appeared, it was eclipsed by another Latin history arguing precisely the opposite, George Buchanan's *Rerum Scoticarum historia* (1582). Like Knox, Buchanan had advanced many of the more contentious arguments of his history in earlier polemical writings, most notably *De iure regni apud Scotos* (1579). Buchanan had also been closely involved in some of the propaganda produced after the deposition of Mary and designed to justify it to the wider world. Buchanan had been Mair's pupil, and in both *De iure* and his history he builds on his teacher's arguments for the rightful deposition of fallible monarchs by their people. But in Buchanan's writing this assumes a far greater ideological significance, linking him more closely to Knox in this respect. And his history provided the prehistory in Scottish historical tradition for the Marian deposition which Knox's had ignored. Although Buchanan dispensed with the Gathelus–Scota story, he retained Boece's list of forty kings between Fergus I and Fergus II. On one level the aim of this was strongly nationalist: Buchanan shared his pre-Reformation predecessor's concern to guarantee the longevity of Scot-

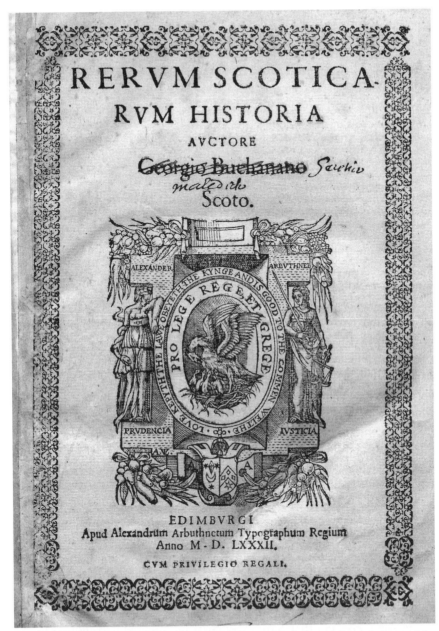

RERVM SCOTICA-
RVM HISTORIA

AVCTORE

~~Georgio Buchanano~~ *Scotir*
maledich
Scoto.

EDIMBVRGI
Apud Alexandrum Arbuthnetum Typographum Regium
Anno M·D·LXXXII.

CVM PRIVILEGIO REGALI.

THE PUBLICATION OF George Buchanan's *Rerum Scoticarum Historia* (printed by Alexander Arbuthnet in 1582) caused a furore because of its contentious arguments on kingship, and parliament ordered copies of the book to be recalled. It was not published again in Scotland in the sixteenth century, but it was printed many times on the Continent.

land's history as an independent nation. But on another, the catalogue provided Buchanan, as it had provided Boece, with the opportunity to include examples of rulers deposed by the nobility on the grounds of tyranny. Buchanan also suggests that the move from an elective monarchy to a hereditary monarchy carried out under Kenneth III was imposed on an intimidated nobility by a corrupted ruler, who had recently also murdered his most likely successor under the old system.

Like Knox, Buchanan also provided an eloquent, and highly prejudiced, reading of the reign of Mary queen of Scots. He stresses throughout this that Mary's deposition was 'rightful, in accordance with the laws and ancient practices of the people'. The appeal to the 'ancient constitution' here, invoking customs argued to go back to Fergus I, in the context of the actual removal of a contemporary Scots monarch, represents the furthest development of the statements on ruler and subject relations in the Declaration of Arbroath outlined early in this chapter. The emphasis in Mary's case was less English leanings than personal morality, but the rejection of her is still couched in terms that appropriate defence of the national interest to the people rather than the monarch.

It is hardly surprising that James VI and several later Stewart monarchs proscribed Buchanan's *De iure* and his history. James also responded in his own way in print with two major publications, *The True Law of Free Monarchies* (1598) and the *Basilikon Doron* (1601), both of which were composed shortly before the Union of the Crowns in 1603. These works deliberately move the emphasis of the debate from history to kingship. James accepts that kings are accountable—but to whom is the crucial issue. The man who had had George Buchanan as his tutor put it thus: 'by remitting them to God (who is their only ordinary juge) I remit them to the sorest and sharpest Schoolemaister that can be devised for them.' But he will also deliberately engage with the historical when necessary. In *The True Law* Boece and Buchanan's forty kings have disappeared but Fergus I remains in order to demonstrate that there were kings in Scotland before any estates or parliaments were thought of, 'And so it follows of necessitie, that the Kings were the authors and makers of the lawes, and not the lawes of the Kings.' This was not the end of the argument, as the fate of James's son Charles would conclusively show, but it was a position that James sustained in Scotland and, following the Union of the Crowns, in England. Scottish notions of kingship and national identity may have been dramatically affected by that union, but so, it should not be forgotten, were those of England.

FURTHER READING

1. Origins: Scotland to 1100

Adomnan of Iona, *Life of St Columba*, ed. and trans. Richard Sharpe (Harmondsworth, 1995), Adomnan's celebrated, and highly readable, saintly biography of Columba with copious notes from Sharpe on the geographical, historical, and cultural context.

Leslie Alcock, *Kings and Warriors, Craftsmen and Priests in Northern Britain AD 550–850* (Edinburgh, 2003), history and especially archaeology interwoven into a coherent picture of diverse aspects of life among the Picts, Gaels, Britons, and Angles; heavily illustrated.

J. Romilly Allen and Joseph Anderson, *Early Christian Monuments of Scotland* (Edinburgh, 1903; repr. 1993), The 'bible' of early Scottish sculpture: a detailed, descriptive catalogue of stone monuments carved by all the peoples of Dark Age Scotland; includes Pictish symbol stones and cross-slabs, Gaelic high crosses, Anglian, Norse, and British material. Fully illustrated.

A. O. Anderson, *Early Sources of Scottish History AD 500–1286*, 2 vols. (Edinburgh, 1922; repr. Stamford, 1990), a handy compendium of virtually all the historical sources available for the history of Scotland, in translation with useful notes. Most of the sources are now available in better modern editions, but these are scattered and not always so readily accessible.

T. O. Clancy (ed.), *The Triumph Tree: Scotland's Earliest Poetry AD 550–1350* (Edinburgh, 1998), the first 800 years of Scotland's literature; translations of poetry in five languages—Latin, British/Welsh, Gaelic, Old English, and Norse.

A. A. M. Duncan, *Scotland: The Making of the Kingdom*, Edinburgh History of Scotland 1 (Edinburgh, 1975), a classic modern account: although the account of the earlier periods has been superseded by some of the other works mentioned here, this broader perspective is still of great value.

George Henderson and Isabel Henderson, *The Arts of the Picts: Sculpture and Metalwork in Early Medieval Scotland* (London, 2004), magisterial art historical survey, lavishly illustrated.

Isabel Henderson, *The Picts*, Ancient Peoples and Places Series (London, 1967), a classic which has stood the test of time, particularly as regards Pictish art. Sadly long out of print.

John T. Koch, *The Gododdin of Aneirin: Text and Context from Dark-Age North Britain* (Cardiff, 1997), a challenging interpretation of the Gododdin poems as a source for the history and culture of northern Britain in the sixth, seventh, and eighth centuries.

Alan Macquarrie, *The Saints of Scotland: Essays in Scottish Church History AD 450–1093* (Edinburgh, 1997), not an account of the early Church as such, but an exploration of the life and cult of figures such as Patrick, Ninian, Kentigern, Columba, and Margaret as well as other important, though more obscure Scottish saints.

Alfred P. Smyth, *Warlords and Holy Men: Scotland AD 80–100*, The New History of
    Scotland 1 (Edinburgh, 1984), again, although in need of heavy modification in the light
    of more recent scholarship, still a highly readable and useful introductory account.
W. J. Watson, *The History of the Celtic Place-Names of Scotland* (Edinburgh, 1926; repr.
    1993), another 'bible', more wide-ranging than the title might suggest, and especially
    valuable on the Church.

Specialist works on the vikings include, on the historical side: Barbara Crawford, *Scandinavian Scotland* (Leicester, 1987); and on the archaeological, James Graham-Campbell
and Colleen Batey, *Vikings in Scotland: An Archaeological Survey* (Edinburgh, 1998).

Three books published by Historic Scotland in conjunction with Batsford provide excellent, up-to-date, introductory overviews to this period. All are heavily illustrated and,
though primarily archaeological in perspective, incorporate historical material as appropriate. They are: Ian Armit, *Celtic Scotland* (1997), David Breeze, *Roman Scotland*
(1996), and Sally Foster, *Picts, Gaels and Scots* (1996).

Another Historic Scotland-sponsored project is the Canongate/Birlinn 'Making of Scot-
land' series. Again well illustrated and primarily archaeological, these shorter works pro-
vide more focused, personal perspectives on the period. Richard Hingley, *Settlement and
Scarifice: The Later Prehistoric People of Scotland* (1998); Chris Lowe, *Angels, Fools and
Tyrants: Britons and Anglo-Saxons in Southern Scotland AD 450–750* (1999); Ewan
Campbell, *Saints and Sea-Kings: The First Kingdom of the Scots* (1999); Martin Carver,
Surviving in Symbols: A Visit to the Pictish Nation (1999); Olwyn Owen, *The Sea Road: A
Viking Voyage through Scotland* (1999); Stephen T. Driscoll, *Alba: The Gaelic Kingdom of
Scotland AD 800–1124* (2002).

A guide to recent specialist scholarship will be found in the bibliographies of these more
general works.

2.   The Emergence of a Nation-State, 1100–1300

GENERAL

G. W. S. Barrow, *Kingship and Unity: Scotland 1000–1306* (2nd edn. Edinburgh, 2003), a
    brief but masterly analysis.
A. A. M. Duncan, *Scotland: The Making of the Kingdom* (Edinburgh, 1975), detailed,
    stimulating, and indispensable.
Michael Lynch, *Scotland: A New History* (2nd edn. London, 1991), including a sparkling
    review of the twelfth and thirteenth centuries.

Collections of essays
There are three wide-ranging collections covering many crucial topics:

G. W. S. Barrow, *Scotland and its Neighbours in the Middle Ages* (London, 1992).
G. W. S. Barrow, *The Kingdom of the Scots: Government, Church and Society from the
    Eleventh to the Fourteenth Century* (2nd edn. Edinburgh, 2003).
A. Grant and K. J. Stringer (eds.), *Medieval Scotland: Crown, Lordship and Community*
    (Edinburgh, 1993; repr. 1998).

SCOTLAND IN ITS BROADER SETTING

R. Bartlett, *The Making of Europe: Conquest, Colonization and Cultural Change, 950–1350* (London, 1993), a highly influential book on the contemporary 'Europeanization of Europe', with much relevant commentary concerning Scotland.

R. R. Davies, *The First English Empire: Power and Identities in the British Isles, 1093–1343* (Oxford, 2000), an outstanding analysis which, despite its focus on the advance of English power, stresses the unique features of the Scottish experience.

David Ditchburn, *Scotland and Europe: The Medieval Kingdom and its Contacts with Christendom, c.1215–1545*, i: *Religion, Culture and Commerce* (East Linton, 2001), a rich and dynamic investigation.

Robin Frame, *The Political Development of the British Isles, 1100–1400* (rev. edn. Oxford, 1995), a penetrating study by a leading British historian entirely at home with the Scottish material.

KINGSHIP, GOVERNMENT, AND ADMINISTRATION

G. W. S. Barrow, *Robert Bruce and the Community of the Realm of Scotland* (3rd edn. Edinburgh, 1988), a justly famous book, with six fine chapters on the pre-1300 period.

A. A. M. Duncan, *The Kingship of the Scots, 842–1292: Succession and Independence* (Edinburgh, 2002), including a rigorous appraisal of the relationship between Scotland and the English state.

R. A. McDonald, *The Kingdom of the Isles: Scotland's Western Seaboard, c.1100–c.1336* (East Linton, 1997), a full and lucid account of the struggle for supremacy between Norse-Gaelic sea-kings and the kings of Scots.

Hector L. MacQueen, *Common Law and Feudal Society in Medieval Scotland* (Edinburgh, 1993), an authoritative analysis of legal developments and the growth of state power.

NOBLE SOCIETY AND POWER

G. W. S. Barrow, *The Anglo-Norman Era in Scottish History* (Oxford, 1980), a detailed examination of Anglo-Norman colonists and settlement; stresses the impact of *English* influences and the underlying continuities.

K. J. Stringer, *Earl David of Huntingdon, 1152–1219: A Study in Anglo-Scottish History* (Edinburgh, 1985), dealing with a major Scottish magnate and the development of cross-Border landholding.

Alan Young, *Robert the Bruce's Rivals: The Comyns, 1212–1314* (East Linton, 1997), an account of thirteenth-century Scotland's pre-eminent noble family.

CHURCH AND RELIGION

Ian B. Cowan, *The Medieval Church in Scotland*, ed. J. Kirk (Edinburgh, 1995), a notable set of papers.

Ian B. Cowan and D. E. Easson, *Medieval Religious Houses: Scotland* (2nd edn London, 1976), an indispensable guide to all new foundations, with an authoritative introduction.

ECONOMY

M. Lynch, M. Spearman, and G. Stell (eds.), *The Scottish Medieval Town* (Edinburgh, 1988), the most comprehensive work to date on urbanization and trade.

Ian D. Whyte, *Scotland before the Industrial Revolution: An Economic and Social History, c. 1050–c. 1750* (London, 1995), a reasonably successful attempt to fill a major gap.

SCOTTISH IDENTITY AND NATIONHOOD

D. Broun, R. Finlay, and M. Lynch (eds.), *Image and Identity: The Making and Re-making of Scotland through the Ages* (Edinburgh, 1998), with a crucial reinterpretation by D. Broun.

Bruce Webster, *Medieval Scotland: The Making of an Identity* (London, 1997), a concise introduction.

ARCHAEOLOGY AND ARCHITECTURE

Richard Fawcett, *Scottish Abbeys and Priories* (London, 1994), and *Scottish Cathedrals* (London, 1997), helpful, well-illustrated introductions.

C. Tabraham, *Scotland's Castles* (London, 1997), an important survey.

P. A. Yeoman, *Medieval Scotland: An Archaeological Perspective* (London, 1995), an interesting interdisciplinary approach.

3. Survival and Revival: Late Medieval Scotland

GENERAL HISTORIES

There are two recent single volume works that have useful observations on the late medieval kingdom:

D. Ditchburn and A. J. MacDonald, 'Medieval Scotland, 1100–1500', in R. A. Houston and W. Knox (eds.), *The New Penguin History of Scotland* (London, 2001).

Michael Lynch, *Scotland: A New History* (2nd edn, London, 1992).

Three volumes in *The New History of Scotland* series cover the late medieval period in an engaging and thoughtful way:

G. W. S. Barrow, *Kingship and Unity: Scotland, 1000–1306* (London, 1981).

Alexander Grant, *Independence and Nationhood: Scotland, 1306–1469* (London, 1984).

Jenny Wormald, *Court, Kirk and Community: Scotland, 1469–1625* (London, 1981).

Ranald Nicholson's *Scotland: The Later Middle Ages* (Edinburgh, 1974) is more narrative in approach but offers a sound introduction to the political history of the kingdom.

Michael Brown's lucid *The Wars of Scotland 1214–1371* (Edinburgh, 2004) is the first of the New Edinburgh History of Scotland series to appear.

KINGSHIP, POLITICS, AND GOVERNMENT

Political biographies of individual monarchs include:

Stephen Boardman, *The Early Stewart Kings: Robert II and Robert III, 1371–1406* (East Linton, 1996).

M. H. Brown, *James I* (Edinburgh, 1994).
Norman Macdougall, *James III* (Edinburgh, 1982).
Norman Macdougall, *James IV* (Edinburgh, 1989).
Christine McGladdery, *James II* (Edinburgh, 1990).
Michael Penman, *David II* (East Linton, 2004).

Discussion of general issues of the exercise of royal and aristocratic power and crown-magnate relations can be found in:

Michael Brown, *The Black Douglases* (East Linton, 2000).
Michael Brown, 'Scotland Tamed? Kings and Magnates in Late Medieval Scotland: A Review of Recent Work', *Innes Review*, 45 (1994), 120–46.
Roger A. Mason, 'Kingship, Tyranny and the Right to Resist in Fifteenth Century Scotland', *Scottish Historical Review*, 66 (1987), 125–51.
Jenny Wormald, *Lords and Men in Scotland: Bonds of Manrent 1442–1603* (Edinburgh, 1985).
Jenny Wormald, 'Taming the Magnates?', in K. Stringer (ed.), *Essays on the Nobility of Medieval Scotland* (Edinburgh, 1985), 270–80.

The development of Scottish legal and representative institutions is traced in:

John Finlay, *Men of Law in Pre-Reformation Scotland* (East Linton, 2000).
Hector L. MacQueen, *Common Law and Feudal Society in Medieval Scotland* (Edinburgh, 1993).
Roland Tanner, *The Late Medieval Scottish Parliament: Politics and the Three Estates, 1424–1488* (East Linton, 2001).

SOCIETY AND CULTURE

The distinctive features of burghal life and the importance of burghs within the kingdom are discussed in a number of recent studies:

E. P. Dennison, 'Power to the People? The Myth of the Medieval Burgh Community', in S. Foster, A. Macinnes, and R. MacInnes (eds.), *Scottish Power Centres* (Glasgow, 1998), ch. 5.
E. P. Dennison, D. Ditchburn, and M. Lynch (eds.), *Aberdeen before 1800: A New History* (East Linton, 2002).
E. P. Dennison and G. G. Simpson, 'Scotland', *Cambridge Urban History of Britain* (Cambridge, 1990).
Elizabeth Ewan, *Townlife in Fourteenth-Century Scotland* (Edinburgh, 1990).
M. Lynch, M. Spearman, and G. Stell, *The Scottish Medieval Town* (Edinburgh, 1988).

Architectural and literary themes are explored in:

John Dunbar, *Scottish Royal Palaces: The Architecture of the Royal Residences during the Late Medieval and Renaissance Periods* (East Linton, 1999).
Carol Edington, *Court and Culture in Renaissance Scotland: Sir David Lindsay of the Mount* (East Linton, 1994).
Richard Fawcett, *Scottish Architecture from the Accession of the Stewarts to the Reformation, 1371–1560* (Edinburgh, 1994).

Michael Lynch (ed.), *The Renaissance in Scotland: Studies in Literature, Religion, History and Culture* (Leiden, 1994).

Sally Mapstone (ed.), *A Palace in the Wild: Essays on Vernacular Culture and Humanism in Late-Medieval and Renaissance Scotland* (Leuven, 2000).

Sally Mapstone and Juliette Wood (eds.), *The Rose and the Thistle: Essays on the Culture of Late Medieval and Renaissance Scotland* (East Linton, 1998).

Some aspects of the religious life of the kingdom are examined in:

Ian. B. Cowan, 'Church and Society', in Jennifer M. Brown (ed.), *Scottish Society in the Fifteenth Century* (London, 1977).

D. Forrester and D. Murray (eds.), *Studies in the History of Worship in Scotland* (Edinburgh, 1984).

Alexander Grant, *Independence and Nationhood: Scotland 1306–1469* (Edinburgh, 1984), ch. 4.

P. Yeoman, *Pilgrimage in Medieval Scotland* (London, 1999).

The history of Gaelic Scotland is addressed by:

J. W. M. Bannerman, 'The Lordship of the Isles', in Jennifer M. Brown (ed.), *Scottish Society in the Fifteenth Century* (London, 1977).

E. J. Cowan and R. A. MacDonald (eds.), *Alba: Celtic Scotland in the Middle Ages* (East Linton, 2000).

Alexander Grant, 'Scotland's "Celtic Fringe" in the Late Middle Ages: The MacDonald Lords of the Isles and the kingdom of Scotland', in R. R. Davies (ed.), *The British Isles, 1100–1500* (Edinburgh, 1988).

M. MacGregor, 'Church and Culture in the Late Medieval Highlands', in J. Kirk (ed.), *The Church in the Highlands* (Edinburgh, 1998).

4.   Renaissance and Reformation: The Sixteenth Century

GENERAL

Gordon Donaldson, *Scotland: James V–James VII* (Edinburgh, 1965), now dated, but still offering a valuable narrative.

Michael Lynch, *Scotland: A New History* (London, 1991), particularly strong on the sixteenth century.

Roger A. Mason, *Kingship and the Commonweal: Political Thought in Renaissance and Reformation Scotland* (East Linton, 1998), a series of studies of sixteenth-century Scottish political culture.

Jenny Wormald, *Court, Kirk and Community: Scotland, 1470–1625* (London, 1981) the liveliest introduction to the period covered here.

THE SOCIAL AND ECONOMIC CONTEXT

R. A. Houston and I. D. Whyte (eds.), *Scottish Society, 1500–1800* (Cambridge, 1989), a valuable collection of essays.

Margaret Sanderson, *Scottish Rural Society in the Sixteenth Century* (Edinburgh, 1982), the only major study of the impact of the feuing movement.

Jenny Wormald, *Lords and Men in Scotland: Bonds of Manrent, 1442–1603* (Edinburgh, 1985), an innovative study of the roots of noble power.

RENAISSANCE MONARCHY

Jamie Cameron, *James V: The Personal Rule* (East Linton, 1998), predominantly concerned with crown–magnate relations, but the first scholarly study of the reign.

Carol Edington, *Court and Culture in Renaissance Scotland: Sir David Lindsay of the Mount* (East Linton, 1994), invaluable insights into James V's court culture.

Norman Macdougall, *James IV* (Edinburgh, 1989), required reading, though essentially a political biography.

J. H. Williams (ed.), *Stewart Style 1513–1542: Essays on the Court of James V* (East Linton, 1996), a useful if diffuse collection of essays.

THE REFORMATION

Ian B. Cowan, *The Scottish Reformation: Church and Society in Sixteenth-Century Scotland* (London, 1982), a solid survey.

Gordon Donaldson, *The Scottish Reformation* (Cambridge, 1960), misleading in places but still valuable.

David McRoberts (ed.), *Essays on the Scottish Reformation* (Glasgow, 1962), much valuable material from a Catholic perspective.

Roger A. Mason (ed.), *John Knox and the British Reformations* (Aldershot, 1998), a wide-ranging collection.

THE REIGN OF MARY

Gordon Donaldson, *All the Queen's Men: Power and Politics in Mary Stewart's Scotland* (London, 1983), an important study of political allegiances from the 1540s to the 1570s.

Michael Lynch (ed.), *Mary Stewart: Queen in Three Kingdoms* (Oxford, 1988), the case for the defence.

Jenny Wormald, *Mary Queen of Scots: A Study in Failure* (London, 1988; revised edn, *Mary Queen of Scots: Politics, Passion and a Kingdom Lost*, London, 2001), the case for the prosecution.

THE REIGN OF JAMES VI

Keith M. Brown, *Bloodfeud in Scotland, 1573–1625: Violence, Justice and Politics in an Early Modern Society* (Edinburgh, 1986), a detailed study of the demise of Scotland's feuding culture.

Julian Goodare and Michael Lynch (eds.), *The Reign of James VI* (East Linton, 2000), a valuable collection focused on James's Scottish kingship.

James Kirk, *Patterns of Reform: Continuity and Change in the Reformation Kirk* (Edinburgh, 1989), an important series of essays.

Maurice Lee, Jr., *Great Britain's Solomon: James VI and I in his Three Kingdoms* (Urbana, Ill., 1991), the only recent study of the king's entire career.

5.   Confidence and Perplexity: The Seventeenth Century

GENERAL

Gordon Donaldson, *Scotland: James V–VII* (Edinburgh, 1965), a book that has stood the test of time: a highly informative work.

William Ferguson, *Scotland: 1689 to the Present* (Edinburgh, 1968), a must for the events leading up to the union of 1707, and the union itself.

William Ferguson, *Scotland's Relations with England: A Survey to 1707* (Edinburgh, 1977), chronologically covers a huge sweep, and has very pertinent things to say about the seventeenth century.

Rosalind Mitchison, *Lordship to Patronage: Scotland 1603–1745* (London, 1983), very enjoyable to read, fast-moving, sometimes attractively idiosyncratic, and full of insights, especially on social history.

T. C. Smout, *A History of the Scottish People, 1560–1830* (London, 1969), a classic; not to be missed.

POLITICS AND RELIGION

Keith M. Brown, *Kingdom of Province? Scotland and the Regal Union, 1603–1715* (London, 1992), short but essential and compelling reading.

Julia Buckroyd, *Church and State in Scotland, 1660–1681* (Edinburgh, 1980), a solid and informative guide to a complex period.

E. J. Cowan, *Montrose: For Covenant and King* (London, 1977), an unusually balanced and useful account of an over-romanticized figure.

Ian B. Cowan, *The Scottish Covenanters, 1660–1688* (Southampton, 1976), dispassionate and demythologizing.

Frances Dow, *Cromwellian Scotland, 1651–1660* (Edinburgh, 1979), detailed, and very interesting and informative.

Bruce Galloway, *The Union of England and Scotland, 1603–1608* (Edinburgh, 1986), an excellent analysis of the uneasy first years of union and of why the king's idea of a more incorporating union failed.

Clare Jackson, *Restoration Scotland 1660–1690: Royalist Politics, Religion and Ideas* (Woodbridge, 2003), an examination of the collapse of popular royalism by setting it in the intellectual context of the age; a pioneering and important book.

Maurice Lee Jr., *Government by Pen: Scotland under James VI and I* (Chicago, 1980): this and the following book are splendid, clear, and wide-ranging accounts by an acknowledged expert.

Maurice Lee Jr., *The Road to Revolution: Scotland under Charles I, 1625–37* (Chicago, 1985).

Alan R. MacDonald, *The Jacobean Kirk, 1567–1625: Sovereignty, Polity and Liturgy* (Aldershot, 1998), challenges the idea that James VI's ecclesiastical policy was a success and sees a high level of religious tension before the reign of Charles I.

Allan I. Macinnes, *Charles I and the Making of the Covenanting Movement, 1625–1641* (Edinburgh, 1991), essential reading for an understanding of Charles I's Revocation Scheme as well as his other follies, which are convincingly analysed.

Allan I. Macinnes, *Clanship, Commerce and the House of Stuart, 1603–1788* (East Linton, 1996), another essential read, for the Highlands and the collapse of clanship.

Walter Makey, *The Church of the Covenant, 1637–1651* (Glasgow, 1979), very sensitive and compelling discussion.

Roger A. Mason (ed.), *Scotland and England, 1286–1815* (Edinburgh, 1987), contains important articles for the seventeenth and early eighteenth centuries.

John Morrill (ed.), *The Scottish National Covenant in its British Context* (Edinburgh, 1990), a marvellous collection of essays on this crucial subject.

David G. Mullan, *Episcopacy in Scotland: The History of an Idea, 1560–1638* (Edinburgh, 1986), subtle and interesting discussion of conflicting ideas about what the Scottish Kirk should be.

David G. Mullan, *Scottish Puritanism, 1590–1638* (Oxford, 2000), a fascinating attempt to understand the minds of Presbyterians and Episcopalians and their common beliefs as well as their conflicts.

Steve Murdoch, *Britain, Denmark-Norway and the House of Stuart, 1603-1660* (East Linton, 2003) brings a new and compelling dimension to Stuart foreign policy.

David Stevenson, *The Scottish Revolution, 1637–41: The Triumph of the Covenanters* (Newton Abbot, 1973); this and the following book are essential reading for the period.

David Stevenson, *Revolution and Counter Revolution in Scotland, 1644–1651* (London, 1977).

Margo Todd, *The Culture of Protestantism in Early-Modern Scotland* (New Haven, 2002), a ground-breaking work which looks below the preoccupations of the elite and opens up the world of the ordinary parishioner.

SOCIAL AND ECONOMIC

Julian Goodare (ed.), *The Scottish Witch-Hunt in Context* (Manchester, 2002), a collection of articles which build on, extend, and challenge the work of C. Larner (see below).

R. A. Houston and I. D. Whyte (eds.), *Scottish Society 1500–1800* (Cambridge, 1989), a collection of wide-ranging and very interesting articles.

Deborah Howard, *Scottish Architecture from the Reformation to the Restoration, 1560–1660* (Edinburgh 1995), a lovely book, for its content and its illustrations; the 'lay' reader learns much.

Christina Larner, *Enemies of God: The Witch-Hunt in Scotland* (London, 1981), the classic work on Scottish witchcraft and the starting point for all interested in the subject.

Michael Lynch (ed.), *The Early-Modern Town in Scotland* (London, 1987), a combination of detailed case studies and more general analyses, which make a fascinating book.

Alastair J. Mann, *The Scottish Book Trade 1500–1720: Print Commerce and Print Control in Early-Modern Scotland* (East Linton, 2000), opens up a neglected and important subject and adds to our understanding of early modern Scotland.

T. C. Smout, *Scottish Trade on the Eve of Union, 1660–1707* (Edinburgh, 1963), crucial to understanding why the union of the parliaments came about.

Ian D. Whyte, *Agriculture and Society in Seventeenth Century Scotland* (Edinburgh, 1979), another pioneering and very influential book.

6.   Scotland Transformed: The Eighteenth Century

GENERAL

David Allan, *Scotland in the Eighteenth Century* (Harlow, 2002), brief accessible survey.

Linda Colley, *Britons: Forging the Nation 1707–1837* (New Haven, 1992), clever analysis of Britishness as a function of 'otherness'.

T. M. Devine and J. R. Young (eds.), *Eighteenth Century Scotland: New Perspectives* (East Linton, 1999), varied essays with a social slant.

N. T. Phillipson and Rosalind Mitchison (eds.), *Scotland in the Age of Improvement* (Edinburgh, 1970), solid collection of essays that has aged well.

T. C. Smout, *A History of the Scottish People 1560–1830* (London, 1969), masterful synthesis.

POLITICS

Michael Fry, *The Dundas Despotism* (Edinburgh, 1992), a major reassessment, stressing the political effectiveness of Henry Dundas.

Bruce P. Lenman, *The Jacobite Risings in Britain 1689–1746* (London, 1980; repr. Aberdeen, 1995), lucid survey of the Jacobite rebellions.

Alexander Murdoch, *The People Above: Politics and Administration in Mid-Eighteenth Century Scotland* (Edinburgh, 1980), expert analysis of politics in the pre-Dundas era.

John Robertson (ed.), *A Union for Empire: Political Thought and the Union of 1707* (Cambridge, 1995), a milestone in Union scholarship.

ECONOMY AND SOCIETY

T. M. Devine, *The Tobacco Lords* (Edinburgh, 1975), classic study of a formidable commercial elite in Glasgow.

T. M. Devine, *The Transformation of Rural Scotland: Social Change and the Agrarian Economy 1660–1815* (Edinburgh, 1994), comprehensive analysis of agriculture and society.

T.M. Devine, *Clanship to Crofters' War: The Social Transformation of the Scottish Highlands* (Manchester, 1994), perceptive essays on clanship, Jacobitism, whisky-making, migration, the concepts of Gaeldom and Highlandism, and more.

T. M. Devine and G. Jackson (eds.), *Glasgow, i: Beginnings to 1830* (Manchester, 1995), urban history on a grand scale, with a social and economic focus.

T. M. Devine and R. Mitchison (eds.), *People and Society in Scotland, i: 1760–1830* (Edinburgh, 1988), lively, readable essays in social history.

Leah Leneman, *Alienated Affections: The Scottish Experience of Divorce and Separation, 1684–1830* (Edinburgh, 1998), path-breaking account of a previously unexplored subject.

Alan I. Macinnes, *Clanship, Commerce and the House of Stuart, 1603–1788* (East Linton, 1996), perceptive reassessment of Highland society and economy.

Christopher A. Whatley, *Scottish Society, 1707–1830: Beyond Jacobitism, Towards Industrialization* (Manchester, 2000), fine social history.

Charles W. J. Withers, *Urban Highlanders: Highland–Lowland Migration and Urban*

Gaelic Culture, 1700–1900 (East Linton, 1998), interdisciplinary study of changing patterns of demographics, labour, and culture.

CULTURE AND ENLIGHTENMENT: IDEAS AND CONTEXTS

Christopher J. Berry, *Social Theory of the Scottish Enlightenment* (Edinburgh, 1997), the first comprehensive account of its subject in more than fifty years.

Alexander Broadie (ed.), *The Cambridge Companion to the Scottish Enlightenment* (Cambridge 2003), state of the art essays.

James Buchan, *Capital of the Mind: How Edinburgh Changed the World* (London, 2003), readable popular account of the Edinburgh Enlightenment.

Jenifer J. Carter and Joan H. Pittock (eds.), *Aberdeen and the Enlightenment* (Aberdeen, 1987), useful if uneven collection.

David Daiches et al. (eds.), *A Hotbed of Genius: The Scottish Enlightenment, 1730–90* (Edinburgh, 1986; repr. 2000), splendidly illustrated introduction to the Edinburgh Enlightenment.

John Dwyer, *Virtuous Discourse: Sensibility and Community in Late Eighteenth-Century Scotland* (Edinburgh, 1987), a landmark study, centring on the Henry Mackenzie circle of sentimental moralists.

Andrew Hook and Richard B. Sher (eds.), *The Glasgow Enlightenment* (East Linton, 1995), the only volume on a neglected topic.

Richard B. Sher, *Church and University in the Scottish Enlightenment: The Moderate Literati of Edinburgh* (Princeton, 1985), the William Robertson circle of clergymen of letters.

M. A. Stewart (ed.), *Studies in the Philosophy of the Scottish Enlightenment* (Oxford, 1990), rigorously contextual studies focusing on moral philosophy and natural science.

Paul Wood (ed.), *The Scottish Enlightenment: Essays in Reinterpretation* (Rochester, N.Y., 2000), more recent essays on Enlightenment philosophy and science.

CULTURE AND ENLIGHTENMENT: LITERATURE, THE ARTS, AND NATIONAL IDENTITY

Thomas Crawford, *Burns: A Study of the Poems and Songs* (Stanford, Calif., 1960; repr. Edinburgh, 1994), rich and insightful.

Leith Davis, *Acts of Union: Scotland and the Literary Negotiation of the British Nation 1707–1830* (Stanford, Calif., 1998), stimulating treatment of literature and national identity from Defoe to Scott.

F. W. Freeman, *Robert Fergusson and the Scots Humanist Compromise* (Edinburgh, 1984), unusual and important.

Ian G. Lindsay and Mary Cosh, *Inverary and the Dukes of Argyll* (Edinburgh, 1973), handsome social history of architecture with much on Ilay.

Duncan Macmillan, *Painting in Scotland: The Golden Age* (Oxford, 1986), good coverage of Ramsay, Raeburn, Runciman, and Allan.

A. J. Youngson, *The Making of Classical Edinburgh* (Edinburgh, 1966; repr. 1988), classic, starkly illustrated study of the creation of the New Town.

7. Workshop of Empire: The Nineteenth Century

The following are all excellent studies, and highly recommended reading.

GENERAL

T.M. Devine, *The Scottish Nation, 1700–2000* (London, 1999).
John McCaffrey, *Scotland in the Nineteenth Century* (Basingstoke, 1998).
T. C. Smout, *A Century of the Scottish People, 1830–1950* (London, 1986).

CULTURE

Douglas Gifford (ed.), *The History of Scottish Literature, iii: The Nineteenth Century* (Aberdeen, 1988).

ECONOMIC

R. H. Campbell, *The Rise and Fall of Scottish Industry. 1707–1939* (Edinburgh, 1980).
Christopher A. Whatley, *The Industrial Revolution in Scotland* (Cambridge, 1997).

EDUCATION

R. D. Anderson, *Education and Opportunity in Victorian Scotland* (Oxford, 1983).
R. D. Anderson, *Education and the Scottish People, 1750–1918* (Oxford, 1995).

EMPIRE

Michael Fry, *The Scottish Empire* (East Linton, 2001).

HIGHLANDS

T. M. Devine, *Clanship to Crofters War: The Social Transformation of the Scottish Highlands* (Manchester, 1994).
James Hunter, *The Making of the Crofting Community* (Edinburgh, 1976).
Eric Richards, *The Highland Clearances: People, Landlords and Rural Turmoil* (Edinburgh, 2000).

POLITICS

W. H. Fraser, *Scottish Popular Politics: Radicalism to Labour* (Edinburgh, 2000).
Michael Fry, *Patronage and Principle: A Political History of Modern Scotland* (Aberdeen, 1987).
Christopher Harvie, *Scotland and Nationalism: Scottish Society and Politics, 1707–1994* (London, 1994).
I. G. C. Hutchison, *A Political History of Scotland, 1832–1924: Parties, Elections, Issues* (Edinburgh, 1986).

RELIGION

Callum G. Brown, *Religion and Society in Scotland since 1707* (Edinburgh, 1997).

S. J. Brown and Michael Fry (eds.), *Scotland in the Age of the Disruption* (Edinburgh, 1993).

SOCIAL

T. M. Devine (ed.), *Irish Immigration and Scottish Society in the Nineteenth and Twentieth Centuries* (Edinburgh, 1991).

T. M. Devine and R. Mitchison (eds.), *People and Society in Scotland i: 1760–1830* (Edinburgh, 1988).

W. H. Fraser and I. Maver (eds.), *Glasgow, ii: 1830 to 1912* (Manchester, 1996).

W. H. Fraser and R. J. Morris (eds.), *People and Society in Scotland, ii: 1830–1914* (Edinburgh, 1990).

G. Gordon (ed.), *Perspectives of the Scottish City* (Aberdeen, 1985).

W. W. Knox, *Industrial Nation: Work, Culture and Society in Scotland, 1800 to the Present* (Edinburgh, 1999).

Christopher A. Whatley, *Scottish Society, 1707–1830: Beyond Jacobitism, towards Industrialisation* (Manchester, 2000).

8. The Turbulent Century: Scotland since 1900

The following are all excellent studies and highly recommended reading.

GENERAL

T. M. Devine and R. J. Finlay (eds.), *Scotland in the Twentieth Century* (Edinburgh, 1996).

A. Dickson and J. H. Treble (eds.), *People and Society in Scotland, iii: 1914–1990* (Edinburgh, 1992).

Christopher Harvie, *No Gods and Precious Few Heroes: Scotland 1914–2000* (Edinburgh, 1999).

David McCrone, *Understanding Scotland: The Sociology of a Stateless Nation* (London, 1992).

POLITICS

A. Brown, D. McCrone, and L. Paterson, *Politics and Society in Scotland* (Basingstoke, 2000).

D. Denver, J. Mitchell, C. Pattie, and H. Bochel, *Scotland Decides: The Devolution Issue and the Scottish Referendum* (London, 2000).

I. Donnachie, C. Harvie, and I. S. Wood (eds.), *Forward: Labour Politics in Scotland 1888–1988* (Edinburgh, 1989).

I. G. C. Hutchison, *Scottish Politics in the Twentieth Century* (Basingstoke, 2000).

C. M. M. MacDonald (ed.), *Unionist Scotland 1800–1997* (Edinburgh, 1998).

James Mitchell, *Strategies for Self-Government* (Edinburgh, 1996).

ECONOMY

R. H. Campbell, *The Rise and Fall of Scottish Industry 1707–1939* (Edinburgh, 1980).

C. H. Lee, *Scotland and the United Kingdom: The Economy and the Union in the Twentieth Century* (Manchester, 1995).

Peter L. Payne, *Growth and Contraction, Scottish Industry 1860–1990* (Glasgow, 1992).

Richard Saville (ed.), *Economic Development of Modern Scotland 1950–1980* (Edinburgh, 1985).

SOCIETY

E. Breitenbach and E. Gordon (eds.), *Out of Bounds: Women in Scottish Society 1800–1945* (Edinburgh, 1991).

Callum G. Brown, *Religion and Society in Scotland since 1707* (Edinburgh, 1997).

C. Macdonald and E. Macfarland (eds.), *Scotland and the Great War* (East Linton, 1999).

T. C. Smout, *A Century of the Scottish People 1830–1950* (London, 1986).

CULTURE

Cairns Craig, *Out of History* (Edinburgh, 1996).

George E. Davie, *The Crisis of the Democratic Intellect* (Edinburgh, 1986).

D. Gifford and D. McMillan (eds.), *A History of Scottish Women's Writing* (Edinburgh, 1997).

W. M. Humes and H. M. Paterson (eds.), *Scottish Culture and Scottish Education 1800–1980* (Edinburgh, 1983).

9. The Scottish Diaspora

The following are all excellent studies and highly recommended reading.

GENERAL

R. A. Cage (ed.), *The Scots Abroad: Labour, Capital, Enterprise, 1750–1914* (London, 1985).

T. M. Devine (ed.), *Scottish Emigration and Scottish Society* (Edinburgh, 1992).

Gordon Donaldson, *The Scots Overseas* (London, 1966).

Marjory Harper, *Adventurers and Exiles: The Great Scottish Exodus* (London, 2003).

Grant Simpson (ed.), *The Scottish Soldier Abroad 1247–1967* (Edinburgh, 1991).

T. C. Smout, Ned C. Landsman, and T. M. Devine, 'Scottish Emigration in the Seventeenth and Eighteenth Centuries', in Nicholas Canny (ed.), *Europeans on the Move: Studies on European Migration, 1500–1800* (Oxford, 1994).

Donald Whyte, *The Scots Overseas: A Selected Bibliography* (Aberdeen, 1995).

SCOTLAND AND EUROPE

J. Berg and B. O. Lagencrantz, *Scots in Sweden* (Edinburgh, 1962).

Paul Dukes (ed.), *The Caledonian Phalanx: Scots in Russia* (Edinburgh, 1987).

Michael Perceval-Maxwell, *The Scottish Migration to Ulster in the Reign of James I* (London, 1973).

Grant Simpson (ed.), *Scotland and Scandinavia, 800–1800* (Edinburgh, 1990).
Grant Simpson (ed.), *Scotland and the Low Countries, 1124–1994* (East Linton, 1995).
Basil Skinner, *Scots in Italy in the Eighteenth Century* (Edinburgh, 1966).
T. C. Smout (ed.), *Scotland and Europe 1200–1850* (Edinburgh, 1986).

SCOTLAND AND THE AMERICAS

William R. Brock, *Scotus Americanus: A Survey of the Sources for Links between Scotland and America in the 18th Century* (Edinburgh, 1982).
J. M. Bumsted, *The People's Clearance: Highland Emigration to British North America, 1770–1815* (Edinburgh, 1982).
Allan Karras, *Sojourners in the Sun: Scottish Migrants in Jamaica and the Chesapeake, 1740–1800* (Ithaca, NY, 1992).
Ned C. Landsman (ed.), *Nation and Province in the First British Empire: Scotland and the Americas, 1600–1800* (Lewisburg, Pa., 2001).
W. Stanford Reid (ed.), *The Scottish Tradition in Canada* (Toronto, 1976).

SCOTLAND AND THE EMPIRE

Alex M. Cain, *The Corn Chest for Scotland: Scots in India* (Edinburgh, 1986).
T. M. Devine, *Scotland's Empire, 1600–1815* (London, 2003).
Michael Fry, *The Scottish Empire* (East Linton, 2001).
John M. MacKenzie, *Empires of Nature and the Nature of Empires: Imperialism, Scotland and the Environment* (East Linton, 1997).
Martha McLaren, *British India and British Scotland, 1780–1830: Career Building, Empire Building and a Scottish School of Thought on Indian Governance* (Akron, Oh., 2000).
D. S. Macmillan, *Scotland and Australia, 1788–1850: Emigration, Commerce and Investment* (Oxford, 1967).

10.   Scotland's Stories

PRIMARY SOURCES

Barbour's *Bruce*, ed. Matthew P. McDiarmid and James A. C. Stevenson, 3 vols. Scottish Text Society (Edinburgh, 1980–5), standard scholarly edition.
Hector Boece, *Scotorum historiae a prima gentis origine* (Paris, 1527), there is a contemporary translation, *The Chronicles of Scotland Compiled by Hector Boece and Translated into Scots by John Bellenden*, ed. R. W. Chambers, Edith C. Batho, and H. Winifred Husbands, 2 vols. Scottish Text Society (Edinburgh, 1935–41); should not be regarded as a literal crib; Bellenden often inserts his own material.
Walter Bower, *Scotichronicon*, ed. D. E. R. Watt et al., 9 vols. (Aberdeen, 1987–98), facing-page English translation of the Latin text; last volume is analytical studies of the chronicle.
George Buchanan, *Rerum Scoticarum Historia auctore Georgio Buchanano* (Edinburgh,

1582), there is a serviceable translation, *The History of Scotland Translated from the Latin of George Buchanan*, ed. James Aikman, 4 vols. (Edinburgh, 1827).

T.O. Clancy (ed.), *The Triumph Tree: Scotland's Earliest Poetry, AD 550–1350* (Edinburgh, 1998), includes English translations of Taliesin's poems and *The Gododdin*.

William Hamilton of Gilbertfield, *Blind Harry's Wallace*, introd. Elspeth King (Edinburgh, 1998).

Hary's Wallace, ed. Matthew P. McDiarmid, 2 vols., Scottish Text Society (Edinburgh, 1968–9), with maps and notes.

John Knox's History of the Reformation in Scotland, ed. William Croft Dickinson, 2 vols. (Edinburgh, 1949), modernized spelling and punctuation.

John Lesley, *The History of Scotland from the Death of King James I in the Year 1436 to the Year 1561*, Bannatyne Club (Edinburgh, 1830).

Robert Lindesay of Pitscottie, *The Historie and Cronicles of Scotland*, ed. Æ. J. G. Mackay 3 vols., Scottish Text Society (Edinburgh, 1898–1907).

John Mair, *Historia Majoris Brianniae tam Angliae quam Scotae* (Paris, 1521); the translation also has a useful introduction and notes on Mair's career: John Major, *A History of Greater Britain*, ed. Archibald Constable, Scottish History Society, 10 (Edinburgh, 1892).

The Original Chronicle of Andrew of Wyntoun, ed. F. J. Amours, 6 vols., Scottish Text Society (Edinburgh, 1902–9).

HISTORICAL AND LITERARY CONTEXT

G. W. S. Barrow, *Robert Bruce and the Community of the Realm of Scotland* (3rd edn. Edinburgh, 1992), standard study of the Wars of Independence.

Stephen Boardman, *The Early Stewart Kings: Robert II and Robert III*, The Stewart Dynasty in Scotland (East Linton, 1996), excellent analysis of the reigns of the two Stewart kings of the late fourteenth and early fifteenth centuries.

R. James Goldstein, *The Matter of Scotland: Historical Narrative in Medieval Scotland* (London, 1993), covers chroniclers and poets.

Alexander Grant, *Independence and Nationhood 1306–1469*, (London, 1984), trenchant political, social, and economic history.

Norman Macdougall, *James III: a Political Study* (Edinburgh, 1982).

POLITICAL THOUGHT

J. H. Burns, *The True Law of Kingship: Concepts of Monarchy in Early Modern Scotland* (Oxford, 1996), lucid account of key concepts in Scottish political thought from the fifteenth to the seventeenth centuries.

Roger A. Mason, *Kingship and the Commonweal: Political Thought in Renaissance and Reformation Scotland* (East Linton, 1998), particularly valuable on Mair, Knox, and Buchanan.

Chronology

	of Alba under Constantin, the Cumbrians under Owein, and the Dublin Norse under Olaf son of Gothfrith. West Saxon control of Northumbria strengthened
945	Overlordship of Cumbria granted to Máel-Coluim, king of Alba, by Athelstan's successor Edmund
954–62	Reign of Indulf, son of Constantin, king of Alba. Secures overlordship of Lothian
997–1005	Reign of Kenneth III
1018	Battle of Carham. Men of Alba, under Máel-Coluim, victorious over the Bernicians, thereby confirming their control over Lothian and establishing the Tweed as the southern boundary of the kingdom
1040–57	Mac-bethad (Macbeth) of Moray king of all 'Scotia'
1058–93	Máel-Coluim son of Donnchad (Malcolm Canmore) rules over Scotia, Cumbria, and Lothian
1093	Death of Máel-Coluim. Succession contested between his brother, Domnall bán (1094–7), and his sons, Donnchad son of Ingebjorg (1094) and Edgar son of Margaret (1094/7–1107)
1113	Henry I of England grants to David (brother of Alexander I) the earldom of Huntingdon
1124–53	Reign of David I
1141–53	David I rules northern England to the Ribble and the Tees
1157	Malcolm IV surrenders Northumbrian territories to Henry II of England
1165	Death of Malcolm IV; accession of William I 'the Lion'
1173–4	William I invades northern England and is captured. Treaty of Falaise: William I recognizes Henry II as superior lord of Scotland
1189	Quitclaim of Canterbury: Richard I of England restores Scottish independence
1192	Pope Celestine III guarantees the independence of the Scottish Church as a 'special daughter' of Rome
1214	Death of William I. Accession of Alexander II
1215–17	Alexander II invades northern England
1222–35	Alexander II finally subdues Ross, Caithness, and Galloway
1237	Treaty of York: Alexander II renounces Scots claims to the English Border counties
1249	Death of Alexander II while leading an expedition to the Western Isles. Accession of Alexander III
1250	Translation and enshrinement of St Margaret's body at Dunfermline Abbey
1263	Hakon IV, king of Norway, is repulsed at Largs

1266	Treaty of Perth: Norway cedes to Scotland the Hebrides and Man
1284	Margaret 'the Maid of Norway' is recognized as heir presumptive to Alexander III, her grandfather
1286	Death of Alexander III
1290	Treaty of Brigham: Margaret Maid of Norway is betrothed to the son and heir of Edward I of England. Death of Margaret two months later
1291–2	The 'Great Cause': claims to the Scottish crown are adjudicated by Edward I as superior lord of Scotland. Accession of John Balliol
1296–1328	Wars of Independence
1296	Edward I defeats the Scots army at Dunbar. King John submits and abdicates. Parliament at Berwick. Submission of Scots
1297	Rebellions against Edward I. William Wallace destroys an English army at Stirling Bridge
1298	William Wallace named as Guardian. Edward I defeats Wallace's army at Falkirk
1304–5	Edward I leads army through eastern Scotland
1305	Execution of William Wallace. Ordinance for the government of Scotland issued
1306	Robert Bruce kills John Comyn at Dumfries. Inauguration of Robert I at Scone
1307	Death of Edward I at Burgh-by-Sands
1307–8	Robert I campaigns against his northern enemies
1309	Parliament held at St Andrews: declarations acknowledging Bruce as king
1314	Battle of Bannockburn
1320	Letters from Scottish community to Pope John XXII issued, including the Declaration of Arbroath
1328	Treaty of Edinburgh–Northampton: English recognition of Scottish independence
1329	Death of Robert I at Cardross
1331	Coronation of David II at Scone
1332	Edward Balliol crowned king of Scots at Scone
1333	Battle of Halidon Hill
1334	David Bruce sent to France. Edward Balliol does homage to Edward III at York
1337	Outbreak of Hundred Years War between England and France distracts Edward III from Scotland
1341	David II returns to Scotland
1346	Battle of Neville's Cross; David II taken prisoner by the English

1349	Plague arrives in Scotland
1356	'Burnt Candlemas': Edward III harries Lothian
1357	Treaty of Berwick. Release of David II, with ransom
1360–70	Chronicle of John of Fordun
1360	Treaty of Bretigny: Anglo-French peace
1363	Unsuccessful rebellion of Robert the Steward and the earls of Douglas and Dunbar against David II. Marriage of David to Margaret Logie
1364	Parliament held at Scone to consider English peace proposals
1368	Arrest and imprisonment of Robert the Steward at Lochleven
1371	Death of David II without children; Robert the Steward becomes the first Stewart king of Scotland as Robert II
1375	John Barbour's epic poem *The Bruce*
1377	Death of Edward III
1384	Creation of a lieutenancy for Robert II's eldest son, John, earl of Carrick
1388	Battle of Otterburn; Scottish victory, but James, 2nd earl of Douglas, killed. Carrick replaced as guardian of the realm by his brother Robert, earl of Fife
1390	Death of Robert II. Carrick succeeds to the throne as Robert III; Fife retains guardianship
1398	Two royal dukes created, a new peerage title for Scotland: Robert III's son and heir David as duke of Rothesay and his brother Robert, earl of Fife, as duke of Albany
1399	Duke of Rothesay becomes lieutenant
1400	Unsuccessful invasion of Scotland by Henry IV
1402	Death of the duke of Rothesay in Albany's custody. Battle of Humbleton (Homildon Hill)
1406	Robert III's surviving son and heir James (future James I) captured at sea by English vessels while journeying to France. Death of Robert III; governorship of Robert duke of Albany established
1409	Destruction of Jedburgh castle, captured from the English
1411	Battle of Harlaw: lord of the Isles defeated by earl of Mar
1412	Foundation of the University of St Andrews
1419	*Garde Ecossaisse* founded as French royal bodyguard
c.1420	Andrew of Wyntoun, *Orygynale Cronykil of Scotland*
1420	Death of Robert duke of Albany; his son Murdoch succeeds as governor
1423	Treaty of London: agreement on James I's release from English captivity in return for substantial ransom
1424	Return of James I to Scotland; battle of Verneuil results in death of Archibald, 4th earl of Douglas, and John, earl of Buchan

1425	Execution of the Albany Stewarts
1426	James I and Queen Joan found Carthusian monastery at Perth
1428	Renewal of Franco-Scottish alliance
1430	Birth and baptism of heir, future James II
1436	Unsuccessful siege of Roxburgh Castle [the Marchmont] by James I
1437	Assassination of James I; execution of Walter, earl of Atholl, and his co-conspirators.
1445	Completion of Walter Bower's *Scotichronicon*
1449	Marriage of James II to Mary of Guelders
1450–1	William, earl of Douglas, and many others travel to Rome for the papal jubilee
1451	Foundation of the University of Glasgow
1452	Killing of William, 8th earl of Douglas, by James II and his courtiers; exiling of James, 9th earl of Douglas, and his brothers
1455	Battle of Arkinholm. Deaths of the Douglas earls of Moray and Ormond
1458	Parliament passes an act encouraging crown and other landowners to adopt feu-farme tenure
1460	Death of James II at siege of Roxburgh
1468	Marriage of James III to Margaret of Denmark
1472	Archbishopric of St Andrews created for Patrick Graham
1474	Proposed marriage treaty with England
1475–6	Crown-led assault on John, lord of the Isles, results in forfeiture of the earldom of Ross and lordship of Kintyre
*c.*1475–9	Completion of Blind Hary's *Wallace*. A critique of James III's pro-English diplomacy?
1487	Papal Indult allowing Scottish king eight months to appoint candidates to vacant benefices
1488	Rebellion against James III nominally led by his own son, the future James IV; death of the king at the battle of Sauchieburn
1492	Archbishopric of Glasgow created. Renewal of Franco-Scottish alliance and treaty with Denmark-Norway
1493	Forfeiture and suppression of the lordship of the Isles
1494	Foundation of the University of Aberdeen: King's College
*c.*1500–2	Building of Great Hall at Stirling Castle
1502	Treaty of Perpetual Peace between England and Scotland. Attack on Sir Robert Menzies of Weem
1503	Marriage of James IV and Margaret Tudor
1507	Introduction of printing to Scotland: Chepman and Myllar

1509	Accession of Henry VIII to the English throne
c.1509	*Wallace* printed by Chepman and Myllar
1512	Gavin Douglas, *Eneados*. Foundation of St Leonard's College, St Andrews
1513	Battle of Flodden; death of James IV; accession of James V
1513–28	Minority of James V
1515–17	First regency of John Stewart, duke of Albany. Treaty of Rouen renews alliance with France (1517)
1521	John Mair, *Historia Majoris Britanniae tam Angliae quam Scotiae*, printed by Ascensius in Paris
1525	Parliamentary act against heretical—Protestant—literature
1526–8	King held by Archibald Douglas, 6th earl of Angus
1527	Hector Boece, *Scotorum Historia*, printed by Ascensius in Paris
1528	Beginning of James V's personal rule; Angus exiled; Patrick Hamilton burned for heresy
1530	King leads punitive royal raid in the Borders
1531	Papacy sanctions heavy taxation of the Church
1532	Establishment of College of Justice, from former court of session
1533	Thomas Doughty founds Loretto hermitage at Musselburgh
1533–4	Henry VIII repudiates papal authority
1535	Renewal of heresy legislation
1536–7	James V visits France; marries Madeleine, daughter of Francis I (Jan. 1537); Madeleine dies shortly after return to Scotland (July 1537)
1538	James V marries Mary of Guise
1540	King embarks on naval expedition to Orkney and the Western Isles
c.1540	John Bellenden, *Chronicles of Scotland* (prose translation of Boece's *Historia*); William Stewart, *The Buik of the Croniclis of Scotland* (verse translation of Boece's *Historia*)
1541	Further anti-heresy legislation. James V fails to meet Henry VIII at York
1542	Scottish defeat at battle of Solway Moss (Nov.); death of James V (Dec.); accession of week-old daughter Mary
1542–61	Minority of Mary queen of Scots
1543–54	Regency of James Hamilton, earl of Arran and (from 1549) duke of Châtelherault
1543	Treaties of Greenwich, proposing Mary's marriage to Henry VIII's son Edward, negotiated (July) and then repudiated (Dec.)
1544–5	Beginning of 'Rough Wooing'; punitive military campaigns levied by England against Scotland
1546	Burning of George Wishart for heresy (March); assassination of Cardinal

Beaton (May); siege of St Andrews Castle; John Knox preaches first sermon

1547   Death of Henry VIII (Jan.); fall of St Andrews Castle to French force; defeat of Scots by Protector Somerset at battle of Pinkie (Sept.); English military occupation of Lowlands

1548   Treaty of Haddington: Mary to marry French dauphin; Mary sent to France

1549   First major Scottish reforming Catholic church council

1550   Visit of Mary of Guise to France

1552   Second major reforming church council; Hamilton's *Catechism* printed

1553   Death of Edward VI of England; accession of Mary Tudor

1554   Châtelherault ousted from regency by Mary of Guise

1555–6   Knox on clandestine preaching mission to Scotland

1557   First Band or Covenant of the Protestant lords of the Congregation

1558   Marriage of Mary and Dauphin Francis (Apr.); burning of Walter Myln for heresy (Apr.). Death of Mary Tudor and accession of Elizabeth (Nov.)

1559   Treaty of Cateau-Cambrésis (Apr.): Knox preaches at Perth and ignites Protestant rebellion (May); death of Henry II of France and accession of Francis II and Mary (July); attempted deposition of Mary of Guise as regent (Oct.)

1560   Treaty of Berwick (Feb.): Elizabeth to intervene to aid Scottish Protestants; siege of Leith (Mar.); death of Mary of Guise (June): Treaty of Edinburgh - French and English troops to withdraw (July); Reformation parliament (Aug.); death of Francis II (Dec.); *First Book of Discipline* drawn up

*c.*1560–72   John Knox, *History of the Reformation of Religion within the Realm of Scotland*

1561   Mary returns to Scotland (Aug.)

1562   Mary takes military action against the Catholic earl of Huntly. Thirds of Benefices offer financial support to Protestant Kirk

1565   Mary marries Henry Stewart, Lord Darnley; failed rebellion of her half-brother James, earl of Moray

1566   Murder of David Riccio (Mar.); birth of Prince James (June); baptism of James (Dec.)

1567   Murder of Darnley (Feb.); marriage of Mary to James Hepburn, earl of Bothwell (May); surrender by Mary to Confederate lords at Carberry and flight of Bothwell (June); Mary imprisoned and forced to abdicate (July); James crowned (July); and Moray made regent (Aug.)

1568   Mary escapes imprisonment, but is defeated at battle of Langside and flees to England

1570s   Robert Lindsay of Pitscottie, *Historie and Chronicles of Scotland*

1570   Assassination of regent Moray and intensification of civil war between King's Men and Queen's Men

1572	James Douglas, earl of Morton, made regent, following brief regencies of earls of Lennox and Mar. Death of Knox
1573	Pacification of Perth and fall of Edinburgh Castle sees final defeat of Queen's Men
1574	Return of Andrew Melville from Geneva. First Poor Law
1578	*Second Book of Discipline* drawn up. Morton ousted from regency, but reasserts his authority. John Leslie, bishop of Ross, *De Origine, Moribus et Gestis Scotorum*
1579	Arrival from France of Esmé Stuart, lord d'Aubigné; created earl of Lennox (1580) and duke of Lennox (1581). Second Poor Law. George Buchanan, *De Iure Regni apud Scotos Dialogus*. Scots Brigade founded in Holland
1581	Negative Confession of Faith. Execution of Morton
1582	Ruthven Raid: King James seized by earl of Gowrie. George Buchanan, *Rerum Scoticarum Historia*
1582–3	Foundation of the University of Edinburgh
1583	King escapes Ruthven Raiders; Gowrie executed and Melville and others seek refuge in England
1584	The 'Black Acts' reassert crown control over the Kirk
1586	League with England; James to receive annual pension from Elizabeth
1587	Execution of Mary queen of Scots
1588	Spanish Armada defeated
1589	Marriage of James VI to Anne of Denmark. Letters from Huntly to Philip II intercepted by English
1590	Trial of North Berwick witches; Francis Stewart, earl of Bothwell, outlawed
1592	Murder of earl of Moray by Huntly. 'Golden Act' underwrites Presbyterian Kirk
1593	Foundation of second University of Aberdeen: Marischal College
1595	Catholic earls Huntly and Erroll, and the earl of Bothwell, exiled
1596	Catholic earls reconciled with king and Kirk. Octavians appointed to manage king's finances. Religious riot in Edinburgh used by James to turn tables on Presbyterian hardliners
1596–7	Second period of witchhunting. James VI, *Daemonologie*
1597	Anglo-Scottish commission established to deal with borders
1598–9	James VI, *True Law of Free Monarchies* (1598); *Basilikon Doron* (1599)
1599	Fife Adventurers' first attempt at colonization of Lewis; second attempt 1602
1600	Three 'parliamentary' bishops appointed. Unsuccessful Gowrie conspiracy. Scots College in Rome founded
1603	Death of Elizabeth. Accession of James VI to English throne as James I: the Union of the Crowns

1605–6	Further attempts to settle Lowlanders in Lewis
1606	Andrew Melville and seven Presbyterian ministers summoned to Hampton Court and imprisoned
1607	King's hopes for closer union finally dashed by English parliament
1609	Statutes of Iona. Scottish plantation in Ulster
1609–10	Acts setting out comprehensive scheme for commissioners of the shires; appointment of JPs
1610	Restoration of diocesan episcopacy
1612	Opposition in parliament to level of taxation
1616	Privy council ordinance on establishing parish schools
1617	King's visit to Scotland. Opposition to his introduction of the Five Articles of Perth, rejected by the General Assembly
1618	General Assembly accepts Five Articles
1621	Parliament: Five Articles and new form of taxation passed, but with considerable opposition. James VI grants Nova Scotia to Sir William Alexander
1622–3	Severe famine
1625	Death of James VI and I. Accession of Charles I. Interference with composition of privy council and court of session. Highly damaging and dubiously legal Act of Revocation issued
1630	Short-lived Scots colony on Cape Breton Island
1630s	Charles begins to appoint Arminian bishops
1633	Charles I comes to Scotland for coronation. Parliament: voting procedure changed
1636	Canons, modelled on English, imposed on Kirk
1637	Introduction of Prayer Book—'Laud's Liturgy'. Widespread riots and resistance. Collapse of king's government, and alternative, the Tables, set up
1638	The National Covenant. General Assembly at Glasgow: episcopacy abolished and Five Articles abjured
1639	Charles I's unsuccessful attack on Scotland: First Bishops' War
1640	Parliament: dismantling of king's powers. English Short Parliament meets. Second Bishops' War.
1641	English Long Parliament summoned. Charles I visits Scotland. Irish rebellion breaks out
1642	First English civil war begins
1643	Solemn League and Covenant; Scots agree to support English parliamentarians
1644	Scottish army takes part in first serious defeat of Charles I at Marston Moor
1644–5	Montrose's year of victories and ultimate defeat at Philiphaugh

1647   The Engagement, made between dissident group of covenanters and
            Charles I

1648   Second English civil war. Defeat of Engager army at Preston. Cromwell
            comes to Scotland

1649   Execution of Charles I. Charles II proclaimed by Scots as British king. Poor
            Law. Abolition of lay patronage in kirk

1650   Covenanters defeated at battle of Dunbar

1651   Charles II crowned; last king to be crowned in Scotland. Covenanters defeat-
            ed at Worcester. Military rule now imposed from England, along with the
            'happy union'; Scottish parliament suppressed

1653–4   Glencairn's rising

1656   JPs reintroduced

1657–9   Extensive witchhunting

1658   Death of Oliver Cromwell

1660   Restoration of Charles II. English Navigation acts exclude direct Scottish
            trade with the American colonies

1660–80   Charles II rules Scotland through the earl of Lauderdale, secretary and, from
            1663, commissioner

1661–2   Renewed witchhunting

1662   Episcopacy restored; lay patronage re-established in Kirk

1666   Pentland Rising

1667   Robert Sibbald founds Physic Garden in Edinburgh, later the Royal Botanic
            Garden

1669   Indulgence granted to Presbyterian ministers; repeated 1672

1672   Act restricting privileges of the royal burghs

1679   Murder of Archbishop Sharpe of St Andrews; armed rising in the west sup-
            pressed at Bothwell Bridge; covenanters proclaim Charles II as enemy of
            God

1679–81   James, duke of York, in Scotland

1681   Act acknowledging royal supremacy in all matters, secular and ecclesiastical.
            Royal College of Physicians founded. James Dalrymple, Viscount Stair's
            Institutions of the Law of Scotland published

1680s   The 'killing times': supposed savage persecution of covenanters

1684   Scots colonies founded in East New Jersey and Charlestown, Carolina

1685   Death of Charles II. Accession of Catholic James II and VII. Monmouth's
            rebellion; Argyll's collusion leads to his execution

1687   Two indulgences, granting complete religious toleration

1688   Edinburgh University given new charter: 'King James's university'. James II
            deposed

1689	Claim of Right; crown offered to William and Mary
1690	Presbyterianism established in kirk
1690s	'King William's Seven Ill Years': severe famine
1692	Massacre of Glencoe
1695	William Patterson founds the Bank of Scotland. Company of Scotland trading to Africa and the Indies chartered
1697	Execution of student Thomas Aitkenhead for blasphemy
1698	Scots colony attempted at Darien
1700	Darien colony abandoned
1701	English Act of Succession, settling thrones of England and Scotland on Sophia, electress of Hanover, after Anne's death
1702	Death of William III. Accession of Anne
1703	Scottish Act of Security, refusing to acknowledge acceptance of Sophia as Anne's heir. Act anent War and Peace, preventing Scotland from being embroiled in English wars
1705	English Alien Act, threatening Anglo-Scottish trade
1707	Act of Union with England: the union of the parliaments. Scottish parliament suppressed. Scots admitted to colonial trade
1708	Abolition of Scottish privy council
1712	Parliament restores rights of patrons to nominate parish ministers
1713	Motion to repeal union of 1707 narrowly defeated in House of Lords
1715	Jacobite uprising defeated at Sheriffmuir
1725	Malt tax riots in Glasgow
1730	Francis Hutcheson occupies Glasgow chair of moral philosophy
1733	Secession from Church of Scotland begins
1736	Porteous riot in Edinburgh
1739	Books I and II of David Hume's *Treatise of Human Nature* published
1743	Archibald Campbell, Lord Ilay, becomes 3rd duke of Argyll
1745	Charles Edward Stuart (Bonnie Prince Charlie) leads Jacobite uprising
1746	Jacobite armies defeated at battle of Culloden
1747	Seceders divide into burghers and antiburghers
1756	John Home's *Douglas* performed in Edinburgh
1759	Carron Iron Works established near Falkirk
1761	Death of Ilay; rise of 3rd earl of Bute; Relief Church established; Joseph Black demonstrates principle of latent heat
1762	William Robertson assumes office as principal of Edinburgh University
1763	Bute resigns amid Wilkite opposition

1768	*Encyclopaedia Britannica* begins to appear
1769	William Robertson's *History of Charles V* and William Buchan's *Domestic Medicine* published
1771	Henry Mackenzie's *Man of Feeling* and Tobias Smollett's *Humphry Clinker* published
1772	Failure of Ayr Bank triggers economic crisis
1775	Henry Dundas becomes lord advocate for Scotland; Watt and Boulton commence partnership to build steam engines. Scots emigration to America halted
1776	Adam Smith's *Wealth of Nations* published; death of David Hume
1777	First volume of Hugh Blair's popular *Sermons* published
1779	'No Popery' riots in Edinburgh and Glasgow
1781	*The Mirror* published by Henry Mackenzie and the Mirror Club
1783	Royal Society of Edinburgh founded
1785	New Lanark cotton mill co-founded by David Dale
1786	Robert Burns's Kilmarnock edition of *Poems, Chiefly in the Scottish Dialect* published
1788	Charles Edward Stuart dies in Rome
1790	Forth & Clyde Canal and Monkland Canal completed
1791	James Boswell's *Life of Samuel Johnson* and first volume of Sir John Sinclair's *Statistical Account of Scotland* published
1792	Scottish Episcopal relief legislation enacted
1793	Roman Catholic relief legislation enacted; government commences sedition trials against Scottish radicals
1795	James Hutton's *Theory of the Earth* published
1797	Scottish Militia Act provokes anti-militia riots
1799	General Sir David Baird defeats Tipu Sultan at Seringapatam
1801	Union with Ireland and establishment of United Kingdom
1802	*Edinburgh Review* published
1812	*Comet*, first steamboat, launched on Clyde
1814	Walter Scott's *Waverley* published
1816	Trial of Patrick Sellar
1820	Radical war
1822	Visit of George IV to Scotland
1828	Hot blast technique of smelting iron developed by J. B. Neilson
1832	First Reform Act (Scotland)
1833	Burgh Reform Act

1842	Edinburgh–Glasgow railway opened
1843	Disruption in Church of Scotland and formation of Free Church of Scotland
1845	Poor Law (Scotland) Amendment Act
1846–8	Highland famine
1847	United Presbyterian Church formed by merger of United Secession and Relief Churches
1862	General Police Act (Scotland)
1866	Glasgow Improvement Act
1868	Second Reform Act (Scotland)
1872	Education (Scotland) Act
1874	Patronage Act repealed
1878	Restoration of the Roman Catholic hierarchy
1879	First steel oceangoing ship built on Clyde
1881–3	Crofters' war
1884–5	Third Reform Act
1885	Creation of Secretary for Scotland
1886	Crofters' Holdings (Scotland) Act. Formation of Scottish Home Rule Association
1887	Establishment of Scottish Office
1888	Formation of Scottish Labour Party. First Glasgow International Exhibition
1889	Local Government (Scotland) Act-passed
1892	State aid for secondary schools
1893	Women admitted to Scottish universities
1894	Scottish Grand Committee set up
1897	Creation of Scottish Trade Union Congress
1900	General election. Unionist victory in UK and Scotland. Merger of Free Church of Scotland and United Presbyterian Church to form United Free Church resulting in a legal challenge in the House of Lords by the 'Wee Frees'. Boer War continues
1901	Death of Queen Victoria. Second Glasgow International Exhibition
1902	End of Boer War. Arthur Balfour succeeds Lord Salisbury as Prime Minister
1903	Visit to Scotland by King Edward amid controversy about the 'numeral'
1905	Royal Commission on the Relief of the Poor
1906	General election, Liberal Party wins landslide in UK and Scotland. Campbell Bannerman Prime Minister. Beginning of Liberal social reform. Franco-British *Entente Cordiale*
1908	Education (Scotland) Act

1910	Two general elections. Liberals hold Scotland but Conservatives recover lost ground in England. Irish home rulers hold balance of power. Scottish home rule emerges as an issue
1911	Reform of the House of Lords
1912	Scottish Liberal Unionists and Conservative Party merge to form the Scottish Unionist Party.
1914	Scottish Home Rule Bill passes second reading, but delayed by outbreak of war
1915	Coalition government. Labour unrest on the Clyde. Gretna train crash
1916	Lloyd George becomes Prime Minister. Easter Rising in Dublin. Industrial conflict dies down on Clyde
1917	Royal Commission Report on housing. Outbreak of Russian Revolution. Introduction of conscription
1918	Education Act brings Catholic schools within the state system. Armistice. General election in December where women over the age of 30 have the vote. Unionists win as part of Coalition. Former Prime Minister Henry Asquith loses seat in Fife to independent Conservative
1919	Riot in George Square, Glasgow. Forty Hours strike
1920	Labour begins to make breakthrough in local government elections
1921	'Triple Alliance' strike fails
1922	Labour Party makes breakthrough at the general election to become largest single party in Scotland
1923	Minority Labour Government
1924	Wheatley Housing Act
1926	General Strike. Scottish Secretary upgraded to Scottish Secretary of State
1927	Failure of private member's Home Rule Bill
1928:	National Party of Scotland formed. Reform of Scottish Office. Women over 21 get the vote
1929	Reunification of the Church of Scotland and the United Free Church. Reform of local government. Second Labour minority government. Wall Street crash
1931	Formation of the National Government. Conservatives do well in Scotland at general election as part of the National Government. Labour heavily defeated
1932	Independent Labour Party breaks away from Labour
1933	Labour takes control of Glasgow in local elections
1934	Formation of Scottish National Party
1935	General election. First past the post system works against Labour recovery. John Buchan becomes Governor-General of Canada

1936	Scottish Economic Committee formed to deal with problems in the Scottish economy. Marquess of Linlithgow becomes Viceroy of India
1937	Hillington industrial estate established
1938	Glasgow Empire Exhibition
1939	Outbreak of Second World War. Evacuation of children from the cities
1941	Thomas Johnston appointed Scottish Secretary of State. Clydebank Blitz
1942	Beveridge Report published
1945	SNP win first parliamentary seat at a by-election in Motherwell. Labour landslide in general election
1946	National Insurance established. Severe winter
1947	Nationalization of coal and electricity
1948	National Health Service established. Transport nationalized
1950	General election reduces Labour majority
1951	General election. Conservatives win. Rationing ends
1953	Coronation of Queen Elizabeth results in protests over the use of the numeral 'II'. Royal Commission of Scottish Affairs
1955	General election. Conservatives win 50.5 per cent of the popular vote in Scotland
1958	Scotland more dependent on heavy industry than in the 1930s. Economy begins to run into difficulty
1961	Publication of *Toothill Inquiry into the Scottish Economy*
1962	Decision taken to base Polaris submarines at Faslane
1964	Labour wins general election with a narrow majority. Labour makes gains in Scotland
1965	Highland Development Board established
1966	Labour wins general election with increased majority. Publication of *A Plan for Scotland*
1967	Nationalization of the steel industry. SNP wins Hamilton by-election
1968	Royal Commission on the constitution established. Conservative leader Edward Heath backs devolution at the 'Declaration of Perth'
1970	General election returns Conservative government. SNP wins only one seat, in Western Isles
1971	Clyde shipbuilders' crisis
1973	Three-day week. Worsening industrial relations. Kilbrandon Report on the Constitution. SNP wins Govan by-election
1974	General elections in February and October. Labour narrowly returned in both. SNP electoral breakthrough
1975	Scottish Development Agency established. Sex Discrimination Act. Reform

of local government into two tiers of 'region' and 'district'

1976	Devolution Bill presented
1977	Devolution Bill fails. SNP do well in local elections
1978	Scotland and Wales Act to establish regional assemblies passed in House of Commons subject to a referendum requiring support of over 40 per cent of the electorate
1979	Referendum fails on 40 per cent clause. General election. Conservative government returned. Collapse of SNP vote
1982	Falklands War
1983	General election. Conservative victory. Unemployment passes the 300,000 mark
1984	Miners' strike
1986	Gartcosh Steel Works closes
1987	General election. Tactical voting reduces the number of Scottish Tory MPs by half
1988	Margaret Thatcher delivers her 'Sermon on the Mount' speech to the General Assembly of the Church of Scotland. SNP wins by-election in Govan; publication of *Claim of Right for Scotland*. Lockerbie tragedy
1989	Introduction of poll tax, formation of Scottish Constitutional Convention
1990	Conservative government rejects Scottish Constitutional Convention proposals
1991	First Gulf War
1992	General election. Conservative victory. Labour does well in Scotland. Closure of Ravenscraig steelworks. European summit in Edinburgh. Iain Banks, *The Crow Road*
1994	Death of Labour leader John Smith. Mel Gibson film *Braveheart*
1996	Massacre at Dunblane. Return of the Stone of Destiny
1997	General election. Labour landslide. Conservatives win no Scottish parliamentary seats. Donald Dewar drafts Scotland Act. Referendum secures Scottish parliament. British hand over Hong Kong to China
1999	First Scottish parliamentary elections. Labour–Liberal Democrat coalition government in Edinburgh
2000	Death of First Minister, Donald Dewar
2001	UK general election. Labour victory. Election turnout down in Scotland. Labour maintains lead
2003	Scottish election. Labour–Liberal Democrat coalition
2004	New Scottish parliament at Holyrood opened

ILLUSTRATION SOURCES

The editor and publishers wish to thank the following for their kind permission to reproduce the illustrations on the following pages:

INDEX

Note: page numbers in italics indicate illustrations and captions.